C0-AXC-326

STUDIES IN HISTORY, ECONOMICS, AND PUBLIC LAW

EDITED BY THE FACULTY OF POLITICAL SCIENCE
OF COLUMBIA UNIVERSITY

Number 274

FEDERAL WATER-POWER LEGISLATION

FEDERAL WATER-POWER LEGISLATION

BY

JEROME G. KERWIN

AMS PRESS
NEW YORK

COLUMBIA UNIVERSITY
STUDIES IN THE
SOCIAL SCIENCES

274

The Series was formerly known as
Studies in History, Economics and Public Law.

Reprinted with the permission of Columbia University Press
From the edition of 1926, New York
First AMS EDITION published 1968
Manufactured in the United States of America

Library of Congress Catalogue Card Number: 71-76690

AMS PRESS, INC.
NEW YORK, N. Y. 10003

PREFACE

In the preparation of this work on water-power legislation, the author has had the valuable assistance of many people who have given freely of their time and advice. The author wishes especially to acknowledge with deepest gratitude the able guidance given by Professor Lindsay Rogers of Columbia University. To many men prominent in public life the author is greatly indebted: to Mr. Harry A. Slattery, prominent among conservation leaders; to Philip P. Wells, Deputy Attorney General of Pennsylvania and member of the Giant Power Commission of the same state; to the former congressmen John J. Esch of Wisconsin, William Kent of California, Thetus Sims of Tennessee—all of whom were active during the water-power controversy; to Senators George W. Norris of Nebraska, James Wadsworth of New York, and Thomas J. Walsh of Montana; to Judson King, to Mr. O. C. Merrill, and to ex-Secretary of the Interior Walter L. Fisher. To all of these men who have supplied valuable suggestions and helpful documentary sources the writer extends his thanks. In the trials of proofreading the author has been greatly aided by Miss Gertrude Chalmers of the University of Chicago Library, by Edward P. Kerwin, Paul Kirkley, and William Klevs.

For any blame for errors of fact, judgment, or composition in the text the author absolves all of the above and through this preface cheerfully accepts the responsibility for his work.

JEROME G. KERWIN.

UNIVERSITY OF CHICAGO,
CHICAGO, ILLINOIS,
APRIL 14, 1926.

CONTENTS

INTRODUCTION

After the great fifteen-year struggle for water-power legislation, it is doubtful if the public to-day recalls the legislative complexities that marked the passage of the Act of 1920. It is doubtful if the average citizen understands the important relation of government to this new source of energy, if he understands what is involved in that relation which touches so nearly his own happiness. Throughout the United States the vast resource of water power, belonging primarily to the people, has been harnessed for man's service by great private corporations which are bound by state legislation and the federal Water Power Act to serve the public. These laws are the result of years of struggle in the state legislatures and in Congress. In the Congress especially the conflict was prolonged and bitter. The struggle should not be forgotten, for it holds valuable lessons for the people of this and other generations.

During the years when the question of effective power legislation was being debated in Congress, a great deal was heard and written about the amazing corruption of the press and of legislators by the power companies. Like most generalities given out in the midst of heated controversy such statements were many times misleading and at time absolutely false. A student delegated to dig up the iniquities of the power trust may well be likened to one of the charter members of the famous Royal Society of England, for when King Charles created that august body he asked its members to find out why a fish weighed more in water than out of it; after several days of investigation the members returned with a reply to the effect that they could not determine why a fish weighed more in water than out of it. To which the King replied, "Well, does it?" So the research student may ask of himself, "Well, was there a corrupt lobby?" The careful student cannot treat as of value grave charges of corruption unless they are supported by unquestionable evidence. Such evidence is difficult to discover. There is nothing very tangible to show that the baser forms of corruption were used. On the other hand, no one can deny the influence and power of an enormous business interest with funds to employ talented, persuasive, lobbying attorneys. For ten years, tremendous pressure was brought to bear upon Congressmen by power companies. It is not to be wondered at. It is the old story. When clever legal representatives of rich corporations could fashion their arguments to play upon those prejudices of legislators built upon theories of state sovereignty or of *laissez-faire,* they were all but invincible.

Opposed to the representatives of the power companies stood the conservationists. Starting out as a small, determined band under the leadership of Gifford Pinchot, the progress of this group illustrates the power of an aggressive, coherent minority. It was into this movement that Theodore Roosevelt injected a spirit endowed with much of his own persistence and energy. The conservationists never once wavered in their support of strong federal control of water-power development. To their influence may be ascribed those safeguards in the national power act which effectively protect popular interests.

But the struggle over power legislation was more than a struggle between power companies and conservationists. There was a clash of ideas on federal government as old as federalism itself. The old issue of states' rights was involved. The answer to the question whether the states or the government at Washington should regulate power development within state boundaries determined the role of not a few Congressmen. Consequently, Congressmen from the South, Congressmen from states with great water-power resources such as New York, and Congressmen from the public domain states of the West found themselves fighting a common battle for limited federal control. Among this group the power interests found valuable allies.

That the government should not meddle in the water-power business was the contention of the conservative, individualist legislator. Now and then one notes in the debates on the power question references to "socialism" and "socialistic proposals", but there is a noteworthy absence of spirited replies on the one side or the other to such statements. Few seemed to be greatly excited about the passing of *laissez-faire*. Especially was this true during the war years. Yet there were Congressmen who based their opposition to a national water-power act on the old theories of individualism. Their number was about equally matched by the few who were opposed to the Act of 1920, as finally passed, because the principle of public ownership was not incorporated.

Prominent among the great issues of water-power legislation was the question of the jurisdiction of administrative officials. The dread of a bureaucracy is ever very real in Congress. The granting of wide discretionary powers to executive officials and the resultant increased importance of the ordinance power were strongly opposed in the water-power debates as strengthening the already growing administrative "tyranny" in Washington. If an administrative officer is to be something more than a routine clerk he must be given opportunity to exercise discretion and to determine the necessary details for the effective administration of the law. But legislators have been wary. Our legislators have held on tenaciously to the privilege of prescribing the minutest details in every big piece of legislation. It can not be seriously questioned that in the governments of Europe the powers of discretion placed in the hands of executive officials by the legislatures are quite extensive and for the most part soberly exercised. In our own case, nevertheless, an increase in administrative power both in state and central governments has taken place within the past decade. Along this path we move slowly.

In the case of power legislation the proposals to place ample control over power sites in the hands of cabinet officials were loudly condemned as distinctly unwise and undoubtedly mischievous. This feature of the debates is interesting among other things as showing the jealousy of the Congress for its prerogatives, and as showing a certain lack of confidence in partisan administration which the legislators themselves help to perpetuate.

In the end, however, the Congress granted to a Cabinet commission large discretionary powers over water-power sites. This outcome may be ascribed to a war crisis and executive dictation. After years of fruitless wrangling it was President Wilson's mandamus that broke the apparently hopeless deadlock. No better illustration may be found of the ascendency of the executive branch of the government during the Wilson administration.

The question of the constitutionality of adequate water-power legislation, more than any other question involved, delayed the passage of a federal power law. No question was debated with more heat—but often with little light—no question was given more time and attention than the constitutional power of the federal government to make charges for power privileges on navigable streams where the government had no riparian rights. The charge question was thoroughly considered by congressional committees, attorneys-general, presidents, and hosts of private attorneys until no single phase of it remained unstudied. Page after page of the *Congressional Record* is filled with discussions on this point. Hours were wasted in academic debate. When the power struggle reached its final stage, veteran members of Congress arose and talked at great length in phonographic fashion on the constitutionality of charges. The friends and the opponents of charges knew exactly what the other would say, how he would say it, and about how long it would take to repeat the old story. No power bill would have been worthwhile without privilege charges or full consideration of them, but it is a matter of honest doubt whether the amount of time given to a minor constitutional point was altogether necessary. In this particular case debate on the legal problem provided a convenient means of delaying the progress of effective power legislation besides obscuring many important questions of policy, such as recapture, upon which the future control of the public depended. Although little evidence is available to prove the point, one is led to wonder whether or not there were forces at work endeavoring to perpetuate the discussion of constitutionality in order to becloud the greater issues.

Finally, a study of the water-power struggle reveals the workings of the national legislative machinery in the process of turning out a major piece of legislation. The complexity of congressional rules, the cumbersomeness of the committee system, the conflicts of committee chairmen,—all are best revealed in a study of legislation that hangs fire through the years.

The author has prefaced the chapter on the legislative history of water power with two chapters which he hopes will afford a background for an intelligent understanding of the whole problem. Chapter I contains a survey of the physical and economic side of the water-power problem.

Chapter II treats of the legal problem, especially of the constitutional questions which so agitated Congress. The author feels apologetic in offering a long chapter on a point which he believes to have been overemphasized. Since, however, this question was able to prevent for many years the enactment of legislation, it deserves to be thoroughly considered and thoroughly understood. Following the chapters on the legislative history of water power, a brief consideration of the progress of power development is taken up with special emphasis placed upon the Muscle Shoals controversy.

CHAPTER I

Economic Aspects of Water-Power

The demand today is for mechanical power to supplant the manual labor of man. Scientists look forward hopefully to the time when economical means of extracting vast stores of energy from tide-water, sun power, earth heat, atmospheric electricity, earth rotation, and sources now unforeseen will lighten man's burden and give him a larger measure of time for recreation and mental improvement. Until that time comes our problem is to use with the greatest economy consistent with efficiency the resources which lie at hand. The four great natural resources of the modern world are: coal, petroleum, gas and water. These resources must furnish in the United States about 150 million horsepower every year to run factories, to light homes and streets, to haul freight, to operate traction lines—in brief, to keep the vast American industrial system going.[1] Every year we are drawing upon our resources in the following estimated amounts: three quarters of a billion tons of coal, one half of a billion barrels of petroleum, seven hundred billion cubic feet of natural gas, and from six to ten million horsepower of hydroelectricity.[2]

[1] North America has nearly two-thirds of the world's supply of coal, one-fourth of the world's supply of oil, and one-sixth of the world's potential water power. George Otis Smith, address before International Power Conference, London, 1924.

[2] Gilbert and Pogue, *America's Power Resources* (New York, 1921), p. 15.

NATURAL GAS

Natural gas is today supplying two million people with illumination for their homes, besides furnishing cheap fuel for manufacturing.[1] In 1915 natural gas furnished 88,364 horsepower in the United States—less than four percent of the water-power record and about two per cent of the coal power. Pennsylvania led with 16,088 horsepower, eighteen per cent of the total within the United States. This state together with Texas, Oklahoma, and New York have over forty percent of the total gas power.[2] The production of natural gas in 1917 was 800,000,000,000 cubic feet. Since that time production has declined considerably, being 650,-000,000,000 cubic feet in 1920. About two-thirds of this supply is used for manufacturing purposes.

This resource—like coal and petroleum—has been extravagantly used.[3] Samuel S. Wyer of the United States Fuel Administration estimated in 1918 that our waste in natural gas was equal to our consumption—800,000,000,000 cubic feet a year.[4] A poster of the United States Fuel Administration spread broadcast during the War said: "Natural gas is becoming scarce; the demands for natural gas are now greater than the available supply. When the present supplies are exhausted we must go back to the more expensive and inferior manufactured gas. The use of natural gas is not an inalienable right, but a privilege enjoyed by about 10 per cent of our entire population in the United States

[1] The manufacture of glass and pottery as well as the manufacture of steel where enormous amounts are required to furnish high heat.

[2] Report of the Secretary of Agriculture, *Senate Document 316*, 64th Cong., 1st Sess., p. 28.

[3] "Natural gas is the least appreciated and consequently the most abused of mineral resources." Gilbert and Pogue, *op. cit.*, p. 155.

[4] It would take 1,200,000,000,000 cubic feet of manufactured gas to replace this. Manufactured gas is more expensive and of a lower grade.

and used in a most extravagant and wasteful manner with no regard for the future and not appreciated until it is gone."

Because natural gas is easily had, it is easily wasted. It is furnished at a very low cost [1] to the consumer who finds that low cost an invitation to waste. Much of this valuable resource is lost through leaks in transmission, a source of waste not readily detected because natural gas is lacking in odor. When oil and gas are found together, prospectors prefer to take the oil, which in any case is more valuable, and to disregard the gas entirely. Competition in the field has resulted in a duplication of lines, an overabundance of wells, increased costs, and in many cases a failure to remove all the gas. It is not unusual to find the operators drilling into the same pool and drawing off the gas from each other's holdings. As in the case of coal and of petroleum, substitutes for natural gas have not been used even where easily obtainable.

COAL

The most important source of power is coal. This vital source of energy underlies nearly five hundred thousand square miles of the United States and is widely distributed.[2] Practically all of the anthracite comes from Pennsylvania, while the highest grade of bituminous coal is found in the Appalachian field extending from Pennsylvania through Ohio, West Virginia, Kentucky, Tennessee, and Alabama. The other deposits of bituminous coal of an inferior grade are found in the Middle West and in the Rocky Mountain region. The total production from all our fields for the years 1916 to 1923, in gross tons, was as follows: [3]

[1] In 1915 the price of natural gas was ten cents per 1000 cubic feet, of manufactured gas twenty-eight cents per 1000 cubic feet.

[2] Gilbert and Pogue, *op. cit.*, p. 39.

[3] These figures are from the New York *World Almanac*, 1925.

	Anthracite	Bituminous	Total
1916	78,195,083	448,678,288	526,873,371
1917	88,939,117	492,670,146	581,609,263
1918	88,237,575	517,308,768	605,546,343
1919	78,501,931	408,908,482	487,410,413
1920	80,032,175	496,975,892	577,008,067
1921	80,779,867	415,921,950	444,105,760
1922	48,824,127	407,894,000	456,718,127
1923	83,338,401	486,964,286	570,302,687

The late Charles P. Steinmetz gives a graphic illustration of what these figures really mean in terms of quantity and power:

Using the coal produced in one year as building material, we could with it build a wall like the Chinese wall, all around the United States, following the Canadian and Mexican frontiers, the Atlantic, Gulf, and Pacific Coast, and with the chemical energy contained in the next year's production, we could lift this entire wall into space 200 miles high. Or, with the coal produced in one year used as building material, we could build 400 pyramids, larger than the largest pyramid in Egypt.[1]

All authorities are agreed that this phenomenal output can not continue for any great length of time. Nor can it be said, despite various means of conservation adopted in late years, that such a large production is altogether necessary. It is true that less than one-half of one per cent of our coal resources have been exploited, yet a large part of the highest grade coal is contained in that one-half of one per cent. The best of the coal is now being used.[2] According to the figures of the United States Geological Survey, the unmined coal resources of the world are 7,685,000,000,000 tons of which 3,500,000,000,000 tons are in the United States.[3] This may seem to be an inexhaustible supply, but

[1] Gilbert and Pogue, *op. cit.*, pp. 31-33.

[2] Mr. Campbell of the United States Geological Survey has estimated that within fifty years the anthracite supply will be exhausted and that almost within the same time the best of our bituminous coal will have been mined.

[3] 16,000,000,000 tons of these are anthracite.

it is well to keep in mind a statement of Mr. O. C. Merrill, Executive Secretary of the Federal Power Commission: "even if we could assume that our ultimate coal resources can be measured in centuries of supply, they are, in depth beneath the ground, in distance from point of use, in cost of production, and in difficulty in transportation, becoming consistently less accessible."[1] And George Otis Smith, Director of the United States Geological Survey, has said:

The fact that more than half of the world's coal reserves are believed to be within the territory of the United States has led many of us into unwarranted optimism. The captains of the great industries concentrated along the Atlantic seaboard will do well to think less of the millions of tons that are said to lie awaiting their need in various parts of this continent-wide country of ours, but rather to ask for details as to where this coal is and how available it is for the use of this and the next generation. The total tonnage involves strings of figures hard for us to comprehend, but the tonnage remaining in the great producing fields of the East is so limited as to compel us to foresee their exhaustion within periods of the same magnitude as those which you executives figure as the expectancy of life for your industrial enterprises. For example, the Pittsburgh bed in Pennsylvania was estimated forty years ago as good for thirty generations, but the rate of mining has so greatly increased that now we must measure the exhaustion of this largest bed in the Keystone State by the space of a single generation. This is not an exceptional illustration of the shortened life due to unexpected increase in drafts upon our coal resources, for in the George Creek field in Maryland this same bed there called the "Big Vein" was believed forty years ago to have a life of at least 150 years, but today the field is regarded as almost worked out.[2]

[1] "White Coal, the Power of the Future," *Financial World*, July 6, 1922.

[2] Gilbert and Pogue, *op. cit.*, p. 57.

Only within late years have Americans given adequate attention to the waste in coal resources. A comprehensive description of the reasons for this waste would require many volumes; it is sufficient to note here that there is waste and inefficiency all along the line from the time the coal is taken from the mines until it is consumed in the furnaces of homes, factories, or locomotive boilers. Herbert Hoover has told us that the coal industry is the "worst functioning industry in the country"—and that is only part of a sad story. Conservation of our coal reserves depends upon a less wasteful system of mining, greater efficiency in consumption,[1] *and curtailment of use by the substitution of some other source of power.*

PETROLEUM

Petroleum is a substitute energy material for coal. The demands upon our coal resources have been lessened to some degree by the use of petroleum. Ten years ago geologists were predicting that the world's coal supply would be exhausted in 100 years; they now put the limit at 1000 years. The production of petroleum in the United States may be shown by the following table:[2]

1917	14,083,255,242	gallons
1918	14,948,964,072	"
1919	15,864,198,000	"
1920	18,622,884,000	"
1921	19,831,686,000	"
1922	23,416,302,000	"
1923	30,861,094,000	"

[1] The United States Geological Survey is of the opinion that of every ton of coal exploited in this country, 600 pounds are lost in mining, 126 pounds are consumed between the underground working and the boiler rooms, 446 pounds are lost in gases going up the stack, 102 pounds are lost by radiation and in the ash-pit, 650 pounds are lost in converting heat energy into mechanical energy, and only 76 pounds are left for useful work.

[2] These figures are from the New York *World Almanac*, 1925.

From this source are derived four main products—gasoline, kerosene, fuel oil and lubricating oil. Numberless by-products such as benzine, vaseline, paraffin, road oil, asphalt and petroleum coke are also derived. The greatest demand has been for crude oil.

On the Pacific Coast, where there is little or no coal, power is produced largely by means of petroleum and water. About seven years ago people began to wonder how long petroleum would be available as a power resource. The Great War increased the fear that our supplies were being unnecessarily depleted, and in July 1917 we find the California State Council of Defense reporting that a decline had already set in in petroleum production. Over-production, ruinous competition, inadequate application of the best technique in drilling and mining, inordinate waste in the use of petroleum, needless use where coal or water power could be had more readily have caused conservationists throughout the land to enter upon a campaign of education to bring Americans to a realization of the profligate waste of their resources. In 1917 the Director of the Bureau of Mines wrote:

What effort have we made to conserve this supply and to utilize it to its greatest advantage? We have made little effort until very recently to do these things. We have been wasteful, careless and recklessly ignorant. We have abandoned oil fields while a large part of the oil was still in the ground. We have allowed tremendous quantities of gas to waste in the air. We have let water into the oil sands, ruining areas that should have produced hundreds of thousands of barrels of oil. We lacked the knowledge to properly produce one needed product without overproducing products for which we have little need. We have used the most valuable parts of the oil for purposes to which the cheapest should have been devoted. For many years the gasoline fractions were practically a waste product during our quest for kerosene; with the development of the internal combustion engine, the kerosene is now almost a waste product in our strenuous efforts to increase the yields of lighter distillates.[1]

The United States Geological survey after a thorough review of the whole field puts our petroleum reserves at 212,310,000,000 gallons. If over twenty billion gallons is to be our annual production it is not difficult to figure out our supply in terms of years. More and more, therefore, will the United States be dependent upon imported supplies and more and more will it become a competitor in the mad, international scramble for oil. In the production of power, petroleum must cease to be a competitor with coal and water, and must be used complementary to them. Max W. Ball in a paper before the American Mining Congress in 1916 said:

There is the root of the whole trouble—the small holding. Let us go back over the history of the field. We saw that as soon as the field was discovered it was leased up in small tracts. Then we saw the Smiths, the Browns, the Joneses and the Standard Oil drilling for dear life, each trying to get the oil from under his little tract and a bit of the other fellow's before the other fellow could get it. Why? Because each tract was so small that it could be drained by wells on the surrounding tracts.

We saw that the race was so keen that wells were improperly drilled, that gas was allowed to waste into the air or dissipate itself through barren formations, that water was allowed to enter the oil sands, and that great quantities of oil were left underground, never to be recovered. Why? Because the small holding forced each man to race with his neighbor. We saw the entire flush production of the field thrown on the market at once, demoralizing market prices, forcing the premature abandonment of wells in other fields, resulting in the burning of unrefined crude and the waste of the more valuable products.

[1] Quoted from Gilbert and Pogue, *op. cit.*, pp. 107-108.

We saw the maximum productions of the fields go into storage where the losses from evaporation were enormous, and where the cost of the old was nearly doubled. What caused these things? The fact that every holder of a small lease must drill it up as soon as possible.

Lastly, we saw the cost of production more than 300 percent what it should have been. And what was the reason? That every man must drill his lines as fast as might be and must completely drill up his land at the earliest moment. Why? Because the oil under his small holding could be taken from him by wells on surrounding tracts.

Ignorance there may be, carelessness there undoubtedly is, but back of ignorance, of carelessness, of reckless, headlong methods is the real cause—the fact that the average holding is so small that speed is the owner's sole protection. Let him be careful if he can; let him be economical if he can find a way; but careful or careless, reckless or conservative, he must be speedy if he would survive. The small holding is his master.

WATER POWER—FIRST USES

The first power resource used in this country was water. Eight years after the Pilgrims landed at Plymouth, Governor Endicott's colony erected a grist mill at Dorchester.[1] In 1638 the General Court of Massachusetts issued regulations respecting corn mills, and in the same year it set up a saw mill. In 1639 Maryland raised funds by subscription for the building of a water-power mill. Settlers coming with William Penn to the banks of the Delaware in 1682 brought a mill frame with them. By the close of the seventeenth century, many mills were operating in New Jersey, New Hampshire, and Maine. Serious competition with English textiles in time brought an act from Parliament (1700) prohibiting the exportation from England of water-

[1] Fanning, "Progress in Hydraulic Development," *Engineering Record*, vol. xlvii, pp. 24-25.

power machinery for the manufacturing of textiles in America. Along with this spread of manufacturing by means of water power came a series of colonial and later, state, regulations aiming to control the exploitations of water powers.[1]

Mills had to be located at the water sites as transmission of power was unknown. Early water-power enterprises were largely confined to New England and the Middle States and figured prominently in the development of those regions, but water resources soon found extensive use in more remote sections. The extent of the use of water for manufacturing purposes before the introduction of electricity may be seen in the following list of the principal plants established between the years 1822 and 1866.[2]

Place	Year	Fall Ft.	Minimum Horsepower	Watershed Square Miles
Lowell, Mass	1822	35	11,845	4,083
Nashua, N. H.	1823	36	1,200	516
Cohoes, N. Y.	1826	104	9,450	3,490
Norwich, Conn	1828	16	700	1,240
Augusta, Me.	1834	17	3,500	5,907
Manchester, N. H	1835	52	12,000	2,839
Hocksett, N. H	1841	14	1,800	2,791
Lawrence, Mass	1845	30	11,000	4,625
Augusta, Ga.	1847	50	8,500	8,830
Holyoke, Mass.	1848	50	14,000	8,000
Lewiston, Me.	1849	50	11,900	3,200
Columbus, Ga.	1850	25	10,000	14,900
Rochester, N. Y.	1856	236	8,000	2,474
St. Anthony Falls, Minn	1857	50	15,500	19,736
Niagara, N. Y.	1861	90	15,000	271,000
Turner's Falls, Mass	1866	35	10,000	6,000
Fox River, Wis	1866	185	....	6,449

[1] Laws and Ordinances of New Netherlands, 1638-1674, p. 3. Also Myers, "Narratives of Early Pennsylvania, West New Jersey and Delaware." Also the charters and general laws of the colony and province of Massachusetts Bay, Charter CXI, p. 405 (1714). Also acts and laws of the General Assembly of the State of Vermont, 1779. Also the acts of the Council and General Assembly of New Jersey, 1777.

[2] Fanning, "History of the Development of American Water Powers," American Pulp and Paper Association, *Proceedings*, 1899, vol. xxii, pp. 16-24.

WATER POWER—PRESENT USE

The introduction of coal for industrial uses together with the improvement of transportation methods made possible the development of industry far from the points of the production of power. Because of this, water power declined and for many years was unable to compete with steam power. With the development of electricity in the seventies, water power again became a competitor of steam power. For fifteen or twenty years this competition was not of any great significance, for successful high-tension transmission over long distances was not at first economically practicable, nor had the mechanical inventions for the generation of electricity by water power reached that stage of perfection which would invite the serious consideration of investors. Pioneers in hydroelectric development took great risks and suffered losses commensurate with the risks. The new era in hydroelectric development began during the first years of the twentieth century. Water power had entered a stage where it could provide illumination for cities and power for manufacturing. Great combinations of capital were invested in the new enterprises; the best of the water-power sites were monopolized. Coal remained, and still remains, the chief means of power generation, but a substitute for it had been found. The problem of harnessing this new source of power to conserve our diminishing coal, oil and gas reserves brought about a twenty-year battle in the press, on the lecture platform, in the state legislatures and in the Congress.

What are the possibilities of water power? It is to be feared that countless numbers of citizens have been led to expect more from this resource than the facts warrant. Pictures of an electric paradise have been painted in our magazines; the magic term *superpower* has awakened the imagination of millions of people who seem to believe that a system of superabundant electric power is in the process of creation. Two typical quotations, bordering on the rhapsodical, show how enthusiastic some people have become at the thought of water power.

> White coal! Shall we change our black diamonds for it one of these days? Already we are hearing the cry like that which came to Aladdin in the narrow streets of a city of Cathay—the call to exchange old lamps for new. . . . In some parts of the country the day is already come, with its dustless, noiseless, clinkerless sources of light and heat and power. White coal is made in the roar of the cataract and the whirl of the rapids, in the sure flow of the rivers, and in the ceaseless beat of the waves. It is the power of the waters harnessed to do the bidding of mortals. Electra waves over it her magic wand, while Iris bends over it the prismatic bow.[1]

And again:

> If the water power of the United States were converted into electric energy, there would be more than enough current to turn every industrial wheel and to light every electric lamp now in service throughout the length and breadth of the land.[2]

It is true that all the *potential* water power in the United States converted into electric energy could turn every industrial wheel and light every home—*if* every water site were reasonably near a market, *if* every swift-flowing stream had a constant flow, *if* at each site storage of water were possible, *if*—and so forth—. One must assume ideal conditions at each water-power site to expect hydroelectric power completely to supplant steam.

Africa possesses the greatest source of hydroelectric power

[1] Harrington, J. W., "White Coal for Black," *Outlook*, September 21, 1921, p. 91.

[2] Roberts, S. G., "Harnessing Our Water-Power," *Scientific American*, May 8, 1920, p. 514.

in the world. More than one fourth of the potential water power of the world is found in the basin of the Congo River. One hundred million horsepower![1] But as one authority puts it: "it is as useful to us as the ice at the North Pole is useful to the iceman."[2] It is beyond the reach of markets, and it presents almost insuperable engineering difficulties. There is, of course, always the possibilty that science will find a way in which to use out-of-the-way water powers, but dealing with the "living present" and the immediate future, certain common sense facts should prevent our growing too enthusiastic on the wonders of water power. Electricity cannot be stored in any great quantity; production and use are almost simultaneous. If it were possible to store power for times when demands for it were heaviest, many of our most roseate dreams would come true. Furthermore, stream flow is not constant. There are seasons when some rivers are at flood stage and other seasons when the same rivers are practically non-existent. The demand for electricity is constant and no city and no industry will tolerate the shutting-off of power because a power company has failed to figure on a stream's drying-up. Sometimes a plant will be able to get sufficient power from a stream during the first year, during the second year, and during the third year; then the fourth year comes along, a dry year, when it is possible to develop only half the power for which

[1] "Stanley Falls consist of seven cataracts having a total fall of about 200 feet in sixty miles. From 10,000,000 to 15,000,000 horsepower may possibly be developed in this locality, though the engineering problems are difficult. On the lower Congo, below Stanley Pool, there are eighteen falls and rapids that have a total drop of 500 feet in less than ninety miles and just above the tidewater there are ten falls and rapids that have a total drop of 300 feet in less than sixty miles. More than 100,000,000 horsepower could be developed in those two stretches." *New York Times*, September 7, 1924.

[2] Claudy, C. H., "Turning the Wheels of a Century Hence," *Scientific American*, July 10, 1920, p. 36.

the plant has been built. Lack of means for storing electricity and for regulating stream flow has been met by the utilization of steam plants during the slack seasons or by the storage of water in large quantities or by both methods. It is superfluous perhaps to point out that the hauling of coal to distant water-power sites is expensive and, in many cases, impracticable. Furthermore, the storage of water means the flooding of lands which are often valuable for other uses. Without assenting to the facts as applied to the particular case, it is of interest to note the difficulties of storage which are shown in the following quotation:

. . . . consider the Great Falls of the Potomac, eighteen miles north of Washington, D.C. Here is unquestionably a great water power going to waste, which could develop in times of normal flow more than enough power to light the streets and homes of the capital city, run its plants and its elevators, turn its wheels and propel its cars. But the Potomac comes down through a narrow gorge or rocky valley. There is no place available to make a lake of sufficient size to hold water enough to tide over such a plant at times of slack water. The variation between the normal flow and the low water is very large, and between the flood water and low water enormous. A plan calculated upon normal flow would require a storage reservoir much larger than the terrain makes possible.[1]

Then there is the matter of transmission. If a water power is at a great distance from an available market, transmission may be difficult, perhaps impossible. Electricity can be transported economically over a distance of two hundred and fifty miles, or, putting it in another way, a territory of 125,000 square miles can be served from one point, but this marks the limit at the present time. Copper wire must be used to transmit the electricity; if the market is far away, the voltage must be high to force the current through the line, and high voltage means costly insulation

[1] *Ibid.*

to prevent leakage. The problem of securing rights of way for long transmission lines and the keeping of those lines in repair further complicate the situation.

These are facts that many do not seem to consider in writing or talking of our vast water resources. On the other hand, water-power interests have often exaggerated these difficulties to secure favorable terms from the national government to develop sites on the public domain or on navigable streams, sites to which the difficulties noted applied in no great degree. The two extremes of excess of optimism and excess of pessimism have to be avoided.

And what of superpower? The advantages of superpower are not to be denied from the points of view of conservation, convenience, and cleanliness. But there is an evident misunderstanding of just what superpower is and what it does. The following explanatiŏn of superpower is understandable and concise:

Super-power is often mistakenly used as a term to mean more power. It does not mean that. It means power flexibility, and greater utility. System takes from system in accordance with the needs and the economies of production, thus: A rain storm on watershed A produces a heavy runoff or surplus water for power company No. 1. Power Company No. 1 has no need for the surplus water at that time, and it would go to waste if power company No. 1 were not connected with power company No. 2. But power company No. 2 has had no rainfall on watershed B, and would have to generate by steam if the power were not available for the excess of power company No. 1. So power company No. 2 buys from power company No. 1 cheaper than it could be developed by coal. The coal is saved. The economic loss of extra water on watershed A is saved, and power company No. 2 gets its power for its customers. That is only one of the many uses of super-power, which may also be expressed as an interconnection of give and take, or plus and minus.[1]

[1] Hutton, T. R. in the *Knickerbocker Press*, Albany, N. Y., September 10, 1924.

There are at present two great superpower areas where superpower is being supplied. Through the Carolinas and Georgia a great interconnecting system has been established and a similar system has been set up in California. No great enthusiasm on the part of consumers seems to have been awakened in either section, for a lowering of rates has not come to pass. The good citizens have evidently been misled by unwarranted promises of the coming electrical millennium.

All this, however, is not to deny the importance of water power, nor to suggest that its fullest development will not be of great service to the nation. Because the people as a whole have not realized the importance of water-power development and its difficulties, the rhapsody singers, not unlike many other reformers, have promised more than they could deliver. What should we expect?

Within the last four or five years we have become acquainted with a new term—Giant Power. This plan contemplates the development of power from coal at the mouth of the mine, the recovery of the by-products at that source, and the fullest development of water resources. The power from these sources of coal and water is to be pooled and distributed. It is not the interchange of small quantities of surplus power at the ends of the distribution wires of each system as in the case of superpower but is the pooling of supply. This converting of our primary energy sources into electricity and their pooling into regional systems to be integrated into a nation-wide federation of systems offer much encouragement. Here is a plan that may in time "bring cheaper and better electric service to all those who have it now," and "good and cheap electric service to those who are still without it," as Governor Pinchot puts it.

In 1923 the Legislature of Pennsylvania made an appropriation for a Giant Power Survey to study "the water and fuel resources available for Pennsylvania and . . . . the most practicable means for their full utilization for power development and other related uses." Morris L. Cooke and Judson C. Dickerman were placed in charge; the result was a comprehensive report on the subject of Giant Power which promises to be a landmark in electric power development in the United States.[1]

In transmitting the report Governor Pinchot summarizes the Board's recommendations, which clearly show what Giant Power is and what it requires. Those recommendations are as follows:

First: Mass production, with opportunity for by-product recovery. This to be secured by Giant Power generating stations of great capacity in or near the coal fields supplying large capacity transmission lines connecting with all other major transmission lines in the State.

Second: The creation of a common pool of power into which current *from all sources* will be poured, and out of which current for all uses may be taken. This to be secured by making the Giant Power companies common purchasers of surplus power from all generating stations in the State and common sellers to all distributing systems in the State.

Third: Free access by every water-power and steam generating station to every potential purchaser, which means every distributing system in the State which supplies the consumer.

Fourth: Complete, prompt and effective regulation of rates, service, and security issues.

Fifth: Rescue of the regulation of electric service from the destruction now threatened by its conversion into interstate commerce, which will be beyond the control of the states and has not been regulated by Congress. This to be

[1] *Giant Power*, the report of the Giant Power Survey board to the Pennsylvania General Assembly, February, 1925, Harrisburg.

secured by compacts among the states consented to by Congress, as allowed by the Constitution of the United States, or failing that, by Congressional legislation.

Sixth: Systematic extension of service lines throughout the rural districts. This to be secured by farmers mutual companies and by rural electric districts, each authorized to construct and operate distribution systems, and each empowered to tax and borrow money.

Linked in with such a system, water power will render its best service in the future.

The United States Geological Survey in 1921 estimated the amount of potential water power in the world at 445,000,000 horsepower. Of this about 23,000,000 has been developed. According to the same authority the United States has a potential development of 53,905,000 horsepower. The United States Commissioner of Corporations in 1912, after making certain revisions in previous estimates, put the minimum potential water power in the United States at about 30,000,000 horsepower and the maximum at about 61,000,000 horsepower. Mr. O. C. Merrill estimates that between 30,000,000 and 50,000,000 horsepower await development, with even a possibility of 200,000,000 considering storage facilities. These and other figures that are found quoted are at best rough estimates.

Mr. O. C. Merrill testifying before a committee of Congress in 1918 said:

If we are to be prepared for the development that must come, it is necessary to be informed—to have the data ready. Today we know practically nothing about our water-power resources. We know, of course, that there are abundant water powers in the Northwest and in the Southeast, that there are lesser amounts in the Rocky Mountains region of the West and in the Central and Northern Appalachians. Our mineral deposits have been mapped and measured, our timber resources minutely examined, but nobody knows whether our water-power resources are 30,000,000 or 300,000,000 horsepower, or what is the relation of any particular territory to any particular market.[1]

A conservative figure would be about 30,000,000 commercially available horsepower. Forty per cent or more of the estimated minimum power of the country is in the states of California, Oregon, and Washington; these, too, are the states that possess little, if any, coal supply. If the available hydro-power of Montana, Wyoming, and Idaho is added, it will be found that sixty per cent of the water power of the country is located in six states. When Colorado, Arizona and Utah are considered with the foregoing states, the figures show that seventy per cent of the minimum potential power is in nine Western States. Eight per cent of the total is found in the Northeast, and twelve per cent in the area east of the Mississippi and south of the Ohio. Water-power resources are far more evenly distributed than coal resources, and fortunately our coalless regions are bountifully supplied with water power. Eighty per cent of our bituminous coal production is mined in the six states of Pennsylvania, Ohio, Indiana, Illinois, West Virginia and Kentucky, and over fifty per cent of it is used in the first four of these states and New York.[2] It turns out, then, that the major water-power areas are in the west and the major steam-power areas are in the east. Coal will, therefore, be the prime producer of energy in the East for generations to come, even allowing for the fullest development of eastern water-power sites.

[1] *Hearings before the House Committee on Water Power*, 65th Cong., 2nd Sess., pp. 24-25.

[2] Merrill, O. C., in the *Financial World* for July 6, 1922.

How may this water power help in the interests of conservation? The first claim for water-power development would be its saving of fuel. It is said by engineers, that between ten and twelve tons of coal will produce one horsepower year. Using ten tons as the figure, the amount of coal that could be saved by the full development of 30,000,000 horsepower would be 300,000,000 tons per annum. A similar saving in petroleum might be expected, especially in the Pacific Coast states where fuel oil is produced and consumed in vast quantities for the production of power. A saving in our petroleum resources is evident even now because of a greater use of water power. In the east, by development of available water powers, a huge saving in coal would be possible; in the West, development of water power means a saving in oil.

A second point in the development of water power appertains to transportation. One-third of the freight equipment of the railroads is used in hauling coal for other than railroad uses. Very often this coal transportation breaks down because of weather conditions, labor troubles, or sheer inability of the railroads to handle the volume of traffic required of them. A greater saving in coal by the substitution of water power and the development of electric power by steam near the points of coal production, will, undoubtedly, release thousands of freight cars yearly for other purposes and will lighten the heavy burden on our transportation system. Besides this consideration, there is the evident advantage of a greater use of electricity to replace steam in the hauling of freight and passenger traffic. With electrification of railroads, the following results have been noted: fewer locomotives are required to haul the same tonnage; to maintain an electric locomotive requires one-half to one-third of the cost of the steam locomotive, due to the elimination of the fire box and the boiler; there is reduced engineman cost—two or more locomotives can be coupled and their power used under operation by one crew; there is reduced track-maintenance cost due to smoother operation of driving parts; there is lower car-maintenance due to smoother motion; since electric locomotives may be operated at either end, time and space do not have to be taken for turntable operations; there is no necessity for coaling, watering or ash-handling; there is no corrosion in tunnels, due to fuel gases and tunnel moisture; there is greater reliability of operation, especially in cold weather when the electric motor is at its best; [1] the crew is well-housed and comfortable; there is elimination of smoke, and signals therefore are not obscured; comfort and cleanliness of passengers is promoted; and finally cities are rid of one great source of the smoke nuisance. Mr. M. O. Leighton, former chief hydrographer of the Geological Survey, gives the following figures showing the amount of saving brought about on the Butte, Anaconda and Pacific Railway of Montana by the electrification of 92 miles of track: Fuel and power saving, 47.8 per cent; saving on repairs, 26 per cent; saving on enginemen's wages, 32 per cent; saving in engine house expenses, 37.7 per cent; saving in water, 76 per cent; saving in lubricants, 49 per cent; saving in other supplies, 22 per cent. Making a grand average total saving in the operation of that 90 miles of road of $268,728 or 36.2 per cent of the total operating expenses of the road.[2] These are actual accomplishments of an extended use of water power and give promise of greater things in the future.

[1] The capacity of an electric motor depends very much on its ability to get rid of the heat generated by it in the passage of the electric current through it and so the colder the day the easier it is for the motor to get rid of that heat. See the testimony of M. O. Leighton before the House Committee on Water Power, 65th Cong., 2nd Sess., p. 511.

[2] *Ibid.*

The development of hydroelectricity in large units means production of atmospheric nitrogen in the form of nitrate of lime, nitrate of soda and cyanamid, which are used in the manufacture of fertilizers, explosives, cyanide, and other products. The United States has only lately taken up the manufacturing of these vital products.[1] Besides their use in the manufacture of munitions and fertilizers, they are valuable in the dyestuff industry. For the past ten years, some electric plants have been engaged in the manufacture of electrophosphoric acid, produced by electrical treatment of phosphate rock and used extensively by farmers as fertilizer. The production of cheap fertilizer is naturally of great importance to the agricultural interests, and for that reason they have always been found behind every movement for the development of hydroelectricity. The United States has relied heretofore in large measure on Chilean nitrates and on the importation of other products which could be very easily produced within our own borders.

[1] The process of the manufacture of nitrate of lime at Rjukan, Norway, is interestingly described by Mr. Henry J. Pierce: "Eighty per cent of the atmosphere is nitrogen and at Rjukan they have a large number of furnaces, each furnace requiring for operation 1500 horsepower. The furnace contains electrodes, and air is forced under moderate pressure through the intense electric flame..., converting the nitrogen of the atmosphere into nitric acid gas. The nitric acid gas passes through... very large steam boilers to be cooled, and in that way, they utilize the heat and obtain all of the steam power required in the operation of the plant. Then the gas is still further cooled and then passed into immense granite chambers filled with broken quartz. Nitric acid has no effect upon granite or upon quartz. It passes up through the quartz impeded in its progress, and water trickling down through the quartz absorbs the nitric acid gas, and you have nitric acid. The nitric acid afterwards percolates down through broken limestone, which has a strong affinity for it, and the limestone, disintegrated into power, having absorbed the acid, becomes nitrate of lime, containing a large percentage of nitrogen, which is used, mixed with phosphoric acid and potash, in the manufacture of fertilizers." *Hearings before the Senate Committee on Public Lands*, 63rd Cong., 3rd Sess., pp. 195-196.

Other beneficial uses of hydroelectricity may be found in the new fields of electrochemistry and electrometallurgy. A higher degree of heat is attainable through electricity than through ordinary fuel; there is also an absence of destructive gases. Upon these new electrical processes depend the manufacture of chlorine, graphite, alkalies, calcium carbide, and atmospheric nitrogen, together with the production of aluminum and steel-hardening metals and the refining of gold, silver and copper. At present the electrochemical industry of the United States is centered about Niagara Falls; here nearly one-half of the power used goes into electrochemistry. Aluminum produced by electrochemistry costs just one-quarter of the amount it costs when manufactured by purely chemical methods. In mining, much valuable ore has heretofore gone to waste because the metal content being very small could not be economically extracted. Extraction of these small particles is now made possible through electricity. Such particles are often of higher grade and greater purity than the metal extracted through the ordinary methods. This method of extracting and refining ores will constantly assume greater importance as the more accessible deposits of metals become exhausted. Besides these uses, we find the electric furnace coming into greater use in the refining and finishing of steel. Not alone important to the agricultural and the dyestuff industry is the production of nitrates, for in time of war the manufacture of high explosives depends upon the nitrate supply.

The following quotation gives some idea of the future possibilities of electricity in the field of industry:

In the field of manufacturing, electrochemistry occupies a unique place. It has already created a number of products of fundamental usefulness, while the latent opportunities for the future are very great. The development of artificial abrasives, especially carborundum, superior to natural abrasives, has greatly facilitated many processes of mechanical manufacture, such as the making of automobile, ordnance, and other materials; the production of calcium carbide has made the acetylene lamp possible, with inestimable benefit to thousands of mines the world over, which have thus been freed from smoky oil lamps and flickering candles; and the manufacture of artificial graphite is rendering a useful service as a lubricant in conserving energy. These products, which are of much greater significance than may be measured by the pecuniary value of the output, have been developed at Niagara Falls as a result of the abundant electric power available there and are made from raw materials of the commonest and cheapest kinds, such as sand, lime, coke and others.

. . . . An important industry has also developed in the electrolytic manufacture of sodium and chlorine, and their numerous compounds, used in large quantities in a wide variety of other industries, which are made from common salt—a widespread and cheap material. It would appear that one striking characteristic of electrochemistry is its ability to convert into useful products the commonest and cheapest of everyday materials. It holds forth in this sense the prospect of the highest type of constructive economic service.[1]

Consider the importance of water power in the improvement of navigation. By the damming of otherwise unnavigable streams for the development of water power, such streams can be made navigable for many miles and in that way become highways of commerce. Cheaper and more extensive means of transportation will always be the common demand of manufacturer and farmer. The extent to which the present transportation situation can be improved by a further development of water power is evidenced by the following table.[2]

[1] Gilbert and Pogue, *op. cit.*, pp. 307-309.

[2] *Hearings before the House Committee on Water Power,* 65th Cong., 2nd Sess., p. 483.

RIVERS OR PARTS OF RIVERS UNDER UNITED STATES JURISDICTION CONTAINING WATER-POWER SITES, THE POWER AVAILABLE, AND THE MILEAGE OF CANALIZED WATERWAY THAT COULD BE SECURED AT SMALL EXPENSE TO THE UNITED STATES TREASURY UNDER A LAW THAT WOULD ENCOURAGE POWER DEVELOPMENT

River	Power Available Horsepower	Length of waterway Miles
Allegheny	189,000	231
Chattahoochee	138,000	138
Chippewa	120,700	165
Clark Fork	1,110,000	170
Clinch	25,000	136
Columbia	4,498,000	400
Connecticut	30,000	23
Coosa	180,000	76
Cumberland	26,800	71
Des Moines	77,150	201
Flint	46,000	78
French Broad	207,000	222
Gasconade	25,300	107
Hiwassee	85,100	94
Holston	55,800	142
James	95,400	149
Little Tennessee	155,900	84
Upper Mississippi	149,000	148
Missouri	350,000	179
New and Kanawha	410,000	148
Ouachita	50,000	90
Potomac	102,700	60
Rainey	50,000	85
Roanoke	127,500	70
St. Croix (Wis.)	37,800	36
Savannah	78,700	129
Snake	369,000	140
Susquehanna	546,000	60
Tennessee	575,000	273
White (Missouri)	54,600	146
Wisconsin	170,000	200
Yadkin	48,500	73
Total	10,183,950	4,324

This list does not exhaust the possibilities of navigation improvement by means of water-power development, but it gives an idea of what may be accomplished. The steadying of the stream flow of rivers which are a menace to life and property at flood seasons is but another result of water-power improvement.

Irrigation and water-power development stand out as the two great needs of the West. The former is, of course, of more importance than the latter,[1] but in the creation of great irrigation projects, water-power possibilities are improved and in the setting up of great hydroelectric plants, irrigation projects are very often furthered. As an example of the latter case take the plans for the development of power at Priest Rapids on the Columbia River. By damming that stream, according to Mr. Henry Pierce of the Washington Irrigation and Development Co.,[2] a 250,000 all-year-round horsepower will be produced. That means that during the low-water months of November, December, January, February, and part of March, 250,000 horsepower may be made possible. When the summer flow brings a volume of water four times as great, the excess may be used for the operating of electrically driven pumps to raise the water to extensive areas of land lying along the river above the reach of gravity water. That means that in the central part of the State of Washington, which has only a four-inch rainfall for the year, the land will be made to yield crops in abundance. Many projects already developed are now doing what is promised by the Priest Rapids development.

Finally, to be enumerated among the benefits of water power are the quickening of manufacturing and the improvement of manufacturing methods. The absence of smoke in industrial enterprises electrically operated will mean more clean, more habitable, and more healthful cities. To dwell on these points would be but to emphasize the obvious.

[1] Too often this has been overlooked by power men who, having secured permission from the Government for the creation of irrigation projects, have given first consideration to power development to the neglect of irrigation either partially or wholly.

[2] *Hearings before the House Committee on Water Power*, 65th Cong., 2nd Sess., pp. 164-165.

These are the beneficial uses of hydroelectricity at the present time. There is nothing mysterious about this new power; it is not magic. Great things are accomplished by it, but it is subject to limitations in use and development. It is a costly and often a poor competitor of steam where coal is abundant. The financial hazards of development, even where there is no competition, are often forbidding to all but the venturesome and the wealthy.

WATER POWER—DEVELOPMENT

The present development in the United States is about 11,000,000 horsepower.[1] This represents a third of the power which is available in the United States. The total development of steam power used in manufacture and the generation of electricity was estimated in 1916 at 28,000,000 horsepower.[2] Today it would be fair to assume that it is over 30,000,000 horsepower.[3] Federal permits are required for over three-quarters of the water-power developments: those on navigable streams, on the public lands and in the national forests.

Before the passage of the Water Power Act of 1920 much was heard about the retarded growth of water-power improvements in the United States. The blame was generally laid at the door of the Federal Government for failure to adopt an enlightened policy. As evidence of this, the West was pointed out as the great water-power area with the best

[1] In 1921 the exact figure, according to the report of the Federal Power Commission, was 9,242,000 horsepower. The same Commission reports an installation of 2,400,000 horsepower already built or in the process of building for 1923. Allowing for development which nominally would not come under the Commission it would seem that the total developed power must be about 11,000,000 horsepower.

[2] Merrill, O. C., "Water Power Development on the National Forests and Proposed New Legislation," *Annals Am. Acad.*, Jan., 1916, pp. 244-254.

[3] See Appendix I for development in 1924.

sites on public lands where development was held up by the government at Washington. Representatives of the power interests were especially loud in their lamentations, and many others joined with them; the sole idea was to rush through a bill which would lighten the existing government control. As we shall see later the legislative policy of the Congress and the administrative policy of the executive departments were not altogether favorable to the promotion of great water-power enterprises, but these were only two of the many causes for the lack of increase in hydroelectric development in this country. What do the facts show regarding development in the West before 1920?

In the first place it is well to remember that water-power development began in the East about a century ago and that that involved hundreds of small streams used directly in manufacturing. The electric industry is comparatively new; water power in the West is chiefly connected with this industry which has attained its growth only within the last twenty-five years. Furthermore, it is to be expected that the great industrial East should have developed its resources earlier and more extensively. Despite all this the West has not been slow. In proportion to its population and in extent of development the West had accomplished more in the last twenty-five years before the passage of the Act of 1920 than the East had accomplished in a hundred years. In the states west of Kansas, the amount of power used in the generation of electricity by public utility corporations, street railway companies and municipalities had increased from 1906 to 1916 by 440 per cent, or twice as fast as in the remainder of the United States. In proportion to population, the amount of power which was used for the above purposes was two and one half times as much as in the remainder of the United States. Six years before the passage of the Water Power Act, the power plants of public utility corporations in California had an installation of one million horsepower; the sum of the greatest loads carried by the industrial plants was a little over 700,000 horsepower, perhaps 600,000 horsepower would be the greatest requirement. California, therefore, had a reserve above ordinary needs of from three to four hundred thousand horsepower. Mr. Merrill estimated the reserve at about 100,000 horsepower [1] over the reserves needed in the greatest emergency. The obvious conclusion is that in California there was more power than users; in other words, *overdevelopment*. A similar situation prevailed in Oregon and Washington. It used to be contended that most of the development took place on private land under state rather than under federal jurisdiction. In 1916 of the 1,800,000 horsepower developed in the Western states, fifty percent was generated from plants constructed in whole or in part in National Forests and operated under permit from the Department of Agriculture.[2] In that same year about 200,000 horsepower additional was in process of building, with about a million horsepower more contemplated under permits where work had not been started. If plants occupying public lands outside of the National Forests were considered, the development under Government supervision would have been considerably over half of the developed water power in the West. Over half, then, of the development in the West was made under government permits revocable at any time. One western periodical said:

> When it is remembered that half of all the hydroelectric plants in the West are operating parts of their generating, storage, or transmission systems under revocable permits, it becomes clear that even this objectionable feature has failed to stop the growth of the West's hydroelectric industry. In truth, it has so little

[1] O. C. Merrill's article in the *Annals Am. Acad.* for January, 1916, referred to above.

[2] See Appendix II.

stopped or even retarded this growth that in many districts the supply of hydro electric power is larger than the demand for it. In view of these facts the oft-repeated allegation that the normal development of the West's hydroelectric industry is being strangled by the Federal Government is absurd. . . .[1]

It is not to be thought that the policy of the government before 1920 is here approved; nor is there any reason to believe that development might not have been much greater under more satisfactory legislation, but legislation must be looked upon as a contributing, not as the sole cause for lack of development. On all sides people regretted the fact that our water powers were not more fully developed. It is certain, however, that many people were under the impression that water-power progress was at complete standstill.[2] Difficulties in the way of development varied from place to place; certain of these difficulties must be noted.

FACTORS IN GROWTH

The development of electricity by water power is, comparatively speaking, a new enterprise. The use of steam has had the inventions of many years behind it and the confidence of engineers and investors. Hydroelectricity was for many years a matter for experiment and laboratory study. It was regarded as a blessing of the future, still too young to be taken seriously. The failure of project after project because of engineering miscalculations made it particularly difficult to secure the capital to develop water power. One engineer has said:

the failures have not come about from financial legerdemain . . . but the honest mistakes of the engineers. . . . Now, I am an

[1] "The Water Power Situation," *Sunset Magazine*, April, 1916, p. 33.

[2] It is true that development on navigable streams had practically come to a standstill.

engineer and it is not a very pleasant thing for me to say that these difficulties have come about through the mistakes of engineers. . . . The mistakes were honest mistakes in most all of the cases and they included mis-estimates, if you please, of the quantity of water in most cases, running all the way from 30 to 200 per cent. And then the plants always cost a good deal more than the engineer told the banker they would cost, with the result that the financial showing is rarely half as good as what the engineer promised at the outset.[1]

For the development of a hydroelectric project, funds necessary to cover the cost of the maximum development must be at hand. A water-power plant, unlike a steam plant which can be progressively developed, must be built to give its greatest possible power at the very start. Sometimes a market is at hand to take this power in its entirety, at other times the market must be built up to consume the power. This will sometimes take many years. In water-power development, therefore, the initial expense is the big expense. Operating costs are not great. There is no fuel cost as in the case of steam plants; there is a low labor cost, as only few men are required to operate a hydroelectric plant. A distribution of costs in water-power plants as compared with steam plants is shown in the following chart:[2]

Expense	Steam Station (per cent of total gross operating expenses)	Hydroelectric Station (per cent of total gross operating expenses)
Administration	4.0	4.0
Ordinary operating expenses (except coal)	10.6	4.8
Coal	48.9	..
Taxes and Insurance	6.7	2.8
Depreciation	10.8	11.0
Bond interest	19.0	77.4
Total	100.0	100.0

[1] *Hearings before the Senate Committee on Public Lands*, 63rd Cong., 3rd Sess., p. 295.

[2] Gilbert and Pogue, *op. cit.*, p. 181.

To secure this money at the start, the prospector must convince the bankers that the site will produce the power and that a market is at hand to take it. The best sites, it must be remembered, have been appropriated by large and wealthy corporations, so that an independent developer of small means must present an extraordinary case before the funds are forthcoming. This has meant that a few great corporations have come to dominate the field. Difficulties of financing hydroelectric projects have retarded development from the start. Some people have the entirely erroneous idea that every hydroelectric plant is a gold mine, but such is not the case. Some plants are exceedingly prosperous, while others run on, receiving a moderate return, and still others to be of any value at all must tie in with a great system of plants. Dogmatic statements to the effect that water-power plants are more prosperous and more effective than steam plants are generalizations which disregard the facts. It is difficult indeed to make any comparison between the cost of steam and the cost of water power and to say which is the cheaper. In each case one must examine carefully the location of the plant with respect to the proximity of fuel resources and market and with respect to the nature of the whole plant and equipment. Where steam and hydro plants are tied together in one great system, it is almost impossible to get a comparison. This much, however, must be kept in mind: steam plants in the East and Middle West will for some time be cheaper for those sections than water power because of the abundance of coal; the West will find its chief asset in its great water powers, lacking as it does great fuel resources. One kind of power will be cheap in one region and expensive in another and vice versa.

MONOPOLY

Because of the risks involved in financing, because of the highly technical nature of the work, because of the necessity of interlocking many hydroelectric units to give continuous service and maximum efficiency in a community, the hydroelectric industry has from the start shown a tendency towards monopoly and centralization of control. The movement towards concentration is found in every section of the United States. The rate of increase in concentration has been highest in the south Atlantic states, while the extent of concentration is greatest in the western states.[1] In 1909 the Bureau of Corporations reported that thirteen groups of interests controlled one-third of the commercial water-power in the United States. In 1912 the same Bureau reported that ten groups controlled three-fifths of the commercial water power. The best sites have been taken by these groups. Harley W. Nehf of Spokane, Washington, writing in the *Journal of Political Economy* reports that representatives were engaged by a large power company in Colorado to locate the best power sites. He says:

> Its activities were extended, not only to acquire new sites, but also to take over those rights which others found it necessary to relinquish. This was illustrated in the cases of the Glenwood and Kremling sites. A Denver promoter was known as a professional filer for water rights. By filing in the names of his friends he secured many rights which were used for the benefit of a larger power company.[2]

The number of water-power sites affording continuous power and good markets for that power is naturally limited. Ownership of the best sites forms the basis of monopoly. In its trust prospectus the International Paper Company stated competition could hardly prove successful, if attempted, because its valuable water-power sites could not readily be duplicated.[3] Of about one hundred power dams authorized

[1] *Senate Document 316*, 64th Cong., 1st Sess., pt. i, p. 14.

[2] October, 1916, p. 775.

[3] *Commercial and Financial Chronicle*, vol. lxvii, p. 177.

by the Congress from 1879 to just before the passage of the Act of 1920 over one-half were controlled by large water-power companies.[1] In 1915 Secretary Houston reported that the following eighteen companies controlled 2,356,521 water horsepower, more than one-half (51.1%) of the total water power used in public-service operations in the United States:

1. Stone and Webster
2. Montana Power Company
3. Utah Securities Corporation
4. E. W. Clark and Co. (Management Corporation)
5. Southern Power Company
6. Hydraulic Company of Niagara Falls
7. Pacific Gas & Electric Co. (Southern California Electric Co.)
8. Pennsylvania Water & Power Co.
9. Pacific Light and Power Corporation
10. H. M. Byllesly & Co.
11. Niagara Falls Power Co.
12. Washington Water Power Co.
13. Georgia Railway Light & Power Co.
14. New England Power Company of Maine
15. Western Power Co.
16. Alabama Traction, Light & Power Co.
17. Commonwealth Power Railway & Light Co.
18. United Railways Investment Company

Of this group Stone and Webster, through their management of operating companies, controlled according to this report, more total power than any other corporation—340,-

[1] These statements and the subsequent statements on monopoly and concentration found in this chapter are drawn from the comprehensive three-volume report of the Secretary of Agriculture issued as *Senate Document 316*, 64th Cong., 1st Sess. and from an earlier report (1912) of Herbert Knox Smith of the Bureau of Corporations under the title of *Water Power Development in the United States*.

211 water horsepower and 529,854 total horsepower. This control consists in actual ownership of properties, majority stock ownership, in lease or in direct management. The number of plants owned, controlled, or managed by these eighteen corporations is as follows:[1]

Name of Company and State	Number of Stations	Water Power Horse-power	Steam and gas power Horse-power	All power Horse-power
1. Stone & Webster:				
Connecticut	5	16,000	6,505	22,505
Florida	4	1,400	8,615	10,015
Georgia	7	29,426	18,790	48,216
Iowa	3	150,000	....	150,000
Kentucky	1	....	2,350	2,350
Louisiana	1	....	1,400	1,400
Massachusetts	7	....	20,630	20,630
Michigan	2	....	5,750	5,750
Nevada	3	9,800	....	9,800
New York	4	45,800	9,000	54,800
Rhode Island	3	2,485	6,650	9,135
Texas	11	....	71,793	71,793
Washington	11	85,300	38,160	123,460
Total, All States	62	340,211	189,643	529,854
2. Southern California Edison Co.:				
California	24	174,350	158,420	332,770
3. H. M. Byllesby & Co.:				
Alabama	1	....	9,330	9,330
Arkansas	1	....	5,425	5,425
California	6	17,200	20,020	37,220
Colorado	5	2,400	11,894	14,294
Idaho	1	....	900	900
Illinois	1	....	9,660	9,660
Iowa	1	....	3,350	3,350
Kentucky	1	....	33,330	33,330
Minnesota	10	43,350	18,500	61,950
Montana	2	2,820	250	3,070
North Dakota	3	....	6,950	6,950
Oklahoma	5	....	17,215	17,215
Oregon	6	520	6,227	6,747
South Dakota	3	2,065	3,740	5,805
Virginia	3	20,900	7,500	28,400
West Virginia	2	....	6,050	6,050
Wisconsin	2	26,800	....	26,800
Total, All States	53	116,155	160,341	276,496

[1] For concentration by states see Appendix III.

4. E. W. Clark & Co. (management corporation):				
Illinois	4	....	19,100	19,100
Maine	16	37,330	18,390	55,720
Oregon	11	80,000	35,875	115,875
Tennessee	5	45,000	3,0000	75,000
Total, All States	36	162,330	103,365	265,695
5. Pacific Gas & Electric Co.:				
California	13	152,080	108,540	260,620
6. Southern Power Co.:				
North Carolina	4	30,000	38,010	68,010
South Carolina	5	127,850	9,000	136,850
Total, All States	9	157,850	47,010	204,860
7. Utah Securities Corporation:				
Colorado	8	18,630	1,480	20,110
Idaho	10	73,507	300	73,807
Utah	25	79,565	28,594	108,159
Total, All States	43	171,702	30,374	202,076
8. Montana Power Co.:				
Montana	19	179,700	8,300	188,000
9. Commonwealth Power, Railway & Light Co.:				
Illinois	7	....	26,480	26,480
Indiana	1	....	13,070	13,070
Michigan	38	70,813	66,610	137,423
Ohio	1	....	6,000	6,000
Total, All States	47	70,813	112,160	182,973
10. Hydraulic Power Co.:				
New York	3	153,000	....	153,000
11. Georgia Railway & Power Co.:				
Georgia	7	100,400	33,720	134,120
12. Washington Water Power Co.:				
Idaho	1	16,300	....	16,300
Washington	4	92,900	16,000	108,900
Total, All States	5	109,200	16,000	125,200
13. Pennsylvania Water & Power Co.:				
Pennsylvania	2	118,000	....	118,000
14. Niagara Falls Power Co.:				
New York	2	115,000	....	115,000

15. Western Power Co.:				
California	4	73,300	38,670	112,000
16. Alabama Traction, Light & Power Co.:				
Alabama	7	72,500	18,920	91,420
17. United Railways & Investment Co.:				
California	5	65,600	25,330	90,930
18. New England Power Co. of Maine:				
Massachusetts	4	49,400	....	49,400
Vermont	3	31,300	700	32,000
Total, All States	7	80,700	700	81,400
Grand Total, 18 companies	348	2,412,921	1,051,493	3,464,414

A résumé of the extent of the business of one of these corporations, the Pacific Gas and Electric Company, just prior to the Act of 1920, given by one of its officials (John A. Britton), demonstrates the extent of the business and the power for good or evil which even one of these companies holds. This company operates almost entirely in the state of California and in that state generates and distributes electricity, provides gas and water, and operates a street railway. The territory covered by its activities amounted in 1918 to 39,000 square miles and the company served 2,000,000 people in about 230 cities and towns of the state. It operated 1640 miles of high-tension lines (these transmitting anywhere from 11,000 to 110,000 volts) and it had 6,000 miles of distribution systems. Under its management were fourteen hydroelectric plants with a capacity of 164,000 horsepower. Of all the power that it developed, 57,300 horsepower was supplied to electrically operated railways, 144,400 horsepower to factories, 10,000 for the lighting of streets, and 262,000 for lighting of stores, hotels, and residences.

The above groups manage or supervise water-power sites for supplying public-service corporations. But there are other groups that are interested in water-power development—the manufacturers of electrical machinery and apparatus. Such groups are the General Electric and the Westinghouse Companies. If community of directors signifies anything, the General Electric Company is by far the most powerful electrical concern in the world, and exercises an extensive influence over water powers in the United States, although controlling *directly* little water power. Its control is chiefly exercised through three subsidiary concerns:

The United Electric Securities Co. (1890)
The Electrical Securities Corporation (1904)
The Electric Bond and Share Co. (1905)

The common stock of all three of these companies is owned by the General Electric Company. These principal subsidiary corporations are active in determining the policies of the General Electric group. The United Securities Co. and the Electrical Securities Corporation purchase the bonds of electric lighting, power, and railway plants and issue in return their own collateral trust funds. The Electric Bond and Share Company purchases securities of power companies and manages operations.

Herbert Knox Smith of the Bureau of Corporations in a report issued in 1912 showed how the General Electric Company controlled or had influence in some twenty-four water-power companies. The water powers controlled by the General Electric were (in 1912): Group A.

Companies	Locality	Power developed and under construction h. p.
American Power & Light Co.	Oregon and Washington	15,840
Asheville Electric Co.	North Carolina	260
Carolina Power & Light Co.	North Carolina	37,000
Consolidated Power & Light Co.	South Dakota	2,000
Rockford Electric Co.	Illinois	1,760
Schenectady Power Co.	New York	26,000
Total		82,860

The above companies held 5,500 horsepower undeveloped. The Schenectady Power Company is owned outright by the General Electric Company and practically all of its power is used at the General Electric works at Schenectady.

In the next table are those companies of whose securities a portion is held by the General Electric Companies and some of whose officers and directors are officers and directors of the General Electric Companies: Group B.

Companies	Locality	Water Power Developed and under Construction h. p.	Undeveloped h. p.
Butte Electric & Power Co.	Montana	69,260	97,600
Central Colorado Power Co.	Colorado	39,000	50,000
Northwestern Power Co.	Minnesota	39,000	20,000
Pennsylvania Water & Power Co.	Pennsylvania	135,000	....
Sierra & San Francisco Power Co.	California	65,500	50,000
San Juan Water & Power Co.	Colorado	8,000	...
Western Power Co.	California	60,000	300,000
Whatcom County Railway & Light Co.	Washington	3,300	5,000
Total		419,060	522,600

The influence of these companies was summed up by Dr. Smith as follows:

Thus the Butte Electric and Power Company, as already shown, occupies a commanding position in the water-power industry in Montana, while the Central Colorado Power Company together with the San Juan Water and Power Company with which it is affiliated, have an almost complete control of developed water power in Colorado. The power of the Northwestern Company in Minnesota is owned by the Great Northern Power Company, a subsidiary. The Great Northern Power Company owns all the common stock of the Northern Power Company of Wisconsin, through which it distributes electricity in that State. It owns in fee rights of way for transmission lines in the City of Duluth. . . . In the City of Superior it supplies power to the Superior Water, Light and Power Company.

The Sierra and San Francisco Power Company is controlled by the United Railways Investment Company of San Francisco and nearly all of the power generated by it is employed by street railways in that city.

The Western Power Company, the water power of which is owned by a subsidiary, the Great Western Power Company, ... sells a large portion of its power to the Pacific Gas and Electric Company.

The Whatcom County Railway and Light Company does the street railway, electric light and gas business of Bellingham, Washington. It owns the entire capital stock of the Bellingham-Skagit Railway Company.

The exact degree of influence which the General Electric exercised over these corporations could not be determined. It may not have been nearly so great as some trust-busters made it out to be. The significance of the control was greatly exaggerated in some quarters, as in most cases the percentage of securities of the above companies actually owned by the General Electric was comparatively small—that of stock alone seldom amounting to as much as five per cent of the total.

In the next group are those companies some of whose officers and directors were (in 1912) officers and directors in the General Electric, or which were in some way connected with interests allied with the General Electric Company, but without corporate ownership of securities: Group C.

Companies	Locality	Developed Water Power h. p.
Albany Southern R. R.	New York	6,320
Colorado Springs Light, Heat & Power Co.	Colorado	3,000
Manchester Traction, Light & Power Co.	New Hampshire	10,000
Niagara Falls Power Co.	Niagara Falls	118,300 [1]
North American Co	Various	69,750 [2]
Portland Railway, Light & Power Co.	Oregon	48,000
Puget Sound Power Co.	Washington	20,000
Tampa Electric Co.	Florida	1,400
Turners Falls Co.	Massachusetts	9,425
Washington Water Power Co.	Washington & Idaho	151,000
Total		437,195

[1] Not including 62,500 h. p. on the Canadian side owned by an affiliated concern.

[2] Of which 68,000 electrical h. p. (i. e. in form of electricity) is purchased from other companies.

A few of the above cases that show community of interest are:

In the case of the Niagara Falls Power Company a connection with the General Electric was established through the firm of J. P. Morgan and Company which had representation on the directorates of both concerns.

In the case of the Washington Water Power Company, Hinsdale Parsons, vice president of the General Electric Company and a director of the Electric Bond and Share Company was a director of the Washington concern.

The North American Company, a holding company, had among its directors: C. A. Coffin, president of the General Electric Company, George R. Sheldon, president of the Electrical Securities Corporation, and C. W. Wetmore, a director of the Electric Bond and Share Co.

No exact relationship could be observed between the General Electric and Westinghouse interests except that the patents of both groups had been pooled since 1896 and certain common directors could be noted.

Control of localities by certain groups may be briefly stated in the following way: that the General Electric interests control the water-power situation in large portions of Washington, Oregon, Colorado, Montana and elsewhere. The Stone and Webster interests exercise control (management) in localities in Washington, Iowa, and Georgia. The Pacific Gas and Electric Company dominates the power situation in a large number of localities in Northern California. The Southern Power Company controls the power situation in North and South Carolina. The S. Morgan Smith interests dominate the power situation about Atlanta, Georgia, while the Gould interests control the best available power sites in the vicinity of Richmond, Virginia. The Commonwealth Power Company controls the lower peninsula of Michigan; while the control of Southern California by the California Edison Company has become notorious.

In general the situation is the same today as it was in 1909, 1913, and 1915. It is, however, necessary to take in connection with the testimony of Mr. Smith, Mr. Houston, Mr. Pinchot and others a refutation offered by Mr. Dahl of the Electric Bond and Share Company.[1] Mr. Dahl takes the first group alleged to be completely under the control of the General Electric water-power companies where a majority of the common stock is controlled by the General Electric. These he would not argue about, but would emphasize the fact that 82,860 horsepower is all that these concerns control. Turning to the second classification made by Mr. Smith where the General Electric interests are admitted not to control the stock ownership but in which there is some slight ownership of stocks or bonds or both and a common directorate, Mr. Dahl claims that the connection between the groups is far too tenuous for one to say there is control. He takes one illustration:

In group B is listed the Sierra and San Francisco Power Company with a total of 65,500 horsepower developed and 50,000 horsepower undeveloped. According to the figures shown by Mr. Herbert Knox Smith, the so-called General Electric interests own but 9.7 per cent of the bonds of the Sierra and San Francisco Power Company, and Mr. S. Z. Mitchell is shown as a director of the Sierra and San Francisco Power Company. Mr. Mitchell is, of course, a director of the Electric Bond and Share Company and is its president. There is no claim of any stock ownership and in a note to group B, Mr. Smith admits that the 9.7 per cent of bonds owned are second-mortgage bonds. So, without the ownership of any stock or any first-mortgage bonds, but merely through the ownership of 9.7 per cent of second-mortgage bonds and the fact that Mr. Mitchell is a common director to the Sierra and San Francisco Power

[1] Mr. Dahl's testimony will be found in the *Hearings before the Senate Commitee on Public Lands*, 63rd Cong., 3rd Sess., beginning on p. 689.

Company and Electric Bond and Share Company, the conclusion is arrived at that the so-called General Electric interests control 65,500 developed and 50,000 undeveloped horsepower owned or claimed to be owned by the Sierra and San Francisco Power Company.

In taking up the third group (Group C) Mr. Dahl calls attention to the fact that almost 50 per cent of the horsepower said to be controlled by the General Electric Company comes within this group. One common director between one of the companies in this class and one of the General Electric Companies places the company in this group; there need be no ownership of stock or securities. Mr. Dahl figures that out of the ten companies listed in this group each one of eight has one director common to the General Electric Company. In one of these companies of the ten there are two common directors.

Mr. Dahl does well to call attention to the fact that common directorship does not necessarily mean common control. It can not be put down as a general proposition that when one director appears in two corporations there is a concentration of the control. Mr. Smith is not unmindful of this fact when he says, "On the other hand, the mere ownership of a small block of stock or a comparatively small amount of bonds and slight representation upon the board of directors may not indicate any considerable degree of influence." There is nothing unusual in the fact that industries seek the best informed men. The desirability of selecting men prominent in the electrical business may bring about the appearance of the same names again and again in the directorates of several corporations. A great deal will depend upon the financial power of any one individual, his controlling investment, upon the force of his personality, and upon his length of service on the board. Yet it cannot be denied that the director of a concern in which the General

Electric has a controlling interest may be a veritable god from Olympus on the directorship of a smaller corporation. What goes on at the meetings of the directors, who voices control, who shapes the policy are more or less matters of conjecture, but the constant re-appearance of identical names in one corporation after another covering a large territory is, to say the very least, significant.

The concern of many people over this concentration which in the early years of water-power activity was unregulated, and even now is not regulated altogether satisfactorily, was quite justifiable. Great water-power combines are in a position to determine the cost of things used as necessities by the people. The ability to determine power costs makes possible the ability to determine the cost of articles for which power is used. Going a step further it is easily seen that the ability to determine the costs of manufactured articles largely permits the regulation of the conditions of manufacturing those articles.

Some combinations may not only influence production but distribution as well. The control of railway transportation may easily rest in the hands of that concern which supplies the electrical energy for the transportation. Here, too, is an opportunity to influence freight rates. The determination of rates carries with it the possibility of other dictation, such as what commodities may be transported, where they may be carried, and by whom they may be handled.

The relation of such combines with the banking groups brings further possibility of the domination of the industrial life of the nation. To what end intercorporate relations between banking interests and water-power combines may lead we dare not hazard a guess. By their influence on legislation they may dictate the use of agricultural and timber lands, and the development of irrigation projects.

Rigid government control is indeed essential. There are

some who claim that government control can never be adequate while private operation of giant power resources remains. In other words, government ownership and operation is the ultimate goal. So far, government control whether by state or nation has not been an unqualified success. Regulation is on trial. Public ownership and operation will only come as public regulation breaks down.

One thing we have learned: that there can not be free and unlimited competition in water-power development. It is an unquestioned fact that the hydroelectric industry tends towards monopoly. As a natural monopoly it need by no means be an evil *per se.* Secretary of Agriculture Houston has said:

> Monopolization of the supply in any given territory makes possible through interconnection of stations and through diversification of load, economies of operation that would not be possible for isolated independent stations. Interruptions of service may be lessened, the needs of the customer may be better served, and rates may be lower with a single power system than with several.[1]

To this it should be added—as noted before—that large amounts of capital may be easily secured by these combinations. Improvements and extensions can be made as the demand occurs and the opportunity offers itself; corporations can afford to wait for long periods for returns on single units of their investments. The larger the production, the lower the cost per unit of output will be. It is a matter of efficiency and elimination of unnecessary duplication.

Monopoly is inevitable; public regulation or public ownership is essential.

[1] *Senate Document 316,* 64th Cong., 1st Sess., p. 55, pt. i.

CHAPTER II

LEGAL ASPECTS OF WATER-POWER

THE physical and economic difficulties standing in the way of water-power development are generally overlooked and the legislative difficulties are misunderstood. The ordinary citizen, relying upon the promises of a great electric paradise, often asked impatiently: "Well, why don't they go ahead and develop the water power? The water's there. What's the matter with the Government that it doesn't pass the laws to give us superpower?" This anxious type of citizen was easy prey for the water-power promoter and the real estate agent holding for sale large tracts of land about great water-power sites. He seemed to be legion at crucial moments in the struggle for sane water-power control. An understanding of the efforts of conservationists to give the Government a whip hand in power development through the imposition of privilege charges and rate control and of the legal obstacles thrown in the path of such efforts by monopolists, was lacking among the good citizenry of certain sections of the country.

So large a part did the question of the legality of Government control play, that it will be necessary to examine this side of the question before proceeding to a review of the legislative history of the problem.

THE OWNERSHIP OF RUNNING WATER

There is no property in flowing water. From the earliest times down to the present this principle has been understood and asserted. From the *Institutes* of Justinian we learn:

"By natural law these things are common to all, namely: air, running water, the sea, and as a consequence, the shores of the sea."[1] This idea of water as *res communis* passed on down through the centuries and is further emphasized by the great jurist Puffendorff writing in the seventeenth century: "It is usual to attribute an exemption from property to the light and heat of the sun, to the air, to the running water, and the like."[2] This same principle is found in the common law Blackstone notes: "But, after all, there are some few things, which, notwithstanding the general introduction and continuance of property, must still unavoidably remain in common. . . . Such are the elements of light, air, and water."[3] In the United States the same doctrine prevails and is found in the commentaries of jurists and the decisions of the courts. In the case of Mitchell *v.* Warner it was said: "It is too late to enter into the legal character and quality of water; the law having been settled, time out of mind, on this subject and remained uniform and unquestioned. Water is neither land nor tenement nor susceptible to absolute ownership. It is a movable, wandering thing and must of necessity continue common by the law of nature."[4] In a New York case the same idea is found: "Running water in natural streams is not property and never was."[5]

THE RIGHT OF USUFRUCT—COMMON LAW

On the other hand a person may have property in the *use* of running water. This right, called a usufructuary right,

[1] Report of National Waterways Commission, 62nd Cong., 2nd Sess., *Senate Document 469*.

[2] *Puffendorff*, C. 5.

[3] Blackstone, *Commentaries*, bk. ii, p. 14; bk. ii, p. 18.

[4] *Mitchell v. Warner*, 5 Connecticut 519 (1825).

[5] *Syracuse v. Stacey*, 169 New York 231 (1901).

is by common law limited to those owning land on the banks of a stream; it is attached to the land and passes by conveyance of the land. This use of the water must be reasonable, must not interfere with the usual flow of the stream, and must in no way work to the detriment of the riparian owners above or below the user. The rule of usufruct appears in the Roman law where it is clearly stated in the *Institutes* of Justinian;[1] it is found in the common law and has been affirmed in many cases in the English courts.[2] In America the rule as stated in the common law is recognized in the larger number of states, particularly those lying east of the Mississippi river. This doctrine is explained by one authority as follows:

A comprehensive statement of the rights of the riparian owner is that he has a right to have the stream remain in place and flow as nature directs, and to make such use of the flowing water as he can make without materially interfering with the equal rights of the owners above and below him on the stream. This prevents the upper proprietor from diverting the stream, consuming the water for other than natural uses, polluting the water, or interfering with the regular, natural flow of the current to such an extent as materially to injure the lower owner; and it prevents the lower owner from throwing the water back on the land of the upper owner.[3]

Chancellor Kent, in his *Commentaries,* states the same rule when he says:

Every proprietor of lands on the banks of a river has, naturally, an equal right to the use of the water which flows in the stream

[1] I *Instit.*, tit. IV, V, *Pandects* 7.

[2] *Embrey v. Owen,* 6 Exch. 352; *Liggins v. Inge,* 7 Bing. 692; *Lyon v. Fishmongers,* 1 App. Case 673.

[3] *River Club v. Wade,* 100 Wisconsin 86 (1898); *Vernon Irrigation Co. v. Los Angeles,* 106 California 237 (1895).

adjacent to his lands, as it was wont to run, *currere solebat*, without diminution or alteration. . . . Though he may use the water while it runs over his land as an incident to the land, he can not unreasonably detain it or give it another direction, and he must return it to its ordinary channel when it leaves his estate.[1]

In Head *v.* Amoskeag, Justice Gray said:

The right to the use of running water is *publici juris* and common to all those proprietors of the bed and banks of the stream from its source to its outlet. Each has a right to the reasonable use of the water as it flows past his land.[2]

So, also, Chief Justice Shaw in the case of Elliott *v.* Fitchburg Railway Company said:

The right to flowing water is now well settled to be a right incident to property in land; . . . while it is common and equal to all through whose lands it flows, no one can obstruct and divert it, yet . . . . each proprietor has a right to a just and reasonable use of it as it passes through his land; and so long as it is not wholly obstructed or diverted, or no larger appropriation of the water running through it is made than a just and reasonable use, it can not be said to be wrongful or injurious to a proprietor lower down. What is just and reasonable use may often be a difficult question, depending upon various circumstances. To take a quantity of water from a large and running stream for agricultural or manufacturing purposes would cause no sensible or practicable diminution of the benefit, to the prejudice of the lower proprietor; whereas taking the same quantity from a small running brook passing through many farms would be of great and manifest injury to those below. . . . It is therefore to a considerable extent a question of degree.[3]

[1] 3 *Commentaries* 439.

[2] *Head v. Amoskeag Mfg. Co.*, 113 U. S. 9 (1885).

[3] *Elliot v. Fitchburg R. R. Co.*, 10 Cushing (Mass.) 191 (1852).

THE RIGHT OF USUFRUCT—DOCTRINE OF PRIOR APPROPRIATION

In the states of the West, the rule of prior appropriation has in whole or in part superseded the common-law rule. The doctrine had its rise in those mining states where it was often necessary to divert water to places far from riparian lands. Gradually the principle of first in time, first in right came to be accepted, and as far back as 1855 we find a California court declaring that among the most important rights of miners was the right to be protected in the possession of their selected localities and the rights of those who by prior appropriation had taken the waters from their natural beds and by costly artificial works had conducted them for miles over mountains and ravines to supply the necessity of gold diggers, and without which the most important interests of the mineral region would have remained without development—*qui prior est in tempore, potior est in jure.* Continuing the court said:

The miner who selects a piece of ground to work must take it as he finds it, subject to prior rights, which have an equal equity, on account of an equal recognition from the sovereign power. If it is upon a stream the waters of which have not been taken from their bed, they cannot be taken to his prejudice, but if they have already been diverted . . . . he has no right to complain, no right to interfere with the prior occupation of his neighbor, and must abide the disadvantage of his own selection.[1]

The above was a case involving the public lands of the United States to which, in California, the rule of prior appropriation is applied, but between private riparian owners the common-law doctrine prevails.[2] This half-and-half rule is

[1] *Irwin v. Philips,* 5 California 140 (1855).

[2] *Lux v. Haggin,* 69 California 255 (1886).

known as the California doctrine and has been adopted with modifications in Kansas, Montana, North Dakota, South Dakota, Washington, and in a few other states. On the other hand, Colorado goes the whole way in adopting in its entirety the prior appropriation principle. The Colorado doctrine is followed in Idaho, Nevada, New Mexico, Utah, and Wyoming. The rule of prior appropriation, wherever applied to the public lands, was expressly approved by the Federal Government in 1866 and again in 1870.[1] The passage of these statutes was in recognition of a custom obtaining in the public land states for many years during which time the United States made no specific pronouncement of policy in regard to public domain-riparian rights. In the case of Irwin *v.* Philips, quoted above, the position of the state was set forth by the court as follows:

> Courts are bound to take notice of the political and social condition of the country which they judicially rule. In this state the larger part of the territory consists of mineral lands, nearly the whole of which are the property of the public. No right or intent of disposition of these lands has been shown either by the United States or the state governments, and with the exception of certain state regulations, very limited in their character, a system has been permitted to grow up by the voluntary action and assent of the population, whose free and unrestrained occupation of the mineral region has been tacitly assented to by the one government, and heartily encouraged by the expressed legislative policy of the other. If there are, as must be admitted, many things connected with this system, which are crude and undigested, and subject to fluctuation and dispute, there are still some which a universal sense of necessity and propriety have so firmly fixed that they have come to be looked upon as having the force and effect of *res judicata.*

There was no denial on the part of the public land states,

[1] Sections 2339, 2340 *Revised Statutes.*

even before the passage of the acts of 1866 and 1870, of the rule of law now well-established that the United States has an absolute and perfect title to its lands. As the Supreme Court of California said in Lux *v.* Haggin:

> . . . the state courts have treated the prior appropriator on the theory that the appropriation was allowed or licensed by the United States. It has never been held that the right to appropriate waters on the public lands of the United States was derived directly from the state of California. . . . [1]

THE POWER OF THE STATES OVER RIVERS

What is the power of the states over rivers within their borders? The several states are each sovereign over the beds and waters of such streams. Not as property does the state hold the running waters, but as sovereign and as trustee for the public to guarantee that beneficial and reasonable use will be made of them. In the case of Martin *v.* Waddell, the court said:

> For when the Revolution took place the people of each state became themselves sovereign; and in that character hold the absolute right to all their navigable waters, and the soils under them, for their own common use, subject only to the rights surrendered by the Constitution to the General Government. [2]

The same rule is laid down by the United States Supreme Court in the case of Pollard *v.* Hagan, wherein it was held to apply in as full a measure to the newer states as to the thirteen original states of the Union. [3] The states determine whether the common law or prior appropriation is to be applied within their boundaries. [4] They determine by

[1] 69 California 255 (1886).

[2] *Martin v. Waddell's Lessee*, 16 Peters 367 (1842).

[3] *Pollard's Lessee v. Hagan et. al.*, 3 Howard 212 (1845).

[4] *U. S. v. Rio Grande Dam and Irrigation Co.*, 174 U. S. 690 (1898); *Broder v. Water Co.*, 101 U. S. 274 (1879); *Gutierres v. Albuquerque Irrigation Co.*, 188 U. S. 545 (1903); *Boquillas Land Co. v. Curtis*, 213 U. S. 339 (1909).

their constitutions and laws the limits of the riparian owner's rights, his ownership to high or low water or to the thread of the stream, his use of the water for power, fishing, bathing, irrigation, manufacturing, and his building of docks and wharves. The exercise of state powers, however, is always subject to those powers delegated by the Constitution to the Federal Government. Whether it be the common rule of usufruct or the rule of prior appropriation, all rules must be applied by the states in subrogation to the paramount rights of the Federal Government in regard to the maintenance of the navigability of streams.

THE POWERS OF THE FEDERAL GOVERNMENT

The Public Domain

In the western states the Federal Government owns vast tracts of land. The extent of this public domain may be realized from the following figures: in Arizona, 92 per cent of the lands within that state are owned by the United States Government; in California, 52.58 per cent; in Colorado, 56.67 per cent; in Idaho, 83.80 per cent; in Montana, 65.80 per cent; in Nevada, 87.82 per cent; in New Mexico, 62.83 per cent; in Oregon, 51 per cent; in Utah, 80.18 per cent; in Washington, 40 per cent; in Wyoming, 68 per cent.[1] By reason of this, the United States becomes riparian owner of valuable water-power lands. The United States, the same as any riparian owner, enjoys the usufruct of the water appurtenant to its lands; it can dispose of such

[1] See the testimony of Senator John F. Shafroth before the Senate Committee on Public Lands, 63rd Cong., 3rd Sess. on *H. R. 16673*, p. 821. The public lands of the United States are divided into five classes: the Public Domain of which there are 186,000,000 acres; the National Forests of which there are 135,000,000 acres, largely treeless; the National Parks of which there are 8,000,000 acres; the Indian Lands of which there are 34,000,000 acres; and the Mineral Lands of which there are 40,000,000 acres. An investigation of the administration of these lands is now underway in the United States Senate.

water on its own terms the same as other riparian owners. The United States Supreme Court has said: "The Government has with respect to its own land the rights of an ordinary proprietor." [1] Or again: "The United States can prohibit absolutely or fix the terms on which its property may be used."[2] If a corporation wishes to develop hydroelectric power on a stream within the public domain, *having first appropriated the water according to the law of the state,* a practice which, as we have seen, has been voluntarily approved by the United States, it may apply to the Federal Government for a lease of the land and the right to develop water power. The Government may lease on its own conditions for any time and for a rental. Such a lease and such a rental may be used by the Government to regulate the corporation in the interests of the people at large. The question might well be raised: Is not the Federal Government, like the private riparian, subject to conditions for the disposal of water power set down by the state? We have seen how the Government has by statute sanctioned the prior appropriation doctrine of the western states, and it will be found in most instances that the Government is desirous of avoiding any conflict with state laws. Nevertheless, the United States is not bound by state laws in its disposition of the public domain. The Constitution of the United States provides that Congress shall have the power to dispose of and make all needful rules and regulations respecting the territory, or other property belonging to the United States.[3] Of this particular section of the Constitution, the Supreme Court has said: "The full scope of this paragraph has never been definitely settled. Primarily, at least, it is a grant of power to the United States of control over its property." [4] In Butte City

[1] *Camfield v. U. S.*, 167 U. S. 518 (1896)

[2] *Light v. U. S.*, 220 U. S. 536 (1911).

[3] Part ii, section 3, article iv.

[4] *Kansas v. Colorado*, 206 U. S. 89 (1906).

Water Company *v.* Baker,[1] the same court said: "Congress is the body to which is given the power to determine the conditions upon which the public lands shall be disposed of." In Light *v.* the United States,[2] the court said: "And it is not for the courts to say how that trust (i.e. care of the public lands) shall be administered. That is for Congress to determine." At another time the court said:

With respect to the public domain, the Constitution vests in Congress the power of disposition and of making all needful rules and regulations. That power is subject to no limitations. Congress has the absolute right to prescribe the times, the conditions, and the mode of transfering this property, or any part of it. . . . No State legislation can interfere with this right or embarrass its exercise.[3]

Or again:

It may well happen that Congress should embrace in an enactment introducing a new State into the Union legislation intended as a regulation of commerce among the states, or with Indian tribes situated within the limits of such new states, or regulations touching the sale, care and disposition of the public lands or reservations therein, which might be upheld as legislation within the sphere of the plain power of Congress. But in every such case, such legislation would derive its force not from any agreement or compact with the proposed new state, nor by reason of its acceptance of such enactment as a term of admission, but solely because the power of Congress extended to the subject and, therefore, would not operate to restrict the State's legislative power in respect of any matter which was not plainly within the regulating power of Congress.[4]

The states of the West resent this federal control of the

[1] 196 U. S. 119 (1904).

[2] *Op. cit.*

[3] *Gibson v. Chouteau,* 13 Wall. 92, 99 (1871).

[4] *Coyle v. Oklahoma,* 221 U. S. 559, 574 (1911).

public domain as an interference with the sovereign rights of the states. It is pointed out that the states which have no public domain are free of this federal interference and that, therefore, the public land states find themselves on an inequality with their sister commonwealths. It is held that, by holding this land, the Government cuts down the revenues of the western states. Governor Ammons of Colorado said, in testifying before the Public Lands Committee of the Senate:

> I want to say that nineteen-twentieths of the taxes of our state come off of about one-eleventh of the territory, and that only a small fraction over 32 per cent of the territory of our state is now on the tax roll. More than half of that is cheap pasture land and yet we are attempting to maintain all those institutions out there that other states are maintaining. It is a terrific burden . . . . my State of Colorado has just as much right to its resources . . . . as has any other state in this Union to its resources. The old original states themselves made that contract and that promise to every new state that should come into this Union, that it should be admitted on an equal footing with the original states. The original states have their property to tax, and we must have ours or we can not support our state governments.[1]

There may be hardships involved, there may be inequalities, but it is too late to say that the Federal Government has no legal right of regulating the public domain contrary to state law. Such interference may be poor policy, but that is another matter. If the stream on which the water rights are granted not only flows through the public domain, but is also a navigable stream, an added source of control is given the United States. This source of control will be taken up presently. The disposition of water-power rights

[1] Hearings before the Senate Committee on Public Lands on *H. R. 16673*, 63rd Cong., 3rd Sess., pp. 626, 637.

and the imposition of charges for enjoying these rights, and the continual regulation of these rights on the public domain rest indisputably with the Federal Government.

THE POWER OF FEDERAL GOVERNMENT

The Treaty-Making Power

A second source of federal water-power control is the treaty-making power. The president is authorized by and with the advice and consent of two-thirds of the Senate to make treaties with foreign nations. Some of our greatest water powers are found on the streams along the Canadian boundary. How extensive is the power of Congress over boundary streams? In May, 1910, a treaty was drawn up, passed, and signed with Great Britain. Under this treaty it was agreed that the volume of water to be diverted on the American side from the Niagara River should be limited to 20,000 cubic feet per second, and on the Canadian side to 36,000 cubic feet per second.[1] In this particular case, the treaty was made for the purpose, so the preamble sets forth, of preventing the diversion of water from the Niagara River to the extent of affecting the level of Lake Erie and the flow of the stream itself. The main purpose of the treaty, however, was to preserve the scenic beauty of Niagara Falls; such is the motive expressed in the Act of June 29, 1906, urging the agreement with Great Britain.[2] It is superfluous, perhaps, to point out that Congress has no express power to preserve scenic beauty however laudable that motive may be. Here then is an instance of the exercise of the treaty-making power over boundary waters. Other agreements have also been made with Canada regulating the diversion of boundary waters. To effect an agreement with a neighboring state to preserve the uninterrupted flow of a stream would seem to be a legitimate exercise of

[1] Treaty Series No. 548.

[2] 34 *Stat.* 626.

the treaty-making power. Certain it is that the states themselves are debarred from making any such agreements without the consent of Congress. It is unquestionably a matter of great concern affecting the welfare and the good-will of two nations. Professor Burdick outlines the extent of federal treaty-making power when he says:

The sound doctrine with regard to the treaty power seems to be this, that the National Government may by treaty deal with any matter which is an appropriate subject of international agreement, as long as it does not contravene any express prohibition in the Constitution, and that such a treaty and legislation in pursuance of it are the supreme law of the land, though they deal with matters which are ordinarily reserved to the states, and to which the ordinary powers of Congress do not extend. If this were not so, such matters could not be adequately dealt with, since the states are expressly excluded from the field of international relations.[1]

In certain instances, the powers of the states over local affairs have been to a degree limited by this power; for example, the disposal of property and the rules of the inheritance of property of aliens may be regulated by treaty.[2] A treaty with the Indians by which land is ceded to a state may prohibit the introduction of liquor into such territory.[3] So also a treaty which gives to the citizens of a foreign country the right to purchase and hold land in the United States and removes the incapacity of alienage, places the parties in precisely the same situation as if they were citizens.[4]

[1] C. K. and F. M. Burdick, *Law of the American Constitution*, New York, 1922, pp. 76-77.

[2] *Fairfax v. Hunter*, 7 Cranch 603 (1813); *People v. Gerke*, 5 California 384 (1855); *Havenstein v. Lynham*, 100 U. S. 483 (1879); *Geofrey v. Riggs*, 133 U. S. 266 (1890); *Wunderle v. Wunderle*, 144 Illinois 40 (1893).

[3] *U. S. v. 43 Gallons of Whiskey*, 93 U. S. 188 (1876); *Dick v. U. S.*, 208 U. S. 340 (1908); *Clairmont v. U. S.*, 225 U. S. 551 (1912).

[4] *Chirac v. Chirac*, 2 Wheat. 259 (1817).

A recent case of a treaty's taking precedence over state legislation is seen in the case of the Sanitary District of Chicago *v.* the United States.[1] The Sanitary District of Chicago, an agency created by the State of Illinois, was authorized by that state some years ago to reverse the current of the Chicago River which formerly flowed into Lake Michigan and by giving the river an opposite incline caused it to flow into the Des Plaines River which empties into the Illinois River; the Illinois River in turn empties into the Mississippi River. By the reversal of the flow of the Chicago River, the sewage from the city of Chicago was diverted from Lake Michigan, whence the city draws its water supply. The building of the new channel, which was twenty-five feet deep and one hundrd and sixty-two feet wide, caused the withdrawal of about ten thousand cubic seconds feet of water from Lake Michigan. A treaty between the United States and Canada of January 11, 1919,[2] provided that the United States should be limited to the withdrawal of 4,167 cubic seconds feet. In the course of time, the Sanitary District was enjoined from withdrawing more than the legal amount of water. The chief complainants were the states bordering on the Great Lakes; these states contended that the diversion of water above the authorized limit seriously interfered with navigation on the Lakes. The Supreme Court of the United States upheld the contention of the states and the provisions of the treaty.

The treaty-making power is conferred in very general terms, and, perhaps, for this reason it may be invoked to regulate matters over which Congress ordinarily has no jurisdiction. When a statute was passed by Congress in 1913 regulating the killing of migratory birds,[3] the act was

[1] 266 U. S. 405 (1925).

[2] 36 *Stat.* 2448.

[3] 37 *Stat.* 828.

held unconstitutional by the Federal District Courts.[1] Yet in 1916 when Congress reenacted practically the same legislation ancillary to a treaty made with Great Britain on the subject, it was upheld by the Supreme Court.[2] Walter Thompson in his work on *Federal Centralization* says:

> Purely from the standpoint of constitutional law, undoubtedly the federal government could interfere with state powers through the exercise of one of the powers delegated to Congress. To what extent the treaty power might be exercised is entirely an academic question. *The Supreme Court has never declared a treaty unconstitutional.*[3]

There would seem to be ample authority, which no one has seriously questioned, for federal regulation of the flow of boundary streams and the water-power rights upon these streams. That power flows not alone from the treaty-making grants of the Constitution but also from the expansive power over commerce which Congress enjoys.

THE POWER OF THE FEDERAL GOVERNMENT

Navigable Streams

Thirdly, the Constitution grants to the Federal Government the power to regulate commerce among the several states and with foreign nations.[4] The power of Congress over interstate commerce is plenary,[5] and whenever it chooses to use the power, its action is supreme. Congress lays down the rules by which commerce shall be carried on; it may

[1] *U. S. v. Shanner*, 214 Fed. 154 (1914); *U. S. v. McCullagh*, 221 Fed. 288 (1915).

[2] *Missouri v. Holland*, 252 U. S. 416 (1920).

[3] *Federal Centralization*, p. 97. Italics are the author's.

[4] Part iii, section 8, article i.

[5] The states do regulate and place burdens upon interstate commerce, it is true, but these restrictions are merely tolerated by the Federal Government in those cases where a general uniformity of regulation is not called for.

regulate for the public all the avenues of interstate and foreign commerce. Navigation is commerce. On this point Chief Justice Marshall has said:

All America understands, and has uniformly understood, the word "commerce" to comprehend navigation. . . . The word used in the constitution, then, comprehends, and has been always understood to comprehend, navigation within its meaning; and a power to regulate navigation, is as expressly granted, as if that term had been added to the word "commerce".[1]

Many years later in the case of the Gloucester Ferry Company *v.* Pennsylvania, the Supreme Court said:

Commerce among the states . . . consists of intercourse and traffic between their citizens, and includes the transportation of persons and property and *the navigation of public waters for that purpose,* as well as the purchase, sale and exchange of commodities.[2]

Navigable streams when they are interstate in character or when they are highways of interstate trade fall under the jurisdiction of Congress.

Even those navigable waters lying wholly within the boundaries of a state are subject to the controlling authority of Congress. In fact, no distinction is made between a navigable stream running through two or more states and a navigable stream located entirely within one state. They are navigable waters and federally-controlled if they form by themselves or by connection with others a highway for commerce with other states or foreign countries.[3] Canals, too, constructed by a state wholly within its borders, constitute navigable waters of the United States, if connecting

[1] *Gibbons v. Ogden*, 9 Wheat. 1 (1824).

[2] 114 U. S. 196, 203 (1885).

[3] *Rhea v. Newport News Co.*, 50 Fed. 21 (1892); *The Katie*, 40 Fed. 489 (1889); *Decker v. Baltimore*, etc. R., 30 Fed. 724 (1887).

with such waters.[1] In short, the central government has the power to secure the uninterrupted navigability of navigable streams within the United States and upon its borders.[2]

What streams are navigable? The old common-law rule under which only those streams are navigable in which the tide ebbs and flows, and only so far as such ebb and flow, has not been adopted in this country. In the United States navigability is a question of fact, for if a stream can be used for commerce, it is held by the courts to be navigable. Even if a stream is navigable only in part, it comes under the power of Congress. All the non-navigable portions of streams which serve in any way as feeders for the navigable portions also come within the jurisdiction of the United States.[3]

The Supreme Court of Massachusetts has said:

The true test of the navigability of a stream does not depend on the mode by which commerce is, or may be, conducted, nor the difficulties attending navigation. If this were so, the public would be deprived of the use of many of the large rivers of the country over which rafts of lumber of great value are constantly taken to market. It would be a narrow rule to hold that in this country, unless a river was capable of being navigated by steam or sail vessels, it would not be treated as a public highway. The capability of use by the public for purposes of transportation and commerce affords the true criterion of the navigability of a river, rather than the extent and manner of that use. If it be capable in its natural state of being used for purposes of commerce, no matter in what mode the com-

[1] *Ex parte Boyer*, 109 U. S. 629 (1884); *The Robert W. Parsons*, 191 U. S. 17 (1903).

[2] *U. S. v. Rio Grande Dam and Irrigation Co.*, 174 U. S. 690 (1898).

[3] *The Montello*, 20 Wall. 430 (1874); *The Genesee Chief*, 12 How. 443 (1851); *The Daniel Ball*, 10 Wall. 557 (1870); *Barney v. Keokuk*, 94 U. S. 324 (1876); *St. Anthony Falls Power Co. v. Commissioners*, 168 U. S. 349 (1899).

merce may be conducted, it is navigable in fact, and becomes in law a public river or highway. . . . It is not, however, as Chief Justice Shaw said, 'every small creek in which a fish skiff or gunning canoe can be made to float at high water' which is deemed navigable, but, in order to give it the character of a navigable stream, it must be generally and commonly useful to some trade or agriculture.[1]

At best, this description of a navigable stream is not very accurate, yet no specific definition of navigability can replace it. Since the Federal Government may regulate the avenues of interstate commerce, it follows that any interference on the part of states or individuals to close these avenues is illegal. If, for instance, a state or a citizen should divert the tributaries of a navigable highway of commerce, interfering with the stream flow, it would be within the rights of the Federal Government to compel a restoration of the stream to its normal condition. Congress, therefore, maintains a supervision of the feeders of navigable streams along with the water sheds of such streams. The possible limits of this control are unknown. Senator Thomas of Colorado, speaking in the United States Senate, made the rather pertinent inquiry as to whether such control might not extend to the ordinary surface or run-off waters, the clouds of heaven, the dews of the morning, the fogs that come in from the seas, and the melting snows upon the mountains. They are, to be sure, all feeders of our navigable streams, but we may trust in the common sense of our judiciary to prevent the clouds, the dews, the fogs, and the snows from finding a place on the Congressional calendars alongside our rivers and harbors.

The Federal Power Commission in its first annual report describes the extent of congressional power over navigation as follows:

[1] *Rowe v. Granite Bridge Corp.*, 21 Pick. (Mass. 1838) 344.

The commerce clause of the Constitution has been deemed ample to enable it to exercise jurisdiction over the navigable waters of the United States. Under this power Congress may prohibit any structure within or over navigable waters, may abate as nuisances any structures obstructing navigation or erected without its consent, may establish and change harbor lines, limiting extensions of structures into the water, may enter upon any system of improvement designed to stabilize or confine the flow, and may forbid diversion of water from any navigable stream. The right to utilize the waters of a stream for power development can be maintained only by the possession of the legal right to erect structures in that stream and to prevent the diversion of waters from the intake of the power works[1].

SUMMARY OF THE LAW OF WATERS IN THE UNITED STATES

Summarizing briefly what has already been said, we have seen that although the *corpus* of running water belongs to no one—neither state nor citizen—it may be used for beneficial purposes and within reason by riparian owners who enjoy as such a usufructuary right in it according to the principle, *sic utere tuo ut alienum non laedas;* that the extent of this use and the amount of injury that may be imposed on riparian owners above or below the user is determined by the states which hold the sovereignty over the running waters of all streams within their respective borders and act as the trustees of the people; that the Federal Government as owner and regulator of the public domain has riparian rights on all streams that flow by or through its property; that while the public domain states have adopted special rules and restrictions which are imposed upon the users of waters on the public lands, the right to make such rules and restrictions is a purely voluntary grant of power from the United States to the states; and that the United States exercises the paramount right of keeping navigation

[1] Pp. 43-44.

open to the public, all other rights of the state and the riparian owner being subject to this.

THE LEGAL PROBLEM AND FEDERAL WATER POWER LEGISLATION

We have already seen that in the waters of running streams the rights of three distinct parties must be considered: the private riparian owner, the state, and the United States Government. It is not surprising that a conflict of interests should have arisen especially, with the growing demand for an extension of Federal Government activities wherever the states have been unwilling or unable to tackle the stringent regulation and control of trusts and monopolies among which most water-power interests should be classed.

We have seen that where the Government owned the lands, it enjoyed the use of the waters running by or through those lands the same as any riparian owner. The right of the Government to lease on its own terms the water powers developed on these streams is unquestioned. It is only a question of how extensively the Government desires these powers to be developed by private initiative, and that is a matter of policy.

Before the passage of the Water-Power Act of 1920 the Bureau of Forestry in the Department of Agriculture laid down a series of rules for those using water-power sites in the National Forests. Among the regulations for those applying for a permit, we find the following: that the plans for the work in connection with the water plant should be filed and approved by the Department; that no deviation from these plans would be permitted without the consent of the Department; that the work should begin at a certain time and should thereafter be diligently and continually prosecuted; that certain specified parts of the work should be completed on definite dates; that the amount and distribution of horsepower should be named; that rental charges should be paid to the United States; that the Secretary of Agriculture could review and readjust rental charges after ten years; that the power company should keep accurate measurement of the stream flow; that a system of accounting approved by the Secretary of Agriculture should be kept; that the books of the company should at all times be open for inspection by the Secretary of Agriculture; that power should be sold to the United States when requested at as low a rate as is given to any other purchased for like use; that in the transfer of the property of the water-power company to the United States, to a state, or to a municipal corporation, no compensation should be allowed for the national forest lands occupied; that no agreement should be made by the company with any other company to form an unlawful trust or a combination in restraint of trade; that upon demand of the Secretary and the payment of just compensation the works might be transferred to the United States, a state, or a municipality; that the permit to use the national forest lands should run for a time specified by the Secretary unless revoked at an earlier date because of violation of the provisions by the permittee. This demonstrates how far the United States has regulated water-power companies through its ownership of riparian lands. No one seems seriously to have questioned the right of the Government to regulate to this extent although representatives of the power companies often voiced emphatic protests against this regulation.[1]

[1] In *United States v. Grimaud,* 220 U. S. 506 (1910) the Supreme Court said: "From the beginning of the government various acts have been passed conferring upon executive officers power to make rules and regulations—not for the government of their departments, but for administering the laws which did govern. None of these could confer legislative power. But when Congress had legislated and indicated its will, it could give to those who were to act under such general provisions power to fill up the details by the establishment of administrative rules and regulations."

Where the Federal Government builds a dam in a stream for the purpose of improving navigation can a charge be made upon the private riparian user of any water power created by the dam to defray in part the cost of the improvement? It is almost universally admitted that such a charge may be made. The late Senator Nelson of Minnesota, who was never an advocate of Government charges, said: "In the one case where the Government for the purpose of improving navigation constructs a dam . . . though incidentally there is power created in connection with it, the Government according to my opinion has the right to charge compensation."[1] And Senator Bankhead who was an ardent champion of the rights of the states in the development of water power said:

> What I do say is that if the Government builds the dam and the lock and creates power and surplus water, and the corporation wants to use it, the Government might say: "We have built this lock at large expense, and if you will pay us a certain percentage on our investment for the use of the structure you may use it."[2]

In other words, that the Government may charge for the use of a dam (its own property) and lay down equitable conditions for that use does not seem to be open to question. Here too, as in the case of the public lands, there seems to be no question of legal power. If any question does exist, it should be definitely set aside by the decision of the Supreme Court in the Chandler-Dunbar case.[3] Among other things, this case decided that it was wholly within the competence of the Government to charge for excess power developed at Government dams. That the Government may charge for

[1] *Congressional Record,* 62nd Cong., 3rd Sess., pp. 2595-2606.

[2] *Ibid.*

[3] *U. S. v. Chandler-Dunbar Co.,* 209 U. S. 447 (1908).

the water power as such in a case where it has condemned the land for the sole purpose of improving navigation, has been often denied, such denial being based upon judicially determined rights in certain condemnation cases. It has been contended that the riparian land was condemned for navigation purposes only, and that incidental benefits produced by improved navigation belonged to the riparian owner. Such cases as the following might be cited to support such a view; In Alabama a railroad company condemned land for a right of way; in building the road a valuable sand bank was discovered which the company endeavored to sell, but the court held that the original owner was entitled to it because the railroad company had acquired the right to build the road and nothing else.[1] A decision very similar to this was handed down in an Iowa case where a railroad company condemned land for its right of way and in the course of construction, stone was taken from the land and an attempt was made to sell it. Here again the court held that the proceeds from any such sale belonged to the original owner whose land the railroad condemned for the one purpose of securing a right of way.[2] The case of U. S. *v.* Chandler-Dunbar Water Power Company has disposed of all doubts on this question, too. In this case, the court said that whatever rights the riparian owner had in a stream were at all times subject to the paramount power of congress over navigation; that if in exercising this power excess water power should be developed, *it was in no sense a property of the original riparian owner.*[3]

The greatest point of controversy, however, can best be explained by taking an actual instance. The Connecticut

[1] *Nashville, C. & St. L. Ry. v. Karthaus*, 43 Southern 791 (1907).

[2] *Vermilya v. Chicago, M. & St. P. Ry.*, 66 Iowa 606 (1885).

[3] Adjoining lands had been taken by condemnation proceedings.

River between Hartford, Connecticut, and Holyoke, Massachusetts, is not naturally navigable. For many years the people living in that section had endeavored to get Congress to undertake the necessary improvement, but the government engineers had reported that the cost would be too great. In 1913, the Connecticut River Company, a Connecticut corporation, asked permission of Congress to be allowed to build a dam at Enfield Rapids which would develop hydroelectric power and incidentally improve the navigation of the river. All the improvement was to be carried on at private expense. A bill was, therefore, introduced in Congress which authorized the building of the dam and navigation locks but provided that the Secretary of War might impose a charge upon the company for the privilege of being allowed to build and derive water power from the river; such charges when paid to be set aside in a special fund to be used for the further improvement of the Connecticut River. The Connecticut River Company was ready and willing to accept the charge provision. The bill, because of this tolls provision, was decisively defeated in the Senate. In other words, can Congress levy a charge upon a person or corporation that seeks to develop power on a navigable stream where the United States has no interest in the surrounding lands and where it has made no expenditure for improvement at the point of the proposed development?

For ten years this question held up every water-power bill that came before Congress. The House of Representatives in later years favored tolls and provided for them in the House bills; the Senate invariably opposed tolls, omitted tolls provisions in its own bills, and struck out toll provisions in the drafts that came over from the House. The Senate and the House were in disagreement. The checks of our Constitutional system were working as they had worked before, as they have worked since, and as we expect them to work in the future. In this particular case the balances were not in operation.

The chief executives of this period of controversy[1] favored Government charges. President Roosevelt in his vetoes of the James River and the Rainey River Bills, let it be known with his usual vigor that he would sign no bill which failed to provide for a charge upon the water companies using the navigable streams of the United States for the development of hydroelectricity. President Taft took the same position in his veto of the Coosa River Bill. President Wilson held a like position when he gave his endorsement to the Water Power Bill of 1918 introduced in the House of Representatives as an amendment to the Shields Bill of the Senate. That Bill provided "That the licensee shall pay to the United States reasonable annual charges in an amount to be fixed by the commission."[2]

Here was the main source of controversy; here was the barrier to effective water-power legislation; here was the question that helped to keep over thirty million horsepower undeveloped. As an economic problem the question involved the expediency of a charge as a curb upon monopolies and the wisdom of a tax that could eventually be shifted to the consumer. As a legal problem the question involved the constitutional power of the Federal Government to tax and to regulate.

The opponents of tolls contended that the only power of control belonging to the Federal Government came from the commerce clause of the Constitution. In other words, the contention was that Congress had power to regulate navigable streams as highways of trade, but that this power excluded every proprietary element and was a limited power

[1] 1907-1918.

[2] *House Report 715*, 65th Cong., 2nd Sess. See section 103 of the reported bll.

of control for a specific purpose. If there were other rights, sovereign or proprietary, it was argued, these rights had passed to the states which were intrusted with the supervision of streams in the interest of the public. All proprietary elements, it was said, belonged to the riparian owner as a part of the riparian estate; as such they were vested property rights. The private rights of the riparian owner included the right to all the beneficial uses of the natural water powers in the stream opposite his land, including the right to develop and operate and to enjoy the revenues from such power.

If there were any right to charge for the use of the water, to levy taxes or tolls, it was vested in the states. Any attempt of the Federal Government to regulate by way of charges through its commerce power, was regarded as a usurpation of state rights. In the use of a stream for any other purpose outside of navigation, the Federal Government had no property and, hence, had nothing to sell. If the Federal Government could levy a tax, it could not be done under the interstate commerce clause but under Section 8, Article 1—the taxing clause. In such a case, the tribute was either a direct tax or an indirect tax; if it was the former, it would have to be apportioned among the states according to population; if it was the latter, it would be subject to the rule of uniformity and would have to be levied uniformly upon every dam and water power in the United States, not constructed directly by the Federal Government. No proposal for a charge conformed to these requirements. Furthermore, it was argued that the granting of the right to impose a charge to an administrative official, such as the Secretary of War or the Secretary of Agriculture, was a delegation of legislative power and, therefore, unconstitutional.

Supporting this view in Congress and outside of Congress were the champions of the rights of the states, the opponents of federal centralization, the conservatives, and last, but by no means least, the hydroelectric interests and their friends. When put forward by a skilled attorney, this point of view possessed a plausibility which was difficult to combat. As in other cases of controversial legislation, it was difficult to separate those who supported the argument from statesman-like motives from those who supported it merely as the hirelings of selfish interests.

How, then, can the Water Power Act of 1920, which provides for federal control, the imposition of charges, and rate regulation, be justified? The Federal Government is given the power to keep the streams of the country open for navigation. No impediment may be placed in a navigable stream by state or individual without the consent of Congress or its authorized agent. The National Government can give or withhold its consent to those seeking to erect obstructions in navigable streams. A power dam is an obstruction and the privilege of erecting one must come from a federal authority. The power to give or withhold consent is absolute and uncontrolled except by the discretion and judgment of Congress. These facts were not denied by the most ardent of the champions of the rights of the states and the opponents of tolls. What follows from the above facts, if accepted? If a grantor may give or withhold consent, he may give upon terms. The authority to make a grant carries with it the authority to withhold, to impose conditions, to modify, and to terminate. The following precedents are not without significance: When Congress chartered the Pacific railroad, it was stipulated that the Government service in transporting troops, mails, and the like should have preference.[1] In one charter Congress reserved the right to restrict charges for Government trans-

[1] 12 *Stat.* 489, section 6; 12 *Stat.* 772, 773; 13 *Stat.* 365, 370.

portation.[1] In the acts of Congress to aid in the construction of telegraph lines, it was provided that the Government business should have priority over all other business and should be sent at rates to be fixed annually by the Postmaster General.[2] These charters and licenses were granted under the federal authority over interstate commerce and over post roads.

In regard to our river highways, it should be noted that the Government has built many public works in aid of navigation in the nature of dams, locks, and canals. Such was the canalization of the St. Mary's River on the waters of the Great Lakes just as they issue from Lake Superior. Congress has not only undertaken such work itself but has committed in certain cases the task to municipal and private corporations. Private parties have been authorized to aid navigation where practical navigation already existed.[3] Such authorization has also been made for the improvement of the stream where it is not actually navigable.[4] Congress has permitted structures for power development at points in rivers where Government plans of navigation improvement have already been adopted, as at Muscle Shoals on the Tennessee River and on the Coosa River in Alabama. Some years back Congress had given companies the right to build dams, maintain and operate power stations in connection with them in consideration of the construction of the locks and drydocks to be operated in place of existing structures owned and operated by the United States,[5] or the construction was subjected to conditions laid down as in the act of June 21, 1906.[6] In connection with the grant of power to

[1] 14 *Stat.* 292, 297, section 11.

[2] 33 *Stat.* 309.

[3] 33 *Stat.* 309.

[4] 34 *Stat.* 52, 183, 211, 1073, 1094, 1288.

[5] 33 *Stat.* 712.

[6] 33 *Stat.* 100; 34 *Stat.* 130, 929.

build a dam in a stream, Congress has laid down such conditions as the erection of locks suitable for navigation purposes, the submission of all plans for the approval of the Secretary of War, and the reservation of the rights to take possession of the dam without compensation, and to control the same for the purposes of navigation, the imposition of the duty of building in connection with the dam or canal or other works a wagon and foot bridge, and lastly the reservation of the right to alter, amend, and repeal the grant or to require the alteration or removal of the structure.[1] The extent to which Congress had gone in imposing conditions long before the passage of the Act of 1920 is clearly shown in the general acts of 1906 and 1910.[2] Outside of the usual conditions for the benefit of navigation, we find that acts of Congress provided that the person building a dam also erect sluiceways for logs and ladders for fish. The opponents of charges might well have objected to the last condition on the ground that the Constitution does not grant to the Federal Government the care of fish! To cite one more case of the imposition of conditions: in the act of June 29, 1906,[3] permitting the erection of a lock and dam in the White River, Arkansas, it was provided that the licensee should purchase and pay for certain lands necessary for the successful construction and operation of a lock and dam and hand them over to the United States. In consideration of the construction of these structures free of cost to the United States, the Government granted the licensee the privilege of using the water power produced by the dam for a period of ninety-nine years; but, in the meantime, to furnish to the United States free of cost sufficient power to operate the locks and to light the United States buildings and grounds.

[1] 24 *Stat.* 123; 30 *Stat.* 904; 34 *Stat.* 265, 266, 296.

[2] 34 *Stat.* 386; 36 *Stat.* 593.

[3] 34 *Stat.* 628.

The following tabulation taken from a United States Senate report,[1] shows the conditions imposed for water-power privileges from 1888 to 1911:

Name of River	Grantee	Date of Act	Provisions
Muskingum, Ohio.	General Authority.	Aug. 11, 1886.	Secretary of War empowered to grant licenses for use of water powers at such rate and on such conditions and for such periods of time as may seem to him just and reasonable.
Green & Barren, Ky.	General Authority.	Sept. 19, 1890.	Secretary of War empowered to grant licenses for use of water powers at such rate and on such conditions and for such periods of time as may seem to him just and expedient with added condition that leases are not to extend beyond period of 20 years.
Cumberland, Tenn. at Lock 1.	General Authority.	June 13, 1902. (See also Act of June 28, 1902.)	Secretary of War empowered to grant licenses for use of water power at such rate and on such conditions and such periods of time as may seem to him expedient.
Tennessee River at Hales Bar.	City of Chattanooga or other private corporation.	April 26, 1904.	Grantee to purchase necessary lands and deed same to United States to construct a lock and dam and give them to United States completed, free of all costs except expenses connected with preparation of plans, superintendence, cost of lock gates, etc., and to furnish free electric current for operating locks and for lighting. Grantee to have use of water power for 99 years.
Mississippi at Des Moines Rapids.	Keokuk & Hamilton Water Power Co.	Feb. 9, 1905.	Grantee to build a lock and drydock and appurtenant works, and United States to have ownership of them. Grantee to furnish power for lighting and operating locks, drydock and appurtenances and provide fishways.
Cumberland and tributaries.	Cumberland River Improvement Co.	March 3, 1905.	Right to collect tolls to cease at expiration of 40 years from date of completion of lock and Dam No. 21, Cumberland River, and United States may then assume possession, care, operation, maintenance, and management of the lock or locks constructed by the corporation, but without in any way impairing the right or ownership of the water power and dams created by corporations.

[1] *Senate Document 57*, 62nd Cong., 2nd Sess.

Coosa, Alabama, at Lock No. 2.	General Authorization.	May 9, 1906.	United States reserves right to control dams, pool-level and to construct locks. Land for lock and approaches to be conveyed to United States free of charge and United States to have free water power for building and operating locks. Fishways to be constructed.
White, Ark., at Lock No. 1.	Baterville Power Co.	June 28, 1906.	Secretary of War authorized and directed to fix from time to time reasonable charges to be paid for use of power.
Coosa, Alabama, at Lock No. 12.	Alabama Power Co.	March 4, 1907.	Dam to be built so that United States may construct a lock in connection therewith. The grantee to have right to use government land necessary for the construction and maintenance of the dam and appurtenant works, to convey to the United States free of cost such suitable tract as may be selected by Chief of Engineers and Secretary of War for establishment of locks and approaches, and to furnish the necessary electric current to operate locks and for lighting grounds.
St. Mary's, Mich.	General Authorization.	Mar. 3, 1909.	Water power to be leased by the Secretary of War upon such terms and conditions as shall be best calculated, in his judgment, to insure the development thereof. A just and reasonable compensation to be paid for use.
Wabash, Ind., at Mt. Carmel.	General Authorization.	Mar. 3, 1909.	Secretary of War authorized to grant leases or licenses for periods not exceeding twenty years at such rate and on such conditions as may seem to him just and expedient.
Mississippi from St. Paul to Minneapolis.	General Authorization.	June 25, 1910.	A reasonable compensation for leases for water power shall be secured to United States.
Coosa, Alabama, at Lock No. 4.	England Water Power Co.	Feb. 27, 1911.	A dam to be property of United States free of charge. Grantee to have water-power rights for 50 years, United States to have right to construct a lock and to have free electric current for operating and lighting. Grantee to raise height of dam at Lock No. 4 and to stop leaks. Beginning in 1925, grantee to pay United States $1 per 10 horsepower with an increase if natural flowage is increased by storage reservoir.

Wabash at Mt. Carmel, Ill.	Mt. Carmel Development Co.	Feb. 14, 1889. Feb. 12, 1901.	Withdrawal of water shall be under direction and control of the Secretary of War.
Rock River near Sterling.	Sterling Hydraulic Co.	Mar. 2, 1907.	Secretary of War authorized to permit erection of a power station in connection with United States dam. Grantee to waive certain claims against United States.
White, Ark., above Lock No. 3.	J. A. Omberg, Jr.	June 29, 1906.	Grantee to purchase lands, construct lock and dam, give them to United States free of charge and furnish United States electric current to operate locks, light grounds. Grantee to have use of water power 99 years.

While the exercise of an illegal power does not justify it, yet the fact that the Congress for so many years had been placing conditions upon companies desiring to obstruct streams for the development of hydroelectricity shows that the practice had been accepted at least as customary. The lack of cases on the subject gives silent testimony to the fact that few questioned the power of Congress to lay down conditions; if there were some who had doubts, they doubted the strength of their position or the sufficiency of their cash reserves for a battle in the courts.

The startling discovery that the imposition of charges by the Government was *ultra vires* corresponded rather significantly with President Roosevelt's broadside against the greedy power trust. Whatever the motive back of this discovery, it does seem unreasonable that development on navigable streams should have been held up on the point. For days and weeks, Congress wrangled in purely academic discussion. A report of a House committee on the General Dam Act of 1906, quoting an opinion of the Attorney General says:

If the power exists, it is for Congress to say whether the occasion for its exercise is real, and whether the connections between the occasion and the method and the results of the exercise are substantial, and whether the means employed to carry the power into effect are legitimate. . . . The interest of navigation may be a secondary or even a negligible consideration with the licensees of the Government, but that does not make the Government jurisdiction any the less a constitutional control over navigation, and the real object of the licensee, whether it be the development of power or irrigation, is none the less subsidiary and incidental from the Government point of view.[1]

The objection to charges on the ground that they would not be constitutional under the taxation clause was never seriously defended. No proponent of charges thought of levying them in such a way as to conflict with the reserved rights of the states nor to do more than had been done before by Congress in other fields. What they sought to accomplish and how they sought to accomplish it, is set forth in Section 10, division " e " of the Act of 1920:

That the licensee shall pay to the United States reasonable annual charges in an amount to be fixed by the commission for the purpose of reimbursing the United States for the costs of administration of this Act; for recompensing it for the use, occupancy, and enjoyment of its lands or other property; and for the expropriation to the Government of excessive profits until the respective states shall make provision for preventing excessive profits or for the expropriation thereof to themselves, or until the period of amortization as herein provided is reached.

Under this provision the Government is reimbursed for services performed through fees. If Congress has the power to act at all, it can most assuredly provide for raising the money to cover administrative services. The power of the Government to charge a rental for the use of its lands and property is beyond question. The provision for the using of a charge to take excess profits is the vital portion of the

[1] *House Report 337*, 59th Cong., 1st Sess.

present act and was the question about which so much controversy raged. There would seem to be no difference between taking excess profits in this case and taking excess profits by means of a super-income tax. The sixteenth amendment to the Federal Consititution would seem to cover the case.

Would the imposition of a charge by an administrative official or a board be a delegation of legislative power? The doctrine of the separation of powers to which Americans have paid homage since our state and national governments were formed is expressed or implied in most of our constitutions. The principle stated in the federal Constitution is substantially: "All legislative powers herein granted shall be vested in a Congress" or "the executive power shall be vested in a President." The courts throughout the country have generally held that exchange of authority amongst the branches of government is forbidden. The federal courts have not interpreted this doctrine narrowly, but the same can not be said of the state courts. Much beneficial administrative control has been prohibited by such narrow construction. Chief Justice Marshall, as early as 1825, set the federal judiciary on the path of broad interpretation when he said: "It will not be contended that Congress can delegate to the courts, or to any other tribunal powers which are strictly or exclusively legislative. But Congress may certainly delegate to others powers which the legislature may rightfully exercise itself."[1] Later on the Supreme Court said:

> The true distinction . . . . is between the delegation of power to make the law, which necessarily involves a discretion as to what it shall be, and conferring authority or discretion as to its execution, to be exercised under and in pursuance of the

[1] *Wayman v. Southard,* 10 Wheat. 1, 42 (1825).

law. The first cannot be done; to the latter, no valid objection can be made.[1]

Some examples of wide powers of discretion placed upon executive authorities through acts of Congress follow: By the non-intercourse act of 1809, importation from France and Great Britain was forbidden until either one or the other no longer violated our declaration of neutrality, when the President was to restore commercial relations with the country that ceased to offend. This was upheld by the United States Supreme Court.[2] The Tariff Act of 1890 provided that the President had the power to admit the goods from certain countries free of duty or to impose a duty according to the treatment which such countries accorded goods from the United States. The act was attacked in Field *v.* Clark,[3] but the United States Supreme Court held that the act did not involve a delegation of legislative power and was constitutional. The Court said:

It was not the making of law. He was the mere agent of the law-making department to ascertain and declare the event upon which its expressed will was to take effect. It was part of the law itself as it left the hands of Congress that the provisions, full and complete in themselves, permitting the free introduction of sugars, molasses, coffee, tea, and hides, from particular countries, should be suspended, in a given contingency, and that in case of such suspensions certain duties should be imposed.

In recent years Congress has not hesitated to place in the hands of executive officials very broad powers. As evidence of this it is only necessary to note section 315 of the Fordney-McCumber Tariff Act of 1922. That section reads:

[1] *Field v. Clark*, 143 U. S. 649, 695 (1892) quoting from *Cincinnati W. & Z. R. R. Co. v. Commissioners*, 1 Ohio St. 77, 78 (1852).

[2] *The Brig Aurora*, 7 Cranch 382 (1813).

[3] *Field v. Clark*, 143 U. S. 649 (1892).

That in order to regulate commerce of the United States and to put into force and effect the policy of the Congress by this act intended, whenever the President, upon investigation of the differences in costs of production of articles wholly or in part the growth or product of the United States and of like or similar articles wholly or in part the growth or product of competing foreign countries, shall find it thereby shown that the duties fixed in this Act do not equalize the said differences in costs of production in the United States and the principal competing country he shall, by such investigation, ascertain said differences and determine and proclaim the changes in classification or increases or decreases in any rate of duty provided in this Act shown by said ascertained differences in such costs of production necessary to equalize the same. Thirty days after the date of such proclamation or proclamations such changes in classification shall take effect, and such increased or decreased duties shall be levied, collected, and paid on such articles when imported from any foreign country into the United States or into any of its possessions: *Provided,* That the total increase or decrease of such rates of duty shall not exceed 50 per centum of the rates specified in Title I of this Act, or in any amendatory Act.[1]

The Burdicks in their work on the American Constitution say of the delegation of legislative power:

Present-day conditions with their great complexity of personal and economic relations, together with the rapidly increasing governmental supervision of personal, and especially of corporate conduct in the interest of the community at large, have made it practically impossible for legislatures to provide for all the detailed application of the rules and regulations which they adopt. Furthermore, such application can be much more satisfactorily made by persons who are experts in given fields, and who devote their time to the consideration of the problems within those fields. These considerations have led legislatures to delegate a great deal of the power that they might exercise

[1] (1922) 42 *Stat.* 858.

to administrative officers and commissions, and this they may constitutionally do as long as they lay down the guiding principles, and leave only to the administrative agency the application of such principles to facts as they arise.[1]

Closely related with the control of the administrative departments over the water power in navigable streams, is the power of the Secretary of War to prohibit the building of bridges over navigable streams, if they constitute an impediment to navigation. This power of the Secretary of War to prohibit the erection of structures in rivers, to approve of plans for their erection, to cause changes to be made when necessary, and to compel the removal of a bridge when it becomes an obstruction—all this has been approved by the Supreme Court.[2] The Secretary of Agriculture may make regulations regarding the occupancy and use of national forest lands and before the passage of the Water Power Act of 1920 laid down regulations including a rental charge for those developing water power in the forest domain.[3]

Finally, the extensive powers granted the Interstate Commerce Commission over rates and conditions of service by the Interstate Commerce Act of 1887[4] would seem to settle the question of the granting to an administrative agency power over charges for water power. This act, with subsequent amendments, is rather general in its terms and places wide interpretative and ordinance powers upon a federal commission. The act itself together with many of the decisions of the Commission have been upheld in numerous decisions of the United States Supreme Court.[5]

[1] *Law of the American Constitution, op. cit.*, pp. 152-153.

[2] *Union Bridge Co. v. U. S.*, 204 U. S. 364 (1907).

[3] *In re Kollock*, 165 U. S. 526 (1897); *Butterfield v. Stranahan*, 192 U. S. 470 (1904); *U. S. v. Grimaud*, 220 U. S. 506 (1910).

[4] 24 *Stat.* 379.

[5] See *Interstate Commerce Commission Cases in the Federal Courts, 1887-1914*, 2nd ed., U. S. Government Printing Office, Washington, D. C.

THE CHANDLER-DUNBAR CASE

The scope of the federal authority in the sphere of water power is nowhere better set forth than in the case of Chandler-Dunbar Co. *v.* the United States.[1] The eleventh section of an act of Congress of March 3, 1909, provided that all the lands and property of every description north of the St. Mary's Falls Ship Canal throughout its entire length and lying between that canal and the international boundary at Sault Sainte Marie, in the State of Michigan, should be taken by condemnation or negotiation by the Secretary of War for the purpose of improving navigation. It was also provided that every permit, license, or authority granted to the Chandler-Dunbar Water-Power Company and others to build dams and develop water power in that region was revoked by the passage of the Act. Section twelve of the Act gave the Secretary of War power to sell surplus water power after the United States had made the necessary improvements for navigation. The Federal District Court for the Western District of Michigan granted the Chandler-Dunbar Company an award of $550,000 on account of its claim, as riparian owner, *to the undeveloped water power of the river* in excess of the supposed requirements of navigation. All parties took writs of error from this, the United States denying it altogether and the defendant alleging its inadequacy. Justice Lurton of the United States Supreme Court delivered the opinion. In that opinion, Justice Lurton decided that under the fifth amendment to the Constitution, the water-power company was entitled to compensation for the upland taken, but that the company could not be said to have any right to compensation for the water-power capacity of the rapids and falls of the St. Mary's River. The company had contended that as riparian owner it had title to the middle thread of the stream. Over

[1] *U. S. v. Chandler-Dunbar,* 229 U. S. 53 (1913).

this, it was contended, flowed about two-thirds of the volume of water constituting the falls and rapids of the St. Mary's River. By reason of that fact and the ownership of the shore, the Company's claim was that it was the owner of the river and of the inherent power in the falls and rapids, subject only to the public right of navigation. The court reasoned:

This title of the owner of fast land upon the shore of a navigable river to the bed of the river is at best a qualified one. It is a title which inheres in the ownership of the shore and, unless reserved or excluded by implication, passes with it as a shadow follows a substance, although capable of distinct ownership. It is subordinate to the public right of navigation, and however helpful in protecting the owner against the acts of third parties, is of no avail against the exercise of the great and absolute power of Congress over the improvement of navigable rivers. That power of use and control comes from the power to regulate commerce between the states and with foreign nations. *It includes navigation and subjects every navigable river to the control of Congress. All means having some positive relation to the end in view which are not forbidden by some other provision of the Constitution are admissable.*[1] If, on the judgment of Congress, the use of the bottom of the river is proper for the purpose of placing therein structures in aid of navigation, it is not thereby taking private property for a public use, for the owner's title was in its very nature subject to that use in the interest of public navigation. If its judgment be that structures placed in the river and upon submerged land are an obstruction or hindrance to the proper use of the river for purposes of navigation, it may require their removal and forbid the use of the bed of the river by the owner in any way which in its judgment is injurious to the dominant right of navigation.

[1] Italics are the author's.

It was natural that the twelfth section of the act authorizing the Secretary of War to lease, on terms agreed upon, any excess of water power created by means of Government works to be constructed, should be attacked. It was contended that here was a taking of private property for commercial uses and not for the improvement of navigation. To this objection, the Court gave the significant answer:

> But, aside from the exclusive public purpose declared by the eleventh section of the act, the twelfth section declares that the conservation of the flow of the river is primarily for the benefit of navigation and, incidentally, for the purpose of having the water power developed, either for the direct use of the United States or by lease . . . . through the Secretary of War.
>
> *If the primary purpose is legitimate, we can see no sound objection to leasing any excess of power over the needs of the Government.* The practice is not unusual in respect to similar public works constructed by state governments. . . . It is, at best, not clear how the Chandler-Dunbar Company can be heard to object to the selling of any excess of water power which may result from the construction of such controlling or remedial works as shall be found advisable for the improvement of navigation, inasmuch as it had no property right in the river which had been " taken ". It has, therefore, no interest whether the Government permit the excess of power to go to waste or to make it the means of producing some return upon the great expenditure.

If then the Government may permit a private company to develop what it does not care to develop itself, it would seem reasonable that there should be some return to the grantor for the privilege. If the Government can lease water power, or, in bolder terms, go into the power business for a profit, there would seem to be no logical reason why that same Government should be deprived of the authority of licensing some one else as its agent and taking from that agent a share of the profits in return for the privilege as a measure of supervision in the interests of all.

The power of the Federal Government to regulate water-power rates and conditions of service in the absence of state regulation involved another question of difference between the conservationists and their opponents. Even federal regulation of interstate lines was opposed on the ground that it was doubtful whether transmission of electric power over state boundaries was interstate commerce. The costly lesson taught us by our early experience with railroads was lost or ignored. With electric power it is not possible to divide the country into small economic units, each with its own plant investment, its own operators, its own laws, its own court decisions. This arbitrary division failed in railroad regulation, and, like the railroads, giant power is no respecter of state boundaries. Already, while Congress talked, the coupling-up process was in full swing. Today interconnections between companies on the Pacific coast makes possible a continuous line for twelve hundred miles from Portland, Oregon, to San Diego, California; and in our Southern Appalachians through the States of North Carolina, Alabama, Virginia, Tennessee, South Carolina, West Virginia, Kentucky, Mississippi, and Florida, great power plants are linked together. When the day comes, in which the various regions of the United States are similarly linked, forty-eight codes of law, forty-eight schedules of rates, and forty-eight different types of annoyance should not stand in the way of progress. From a practical point of view, there are enough arguments against state regulation of electric power services; from a legal point of view, we may find other arguments.

In Western Union Telegraph Company *v.* Foster [1] the

[1] *Western Union v. Foster and MacLeod,* 247 U. S. 105 (1918).

Supreme Court held void an attempt by Massachusetts to compel service to certain firms within that state of telegraphic news of sales and prices on the New York Stock Exchange, on the ground that electrically conveyed information was interstate commerce and, therefore, beyond the reach of state power. It has also been held by the same court that gas produced by a producing company or transmitted through pipe lines owned by a pipe line company is a public utility, and in Public Utilities Commission *v.* Landon,[1] the Supreme Court, although holding that local natural gas distributing companies were subject as to rates to state regulation, held that the transportation from the wells across state lines to the mains of the distributing companies was interstate commerce. In Pennsylvania Gas Company *v.* Public Service Commission,[2] it was held that gas produced in Pennsylvania and sent into New York is an interstate product and subject to federal rate and service regulation. So also in the case of West *v.* Kansas National Gas Company,[3] the Supreme Court invalidated an Oklahoma statute which sought to prevent the transportation of natural gas out of Oklahoma where it was mined, the Court holding that transportation of gas across state lines is interstate commerce and that the states might not interfere with such commerce. In United States Gas Company *v.* Hallanan,[4] the Supreme Court held that the production of natural gas, a considerable part of which was to cross state lines, was a part of interstate commerce and not subject to taxation. In the fairly recent case of Commonwealth of Pennsylvania

[1] *Public Utilities Commission of Kansas v. Landon,* 249 U. S. 236 (1919).

[2] *Pennsylvania Gas Co. v. Public Service Commission,* 252 U. S. 23, 40 (1920).

[3] *Attorney General of Oklahoma v. Kansas Natural Gas Co.,* 221 U. S. 229 (1911).

[4] *U. S. Fuel Gas Co. v. Hallanan,* 257 U. S. 277 (1921).

v. West Virginia, the Supreme Court held void a statute of West Virginia, which sought to give West Virginia consumers a preferential right to gas produced in that state as against consumers in the States of Ohio and Pennsylvania. "In the matter of interstate commerce we are a single nation," said the Court, "one and the same people. . . . In such (interstate) commerce instead of the states, a new power appears and a new welfare which transcends that of any state."[1] The latest case bearing on this particular subject—that of Missouri *v.* Kansas Natural Gas Company decided by the Supreme Court in May, 1924, demonstrates further what the courts will very likely say in the case of state regulation of hydro rates. In this particular case, the Company developed and purchased natural gas in Oklahoma and Kansas which it transported by pipe line into Kansas and Missouri, and there sold it at wholesale. The company raised its rates; Kansas and Missouri promptly reduced them. Suits were brought in the federal and state courts of both states. The Supreme Court of Kansas decided in favor of state regulation in the absence of federal regulation. The two federal courts held the state action void as an undue interference with interstate commerce. The decision of the United States Supreme Court upheld the two lower federal courts, thus reversing the decision of the Kansas state court.

It would seem, therefore, that state regulation is legally impossible even where the Federal Government has not acted. There is only one authority that can act—Congress.

There arises next the question of the regulation of hydro rates on wholly intrastate lines. In the Act of 1920 is found the following clause:

That in case of the development, transmission, or distribution,

[1] *Pennsylvania v. West Virginia,* 262 U. S. 553 (1923).

or use in public service by any licensee hereunder or by its customer engaged in public service within a state which has not authorized and empowered a commission or other agency or agencies within said state to regulate and control the services to be rendered by such licensee or by its customer engaged in public service, or to rates and charges of payment therefor, . . . it is agreed as a condition of such license that jurisdiction is hereby conferred upon the (water-power) commission,[1] upon complaint of any person aggrieved or upon its own initiative, to exercise such regulations and control until such time as the state shall have provided a commission or authority for such regulation and control.

Objection on the part of certain legislators to this provision, as an undue interference with the rights of the states, did not as a rule receive very serious consideration since most states provide for rate regulation. A recent decision of the Supreme Court has some relation to a question of this nature. The doctrine of the famous Shreveport Case [2] was reaffirmed and extended in the case of Wisconsin *v.* Chicago B. & Q. R. Company.[3] Under the Transportation Act of 1920, the Interstate Commerce Commission granted increases in rates to common carriers. This increase in rates for interstate carriers to be fairly effective required an increase in rates on local carriers. Wisconsin and other states refused the increase. The Supreme Court in upholding the federal law and the Commission, pointed out that the Federal Government might remove any obstructions raised by state regulation which prevented the successful operation of the federal plan. The court said:

. . . . effective control of the one (interstate rates) must

[1] A federal agency.

[2] *Houston, East and West Texas Ry. v. U. S.*, 234 U. S. 342 (1914).

[3] *Ry. Commission of Wisconsin et. al. v. C. B. & Q. Ry.*, 257 U. S. 563 (1922).

embrace some control over the other (intrastate rates) in view of the blending of both in actual operation. . . . The same rails and the same cars carry both. The same men conduct them. Commerce is a unit and does not regard state lines, and while under the Constitution, interstate and intrastate commerce are ordinarily subject to regulation by different sovereignties, yet when they are so mingled together that the supreme authority, the Nation, cannot exercise complete effective control over interstate commerce without incidental regulation of intrastate commerce, such incidental regulation is not an invasion of state authority or a violation of the proviso.

With the rapid increase of vast interconnecting units, it is difficult to see how hydro power can become anything other than an interstate utility with interstate regulation.

Many will regret the Federalist tendencies of these judicial pronouncements. Many will regret that economic tendencies take no heed of state lines, that our Federal Union becomes less federal each decade, that our local governments are losing vitality, and that our Constitution is being grotesquely bent to fit new situations; yet, the sober fact remains that the well-being of the people demands that we adapt ourselves and our institutions to the newer tendencies.

What has been said does not mean that the Washington Government must take immediate steps to control the whole field of power development. Without any constitutional difficulties, it might exercise stringent control over the larger part of the hydroelectric industry through its control of the public domain. Up to this time, its control has been mostly supervisory. These court decisions, however, may remind the states of a latent power. Interstate agreements on rates and conditions of service may, undoubtedly, be made with the consent of Congress. The value of interstate agreements of one kind or another is being realized, as is evidenced by the treaty between New York and New Jersey on the development of the Port of New York; by the agreement among the states bordering on the Delaware River as to the power development on that stream; and by the pact among the six states of California, Nevada, Utah, Wyoming, Colorado, and New Mexico—a seventh, Arizona, necessary for complete agreement still holds out—relative to the building of Boulder Dam on the Colorado River, which would make possible the largest artificial water-power and irrigation project in the world. Such agreements as to power development and rates may in time be arrived at by the states of the northeast; other natural power units for the regulation of rates and exchange of services should be formed. With various regional pacts agreed to, there might be formed a federation of power regions supervised by the National Government. In such a case, Congress would have to assume the responsibility of seeing to it that such interstate agreements were in all respects in line with the public welfare and would be expected to approve or disapprove such agreements with that idea in view. It will, of course, be no easy matter to bring separate states together in agreement on power production, regulation, and transmission, but the prize of great economic gains in return for laying aside a narrow provincialism must not be disregarded. Vast pools of power lie within our reach. Governor Pinchot says:

> The freedom of commerce among the several states, the unrestricted exchange across state lines of services, goods, and resources guaranteed by the Federal Constitution, is the strongest man-made basis of the prosperity of each state. This consideration applies . . . to energy flowing over a wire, whether the burning of fuel or the falling of water is the source.
>
> Such a system must transcend state lines, and is likely to become nation-wide. The new art of electric transmission is already so developed that the Giant Power system with which

we are immediately concerned should now include all power producers and consumers in the northeastern section of the United States, and should perhaps draw also upon resources of water power in Canada.

If this is so, then Pennsylvania should share its fuel with southern New York, and New York should share its water power with western Pennsylvania. I hope and expect that the power resources of Pennsylvania will be intensively developed, enormously increased, and their product greatly cheapened, not only for the people of Pennsylvania but also for the people of New Jersey and New York.

CHAPTER III

The Issue Comes to Light

LEGISLATION TO 1906

For one hundred years the states exercised undisputed control over navigable waters within their boundaries. Without interference from any superior authority, each state regulated the rights and obligations of riparian proprietors.

The first acts of Congress bearing any relation to water-power development were passed under the power of the Federal Government to keep open the lanes of navigation. These acts were largely concerned with the regulation of the building of obstructions in the navigable waters of the United States and the removal of such obstructions when deemed essential. Water-power dams being obstructions naturally came with the purview of such acts. The first general legislation on this subject is found in the rivers and harbors act of July 5, 1884, by which the Secretary of War was directed to report to Congress whether bridges crossing navigable streams or structures then erected or in process of erection were interfering with free and safe navigation. In the rivers and harbors act of September 27, 1890, we find the following regulations:

> The creation of any obstruction, not affirmatively authorized by law, to the navigable capacity of any waters, in respect of which the United States has jurisdiction .... is hereby prohibited. The continuance of any such obstruction shall constitute an offense and each week's continuance of such obstruc-

tion shall be deemed a separate offense. Every person and every corporation which shall be guilty of creating or continuing such unlawful obstruction . . . . shall be deemed guilty of a misdemeanor and on conviction thereof shall be punished by a fine not exceeding $5000, or by imprisonment . . . . not exceeding one year or by both such punishments in the discretion of the court.

Further provisions of this act gave to the Attorney General of the United States power to begin proper proceedings in equity in any United States Circuit Court, within the district in which the obstruction happened to be, for the removal of such obstruction. Under this act every separate dam construction had to be approved by Congress. Owing to the pioneer nature of the electric power industry at this time little was accomplished through the act.[1] It did, however, assert the paramount power of Congress over navigable streams and gave warning to the states that henceforth regulation of navigation by the central government had to be reckoned with. The debates on the bill were mainly concerned with the power given the Secretary of War in certain sections of the bill to cause the removal of structures and with possible interference with the powers of the states over structures which the legislatures had authorized. The fear of placing too much power in the hands of an administrative official caused greater concern than the fear of power corporations, rates, or even the rights of states. This same fear crops out again and again throughout all the years of debate on water-power legislation.

An extension of the act of 1890 was provided in 1899 when Congress assumed full and complete control over navigable streams, forbidding the construction of dams, piers for bridges, or other structures in them without special

[1] The first hydroelectric plant was constructed in 1890. Act of 1890 (26 *Stat.* 454); Act of 1899 (30 *Stat.* 1151).

consent of Congress. Section twelve of the act reads as follows:

> That it shall not be lawful to construct or commence the construction of any bridge, dam, dike, or causeway over or in any port, roadstead, haven, harbor, canal, navigable rivers, or other navigable water of the United States until the consent of Congress to the building of such structures shall have been obtained and until the plans for the same shall have been submitted to and approved by the Chief of Engineers and by the Secretary of War. Provided, That such structures may be built under authority of the legislature of a state across rivers and other waterways the navigable portions of which lie wholly within the limits of a single state, provided the location and plans thereof are submitted to and approved by the Chief of Engineers and by the Secretary of War before construction is commenced.

This act occasioned little comment or debate in the House, perhaps, because the question of each water-power development was still to be decided by the Congress except in the cases where the project was on a stream the navigable portions of which were wholly within a state. In the latter case approval by the state legislature and the Secretary of War was sufficient. In the Senate no objection was raised to the water-power dam provisions. The whole bill, however, narrowly escaped death by a filibuster on the part of those who would authorize the President to acquire the right to build a canal across Nicaragua, but especially on the part of Senator Warren of Wyoming who wanted the bill sent back to conference because no provision was made for irrigation. In the wee hours of the morning of March 4, 1899, Senator Frye agreed to a recommittal which broke the filibuster. A short conference between Senator Warren and the Senate leaders saved the bill before the expiration of the Fifty-fifth Congress.

No evidence of pressure by power interests for or against passage of this act is at hand. Nor is it likely that such pressure was brought, since the power industry was still in its infancy. The motive behind the passage of the Act seems to have been a desire on the part of shipping interests to clear the channels of navigable streams of an ever-increasing number of obstructions in the way of bridge piers, rubbish, dams, and wharves. The house committee in reporting the bill believed that the "interests of commerce" would be served by its passage. This seems to have been the prime reason.[1]

The acts of 1890 and 1899 dealt exclusively with navigable streams. On the public domain, however, were many choice water-power sites which did not come under the regulations of the acts of 1890 and 1899. It was necessary, moreover, in some cases where the power sites were on streams outside of the public lands and forests to secure rights of way for transmission lines. Before 1896 water-power sites on the public lands went to patent either as parts of homesteads or by purchase and were given no attention by the Federal Government. Under this procedure a large number of the best sites were practically given away and in that manner passed into private ownership beyond control. As fast as the new power concerns could grab these valuable sites they did so. Whenever such concerns today occupy land under the old, lax laws, they are beyond federal control as long as the business is intrastate. The acts of 1891 [2] and 1895 [3] authorized the Secretary of the Interior to grant rights of way through the public domain for ditches, canals, and reservoirs for purposes of irrigation. Rights of way were granted for irrigation purposes under these

[1] *House Report 1826*; 55th Cong., 3rd Sess.

[2] 25 *Stat.* 1095.

[3] 28 *Stat.* 635.

acts, it being understood that development of electricity was a subsidiary purpose. Under an act of May 14, 1896,[1] the Secretary of the Interior was

authorized and empowered under general regulations to be fixed by him, to permit the use of a right of way . . . not exceeding 40 acres upon public lands and forest reservations . . . for the purpose of generating, manufacturing, or distributing electric power.

An act of 1901 [2] brought together general rights-of-way acts of previous years and provided that

the Secretary of the Interior be, and hereby is empowered, under general regulations to be fixed by him, to permit the use of rights of way through the public lands, forests and other reservations of the United States . . . . for electrical plants, poles, and lines for the generation and distribution of electrical power.

The act further provided that the permit granted by the Secretary of the Interior might be revoked by him or his successors at will. The bill incorporating the provisions of this act was reported unanimously by both the Senate and the House Committees and passed both Houses of Congress without debate or amendment. Public domain legislation was further extended by an amendment to the Agricultural Appropriation bill of 1911 [3] which provided:

That the Secretary of the Interior be, and he hereby is authorized and empowered, under general regulations to be fixed by him, to grant an easement for rights of way for a period not exceeding 50 years . . . . over public lands, forests, and reservations for electrical poles and lines.

[1] 29 *Stat.* 120.

[2] 31 *Stat.* 790.

[3] 36 *Stat.* 1253.

Although these acts remedied the earlier unsatisfactory situation, yet they were somewhat inadequate. All these acts provided that the Secretary of the Interior might grant permits "under general regulations." This broad language was objectionable. It will be seen that the Secretary had to grant permits under a regulation that was general and hence applied to all projects, despite the fact that certain localities required special arrangements. Here again Congress demonstrated its fear of administrative discretion. In this instance the service was crippled, as one Secretary of the Interior, Mr. Fisher, pointed out, but no remedy was provided until the passage of the Power Act of 1920.

In the short session of the Fifty-eighth Congress [1] a bill [2] for the general regulation of water-power dams in navigable streams was reported from the House Committee on Interstate and Foreign Commerce.[3] The report was divided, those favoring the bill pointing out the advantages of uniform legislation on the subject as well as the advantage to the Government in having private capital develop navigation. The minority of the committee, although granting that some legislation was necessary, objected to the bill on the following grounds:

(1) Citizens should not be denied the use of the water-power of streams simply because they are declared navigable.

(2) No plan for development of these water powers will ever be practical unless some provision is made that the parties building a dam shall be reimbursed by the Government whenever the Government sees proper to use the dam so constructed by the individual or corporation.

[1] Dec. 5, 1904–Mar. 4, 1905.

[2] The provisions of this bill were practically the same as those found in the General Dam Act of 1906.

[3] *House Report 4832*, 58th Cong., 3d Sess.

(3) Not a dollar of capital will be invested under the drastic provisions of the bill.

Mr. Adamson disclosed the reason for seeking legislation at this time when in the debate on the bill in the House (February 28, 1905) he said: "Almost every week and each day somebody is discussing the subject and seeking permission to construct dams for the improvement of water-power." This sentence is significant in showing the growth of the power industry and the increased attention it was receiving from the National Legislature. A present-day touch is given to the debate in the House on this bill by Mr. Richardson (Alabama) who opposed it on the ground that it came too late in the session for proper consideration; that it was not inclusive enough; that its provisions made investment hazardous, and that *no provision was made for the creation of a dam at Muscle Shoals on the Tennessee River where the Government had constructed valuable works and where unused and valuable power awaited investment of capital.* The words might very aptly fit in on many a page of the latest edition of the *Congressional Record.*[1] Mr. Mann of Illinois in sponsoring the bill said that every special permit thus far given by Congress contained a right of repeal and yet private capital was not wary. He looked upon the measure as a proclamation to those interested, giving exactly the terms upon which Congress would grant permits.

This bill, however, was not passed in the fifty-eighth Congress.

In June, 1906, Congress passed a general act fixing conditions which would thereafter apply to each specific power project in the navigable waters of the United States.[1] The act required the consent of Congress for each project and

[1] 69th Congress.

[2] 34 *Stat.* 386.

set forth the conditions upon which such consent could be given. The following provisions of this important act should be noted:

1. Plans and specifications for the work had to be approved by the Chief of Engineers and the Secretary of War.

2. As a condition of approval these officers might require:

(a) The construction, maintenance, and operation by the grantee without expense to the United States of locks and over navigation facilities.

(b) If the above facilities were constructed by the United States, the conveyance by the grantee at his own expense of the lands needed by the United States for such purposes, together with free use of water power for the operation of such facilities.

3. The United States had authority to construct locks in the dams at any time and to control water discharges and pool levels.

4. Grantee had to maintain, at his own expense, lights, signals, and fishways.

5. Construction had to be begun within one year and completed within three.

6. The act might be repealed at any time by Congress.

7. Or the grant might be terminated in the event of refusal on the part of the grantee to comply with any lawful order of the Chief of Engineers or the Secretary of War.

8. Any dam or structure found a hindrance to navigation had to be removed by the grantee at his own expense; if he failed to do so, the United States could remove the obstruction and charge the expense of removal to him.

9. No time limit was placed on the duration of the grant itself.

Such was the Act of 1906. Introduced in the House of Representatives by Congressman Mann of Illinois in December of 1905, it was reported favorably without amendment from the Committee on Interstate and Foreign Commerce in the early part of January, 1906.[1] The Committee in reporting the bill called attention to the fact that if the bill were passed it would only be necessary in the future in authorizing the construction of a dam to provide a simple sentence granting the authority to construct the dam in accordance with the provisions of the act. The committee had for sometime past given a considerable degree of attention to the question of authorizing the construction of dams in navigable streams for the development of water power and had come to the conclusion that there should be adopted some uniform regulations which would govern in each case. The effort of the Committee had been to frame a bill which would permit the development of water power and at the same time render it easier and cheaper for the Government to improve the navigation of streams through private capital. To prepare many streams for navigation would have required more money than the Government would have been willing to appropriate. The framers of the bill expressed the hope that not alone would the interests of navigation and of the Government be protected, but that the terms of the bill would profit the owners of water rights. The committee called attention to the way in which both Government and private riparian owner might do this in the following words:

These terms and conditions (i. e. to the private owner) should vary with different circumstances. On important streams with valuable water power and large commerce the owners of water rights might accept conditions largely beneficial to the Government. On smaller streams with less water power and trivial commerce, with little prospect of increase, the Government would be expected to impose very mild terms and light conditions.[2]

[1] *House Report 337*, 59th Cong., 1st Sess.

[2] *Ibid.*, p. 2.

To those who feared that the Government might through its unlimited right to modify or repeal the terms of the grant jeopardize or destroy the investment of the private owner the committee gave the following assurance:

There is little probability of amending or modifying so as to injure property constructed under the provisions of this bill. Only in rare cases of great necessity would it be probable and in such cases there is no doubt that the Government would be prompt and liberal in making compensation.[1]

The bill as proposed passed the House without opposition June 4, 1906; it passed the Senate without opposition June 16, 1906, and was signed by the President June 25, 1906. The lack of opposition or discussion of any kind is particularly interesting in view of the impending battle on water power which was soon to begin. No evidence of lobbying one way or another, no pressure on the part of the press, no fear for the interests of conservation come to light at this time. Only a desire on the part of legislators to adopt a *uniform policy* with respect to the ever increasing number of applications for permits to dam navigable streams, seems to have brought about the legislation of 1906. The reason for the legislation stated by Representative Hepburn (Iowa) in the previous session when discussing a similar bill was:

The bill does not authorize the erection of dams or other impediment in any navigable river. It simply provides that when such authority is hereafter given the conditions of this bill shall be observed. *It is solely to save the time of the House.*[2]

LEGISLATION 1906-1913

Some twenty-five special acts had been authorized by Congress under the Act of 1906—all being signed by Presid-

[1] *Ibid.*, p. 2.

[2] *Congressional Record*, 58th Cong., 3rd Sess., p. 3665.

ent Roosevelt—when a bill was introduced in the House of Representatives providing an extension of time for the completion of water-power works on the Rainey River, a boundary stream between the State of Minnesota and the Dominion of Canada. The Rainey River Improvement Company had been organized in 1898 under the laws of Minnesota. Its first permit to build a dam across the Rainey River was granted by an act of May 4, 1898,[1] when a time limit for commencing the work was fixed at one year and for completion in three years. An added extension of time was granted by an act of May 4, 1900;[2] this act set the time for commencing at three years and for completion at five years. An act of June 28, 1902,[3] extended the time for construction until May 4, 1907. An act of February 25, 1905,[4] set the time for completion at July 1, 1908. In other words the patentees had enjoyed the exclusive privilege of constructing the work for more than ten years and apparently nothing had been done. So in January, 1908, Mr. Bede introduced his bill for a further extension of time until July 1, 1912. An amendment to the bill in committee extended the time to July 1, 1911, and brought the whole project under the Dam Act of 1906. Brigadier-General Makenzie, Chief of Engineers of the War Department, approved the act with minor changes saying:

It is understood that the dam is now under construction and that operations are being so conducted as to in no way interfere with navigation interests. I see no objection, therefore, to favorable consideration of the proposition set forth in the bill.[5]

[1] 30 *Stat.* 398.
[2] 31 *Stat.* 167.
[3] 32 *Stat.* 485.
[4] 33 *Stat.* 814.
[5] *House Report 1061*, 60th Cong., 1st Sess.

Everyone assumed that all would now be fair sailing. The bill passed both Houses with little discussion and few amendments. On April 6, 1908, it was presented to President Roosevelt. Mr. Roosevelt was astonished at the number of times extensions had been given to the grantee. Indeed, the monotonous repetition of further grants might have excited a man of milder temperament than the two-fisted Mr. Roosevelt. Although he did not act hastily, he did act without full consideration of the circumstances when he despatched his veto message to Congress on April 13, 1908. This message is a landmark in the history of water-power legislation. It may be looked upon as the Confession of Faith of the Conservationists. Because of its importance the larger part of it follows:

I do not believe that natural resources should be granted and held in an undeveloped condition either for speculative or other reasons. So far as I am aware, there are no assurances that the grantees are in any better condition, promptly and properly to utilize this opportunity, than they were at the time of the original act, ten years ago.

In all permits of this character the duty of declaring a forfeiture, after notice and hearing, for failure to begin or complete construction within the time limited by the permit, or for other breach of conditions, should be definitely imposed by the proper administrative officer (in this case the Secretary of War). There have been many unfortunate experiences resulting from conditional grants which, though on their face apparently terminable for breach of condition, proved practically indeterminate because no one official was specifically given power to discover and declare the breach. The general statute regulating dams in navigable waters (act of 1906) though representing an advance, yet leaves uncertain much that should be definitely expressed in each act permitting the construction of dams under this statute. *A definite time limit is one of these*[1] *important*

[1] Italics throughout message are the author's.

omissions. . . . It is essential that any permit to obstruct them (rivers) for reasons and on conditions that seem good at the moment should be subject to revision when changed conditions demand. The right reserved by Congress to alter, amend, or repeal is based on this principle. . . . *Each right should be issued to expire on a specified day without further legislative, administrative or judicial action.*

Every permit to construct a dam on a navigable stream should specifically recognize the right of the Government to fix a term for its duration and to impose such charge or charges as may be deemed necessary to protect the present and future interests of the United States in accordance with the act of June 21, 1906. *There is sharp conflict of judgment as to whether this general act empowers the War Department to fix a charge and set a time limit. All grounds for such doubts should be removed henceforth by the insertion in every act granting such a permit of words adequate to show that a time limit and a charge to be paid to the Government are among the interests of the United States which should be protected through conditions and stipulations* to be approved either by the War Department, or, as I think would be preferable, by the Interior Department.

The provision for a charge is of vital importance. The navigability of every inland waterway . . . . should be improved for the purposes of interstate and foreign commerce upon a consistent unified plan by which each part should be made to keep every other. One means available for the improvement of navigation at a particular point on any river may be a dam creating a water pool of sufficient depth. Such a dam may . . . . develop power of sufficient value to pay in whole or in part for the improvement of navigation at that point, and if there is any surplus it can be spent upon improvements at other points in accordance with the general plan. *Since the Government can do by any proper agency what it can do directly, it is in principle immaterial whether this income to construct needed improvements is derived from works constructed directly by the Government or by a corporation acting under federal authority, since federal authority is the one indispensable legal prerequisite for the work,* though the charge to be paid to the Government for the power would of course differ in two cases; indeed the charge would necessarily vary greatly, for where the improvement was both costly and of great benefit to the public, the charge would naturally be made low, the time limit long.

The income derivable from this source would materially aid in the complete improvement of our navigable waters. . . . This natural wealth (water powers) is the heritage of the people. I see no reason for giving it away, though there is every reason for not imposing conditions so burdensome as to prevent the utilization of the power. . . .

We are now at the beginning of a great development in water power. Its use in electrical transmission is entering more and more largely into every element of the daily life of the people. *Already the evils of monopoly are becoming manifest;* already the spirit of the past shows the necessity of caution in making unrestricted grants of this power.

The present policy pursued in making these grants is unwise in giving away the property of the people in the flowing waters to individuals or organizations practically unknown, and granting in perpetuity these valuable privileges in advance of the formulation of definite plans as to their use. *In some cases the grantees apparently have little or no financial or other ability to utilize the gift, and have sought it merely because it could be had for the asking.*

In place of the present haphazard policy of permanently alienating valuable public property we should substitute a definite policy along the following lines:

First. *There should be a limited* or carefully guarded *grant* in the nature of an option or opportunity afforded within *a reasonable time for development of the plant* and for execution of the project.

Second. Such a grant of concession should be accompanied in the act making the grant by a provision expressly making it the duty of the designated official to *annul the grant if the work is not begun or plans are not carried out in accordance with the authority granted.*

Third. *It should also be the duty of some designated official to see to it that in approving the plans the maximum development of the navigation and power is assured,* or at least that in making the plans these may not be so developed as ultimately to interfere with the better utilization of the water or complete development of the power.

Fourth. *There should be a license fee or charge* which, though small or nominal at the outset, can in the future be adjusted so as to secure a control in the interest of the public.

Fifth. *Provision should be made for the termination of the grant or privilege at a definite time, leaving to future generations the power or authority to renew or extend the concession* in accordance with the conditions which may prevail at the time.[1]

The message and bill were referred to the House Committee on Interstate and Foreign Commerce on the motion of Mr. Mann (Illinois). The committee held hearings on the bill during which they were informed by the Secretary of the Interior, James R. Garfield, that the administration had not been cognizant of all the facts in connection with the bill.[2] He pointed out that the Rainey River Company had evidently proceeded with due diligence in carrying out its work and had spent more than $750,000 on partial construction without issuing bonds or stock. It is true the company had done all of this. Furthermore, the Dominion Parliament and the Parliament of Ontario had granted rights and licenses to an associate company of the Rainey River Company to do the Canadian portion of the work; as the whole project was a unit it was quite proper that the work be taken over by one company. Much of the time and the capital had been spent in trying to induce the railroads to come to the place of construction. The dam could not be

[1] *Congressional Record*, 60th Cong., 1st Sess., pp. 4698-4699.

[2] *Congressional Record*, 60th Cong., 1st Sess., p. 6863.

built until the railroads came. Besides this source of delay, it took seven years to get the consents of the Dominion Parliament and of the Provincial Parliament. When work actually began in 1905, there seemed to be no reason why the work should not be consistently and steadily prosecuted, but a severe financial panic in 1907 brought another cessation of the work. The trials and tribulations of this Job of water-power companies had found no ear at the White House. Then, too, it was known to those familiar with the project that the building of the dam would not only furnish power but would improve navigation and would maintain the waters of Rainey Lake at a high level during the low water period. Lieutenant Colonel Hoxie of the Corps of Engineers of the Army had reported in 1905 that the improvement of navigation would be too costly for the United States to undertake.[1]

These considerations greatly changed the whole situation from the administration's standpoint, but in themselves counted as little compared with an important written agreement arrived at between the Secretary of War and the Rainey River Company. In that agreement the company agreed to come under the general Dam Act of 1906 and to submit its new plans and specifications for approval by the War Department. It agreed to submit to a time limit, to remove without expense to the United States obstacles to navigation, to pay a charge for the privilege of building a dam in navigable waters, and to submit to any general law or special modification thereafter laid down by Congress.[2]

President Roosevelt requested the Congress to pass the bill over his veto. This was done on May 23, 1908.

In February, 1908, Representative Russell of Missouri introduced a bill to authorize William H. Standish to con-

[1] *Ibid.*

[2] *Ibid.*

struct a dam across James River in Stone County, Missouri, and to divert a portion of its waters through a tunnel into the said river again, to create electric power. The bill was referred to the House Committee on Interstate and Foreign Commerce and was reported with amendments March 17, 1908. The chief amendment provided that the Secretary of War should at all times control the use of the water even to the extent of causing the persons taking advantage of the privileges granted to cease using the water when such should be necessary for navigation.[1] The bill was subject to all the conditions of the Dam Act of 1906. As amended by the committee the bill passed the House March 18, 1908. It was not passed in the Senate until the beginning of the next session[2] January 4, 1909. On January 15, 1909, a veto message came from President Roosevelt. Again the President laid down the gospel of the conservationists. The message was very much like the Rainey River veto; summarized it was as follows:[3]

[1] The James River Bill: Be it enacted, etc., That William H. Standish, of Reeds Springs, Stone County, Missouri, his heirs and assigns, be, and they are hereby authorized to construct, maintain, and operate a dam in the big bend of the James River in township 23 north, range 24 west, in the County of Stone and State of Missouri, across the said James River at said point. And that at the narrows in said bend be and they are hereby authorized to impound and by canal and tunnel to divert and conduct across said narrows such portion of the water in said river, through said tunnel, into said river again as may be necessary for electric power purposes, all subject to and in accordance with the provisions of the act of Congress entitled "An Act to regulate the construction of dams across navigable waters" approved June 21, 1906.

Section 2. That the construction of said dam and tunnel shall be commenced within two years of the passage of said act, and be completed within five years from the date of the passage of this act.

Section 3. That the right to alter, amend, or repeal this act is hereby expressly reserved. (*H. R. 17707*, 60th Cong., 1st Sess.)

[2] 60th Cong., 2nd Sess.

[3] *House Document 1350*, 60th Cong., 2nd Sess.

1. The bill gives to the grantee a valuable privilege which is monopolistic and does not contain conditions essential to protect the public.

2. No rights should be granted unconditionally to any corporation.

3. He (the President) would sign no bills which did not contain a *charge* and a *time limit*.

4. The Government is met with new conditions of industry seriously affecting the public welfare and it should not hesitate to adopt measures for the protection of the public.

5. "*When the public welfare is involved, Congress should resolve any reasonable doubt as to its legislative power in favor of the public and against the seekers for a special privilege.*"

6. *The people of the country are threatened by a monopoly far more powerful*—because in closer touch with their domestic life—than anything known to experience.

7. The water power alone if fully developed and wisely used is probably sufficient for our present transportation, industrial, municipal, and domestic needs and should be protected from monopolistic control. . .

8. If care is not taken now, future generations will find themselves face to face with powerful interests intrenched behind the doctrine of 'vested right' and strengthened by every defense which money can buy and the ingenuity of corporation laws can devise.

9. "*The great corporations are acting with foresight, singleness of purpose and vigor to control the water powers of the country. They pay no attention to state boundaries and are not interested in the constitutional law affecting navigable streams except as it affords what has been aptly called a 'twilight zone' from any regulation.*"

10. *He charged that there were several bills pending in*

Congress either drafted by representatives of the power companies or containing the provisions they approved.

11. In repeating the terms of the administration, the President laid down the following conditions:

(a) A limited and carefully guarded opportunity to develop the project.

(b) Provisions for annulling the grant after a reasonable period if the work has not been begun or the plans not carried out.

(c) Plans to provide for maximum development.

(d) A license fee or charge which could be adjusted to profits in the future.

(e) A time limit for the grant (about 50 years) giving the chance to future generations to renew concessions or to revoke them.

(f) Provisions for revoking the permit upon proof that the licensee has engaged or is engaging in any unlawful combination in restraint of trade.

12. The President concludes: "*I esteem it my duty to use every endeavor to prevent the growing monopoly, the most threatening which has ever appeared, from being fastened upon the people of this nation.*"

The fight was now on.

What reasons can be assigned for this sudden hostility on the part of the President to certain types of water-power bills? It had not been the rule during Roosevelt's administration to incorporate the Roosevelt provisions into the special laws. Congress had granted (March 4, 1907) to the Alabama Power Company the right to build a dam across the Coosa River in Alabama for the development of water power. In return the Alabama Power Company had to furnish the electric current necessary to operate the lock in connection with the navigation dam. *The grant was given in perpetuity and signed by the President.*

Chief among the reasons for the change in attitude may be assigned the conservation movement, the great exponents of which in the administration were Gifford Pinchot and Henry Graves of the Forestry Bureau.[1] The nation owes eternal gratitude to these champions of a great cause. The waste in our national resources was ably presented by them, and as a result of their activities we find President Roosevelt in 1908 calling a conference of Governors to consider all phases of the problem. At the same time he appointed a Conservation Commission of fifty members with Mr. Pinchot as chairman. The commission did not report before the Rainey River veto, but it had been actively investigating before that time. The Bureau of Corporations, the Bureau of the Census, and the Geological Survey gave active aid in the preparation of reports on water power. All investigation pointed to a concentration of control of the power industry in the hands of about thirteen major corporations such as the General Electric Company, and the Westinghouse Company and certain banking groups.[2]

Besides knowing the activities of the conservation group, the President was cognizant of the work of the power group. The administration had come into direct contact with them during the Fifth-ninth Congress in a series of conferences in which the power people demanded grants in perpetuity.[3] The power interests or their friends had incorporated perpetual and unregulated grants in several bills of the Sixtieth Congress;[4] among them Senate bill 6626 to subject lands held

[1] *Autobiography* Theodore Roosevelt, New York, p. 394.

[2] See the report of Dr. Herbert Knox Smith, United States Commissioner of Corporations, entitled *Water-Power Development in the United States* (Washington, 1912). A brief report from the Commissioner to the President (January, 1909) is found in the *Congressional Record*, 60th Cong., 2nd Sess., pp. 3413-3414.

[3] Roosevelt tells us this in his James River Veto Message, *House Document 1350*, 60th Cong., 2nd Sess.

[4] Second Session.

by the United States to condemnation by state courts; House bill 11356 and Senate bill 2661 granting locations and rights of way for electric and other power purposes through the public lands of the United States. That the private corporations had been active in drafting legislation is evident from a speech by Representative Mann (Illinois) in the House during the debate on the Coosa River Bill. He said:

Some years ago, while I was serving on the Committee on Interstate and Foreign Commerce, I found that the practice in regard to bills relating to the construction of dams was for the attorney of some company that desired the privilege to prepare a bill, in some cases one section long, occupying half a page of bill form, and in some cases 9 or 10 or 12 sections long, occupying several pages of bill forms. There was no pretense of preserving any rights of the general government in most of these cases.[1]

Furthermore, in his veto of the Rainey and James River bills the President had in mind a general change in water-power legislation, especially in regard to navigable streams. Opinion was divided as to whether or not the Act of 1906 gave to the Secretary of War the right to impose a charge. The President desired a very definite provision for the imposition of a time limit and a charge.

New legislation was needed. No further navigable stream legislation was possible so long as President Roosevelt demanded a definite time and a charge limit which many wise counsellors believed impossible under the Act of 1906. The House Committee on Interstate and Foreign Commerce had long been busy on a new bill, but the chairman of that committee, Mr. Stevens of Minnesota, reported to the House on February 27, 1909, that no bill would be presented immediately. For his reasons he assigned the following:

[1] *Congressional Record*, 52nd Cong., 2nd Sess., p. 11584.

1 The time was not feasible (end of session near).

2 Legislation would have to be carefully drawn to protect the whole community as well as the property rights of private interests.

3 The conflicting rights of the National Government and of the states made the subject particularly difficult to deal with.

4 And his last reason:

> But when the power of the National Government is so carefully defined and limited by the Constitution of the United States, and when so large a part of the authority over this subject must necessarily remain with the states, and when the boundary of private rights must be ascertained and respected in the instances where such rights exist, and yet the whole range of utilization, control, rights, and charges must be considered in the preparation of any legislation to be passed by Congress, the difficulties of ascertaining accurately the respective powers of the National Government, the states, and the individual owners, of considering the divergent views and interests, and of formulating such provisions as shall be adequate to secure development of these great natural resources, are vastly increased and require much time for their proper understanding, thorough consideration, and final settlement.[1]

There was something ominous in the last reason. The committee was not a unit. Mr. Roosevelt's ideas of time limits, charges, and regulation had aroused a bitter antagonism. What Mr. Roosevelt's answer was to this statement of the Committee's difficulties with the legal questions involved may be gathered from a letter from the President to Representative Bede in May, 1908.

> In my judgment *it is not a case as to whether the Constitution authorizes the actions,* but as to whether the National Government does or does not choose to take the position that, as a

[1] *Congressional Record,* 60th Cong., 2nd Sess., p. 3409.

grant of this kind is an exclusive and therefore a monopolistic grant, it is fair that the holder as a condition of the enjoyment, should give just compensation to the public at large. . . . It seems to me unwise for Congress to take any other position.[1]

One catches in this statement a glimpse of the "twilight zone."

There may have been one very good reason for the delay which the committee sought to justify—a reason not stated. Mr. Taft, the incoming President, was known to be opposed to charges for water-power privileges. As Secretary of War his position on that point was quite clear.[2] At any rate the committee decided to wait. To the power interests the wait was justified.

In August, 1909, a bill was introduced and debated in the House permitting J. L. Hankinson, N. B. Dial, and others to construct, maintain, and operate a dam across the Savannah River in accordance with the provisions of the general Dam Act of 1906. Mr. Mann of Illinois in advocating the passage of the measure made the following significant statement:

I understand after talking with the present President (Mr. Taft) that he is inclined to think—not to state it more strongly—that Congress is not entitled in granting permits for the construction of a dam to charge for that right upon the theory that the Government is the owner of anything, and probably—I say probably—if a dam bill like this were passed it would not be vetoed by the President.[3]

The Bill was passed and signed by President Taft. What joy this must have brought to the hearts of the power people, the anti-conservationists, and to the lovers of the rights of

[1] *Congressional Record,* 60th Cong., 2nd Sess., p. 3410.

[2] *Congressional Record,* 64th Cong., 1st Sess., p. 2580.

[3] *Congressional Record,* 61st Cong., 1st Sess., p. 4822.

states! We have no record of Ex-President Roosevelt's comments on this turn of affairs.

On April 11, 1910, there came from the House Committee on Interstate and Foreign Commerce the long-awaited general act. The provisions of this act, which was the last piece of general water-power legislation before the passage of the Act of 1920, were briefly as follows:

1 A person or corporation desiring to construct a dam for power purposes across a navigable stream had to submit to the Secretary of War and the Chief of Engineers for their approval the plans and specifications for such dam and accessory works.

2 In approving such plans the Secretary of War and the Chief of Engineers might make certain stipulations such as requiring the person building the dam to construct, maintain and operate in connection with the dam, without expense to the United States, a lock or locks, booms, or sluices, or any other structure which the Secretary of War and the Chief of Engineers at any time might deem necessary in the interests of navigation.

3 Whenever Congress should authorize the construction of a lock or other structure necessary for navigation purposes in connection with such a dam, the persons owning such dams would have to convey to the United States free of cost, title to such land as might be required for such construction and would have to convey to the United States free water power or power generated from water power for the construction work.

4 *Provided further that in acting upon such plans the Chief of Engineers and the Secretary of War shall consider the bearing of such structure upon a comprehensive plan for the improvement of the waterway over which it is to be constructed and for the full development of water power . . . as a part of the conditions and stipulations imposed by them,*

shall provide for improving and developing navigation, and fix such charge or charges for the privilege granted as may be sufficient to restore conditions with respect to navigability .... or reimburse the United States for doing the same, and for such additional or further expense as may be incurred by the United States with reference to such project.

5 The Secretary of War and the Chief of Engineers were authorized to fix charges where any direct benefit was received from the construction, operation, and maintenance by the United States of storage reservoirs at the headwaters of any navigable stream.

6 The person building any dam in accordance with the provisions of the act was liable for any damage inflicted upon private property.

7 The grantee was required to maintain lights and fishways as ordered by the Secretary of Commerce.

8 The Secretary of War might revoke the permit for non-performance of the rules.

9 In case the United States found it necessary to take over the property for a public purpose, the grantee was to be paid the reasonable value of his works exclusive of the value of the privilege granted; the reasonable value to be determined between the Secretary of War and the grantee or failing an agreement, by the United States District Court.

10 The permit was to run for fifty years.[1]

This was indeed a compromise measure—so compromised that it was ineffective. It struck in all directions. It provided charges and it did not; it provided regulation and it did not. While the bill was being debated it was pointed out that the basis for the charge was very inaccurate. Surprisingly little debate was expended on the measure, and, after passing both Houses, it was signed by President Taft in June, 1910.

[1] 36 *Stat.* 593.

Although more stringent than the Act of 1906, it was not an improvement over that act. Charges were provided but not on the conservationist principle of regulation. Compensation was required for restoring prior conditions of navigability and for benefits from headwater improvements or forested watersheds operated or maintained by the United States, but no provision was made for the collection of charges for the privilege itself. Investment under the act was bound to be precarious for the following reasons: first, no disposition of the properties at the termination of the fifty-year grant was provided; secondly, it was possible that the permittee might be required some time in the future to undertake at his own expense navigation improvements of undetermined cost; thirdly, the right was reserved by the Congress to alter, amend, or repeal the act at any time without any liability on the part of the United States.

The Act of 1910 was an administration measure, for Mr. Stevens of Minnesota stated before the House Committee on Interstate and Foreign Commerce that it was prepared in consultation with the President and his advisors. It was quite evidently the result of an effort to satisfy the conservationists by certain stringent provisions and the grabbers by dropping the charge-for-privilege provisions.

One of the most dramatic efforts of the grabbers to secure the old privileges which were common when the water-power industry was young occurred in the summer of 1912. The presidential nominating conventions were over, and the campaign was on. The intensity of the political combat was reflected in the Congress where, despite the torrid summer heat, the Senate and the House were engagd in a bitter struggle over tariff legislation. Everything else seemed to have been forgotten in this one giant struggle. Suddenly on July twenty-second there came from the House Committee on Interstate and Foreign Commerce a water-power bill of the omnibus type. Seventeen dam projects were grouped together in a single measure in order to secure the favor of the members of various committees interested in its enactment. It was drawn up on the pork-barrel principle. No provisions for charges, no provisions for regulation were provided. This was the third such measure introduced since 1906.

From 1789 down to this time, Congress had given one hundred franchises to build dams. Over fifty per cent of them were under the control of some one of the six great water-power groups. Here was a bill which authorized almost one-fifth as many dams as Congress had authorized in 125 years. Yet no hearings were held and no investigation made by the Committee. The bill was reported back to the House without amendment the day following its reference.

In its report the committee said that the first six projects in the bill were reported separately to the House and placed on the Unanimous Consent Calendar, but on objection of Mr. Cooper of Wisconsin all but one were stricken off. The Committee went on to tell of the objection of the Secretary of War (Mr. Stimson) to the bills because they contained no provision for charges. The Committee reported:

The Secretary of War, however, taking up some old suggestions that were insisted upon before the amendment of 1910, has demanded that each of these bills be amended so as to incorporate certain restrictions which the general dam act already permits the Secretary of War to impose.[1] . . . We can not concur in those suggestions, because one wise purpose of the general dam act was to avoid prolixity and multiplicity of detail in each separate bill. . . . The Corps of Engineers and the President are not in accord with the Secretary of War in his demands, and the recommendations of the Chief of Engineers

[1] But the Act of 1910 did not permit general changes.

is favorable . . . , therefore, we have not seen proper to adopt the recommendation of the Secretary of War. . . . Two of these bills have not at this time been reported to us by the War Department. Of course, we expect from the Secretary of War the same letter, in substance, which he has adopted as to the eight bills in which we can not concur, and, therefore, we deem it unnecessary to wait for his letter.[1]

A bitter fight ensued on the floor of the House. Representative Rainey of Illinois, armed with volumes of statistics and with an exposé of the power trust prepared by Mr. Harry Slattery of the conservationist group, led the fight for the conservationists. He charged that in order to get a franchise worth millions of dollars it was only necessary for some person or corporation to persuade a member of Congress to introduce a bill for that purpose and simply to ask the Committee on Interstate and Foreign Commerce to report it out. He claimed that the committee did not even know the post-office addresses of the men who were to receive these valuable franchises. Mr. Rainey's particular target was Representative Austin of Tennessee, a staunch supporter of the bill. The following excerpts will show the temper of the argument:

Mr Austin: The gentleman talks about my room being headquarters for the Water Power Trust. Mr. Paull has been in my room. These two men who came from Morristown, Tennessee, also called to see me. Who else? Why, a man the Member from Illinois in one of his speeches here denominated as a 'lobbyist' for the Water Power Trust called. I did not invite him and I did not insult him. He was the same man that Mr. Rainey dined with at Harvey's the night before he voted for this man's water-power bill in the House on July 25, 1912. What was that bill? It was the White River bill, the Dixie Power bill. You voted for it. Before voting for it you

[1] *House Report 1050*, 62nd Cong., 2nd Sess.

denominated him in your speech as a 'lobbyist'. What else did you do? You corrected your speech and published in the *Record* not that he was a 'lobbyist', but 'a very pleasant gentleman'.

The Speaker: The Chair has admonished the gentleman that he must not use the pronoun 'you'; that is against the rule.

Mr. Austin: .... Now, what was the White River, or Dixie Power bill? I voted for it because it meant the development of Arkansas. ... The Member from Illinois (Mr. Rainey) voted for it. He did not vote for it until after he had spent an evening with a 'water-power lobbyist'. ... The President of the United States gave as one of his reasons for vetoing that bill .... the following:

> The bill also fails to reserve to the Federal Government any right to receive from the grantee of this privilege any compensation therefor.

Why did the great defender of conservation legislation in this House fail .... to vote against it when he knew it carried no compensation for the Government?

Mr. Rainey: In order to throw discredit upon me the gentleman states that I voted in this House for the Dixie power proposition .... The bill was not before the House at all .... It was the report of the conferees. There was no opportunity that afternoon to vote for or against the bill.

Now, the gentlemen makes the further statement that in the discussion of this White River proposition .... I referred to the fact that a lobbyist from St. Louis was here promoting the schemes of the Ozark Power Company .... I left the statement out of the *Record* because I was visited upon this floor, before the speech was revised, by two members of the Arkansas delegation, and they said to me in effect this: 'Do not use the word lobbyist in commenting upon this gentleman. It will injure us in our districts'. ... and, in their presence I wrote the words 'a very pleasant gentleman' ... and that term used sarcastically, as I used it, I thought made my characterization of that particular lobbyist much more objectionable . . . . but it satisfied this gentleman from Arkansas.

The gentleman from Tennessee (Mr. Austin) refers to a dinner I had at Harvey's the night before this matter came up for discussion. I was there. I went there with the gentleman from Mississippi (Mr. Sisson) as his guest. On the way there we met the gentleman from Arkansas (Mr. Oldfield) who was accompanied by this gentleman whom I next day characterized as a lobbyist; I think his name is Mr. Powell. . . . Mr. Sisson invited Mr. Oldfield to accompany us, and his friend being with him, Mr. Sisson invited him also. We went over to Harvey's and had dinner there that evening. It was the day before the Dixie power question came up here . . . . that evening was the first intimation I ever had that any gentleman was here in this city representing the Dixie Power Co., and the gentleman himself told me when he sat down with us at the table: 'You are fighting these power schemes in these States, and it is only fair for me to say to you, before I sit down, that I am here representing one of them'. I think he said he represented the Ozark Power Company. We said to him, 'That makes no difference', and he sat down and had dinner with us. Mr. Sisson paid the bill for that dinner.

Mr. Austin: My understanding of that matter is that the gentleman received a message or information that the Representative of the Dixie Power Co. was looking for him and intended to settle with him for calling him a lobbyist.

Mr. Rainey: I denounce that as absolutely false. I received no such message.

The Speaker: The gentleman from Illinois should not interrupt without asking permission. That applies to both gentlemen.

Mr. Austin: My information is from Mr. Powell himself, who spent a very pleasant evening with the gentlemen from Illinois, who is fighting every power bill except Mr. Powell's of the Dixie Power Co.[1]

[1] This charming dialogue runs through several pages of the *Record*. See *Congressional Record*, 62nd Cong., 2nd Sess., pp. 11370-11380.

The fight went merrily on. The Omnibus Bill was doomed. The advocates of speed in water-power legislation were not altogether disheartened despite the fact that scarcely a month remained before adjournment. Many a greater (if not worthier!) battle had been won in less time.

On July 20, 1912, the fight was carried to a more friendly body when there was introduced in the Senate a bill to authorize the building of a dam across the Coosa River in Alabama at Lock 18. This was one of the projects in the House Omnibus Bill. The prime mover of the bill was the great champion of states' rights and of an unregulated water-power industry—Senator Bankhead of Alabama.

With slight amendments the bill was reported from the Committee on Commerce by Mr. Martin of Virginia. The bill read as follows:

Be it enacted, etc., that the Alabama Power Company, a corporation organized under the laws of the State of Alabama, its successors and assigns, are authorized to construct, maintain, and operate a dam across Coosa River in the State of Alabama, at a place suitable to the interest of navigation about 7½ miles above the city of Wetumpka, in accordance with the provisions of the act approved June 23, 1910, entitled, An act to amend an act entitled 'An act to regulate the construction of dams across navigable waters; approved June 21, 1906.'

Sec. 2. That the right to alter, amend, or repeal this act is hereby expressly reserved.[1]

The Alabama Power Company was organized under the laws of the State of Alabama. The entire capital stock and the bonds of the Company and its subsidiaries—the Birmingham, Montgomery, and Gulf Power Co. and the Muscle Shoals Hydroelectric Co. was at this time controlled by the Alabama Light and Power Co. (Ltd.), a Canadian Corporation. The Birmingham, Montgomery, and Gulf Power

[1] *Congressional Record,* 62nd Cong., 2nd Sess., p. 10882.

Co. and the Muscle Shoals Co. possessed a charter granted in 1900 by the State of Alabama, unlimited in time, not forfeitable for nonuse, and giving the right:

(a) to build dams and resevoirs on the Tallapoosa River or its tributaries,

(b) of eminent domain,

(c) to distribute electricity in all cities and towns in Alabama,

(d) to acquire, by purchase or contract, stocks, bonds, and other securities of any electric railway or electric light company in Alabama,

(e) to exercise all powers belonging to manufacturing companies under the Alabama law,

(f) to be exempt from taxation for 100 years from the commencement of the work.

The Alabama Power Company controlled about two-thirds of the 1,084,000 horsepower capable of development in the State of Alabama.[1]

Upon the introduction of the Coosa River Bill, Senator Burton of Ohio offered the following amendment:

Provided, That the rights here conferred shall not be assigned or transferred except upon the written consent of the Secretary of War;

[1] These companies controlled water powers capable of delivering 400,000 primary horsepower for 10 hours daily even in the driest periods. The following were officers of the Alabama Power Company: James Mitchell, President, 100 Broadway, New York City; Lawrence MacFarland, Vice-president, Montreal, Canada; John B. White, Vice-president, London, England; W. D. Ross, Treasurer, Toronto, Canada; F. S. Ruth, Secretary, and Wyley Alfred, Auditor, Montgomery, Alabama. The Directors were: James Mitchell, James R. Morse, Martin W. Littleton, C. H. Baker, George H. Schuler, John F. Wallace—all of New York; and Frank Washburn of Nashville; J. W. Worthington of Sheffield, Alabama; W. D. Ross of Toronto, Canada; Lawrence MacFarlane of Montreal, Canada; and John B. White of London, England. 62nd Cong., 2nd Sess., p. 11050.

And provided, That the Federal Government reserve the right to control the charges for service to consumers in the event that the public interest may so require.[1]

This amendment together with a tolls amendment offered by Senator Poindexter was turned down, and the bill passed the Senate without a record vote.

In the House, Representative Heflin of Alabama endeavored to get an immediate consideration of the Bill before it was considered by the Committee on Interstate and Foreign Commerce. Heflin explained that he had the written authority from the committee signed by eleven of its members—a quorum, there being twenty-one members in all. The signers were Representatives Adamson, Richardson (by telegram), Covington, Driscoll, Sims, Goeke, W. R. Smith, Martin, Hamilton, Doremus, and Cullop. A meeting of the committee had been called and the few members who did appear indicated that they favored the favorable report on the bill and agreed to sign the paper which Heflin presented. No action as a committee was taken.

Representative Foster of Illinois immediately raised the point of order that the gentleman was not acting in accordance with the rules of the House. To support his point of view he quoted the following from Jefferson's Manual:

A committee meet when and where they please, if the House has not ordered time and place for them, but they can only act when together, and not by separate consultation and consent—nothing being the report of the committee but what has been agreed to in committee actually assembled.

Mr. Heflin contended that the committee was called, that the committee did have a meeting, and that some of the members of the committee assembled in the committee room, took the action of approving the round-robin, informed the other

[1] *Congressional Record,* 62nd Cong., 2nd Sess., p. 10882.

members who were absent of their action and asked them to indorse their action. He contended that a majority of the committee had signed a written authorization to take up the bill on the Speaker's table.

Here was a neat parliamentary question, aside from its being a wilful obstruction by the conservationists to forestall action on the bill. As a matter of sober fact the Coosa River project was included in the Omnibus Bill, had been considered with that bill, and had been favorably reported on as a part of that bill. There was no point in the contention that the bill had not been considered. The objection was, of course, technical, but not without some importance from a parliamentary standpoint. It would, for instance, be possible for a committee meeting to be called with three or four members present. All might be on the same side of the question; no one would raise the point of a quorum. Yet such a group might issue a report as emanating from the committee. Furthermore, it seems but reasonable to contend that the action of a committee is the action of a committee assembled and not the action of a group scattered all over Washington and its environs.

Mr. Heflin, anxious to get a favorable ruling from the Chair, at one point burst forth into a piteous appeal for the folks at home:

> This bill affects my district, my people, and my State. Both Senators and every Member of Congress in this House, the governor of my State, the commissioner of agriculture are all in favor of it, and I appeal to the gentleman from Illinois, if upon no other grounds, that he allow me and my people to say what shall be done in this purely local matter. (Applause) [1]

The Speaker ruled against Mr. Heflin.

The Coosa River Bill was reported and debated on August

[1] *Congressional Record*, 62nd Cong., 2nd Sess., p. 11395.

22, 1912. Mr. Heflin opened debate with a good-humored attack on the conservationists. Many crimes were committed in the name of conservation, he contended. Representative Adamson (later the author of the Adamson Eight Hour Law) paid his respects to the conservationists thus:

I have deprecated the unfair conduct of obstructionists under the false, misleading, and fraudulent name of 'conservationists', unjustly assumed, in objecting to consideration by which only debate on specific propositions could be had and amendments proposed and voted on. Those gentlemen have preferred to hide behind the bulwark of objecting to consideration and then indulge in what they call general debate, which consists in railing at particular individuals, misrepresenting the attitude of the committee, and deluging the country with gush, poppycock, and innuendo, which, boiled down means unconstitutional centralization as imperialistic and autocratic as that of Xerxes or Ptolemy in relation to the particular matter.[1]

Mr. Humphreys of Mississippi offered the usual amendment of the anti-monopolist group providing for charges to be imposed by the Secretary of War. The amendment was vigorously opposed by Representative Mondell of Wyoming who declared the conservationist group guilty of furthering schemes to establish a great centralized bureaucracy, and by Representative Underwood who made a plea for the rights of the states, denied the existence of a water-power trust behind the Coosa project, and endeavored to show the unconstitutionality of tolls. His enthusiasm at one point equaled that of the redoubtable Heflin: "My God, gentlemen," exclaimed Underwood, "have not the people of Alabama a right to use their own resources when you will not do it?"[2]

Mr. Rainey of Illinois figured that the company would be

[1] *Congressional Record,* 62nd Cong., 2nd Sess., p. 11567.

[2] *Congressional Record,* 62nd Cong., 2nd Sess., p. 11586.

able to earn from its 400,000 horsepower about eight million dollars a year, computing on a basis of twenty dollars per horsepower. He claimed that the company could develop hydroelectricity, pay two dollars per horsepower to the Federal Government, charge the consumers less than twelve dollars per horsepower, and make more than ten per cent on the capital invested.[1]

Mr. Foster of Illinois referred to the great point of the manufacture of fertilizers made so much of by the Southern members. He proposed that the members from Alabama accept an amendment which would make the grant null and void as soon as the grantee ceased to manufacture air nitrate fertilizer.[2] The proposal was not taken up.

Mr. Heflin concluded the hectic struggle with a speech quite characteristic; a speech both sarcastic and humorous:

We have gentlemen here who talk about a dam site, and every time they hear of a dam site or see a dam site bill they throw a fit. My friend from Illinois (Mr. Foster), my friend from Mississippi (Mr. Humphreys), and my friend from Wisconsin (Mr. Cooper) all look cross-eyed every time they hear of a dam site bill . . . . the gentleman from Illinois (Mr. Foster) the self-selected Member from the Nation at large, the astute and self-constituted guardian of every district in the United States, drew his little legislative blade, and cutting the air as he came, rushed recklessly into the arena to defend his people against the calamity that would overtake them if Congress should grant a permit to dam the Coosa.

I saw the gentleman from Wisconsin (Mr. Cooper), with an air determined and resolute, rise and lean forward, eager to hear all that was being said about building a dam across the Coosa River, down in my district. I could see his nostrils distend with indignation and his eyes flash with the fire of

[1] *Congressional Record*, 62nd Cong., 2nd Sess., p. 11589.

[2] *Congressional Record*, 62nd Cong., 2nd Sess., p. 11589.

serious concern as he contemplated the outrage about to be perpetrated upon his people by the building of a dam across the Coosa River, way down in Alabama, in my district. (Laughter) Then I could hear his big heart beating with fury as he expressed in lurid language his opposition to the construction of a dam across the Coosa River (Laughter) and as he took his seat I could hear wailing and gnashing of teeth amongst his constituents in far-away Wisconsin (Laughter and applause). Then I seemed to hear his terror-stricken constituents say 'What will become of us and ours? Who will keep the wolf from the door—who will shelter us in time of storm if they dare to dam the Coosa River?' (Laughter and applause.) Then they lifted up their voices and shouted in unison with the gentleman from Wisconsin, 'You may dam the Ohio and dam the Tombigbee, you may dam the Hudson and dam the Tennessee, and you may dam the Mississippi, but dam the Coosa—not by a dam site.' (Loud laughter and applause).[1]

The amendment of Mr. Humphreys was lost by a vote of 89 to 98 with 12 voting present. The bill finally passed the House.

On August 24, 1912, the bill was returned to the Senate without the President's signature. President Taft vetoed the measure for its lack of provison for charges—a reversal of policy on the part of the President. Part of the veto message ran as follows:

If the Federal Government chose to build this dam itself in aid of navigation, its right to the water power incidentally created would be beyond question. When, instead of building the dam itself, it builds it by an agent, as proposed by this bill, I believe it to be equally clear that the dam and all its incidents, including the water power created, is within the regulative power of the Federal Government in respect to navigation . . . . No provision is made in the bill whereby the Secretary of War may, in granting the permit, exact such compensation as in the

[1] *Congressional Record,* 62nd Cong., 2nd Sess., p. 11590.

course of time may prove to be necessary . . . . I think this is a fatal defect in the bill.[1]

The bill did not pass over the veto.

What was the reason for this veto? It seemed entirely inconsistent with the known attitude of Mr. Taft. To many it was a genuine surprise. Senator Bankhead of Alabama a few years later gave an interesting explanation.[2] Bankhead was a firm supporter of the Coosa bill, and also an opponent of tolls. When he learned that President Taft intended to veto the bill he rushed to the White House to remonstrate with the President. Bankhead reminded the President that the bill contained those principles he favored while Secretary of War. Mr. Taft replied: "That is true; those were my views then, and they are my views now."

Mr. Bankhead asked why he vetoed the bill if he favored its principles to which Mr. Taft replied, "Senator, I have a Bull Moose Secretary of War; he insists upon this veto along the lines of a veto message that I have authorized him to write." Mr. Bankhead's comment was, "That is very strange, Mr. President." At which the President said, "Well, it is. I have not changed my opinions upon the same, but I am too near the end of my administration to have a family row."

All of which proves that a President is not at all times leader and boss in his own official household.

This period[3] saw much activity in the field of public domain legislation. Not that the prevailing Act of 1901 with the amendment of 1911 were fundamentally changed, but a great deal of effort was spent in modifying them or framing legislation that would involve a more comprehensive policy in handling water-power problems on public lands.

[1] *Senate Document 949*, 62nd Cong., 2nd Sess.

[2] *Congressional Record*, 64th Cong., 1st Sess., p. 2580.

[3] 1906-1913.

In 1905 the Forest Service was transferred from the Department of the Interior to the Department of Agriculture. From that time on permits for water-power developments on the public domain were issued by two distinct authorities. Permits for water-power sites and transmission lines on and through the national forests were granted by the Secretary of Agriculture; permits outside the national forests were granted by the Secretary of the Interior.

As early as 1906 controversy began in and out of Congress on the question as to whether there was any right on the part of the Secretaries to make a charge for the privilege they were granting. In 1907 the Attorney General informed the Secretary of Agriculture that under existing law it was quite possible to make a charge to permittees. The Secretary of Agriculture took advantage of the opinion. Permittees in the national forests then came in under the following permit:

UNITED STATES DEPARTMENT OF AGRICULTURE

FOREST SERVICE

.................................., Uses,
(Name of forest.)

.................................., Power,
(Name of applicant.)

.................................., ...
(Use applied for.) (Date of Application.)

POWER AGREEMENT

CLAUSE 1. The .... Company, hereinafter called the permittee, a corporation organized and existing under the laws of the State, or Territory, of ...., and its office and principal place of business at ...., in said State, or Territory, hereby applies for permission to occupy and use certain lands of the United States and rights of way reserved by the United States within the

.... National Forest, by constructing, maintaining, and operating thereon, for the purpose of this clause below set forth, the following works:

(Cancel such of the three following items (a), (b), (c), as may not be applicable.)

(a) .... dam—approximately ...... feet in height, respectively; and .... reservoir—to flood approximately .... acres, whereof approximately .... acres are National Forest land;

(b) .... conduit—approximately .... miles in length, whereof approximately .... miles will lie upon National Forest land or land within National Forests over which a right of way for ditches or canals, constructed by the authority of the United States is reserved by the act of August 30, 1890 (26 Stat., 391).

(c) .... power house—and appurtenant structures to occupy approximately .... acres, whereof approximately .... acres are National Forest land; all approximately as shown on ..... certain tracing, executed by ....
....
....
on ....
19—, respectively, filed in ....
.... on ....
....................., 19—, respectively, and marked by the designation hereto prefixed, which tracing .... hereby made a part of this instrument.

The works for which a permit is hereby applied for are to be constructed, maintained, and operated for the purpose of storing, conducting, and / or using water for the generation of electric energy.

The permittee does hereby, in consideration for the permit hereby applied for, promise and agree for itself and its successors to comply with all regulations and instructions of the Department of Agriculture governing National Forests, and especially with the following conditions:

CLAUSE 2. The permittee shall pay to the .... National Bank of .... (United States depository), or such other Government depository or officer as shall hereafter be duly designated by the United States, to be placed to the credit of the United States, a construction charge of .... dollars ($........), annually in advance from .... until the beginning of the use, for the purpose aforesaid, of the work or works for which permit is hereby applied for, being at the approximate rate of one dollar per acre and five dollars per mile for the land occupied by said works, at which time the permittee shall be entitled to a credit toward the operation charge hereinafter provided for; of part of such annual construction charge, so last paid, proportionate to the remaining part of the year for which such last payment was made; and annually thereafter a net operation charge fixed by the forester and calculated as follows: The gross operation charge for any year shall be calculated by the forester upon the basis of the quantity of electric energy generated in such year at a maximum rate which shall not exceed the following amounts per thousand kilowatt hours (KWH):

	Cents
For the 1st year	2
For the second year	4
For the third year	6
For the fourth year	8
For the fifth year	10
For the sixth to 10th years, inclusive	12½
For the 11th to 15th years, inclusive	15
For the 16th to 20th years, inclusive	17½
For the 21st to 25th years, inclusive	20
For the 26th to 30th years, inclusive	22½
For the 31st to 25th years, inclusive	25
For the 36th to 40th years, inclusive	27½
For the 41st to 45th years, inclusive	30
For the 46th to 50th years, inclusive	32½

CLAUSE 3. From the gross operation charge for any year, calculated as aforesaid, deductions shall be made as follows:

(a) A sum bearing approximately the same ratio to one-half such gross operation charge as the area of unreserved lands and patented lands on the watershed furnishing the water stored, conducted, and / or used in the works for which permit is hereby applied for bears to the total area of the watershed, as of the beginning of each year;

(b) A sum bearing approximately the same ratio to one-half such gross operation charge as the length of the conduit, for which permit is hereby applied for, upon unreserved lands and upon patented lands, over which a right of way for ditches and canals is not reserved by the act of August 30, 1890 (26 Stat., 391), bears to the total length of such conduit, as of the beginning of each year;

(c) A sum bearing approximately the same ratio to the balance remaining after said deductions "a" and "b" as the quantity of electric energy generated from water stored artificially by the permittee, over and above what is generated by the natural flow bears to all electric energy.

The sum remaining after all the aforesaid deductions have been made shall be the net operation charge for such year.

Provided That the term "unreserved lands," as above used in this clause, shall be deemed and taken to mean lands of the United States not reserved as a part of any National Forest, and that this permit shall not affect such lands or restrict in any manner the right and duty of the United States to control the occupancy and use thereof through the department or officer lawfully charged with their custody or control.

Provided further: That the term "patented lands," as above used in this clause shall include all lands to which title has been perfected in persons, corporations, States, and Territories; also all lands outside the United States.

Provided further: That the word "conduit," as used in this and other clauses of this permit, shall include ditches, canals, pipe lines, and all other means for the conveyance of a flow of water.

CLAUSE 4. The decision of the Forester shall be final as to all matters of fact upon which the gross operation charge for any year, the deductions for such year, and the net operation charge for such year depend.

CLAUSE 5. The permittee shall install and maintain in good operating conditon, free of any expense to the United States, accurate meters and other instruments approved by the Forester, adequate for the measurement of the electric energy on which said gross operation charge is to be calculated, and accurate measuring weirs and other devices approved by the Forester, adequate for the determination of the quantity of water used in the generation of electric energy from the natural stream flow and, separately, the quantity of water stored by the permittee so used over and above the natural stream flow; and the permittee shall keep accurate and sufficient records to the satisfaction of the Forester and free of any expense to the United States, showing the quantity of electric energy generated in each year, the quantity of water used in such generation of electric energy from the natural stream flow, and separately, the quantity of water stored by the permittee so used over and above the natural stream flow; and the authorized agents of the Forest Service shall at all times have free access to the aforesaid meters, weirs, instruments, devices, and records of the permittee. In case the permittee fails for any year to so install and maintain such meters, weirs, instruments, and devices and to keep such records, the Forester shall fix by estimate the amount of the gross charge and of the deductions for such year, using such information as he can readily obtain.

CLAUSE 6. If the United States shall hereafter, for permits of this nature in national forests, reduce the general scale of maximum rates below those above provided for in clause 2 hereof, or shall wholly abolish charges for permits of this nature, then and thereupon the charges to be calculated and fixed hereunder, as provided in clause 2 hereof shall be reduced or abolished in like degree.

CLAUSE 7. The permittee shall pay to the United States depository or officer, as above set forth in clause 2 hereof, the full value of all merchantable live or dead timber cut, injured, or destroyed in the construction of the said works, title to which, at the time of such cutting, injury, or destruction, is in the United States, according to the scale, count, or estimate of the forest officer in charge or other duly authorized officer or agent of the United States, such full value of timber cut, injured, or destroyed in the construction of said works shall be deemed and taken to be, and payment therefor shall be made in advance as required by such forest officer or other duly authorized officer or agent of the United States.

CLAUSE 8. The permittee shall dispose of all brush and other refuse resulting from the necessary clearing of or cutting of timber on the lands occupied under the permit hereby applied for as may be required by the forest officer in charge.

CLAUSE 9. The permittee, its employees, contractors, and employees of contractors, shall do all in their power, both independently and upon the request of the forest officers, to prevent and suppress forest fires.

CLAUSE 10. The permittee shall, on demand of the District Forester, or other duly authorized officer or agent of the United States, pay to the United States depository of officer, as above set forth in clause 2 hereof, full value as fixed by such District Forester, or other duly authorized officer, for all damage to the National Forests resulting from the breaking of or the overflowing, leaking, or seepage of water from the works constructed, maintained, and / or operated under the permit hereby applied for, and for all damage to the National Forests caused by the neglect of the permittee, its employees, contractors, or employees of contractors.

CLAUSE 11. The permittee shall build new roads and trails as required by the forest officer, or other duly authorized officer or agent of the United States to replace any roads or trails destroyed by the construction work or flooding under the permit hereby applied for, and to build and maintain suitable crossings as required by the forest officer, or other duly authorized officer or agent of the United States, for all roads and trails which intersect the conduit, if any, constructed, operated, and / or maintained under the permit hereby applied for.

CLAUSE 12. The permittee shall within .... months from the date of approval hereof, begin bona fide construction of the works for which permit is hereby applied for, and shall, within .... years from the date of said approval, complete such construction and begin to operate said works for the purpose of clause 1 hereof set forth, unless the time is extended by written consent of the Forester; it being understood that such consent will usually be given only because of physical obstacles of construction, such as floods or engineering difficulties which could not reasonably have been anticipated.

CLAUSE 13. In constructing any dam or reservoir under the permit hereby applied for the permittee shall follow the usual precautions in the ordinary methods of dam construction. This obligation, however, shall not be construed so as to relieve the permittee from any requirement of State law regarding the construction of dams and storage of water.

CLAUSE 14. The permittee shall sell electric energy to the United States when requested at as low a rate as is given to any other purchaser for a like use at the same time: *Provided,* That the permittee can furnish the same to the United States without diminishing the measured quantity of energy sold before such request to any other consumer by a binding contract of sale: *Provided further,* That nothing in this clause shall be construed to require the permittee to increase its permanent works or to install additional generating machinery.

CLAUSE 15. The permit hereby applied for shall be non-transferable (U. S. Rev. Stats., sec. 3737) and shall be subject to all prior valid claims which are not by law subject thereto.

CLAUSE 16. No Member of or Delegate to Congress shall be admitted to any share or part of this agreement or to any benefit to arise thereupon. (U. S. Rev. Stats., sec. 3739 to 3742, inclusive).

CLAUSE 17. No person undergoing a sentence of imprisonment at hard labor imposed by any court of the several States, Territories, or municipalities having criminal jurisdiction shall be employed in the performance of this contract. (Executive Order, May 18, 1905).

CLAUSE 18. The permittee shall, except when prevented by the act of God or the public enemy or by unavoidable accidents or contingencies, continuously operate for the generation of electric energy the works to be constructed under the permit hereby applied for, in such manner as to generate after such generation begins, not less than the following percentages of the full hydraulic capacity of the said works measured in kilowatt-hours: In the first year, ... per cent; in the second year, ... per cent; in the third year, ... per cent; in the fourth year, ... per cent; in the fifth year, ... per cent; and in every year thereafter, ... per cent.

CLAUSE 19. If any of the works for which permit is hereby applied for shall be owned, leased, trusteed, possessed, or controlled by any device permanently, temporarily, directly, indirectly, tacitly, or in any manner whatsoever so that they form part of, or in any way effect, any combination or are in anywise controlled by any combination, in the form of an unlawful trust, or form the subject of any contract or conspiracy to limit the output of electric energy or in restraint of trade with foreign nations or between two or more States or Territories or within any one State or Territory, in the generation, sale, or distribution of electric energy, the permit hereby applied for shall be forfeited to the United States by proceedings instituted by the Attorney General of the United States in the courts for that purpose.

CLAUSE 20. The permit hereby applied for shall cease and be void upon the expiration of fifty years from the date of approval hereof, but it may then be renewed in the discretion of the duly authorized officer or agent of the United States and upon such conditions as he may in his discretion fix: *Provided*, That such officer or agent in fixing such conditions shall consider the actual value at that time for power and all other purposes of the lands and rights of way within national forests occupied and used under the permit hereby applied for, and the actual value at that time of all improvements lawfully made by the permittee within national forests under the permit hereby applied for, but neither the property of the permittee, if any, outside of national forests nor the permit, franchises, bonds, capital stock, or other securities of the permittee shall be considered in fixing such conditions.

CLAUSE 21. Nothing herein contained shall be construed to prevent the Forest Service from having the same jurisdiction over the lands above specified, including the issuance of further permits, as over other National Forest lands not inconsistent with the occupation and use hereby applied for.

In witness whereof the permittee has executed this application in duplicate at .... on this .... day of ...., 19—.

............................,

(SEAL.) By ....,

Attest: *President.*

..........................,

Secretary.

ACKNOWLEDGMENT

STATE OF ....

County of ....*ss:*

On this .... day of ...., 19—, before me, a notary public in and for said county, duly commissioned and sworn, my commission expiring ...., 19—, personally came ...., to me personally known, who, being by me duly sworn, did depose and say that he resides in ....; that he is the .... of the .... company; that said company is the corporation which is described in and which executed the foregoing instrument; that he knows the seal of said corporation; that the seal affixed to such instrument is such corporate seal; that it was so fixed by order of the board of directors of said corporation, and that he signed his name thereto by like order; and the said .... acknowledged said instrument to be the free act and deed of said corporation.

Witness my hand and official seal the day and year first above written.

(Notarial Seal.) ....,

Notary Public in and for .... *County.*

Approved ...., 19——, and permission granted subject to conditions set forth.

............................,

Forester.[1]

A bitter controversy over water-power legislation for public lands took place in Congress during 1907 and 1908. On March 2, 1909, Secretary of the Interior Garfield, before retiring from office revoked about twenty-five permits in order to bring the permittees under regulations similar to those imposed by the Department of Agriculture. Permits might be taken out under the new regulations, providing for tolls and under a more secure tenure. The Department of the Interior had provided in its regulations that any water-power permit was likely to be defeated by any entry of the land, so that if a homesteader or mineral claimant came along after the permit was granted and put a claim upon the land, upon the patenting of that claim the permit *ipso facto* lapsed. The new permit gave the power patentee a right good against everybody but the United States. The conditions stipulated were not onerous and were not new, but the revocation order was somewhat unexpected. Although no vested rights were injured nor the value of investments appreciably affected, the power interests were able to cry aloud that this showed exactly what might happen by arbitrary administrative decree. The permit was revokable at any time, it was pointed out, and therefore investment was very insecure. From the time of the revocation order there was never a debate of consequence in which the

[1] Senate Committee on Public Lands, *Hearings on H. R. 16673*, 63rd Cong., 3rd Sess., pp. 443-448.

water-power people and their allies did not point to this act and very often with telling effect. This formed one of their chief supports for the contention that permits should be practically permanent.

The veto of the Coosa River bill brings to a close the second period of the fight for water-power legislation. The work of Gifford Pinchot and his allies had brought forth a determined conservation sentiment in government circles. Behind the conservation group stood President Roosevelt with the immense prestige that goes with a forceful executive. Powerful allies in the administration were found in Henry Graves of the Forestry Bureau; Herbert Knox Smith, Commissioner of Corporations; James R. Garfield and Walter L. Fisher, Secretaries of the Interior; Henry L. Stimson, Secretary of War. These stood out boldly for government control of water-power corporations, the right of the Government to recapture water rights on fair terms, and the right of the Government to make such charges for water rights as the particular permits required in the interests of the general welfare.

The water-power companies throughout the country presented a united front throughout this period—standing for the old regime with its lack of charges and lack of control. Their representatives flocked to Washington, were present at all the hearings, were busy from morning to night in using those measures best known to lobbyists to persuade the Congress and the administration to yield. Their friends in Congress were well-known: both the Senate and House were largely theirs. Their supporters were of no particular party, nor were their enemies. Yet it must be said that the Senators and Representatives who fought the fight of the water-power interests most consistently were from the South and the far West. The South had valuable power to develop in its streams, and it wanted that power developed quickly.

The wealthy power interests promised development of the water power, improved navigation, cheap and abundant fertilizer—all without expense to the state or to the Government. Southern representatives could see great towns and cities arise under the magic wand of the power industry. To the Southerners the conservationst was a busybody, a meddlesome crank who, having much money and little to do, would check the progress of a great region for a theory. And dear to the hearts of the Southerner has ever been the rights of the sovereign states. The power interests played up this idea, and the Southern Congressmen used it with no little force in congressional debate. The huge, overpowering federal machine was bearing down to crush all local intiative, all local enterprise, and every vestige of progress in the development of water power.

To the Western Congressmen objection was founded on another source. Large portions of the public domain were in the western states—whole dominions within these states were practically withdrawn from state control. To the Westerner these lands were held out of use because of the doctrines of the growing movement for conservation. Many acres had been withdrawn from entry because of their possible value as water-power sites. The Government was not moving fast enough in the development of the vast power resources of these regions; it was making development impossible by prohibitive restrictions. Whether the development was on the public domain or in the navigable streams, the West wanted it and wanted it at once.

To these groups were added Congressmen from the East and Middle West, friends of the corporations and big business who were anxious for development on easy terms to the power companies because of private investment or because of a conscientious and sincere belief in the current stories of the persecuted power man and the unconstitutionality of government regulation.

Whatever the belief, whether of conservationists, of grabbers, of Southerners, or of Westerners, one fact remained—that development was not progressing as steadily as it might have done under favorable legislation. This does not mean, however, that the extreme pessimisim in certain quarters was justified. Development was not at a standstill, as the representatives of the power companies often proclaimed when complaining of harsh and uncertain governmental regulations. It would seem that much of that kind of talk was mere propaganda in behalf of the adoption of a free and wide-open policy favorable to power developers. On the public lands it was sometimes claimed that there was overdevelopment. In an editorial in the *Sunset Magazine,* a Pacific monthly, for April, 1916, there appeared the following:

Contrary to the claims of the electric interests, the development of the West's water power has not been throttled by the lack of comprehensive, liberal laws regulating the use of falling water on the public domain. In the decade between 1902 and 1912 the thirty-four states east of the Rockies merely doubled the capacity of their water power plants, increased it by 98 per cent.

Exact figures of development on the public lands are lacking, but Mr. O. C. Merrill estimates that under the Act of 1901 with subsequent amendments projects aggregating 800,000 horsepower were authorized.[1]

In the case of navigable streams development was practically at a standstill after the Coosa River veto in 1912. In Appendix IV will be found a list of the special acts appertaining to development on navigable streams from 1884 to 1912. It will be noted that according to this list a bare 200,000 horsepower had been developed. Less accurate

[1] *Report of the Federal Power Commission,* 1921.

statistics place the amount of horsepower developed on navigable streams before 1920 at 400,000 horsepower. Allowing for the fact that the list in the Appendix was made public on March, 1918, and more accurate figures would have been available in 1921, it would seem fair to say that development on navigable streams amounted to 300,000 horsepower.

The publication within this period on March 14, 1912, of a report by Commissioner of Corporations, Herbert Knox Smith, on *Water Power Development in the United States* aroused great interest throughout the country. This report showed that ten groups controlled the larger portion of the water power—potential and developed—in the United States. The movement towards concentration, for good or ill, was rapidly progressing. The necessity for a well-defined government plan which would secure for the whole public its proper share in the natural resource was the burden of Dr. Smith's message. One sentence shows with which group the Commissioner stood:

The public can either develop and operate the site, selling the energy at market rates, or the public may lease the site at a rental fairly representing its natural value.[1]

The comment of certain newspapers on the report demonstrated that interest in the problem was no longer latent.

The Philadelphia *North American:*

A gigantic monopoly is grabbing the water power of the nation . . . . the money trust is behind the grab.

The New York *Journal of Commerce:*

the danger of this extensive kind of control is probably magnified in a mind which has been devoting itself to the study of this one subject for a good while. It (i.e. the mind) admits:

[1] P. 19.

there may be involved here a new trust problem, with which public authority will have to deal . . . the only practical suggestion made at present is that of conserving the water power that remains on the public domain and directing its use in a way to yield a revenue to the Government and prevent monopoly control in private hands.

The Salt Lake *Tribune:*

What control has the Federal Government over the waters of the country, aside from the navigable waters? None whatever. By unanimous precedent and universal consent the control of non-navigable waters is in the states. . . . It is not easy, therefore, to say just what the United States can do as a straight forward water proposition; but in the discussion something may be evolved, and the Commissioner does well to set forth his views as strenuously as possible.

Such was the division throughout the country; such, too, was the division in the Congress.

The first break in the united front of the power interests came with the introduction of the Connecticut River Dam Bill of January, 1913.

In 1824 the Connecticut River Company was granted a charter by the State of Connecticut under the terms of which a dam was erected at the head of Enfield Rapids, sixteen miles above Hartford. Navigation was taken care of by locks and a five-mile canal. Originally, the revenue of the company was derived from boats using this canal. Gradually the company passed from a navigation company to a water-power company. With this transition accomplished, tolls on the canal were abolished and the company depended entirely upon the proceeds from its water power. Subsequently the State of Connecticut amended the company's charter of navigation granting it the right to generate, use, and sell hydroelectric power.

The Connecticut River Company, owned by the Stone and Webster Management Association, proposed to build a dam at Windsor Locks for the purpose of developing electric power and improving navigation for many miles north of Hartford. The Federal Government engineers had reported the improving of navigation in this river as too costly a project for the Government.

The Stone and Webster interests agreed to accept a fifty-year permit with annual charges to be levied by the Secretary of War for the privilege of developing water power. Signs of surrender had come at last. It looked as if the battle of the conservationists was nearing an end.

The bill was reported from the Senate Committee on Commerce, January 20, 1913.[1] A majority and minority report was rendered. Senator Burton of Ohio gave the majority report which favored charges and produced a letter from Secretary of War Stimson approving the principle of tolls. A minority report cited all possible reasons—mostly legal—why a charge should not be included; approving the minority report were Senators Bankhead, Nelson, Stephenson, Simmons, Percy, Fletcher, Martin, Reed (Mo.), and Oliver.

Friends of the water-power groups and champions of the wide-open policy of development realized that the enactment of this measure would create a precedent which would embarrass them in the future. They, therefore, bent every effort to end or amend the bill. Senator Bankhead of Alabama led the opposition to the bill on the following grounds:

1. The Federal Government, having no right to control the use of water power in the Connecticut River, could not legally legislate on the subject of control.

2. A valuable resource of the state would be practically confiscated.

[1] *Senate Report 1131*, 62nd Cong., 3rd Sess.

3. The control, regulation, and disposition of water power in the Connecticut River being questions of state policy, Congress had no right to demand compensation in any form.

4. The Federal Government had no right to withhold a permit for the construction of a dam, because it would not interfere with navigation but would improve it.

5. If the Secretary of War were given authority and discretion to fix the amount of the charge, it would be an attempt to delegate to the head of a department the power to levy and collect taxes, a function which belonged to Congress alone.

The debate was almost wholly on the constitutional right of Congress to provide charges and regulation. It was without question a most enlightening discussion of the legal side of the question although to some it appeared academic and without value. Opposition to the measure, however, was not entirely on constitutional grounds. Senator Cummins of Iowa opposed the bill for not providing enough safeguards for the Government in the recapture clause, and Senator Borah opposed the measure for not being extensive enough.

Senator Bankhead was much perturbed at a statement emanating from the headquarters of the Progressive Party in Washington warning the people to beware of the revival of the Coosa River bill and praising the provisions of the Connecticut River bill. The statement was signed by the Legislative Reference Committee of the Progressive Party composed of William Draper Lewis, Chairman, Gifford Pinchot, Jane Addams, James R. Garfield, Francis J. Heney, Charles E. Merriam, Herbert Knox Smith, Ben B. Lindsey, Walter E. Weyl, and Henry F. Cochems. Mr. Bankhead regarded the statement as rank propaganda. He paid his respects to the authors in the following language:

This legislative committee of the Progressive Party are undertaking to poke their noses into everything; they are undertaking to make false impressions upon everybody, and everybody knows who a portion of that committee is. One of them I have the honor to know personally, and only one. He acquired fame as a member of the kitchen cabinet that is now by-gone. He played tennis in the backyard of the White House, and that is all I know of his doing that could be construed as a public service.[1]

Senator Bankhead struck the bill a mortal blow by offering an amendment to take out the tolls provisions. Despite the efforts of Senators Burton, Root, Brandegee, McLean, Newlands, and others to defeat the amendment it was passed, and with it the bill was put through with many of its sponsors voting against it.[2] After passing the Senate on

[1] *Congressional Record*, 62nd Cong., 3rd Sess., p. 2980.

[2] The vote on Bankhead's amendment was as follows:

Yes

Ashurst	Gangle	Sheppard
Bacon	Gardner	Shively
Bankhead	Gronna	Simmons
Borah	Guggenheim	Smith (Ariz.)
Browne	Johnson (Me.)	Smith (Md.)
Bradley	Johnson (Ala.)	Smith (So. C.)
Brady	Jones	Stephenson
Bryon	Kern	Stone
Catron	Lea	Sutherland
Chamberlain	McCumber	Swanson
Clark (Wyo.)	Martin (Va.)	Thomas
Clarke (Ark.)	Myers	Thornton
Culberson	Nelson	Warren
Cummins	O'Gorman	Webb
Curtis	Oliver	Wetmore
Fall	Overman	Williams
Fletcher	Panter	Works
Foster	Percy	

February 17, 1913, the bill went to the House where it was sent to the Committee on Interstate and Foreign Commerce. Although two more weeks remained of the session, the bill expired in committee.

The next great battle took place in Washington outside of the congressional halls. The National Conservation Congress was called to meet in November, 1913. The first meeting of this Congress took place in Seattle in 1909; after that, annual meetings were held to discuss various phases of conservation. The call for the meeting read in part:

This year's congress affords an opportunity for service not enjoyed since the historic conference of Governors at the White House. At that conference the conservation sentiment was crystalized into a movement. At this year's congress it is expected that the conservation movement will be shaped into definite recommendations for legislation by both states and Federal authorities.[1]

Interested organizations in every state sent delegates to the number of 722. Before the assembling of the delegates there was much talk of a bitter fight to be staged. The congress promised to be a huge success.

No

Brandegee	Gallinger	Owen
Bristow	Gore	Page
Brown	Jackson	Penrose
Burnham	Kenyon	Perkins
Burton	LaFollette	Poindexter
Clapp	Lippitt	Pomerene
Crane	Lodge	Richardson
Crawford	McLean	Root
Dixon	Martine (N. J.)	Townsend
duPont	Newlands	

[1] The following account of the Conservation Congress is taken from the *Proceedings*, National Conservation Congress, 1913.

A committee on resolutions composed of one delegate from each state with Captain J. B. White as chairman was appointed at the opening of the convention. Each state appointed its representative on the resolutions committee, and, the President of the congress, Charles J. Pack, appointed the chairman. At the second session there came three reports from the special committee on water power: a majority report signed by George F. Swain, the chairman, Lewis B. Stillwell, M. O. Leighton, Edwin S. Webster, B. M. Hall; a minority report signed by Henry L. Stimson, Joseph N. Teal, Gifford Pinchot; and a unanimous report. The majority report recognized the dangers from unregulated control of water powers by the great monopolies, favored state control, recommended the indeterminate permit system, and on charges advised:

> The preservation of the government rights, whatever they may prove to be, being recognized by the principles that the Government must give a permit and fix its terms, we believe that in many cases the real interests of conservation will be best served by making no government charge, the improvement of navigation brought about by the construction of the dam and locks being accepted in lieu of charge. In other cases, some charge may be desirable.

The report was not specific on the great tolls issue. To the conservationists the vital issue had been evaded in this report.—Hence the minority report which insisted on the following points:

1. A thirty-year permit for the permittee.
2. Power to revoke after that time by the proper administrative official upon one year's notice.
3. At least every ten years after the expiration of the thirty-year grant amount of compensation to be paid the Government and other conditions to be reviewed and revised.

4. Government to have power to take over the plant at any time after the expiration of the thirty-year grant upon a year's notice and upon payment of a reasonable sum for appraised physical value at the time not including consequential damages or the value of the franchise.

5. To prevent monopoly, franchises to be non-assignable and non-transferable.

6. A reasonable annual charge based on the value of the site for power development and adjustable at intervals.

7. Direct Government participation in the profits over and above a percentage to be determined in the franchise.

8. The public to have the right to approve or disapprove issues of capital stock in order to prevent over-capitalization and to have the right to prescribe uniform accounting methods.

9. The right reserved to the Government to regulate rates and service to the consumer should the business be or become interstate or should the state or local authority fail to do so.

10. The franchise to be terminated if at any time the works constructed under it are owned, controlled, or operated by an unlawful trust, or in restraint of trade.

The unanimous report resembled far more the minority report than it did the majority report. It signified a victory for the conservationist members. Differences between the minority and the unanimous report were:

1. The term of the franchise was not in the unanimous report. A franchise for a definite period " sufficient to be financially attractive to investors " was requested.
2. The unanimous report recognized the right of compensation for the privilege of developing the power but to be paid to the Government " State or Federal from whom the privilege comes."

3. The unanimous report further recognized that tne method of exacting compensation should be carefully safeguarded so that in case full compensation by rate regultaion were exacted by local authorities, an additional burden would not be imposed.

Beyond these points all the committeemen recognized the necessity for prompt development, prevention of unregulated monopoly, and good service with fair charges to the consumer.

The first conflict in the convention was on the adoption of the unanimous report. Mr. Pinchot led the fight for its adoption. The friends of the water-power companies and the anti-Pinchot group demanded that the report be sent to the committee on resolutions to be accepted, rejected, or modified by them. In that committee the power people had control, and were prepared to smother all Pinchot propositions. As evidence of the control of the resolutions committee by the power groups we have the undisputed testimony of Mr. C. L. Watts, a militant member of the Alabama delegation, when defying the delegates from his own state he said:

This is the first time I have enjoyed the distinction of sitting as a delegate in this great Congress but I have always regarded it as a congress that was intended to reflect the enlightened public sentiment of this country. I regret to say that that is not the case with respect to the Alabama delegation here, of which I am a member. We have sitting here as delegates the vice-president of the Alabama Power Company, his private secretary, and the counsel for that company, a subsidiary of the Alabama Light and Traction Power Company, a foreign corporation, a Canadian corporation, that owns and has a monopoly of 1,057,000 horsepower in my native state of Alabama.

When I came here yesterday morning with my credentials as

a delegate to this convention—and, by the way, I was appointed at the instance of the vice president of the Alabama Power Company, who did not know how I was going to vote—I found in less than five minutes that the water-power interests of the State of Alabama predominated in and dominated over that delegation. Before he knew how I was going to vote—and I am violating no confidence when I tell you this—he told me what the program was—and, again by the way, he is a member of this remarkable committee on resolutions! He told me that the plan was a dark laid scheme, if you please, to defeat the will of this great Congress; that the proposition was to refer all reports from committees and all resolutions to this remarkable committee on resolutions, and he said, 'When we get it there we will fix it.' They have put a unit rule on us. Of course, I am going to have the delegation polled . . . . When the voting comes to pass, I think it is my duty under all circumstances and facts surrounding the situation, to let you know.

The Chairman, Walter L. Fisher, kept the unanimous report before the congress. In the meantime the convention settled down reluctantly to listen to speeches by Senators Shafroth and Thomas of Colorado, Senator Newlands of Nevada, Senator Bankhead of Alabama, Ex-Secretary of the Interior James R. Garfield, and Representative Keating of Colorado. The restlessness of the delegates became more evident as these talks continued until at the close of Mr. Keating's remarks the proceedings ran as follows:

Mr. Keating: When we appeal to the Constitution and the law, are the officers of this Government to turn on the farmers of my district and call them Shylocks demanding their pound of flesh?
(Cries of 'Question! Vote! Question! Vote!')

Mr. Keating: I want to make that point perfectly clear.
(Continued cries of 'Vote! Vote! Vote!')

Mr. Keating: I have attended so many Democratic conventions that this sort of thing does not frighten me.
(Continued cries of 'Vote! Vote! Vote!')

Chairman Fisher: Gentlemen, we must have order. We are going to hear everybody entitled to speak here if we have to stay all night.

Mr. Keating: I appreciate that perhaps I am trespassing upon your time.

(Cries of 'You are! You are!')

Mr. Keating: Will the one hundred and fifty-nine delegates from the District of Columbia kindly permit me to conclude my remarks?

In this last remark Mr. Keating underestimated the District of Columbia representation which numbered 169.[1] Mr. Pinchot brought into the convention as many employees of the Forestry Bureau as he could gather. Although in voting strength they counted only 20, in noise they dominated the congress. The conservationists had an excellent cheering section. A western delegate remarked that every time a vote was taken the reply of the East was as the roar of Niagara.

Mr. M. T. Bryan of Tennessee moved that the unanimous report be referred to the committee on resolutions. This was voted down by 154 to 434. The question of accepting the unanimous report was then put to a *viva voce* vote and (with the District of Columbia delegates voting) was declared adopted 'overwhelmingly.'

At the eighth session (November 20, 1913) the resolutions committee presented its recommendations containing no reference to the great water-power question, it being contended that the adoption of the unanimous report of the water-power committee took the question from their hands. Mr. Pinchot came forward with the following amendment:

Whereas, Concentrated monopolistic control of water power in private hands is swiftly increasing in the United States, and far more rapidly than public control thereof; and

[1] The largest state delegation was that of New York which numbered 66.

Whereas, This concentration, if it is fostered, as in the past, by outright grants of public powers in perpetuity, will inevitably result in a highly monopolistic control of mechanical power, one of the bases of modern civilization, and a prime factor in the cost of living; therefore,
Be it resolved that we recognize the firm and effective public control of water-power corporations as a pressing and immediate necessity urgently required in the public interest;
That we recognize that there is no restraint so complete, effective, and permanent as that which comes from firmly retained public ownership of the power site;
That it is, therefore, the solemn judgment of the Fifth National Conservation Congress that hereafter no water power now owned or controlled by the public should be sold, granted, or given away in perpetuity, or in any manner removed from the public ownership, which alone can give sound basis of assured and permanent control in the interest of the people.

The congress was thrown into an uproar by the introduction of this resolution. Many delegates had gone home believing that no more of importance was to be done. The water-power interests had lost out by the adoption of the unanimous report; now came this resolution adding insult to their already greatly injured feelings. Would this Pinchot ever be content?

There came at this moment to the defense of the water-power groups Marshall O. Leighton, former chief hydrographer of the United States Geological Survey. Mr. Leighton, an able engineer, had formerly been in the Pinchot camp. Since he had gone into private business as a consulting engineer he had changed his views.

It is my official duty [he told the congress] to meet a great many power men, and since I have left the service and hung out my shingle and tried to do a little business, in the ordinary way, I have met more power men on an honorable business basis. I believe, and my colleagues in committee believed that there is no body of men in the United States who have done more effective work in the bringing about of public utilities regulation within the states than these same predatory water-power interests. . . . I do not mind requiring that the public water powers shall be properly regulated, but why rub it in? It is an accomplished fact I tell you, and what does it do? The water-power industry to-day, as I assure you, is in a state of stagnation.

The "conversion" of Mr. Leighton meant much to the water-power companies. The latter had entered the government service and had taken therefrom one of the most able defenders of the government's and the people's rights. Since that time Mr. Leighton had "met more power men on an honorable business basis." There can be no question of the basis being honorable; it was simply a case of the economic determinism of allegiance.

The fight over Mr. Pinchot's amendment waxed furious. This peaceful, or supposedly peaceful, convention which, according to all accepted traditions of such meetings, should have passed a few pious resolutions, elected officers, determined upon some time in advance, sat down to a happy feast, and left for home with thoughts of the unusual social success the whole affair had been,—this convention had seen nothing but fight and heard nothing but bitter controversy.

Representative Burnett of Alabama gave his idea of the gathering from the point of view of the anti-Pinchot group:

This wonderful stage here is a setting of 'Ex-es;'—Ex-Secretary of War,[1] Ex-Secretary of the Interior,[2] and another Ex-Secretary of the Interior,[3] and an ex-Forester.[4] Why? Be-

[1] Henry L. Stimson.

[2] James Garfield.

[3] Walter L. Fisher.

[4] Gifford Pinchot.

cause the people would have arisen in their might and have scorned the meeting we had yesterday of the 'Ex-es' that so adorned this rostrum. It may be possible, my friends, that the Pie brigade[2] is here in such numbers as to vote down what is right, but, gentlemen, from that body we expect to appeal to the people of the country.

Then followed confusion and bedlam. Cries of "Order, Order," "Mr. President, Mr. President," "The gentleman is not in order," "What business have you here?" "I second the motion," and so forth kept the assemblage in an uproar. At one point Charles L. Pack, President of the congress, exclaimed to Pinchot:

Oh, Gifford, Gifford! We have been friends for years. For ten years I have stood by you in everything that you have urged. But we have reached the parting of the ways. I can not follow you in a course that seems to me destined to disrupt and nullify every bit of good that the Conservation Association has done. I am through.[1]

Nevertheless the Pinchot resolution was passed by a vote 317 to 96. And the convention adjourned *sine die*.

This convention is important in that it received newspaper publicity all over the land informing the people of the issues involved and the leaders in the fight. The water-power interests and the anti-Pinchot groups met with bitter defeat despite the fact that the best the corporations could bring together fought by persuasion and threat to accomplish a victory in the congress. Albert F. Baldwin, writing in the Outlook on the convention, said:

The interests which have been fighting for states' rights were, by the complaisance of Governors or other authorities, able to

[1] New York *Times*, Sunday, November 30, 1913.

[2] Gifford Pinchot's fighting battalion of Government employees.

send a good many delegates to the Congress. Those who had observed the water-power lobbies which had tried to influence legislation before the Federal Congress recognized certain familiar faces among the delegates.[1]

The fight was by no means over. Congress was still hopelessly deadlocked on effective water-power legislation. Once again, therefore, the monopolists turned to the Federal Legislature.

[1] "The Fight for the Nation," *Outlook*, November 29, 1913.

CHAPTER IV

Congress Battles On

1913-1917

At the outset no one was exactly certain where the new Wilson administration stood on the water-power question. It was pledged to a sane conservation policy and the development of natural resources; but it was a Democratic administration and, therefore, pledged to respect the rights of the states. It will be remembered that southern statesmen had attacked the Pinchot conservation policy as a grave interference with the reserved rights of the 'sovereign' states.

Numerous bills, both of a special and of a general nature, were before Congress when the Wilson administration started on its career. Never before were the various groups interested in the water-power problem more active. Water-power development was now a matter of great concern to the whole country; it was before the public as it never had been. It is true that the public at large understood but vaguely the legal technicalities involved, but the public did know of trusts, monopolists, grabbers, conservationists, and theorists as applied to the water-power problem. The papers and magazines were now discussing frequently, even if inadequately, the question of water-power development and effective legislation, Conservationists and water-power lobbyists were making almost daily appeals to the country. The numerous bills in Congress simply reflected the interest of the country at large.

The conservationists could now boast of a House of Representatives friendly to charges and extensive Federal regulation. The Senate remained Bourbon almost to the last. The new Secretary of the Interior, Franklin K. Lane, proved to be a steadfast friend of the conservation group, and his ideas as set forth in the Ferris bill—to be discussed later—were highly satisfactory to Pinchot and his followers. The new Secretary of War, Lindley M. Garrison, under whose jurisdiction fell the navigable streams, believed in the constitutionality of tolls, but doubted the wisdom of a tolls policy.[1]

The first important piece of legislation on water-power development to come to light at this time was the Adamson Bill dealing with water powers on navigable streams. Rumors had been going about in Congressional circles since the early part of February, 1914, that an inspired administration bill was to be introduced. Everyone awaited anxiously to see what the Wilson policy would be in regard to navigable stream legislation. Representative Adamson of Georgia, chairman of the House Committee on Interstate and Foreign Commerce, had been in touch with the White House and with the War Department. There seems to have been much uncertainty in the administration as to the proper course to take. A clash between two members of the Cabinet, Garrison and Lane, over the provisions of the bill as it might or might not have touched the Department of one or the other formed a rather diverting prelude. When the bill made its first appearance in the House a conflict arose between the two important committees on Interstate Commerce and on Public Lands—both of which had jurisdiction of different phases of water-power administration. Suddenly, all operations ceased and the bill was withdrawn from

[1] *Congressional Record,* 63rd Cong., 2nd Sess., p. 12893. See Appendix VIII.

consideration. The matter of committee jurisdiction was beginning to assume the proportions of a tremendous obstacle to progress.[1]

The committee situation was somewhat as follows: The Committee on Public Lands had control of legislation which would effect between 42,000,000 and 44,000,000 potential horsepower on the public domain. A bill from that committee, therefore, would have far greater consequences for good or evil than a bill from any other committee, since the estimated potential horsepower in the country is certainly no more than 61,000,000 horsepower. Yet some of this public domain power was to be found on Indian lands, and under the rules of the House the Committee on Indian Affairs had some jurisdiction; a great deal more of it was to be found on forest reserves which came under the jurisdiction of the Committee on Agriculture, while the Committee on Military Affairs vigorously asserted control over legislation affecting water power on military reservations. This the Public Lands Committee was loath to grant. The Committee on Interstate and Foreign Commerce could not assert unquestioned authority over water-power legislation affecting navigable streams, because the Committee on Foreign Affairs had a deep interest in all matters connected with boundary streams, especially Niagara; while the Committee on Rivers and Harbors had control of legislation relative to dams built in navigable streams by the Government to improve navigation. A better illustration of overlapping jurisdiction and committee conflict could hardly be imagined. The solution was not found until four years later; it was then found with the aid of Presidential dictation.

After the Adamson Bill was withdrawn from the House,

[1] *Congressional Record*, 63rd Cong., 2nd Sess., p. 12329; and also the speech by Representative Murdock of Kansas, same Congress, same Session, p. 12900.

two or three conferences were held with President Wilson which were attended by certain members of both the Public Lands and the Interstate and Foreign Commerce Committees together with the Secretaries of War and the Interior. The President had evidently brought about an agreement, and on June 30, 1914, the Adamson Bill set sail on a stormy voyage through the House.

The hearings on the bill before its introduction into the House were indeed perfunctory. Two witnesses appeared. One was J. W. Worthington of Sheffield, Alabama, interested in the Alabama Power Company. The other was H. L. Cooper, a water-power magnate, who was instrumental in putting through the Keokuk Dam on the Mississippi, a project which promised many blessings for the people in Iowa, Illinois and other States; the power was developed but cheap rates were never realized.[1] One interesting bit of testimony offered by Mr. Cooper was that the Stone and Webster interests were his competitors. In the House Hearings[2] on the Adamson Bill (H. R. 16053) Mr. Cooper said: "I know the Stone and Webster people very well. I would like to say that they are very strong competitors of mine, and they come nearer being idealists in selling things cheaper to the public than they get anywhere else, than anybody I have ever heard of anywhere. They are strong competitors of mine, and I have lost a lot of money and a lot of sleep over the fact that I can not get business that they get away from me."

Moody's Manual for 1913 showed that the Mississippi River Power Company which owned the Keokuk Dam had for its President, Edwin S. Webster and for its Vice President, Hugh L. Cooper. The directorship included E. S.

[1] *Congressional Record*, 63rd Cong., 2nd Sess., p. 12329.

[2] Hearings before House Committee on Interstate and Foreign Commerce on *H. R. 16053*, 63rd Cong., 2nd Sess.

Webster and C. A. Stone. The managing agents were Stone and Webster.

The Adamson Bill may be summarized as follows:

1. Construction of locks to be required to protect navigation.

2. Water resources to be utilized to the best advantage.

3. The Federal Government to charge the grantee for the benefit derived from reservoirs and other headwater improvements to the maximum annual amount of five per cent of total Government investments. (No charge to be made for use of water).

4. The Government to charge five per cent per year for use by the grantee of public lands.

5. Navigation to be the paramount consideration.

6. Limit of $1,000 to be placed for each offense for the violation of requirements.

7. Assignment or transfer of franchises without the approval of the proper government authority to be prohibited to prevent speculation in franchises.

8. The franchise to be for a term of 50 years, or until compensation would be made if the Government decided to take over plant. After that term the Government to be empowered to terminate the franchise on one year's notice, *paying the fair value for the property,* not including good will or value of the franchise.

9. Pending contracts to be assumed if the plant were taken over by the Government or another.

10. Reasonable rates and service without discrimination to be provided.

11. The Government through the Secretary of War to regulate rates and service on interstate business if the state neglected to do so adequately in the opinion of the Secretary of War.

12. Provision for prompt construction—commencement

within one year and completion within three years to meet the community's demands, unless the time were extended by the Secretary of War.

13. The surplus power developed by government plants to be leased.

14. A prohibition against ownership by trusts in restraint of trade, but recognition of natural monopoly and permission for interchange of power with other companies.

The views of Secretary of War Garrison presented to the Committee in a bill of his own should be compared with the above bill. The Garrison Bill made the following provisions:

1. Congress to grant authority to construct dams; permits to be issued by the Secretary of War and the Chief of Engineers.

2. No permit to be granted until the state in which the power plant was to be located had authorized the grantee to become a public utility and had provided adequate laws and instrumentalities for proper regulation.

3. The state to tax the power company.

4. The Secretary of War to regulate interstate business.

5. Government to be empowered to require the grantee to construct navigation locks and to operate them without cost to the Government.

6. The project to provide for the largest use of the water resources.

7. The Government to be empowered to charge grantee a reasonable amount annually for the benefits derived from storage reservoirs, watersheds, and other headwater improvements.

8. The United States to be reimbursed for any expense incurred in supervising the project.

9. The grantee to pay for restoring impaired navigation.

10. Navigation to be given paramount consideration.

11. Five thousand dollars fine for violation of the terms of the grant.

12. Term of franchise to be 50 years; renewals, five years.

13. The United States to take over the plant at the end of the term by *paying the fair value,* not including good will or franchise value, and by assuming good faith contracts.

14. Assignment or transfer of franchises without approval of the Government to be forbidden.

15. Ownership by trust in restraint of trade, and unreasonable rates to be prohibited.

16. The United States to lease power at government plants.[1]

At this time the Pinchot group was consistently advocating strict federal regulation, charges, and reasonable means of recapture of the plant by the Government. A conservation bill would have provided:

1. A 50-year franchise, revocable only for good cause before the expiration of the term; revocable thereafter upon one year's notice and payment of appraised value of material property and improvements; renewal terms, 10 years; franchise to terminate automatically in 50 years, but renewable on new terms to be prescribed by the Government.

2. Franchise to be non-assignable, except with government approval, to prevent speculation in franchises.

3. *An annual charge for the use of the water* and any government land used, and, in addition, participation by the Government in any profits realized above a certain per cent; the proceeds to be devoted to navigation improvement.

4. Development of the project to capacity as required by granting officers to supply the needs of consumers.

5. Public regulation of capitalization.

6. Government regulation of interstate business and of intrastate business if the state failed to regulate satisfactorily.

[1] *H. R. 16053,* 63rd Cong., 2d Sess.

7. Ownership by trust in restraint of trade to be penalized by forfeiture of the franchise.

It will be seen that the Adamson and Garrison Bills were practically at one on the subject of a charge for the water-power privilege, although it was omitted in these bills for different reasons. The committee reporting the Adamson Bill said on this point:

We have not provided for any specific tax upon the business of the enterprise. If the Federal Government should conclude that it is necessary to take away from the states the matter of water power as an object of taxation, we consider that a proper and safe way to do that is for the Ways and Means Committee to report a bill for levying a uniform excise tax upon all water-power, or hydroelectric, or upon water-power sites developed or undeveloped.[1]

This is something which the conservationists would never agree to, for sites varied in value. A site at Niagara could in no way be compared to a site on a small navigable stream with meager flow. To tax the two sites uniformly would not be charging according to benefit received. Proximity to a ready market, size of plant, benefit to navigation, efficiency of service were all matters which the conservationists would take into consideration in levying a charge.

Secretary of War Garrison expressed his viewpoint as follows:

Legally speaking, I do not think there can be any dispute that with respect to the question of power (to make charges) the position of the Federal Government is paramount. Nothing can be done without its consent, and only that can be done to which it consents. The interests to be considered I view as follows: First, there are the communities which will benefit by utilization of the water power. Next is the immediate sovereign

[1] *House Report 592*, 63rd Cong., 2nd Sess.

over them which would direct this matter and have power with respect thereto, were it not for the paramount power above alluded to, which resides in the Federal Government. Finally, there is the Federal Government with absolute power, by reason of its ability to prevent the doing of anything without its consent. I conceive the equitable sphere of the Government to be to see to it that this great public utility shall be availed of in a way that will benefit the greatest number possible under the most favorable terms possible, and to recognize the justice—not as a matter of law—of the state entity receiving a revenue from the operation of this public utility within its confines and regulating it for the benefit of its people.[1]

This represents the idea of the states'-rights Democrat,—a point of view which was quite likely akin to President Wilson's when the latter first tackled the power problem.

The argument of the conservationists ran as follows:

The values made available by water-power franchises should pay a yearly and unfailing compensation in return. The public makes the grant and there should be no uncertainty as to the participation of the public in the profits which arise from the grant. The public can not get its full share of the advantage of power development except by a government charge, collected, so to speak, at the water wheel. It is not sufficient to trust that the public will always receive its proper share by means of regulation of rates alone. Local authorities may neglect or may be unable, under conflict of jurisdiction or for other reasons, to exact in the public's interest the full value of the public's right. The value of a water power may in the course of time increase far beyond the power of local regulation adequately to distribute its benefits. We believe in normal cases the best method is for the Government to share increasingly in the net profits of the enterprise, provided those profits exceed a reasonable per-

[1] Letter taken from the *Christian Science Monitor* (Boston), Wednesday, May 6, 1914. The article from which the letter is taken is an excellent contemporary survey of the water-power issue in Congress.

centage, the right of the Government otherwise to be exercised merely by the imposition of a small annual fee or its equivalent.[1]

The Adamson Bill, when reported, was given a privileged status on motion of the majority leader, Mr. Underwood. It was made the continuing order of business, that is, it might be brought up for consideration at any time when the House was not occupied in consideration of appropriation bills, except on Calendar Wednesdays, District of Columbia Mondays, or pension Fridays. From references made in the debates we may gather that a goodly number of the representatives of the water-power companies occupied seats in the House gallery to watch proceedings in the early days of the bill's progress. There was no doubt of their pleasure with the bill, and of the confidence they felt in the support of such prominent leaders as Representatives Adamson of Georgia, Stevens of Minnesota, and Underwood of Alabama.

For six weeks during the summer, debate dragged on with both sides at times becoming irritable and unreasoning. At one point Representative Adamson broke into a heated discussion with:

I deprecate the exhibition of feeling and indulgence in violent language during the discussion of this bill. . . . No man believes any member of Congress here desires to loot the public nor permit any graft nor hurt the general Government nor rob the people. So far as I am concerned I have had a clean bill of health from all, even the most violent of those who have criticized the bill. I will take the liberty . . . to extend that acquittal to the entire membership. Such language may be indulged with impunity by outsiders who have nothing to lose but everything to gain, and who enjoy access to the sensational papers, but it is improper and unmerited here.[2]

[1] *Ibid.*

[2] *Congressional Record*, 63rd Cong., 2nd Sess., p. 12892.

Mr. Adamson's reference to "sensational newspapers" was meant for the most part for Hearst publications which were stirring up much sentiment against the "water-power trust," "the grabbers," and others.

The crucial point in the House consideration of the bill was reached on July 28, 1914. Mr. Sherley of Kentucky had introduced an amendment which read as follows:

The Secretary of War may provide as a condition of such approval for the payments to the United States of reasonable annual charges for the benefits that accrue to the grantee by the authority given under this act, and at the end of twenty years, and every ten years thereafter, the Secretary of War may re-adjust the annual charges as may then be just and reasonable.[1]

The amendment was vigorously defended by Representatives Kent of California, Stevens of New Hampshire, Murdock of Kansas, Ferris of Oklahoma, and Bryan of Washington. During the discussion a message from Gifford Pinchot as President of the National Conservation Association was read giving the view of that group on the Adamson Bill. Mr. Pinchot characterized the bill as "a direct rebuff to the many patriotic men and women who for the last decade have fought the water-power grabbers." Both important and significant in this message are Pinchot's views on the administration policy:

Every friend of conservation will receive with keen disappointment the recent announcements from the White House that the administration indorses the Adamson dam bill. . . . This is an unfortunate and needless surrender to the power interests on the threshold of victory for the people. . . . In a statement of June 1, I called attention to the fact that the Adamson bill was much more favorable to the water-power interests than to the public interest. It was precisely the kind of bill the power people

[1] *Congressional Record,* 63rd Cong., 2nd Sess., p. 12759.

wanted. . . . Its most important provisions are in conflict with the present dam act and the policies now in force in the Departments of Agriculture and of the Interior. The recent amendments to the bill, approved at the White House conferences, unbelievable as it may seem, fail to bring the bill into line with these policies. The bill as it stands is a thoroughly bad bill. . . . The Adamson bill in its present form is full of jokers, and is lacking in important safeguards to protect the public interest.[1]

The Sherley amendment was adopted by a vote of 143 to 45. The conservationists had won. Amendments affecting the recapture clause and other sections were adopted. By the time the bill came to a final vote, it had become a conservation measure and had become entirely unacceptable to the power people. Several attempts were made to recommit the bill but to no avail; it was adopted by a vote of 191 to 47. Some of the aggressive leaders of the anti-conservationists voted for the bill, for it was known that the Senate would never accept the amended measure. The Senate had its own ideas as we shall see in a study of the Shields Bill.

Turning to the question of the development of power on public lands we find a more determined attitude exhibited on the part of the administration to protect every public interest. Secretary Lane had laid down the following principles early in his administration:

1. The greater the development of power by a company, the lower the charge per horse power would be which the Government would make.—This was intended to assure the full use of the stream.

2. The lower the rate the company charged to the consumer the lower would the government charge be.

3. There would be no charge whatever for a period of

[1] *Congressional Record*, 63rd Cong., 2nd Sess., p. 12901.

five or ten years during which the power company would be finding a market.

4. That the states' jurisdiction over intrastate rates and service would be accepted; but over interstate rates and services the Federal Government would have jurisdiction.

5. There would be absolute prohibition of combination and monopoly. There would be a revocation of the permit if it were established that any unlawful combination existed.[1]

Embodying the Lane ideas, the Ferris Bill was introduced in the House of Representatives.[2] Extensive hearings had been held during which the best talent of the power companies pleaded against the bill.[3] The Ferris Bill passed the House and went to the Senate where more hearings were held. A study of the hearings before the Public Lands Committee of the Senate on the Ferris Bill is enlightening as showing the type of pressure brought upon Congress and the kind of men who formed the famous water-power lobby.[4] Taking the names of those who came to represent the power groups, we find the following:

John A. Britton, Vice President and General Manager of the Pacific Gas and Electric Company of California.

W. A. Brackinridge, Vice President of the Southern California Edison Company.

Clarence M. Clark, of E. W. Clark and Company of Philadelphia, a banking firm engaged in the financing of public utilities.

[1] Honoré Willsie, "Mr. Lane and the Public Domain," *Harper's Weekly,* August 30, 1913, pp. 6-8.

[2] May 19, 1914, see *House Report 842,* 63rd Cong., 3rd Sess.

[3] Hearings before the House Committee on Public Lands on *H. R. 14893,* 63rd Cong., 2nd Sess. These hearings contain a wealth of material on the water-power problem.

[4] Hearings before the Senate Committee on Public Lands on *H. R. 16673,* 63rd Cong., 3rd Sess.

H. L. Cooper, a consulting engineer of New York City, engaged in the building of water-power works.

G. M. Dahl, Vice President of the Electric Bond and Share Company of New York City which engages in the financing of electric light and power companies. This company is closely allied with the General Electric Company.

John H. Finney of Washington, D.C., a director of the American Institute of Engineers, a member of its public policy committee, and manager of the Washington office of the Aluminum Company of America operating at Niagara Falls.

Dennis T. Flynn, banker, of Oklahoma City, Oklahoma. An ex-member of the House of Representatives of the United States.

Franklin T. Griffith of Portland, Oregon, President of the Portland Railway, Light, and Power Company.

C. B. Hemingway of Kentucky representing no one in particular but expressing sympathy for the stand taken by the power companies. When asked what interest he represented he replied: " I do not appear on behalf of any special interest. My concern is the general good." [1]

Samuel Herrick, attorney at law of Washington, D. C., who expressed himself in favor of the principles acceptable to the power companies.

Francis T. Homer, a member of the banking firm of Bertron Griscom and Company of 40 Wall Street, New York City.

Sidney Z. Mitchell, President of the Electric Bond and Share Company of New York City.

Henry J. Pierce of Seattle, Washington, President of the Washington Irrigation and Development Company, a corporation organized under the laws of the State of Washington which was interested in the development of power in the Priest Rapids of the Columbia River.

[1] *Ibid.*, p. 763.

W. V. N. Powelson, a consulting engineer of New York City. In reply to the question of what interests he represented he said: "I am here because of a desire to promote the public welfare. I am not here as the representative of any power company, nor do I represent anybody but myself."[1]

John D. Ryan, President of the Montana Power Company.

Frank H. Short, attorney of Fresno, California, appearing for the San Joaquin Light and Power Corporation. "I have represented the interests of companies that have desired to develop the hydroelectric and water resources on the public lands for about ten years," he replied to the question on representation.[2]

George A. Snow, of Salt Lake City, Utah. As to his connections, he said: "My own business is that of taking something here and there and by putting them together produce something that will be useful to mankind. That is in effect what those are doing who undertake the development of hydroelectric projects. . . . I object to this bill (Ferris Bill) in pretty much its entirety."[3]

S. M. Stockslager of Washington, D.C., a former commissioner of the General Land Office now representing the Northern California Power Company.

George C. Ward, Vice President of the Pacific Light and Power Corporation, Los Angeles, California.

The general tenor of their arguments is summed up in the following testimony.

The companies with which I am identified have built four of these projects, and I feel, and I believe that the people of my state feel, that all of these projects have been fairly conducted, and nothing appears to have developed to call for regulatory

[1] *Ibid.*, p. 267.

[2] *Ibid.*, p. 471.

[3] *Ibid.*, pp. 536-537.

measures either by the State or Government. On general principles I consider it a mistake to discourage individual initiative and business enterprises by unwarranted interference. It will be practically impossible to secure the investment of large sums of money in such enterprises as these unless they can be given encouragement and elasticity with as much freedom as possible from complications, and complications usually follow an attempt to regulate a large and important industry at long range, and particularly is this likely to prove true where that regulatory power is vested in the general Government, which by the very nature of things moves slowly.[1]

Most of this argument is as old as industrial history, but it never ceases to have a terrifying effect. When this argument, however, is supported by long accounts of engineering details, by complex financial statistics, by thrilling stories of failures, hopes, and successes in an industry, a certain feeling of admiration is stirred up for this individualistic endeavor. Surrounded with much excess verbiage the plea is likely to assume an unwarranted complexity. Senator Norris alone seemed to have overcome a tendency towards an inferiority complex and to have made a deep study of the problem at hand which made his questions penetrating and enlightening.

The Government's side of the question—which happened in this case to be that of the conservationists—was presented by:

Edward C. Finney, an assistant attorney in the Interior Department; O. C. Merrill, chief engineer of the Forest Service; George Otis Smith, director of the United States Geological Survey. Upon these men the committee depended for impartial information.

The conservation group was represented by Walter L. Fisher, Ex-Secretary of the Interior; Gifford Pinchot; and

[1] *Ibid.*, p. 537.

Philip P. Wells, formerly an administrative officer in the Forest Service and in the Interior Department. These men, with nothing to gain personally for their fight, stood out for effective government regulation and against the arrayed talent of the water-power industry. Just as the names of the water-power lobbyists appear again and again at congressional hearings, so the names of the conservation lobby are found in every public document connected with the water-power struggle. Verily, the praises of many public benefactors remain unsung.

Other representatives at these hearings who put forth views which coincided with those of the power companies were: Governor Elias M. Ammons of Colorado, Governor-elect George A. Carlson of Colorado, United States Senator Wesley L. Jones of Washington, Representative Frank W. Mondell of Wyoming, United States Senator John D. Shafroth of Colorado, and Governor William Spry of Utah. These public officials represented for the most part the opponents of the public domain policy of the United States.

Over nine hundred pages of testimony were taken from December 9, 1914, to January 2, 1915. About the same amount of testimony—practically from the same people—had been taken before the House committee. Delay, duplication, and added expense is the price the Government pays for its dual committee system.[1]

After the hearings, the Senate Committee on Public Lands struck out all but the enacting clause of the Ferris bill—an event which the anti-conservation groups in the House foretold—and substituted an entirely new bill drawn by Senator Myers of Montana, Chairman of the Public Lands Committee. That the power people were pleased with the substitution one may gather from an address by Henry J. Pierce of Seattle before the National Electric Light Association at

[1] Luce, *Legislative Procedure*, Boston, 1922, chap. viii.

Chicago.[1] He said that the Myers Bill was drawn "along practical, orderly lines fair to the public and the investor."

A comparison of the two bills shows the following differences:

1. The Ferris Bill empowered the Secretary of the Interior to lease public lands of the United States for water-power purposes under such terms and conditions as he chose to prescribe. (His granting of the lease was a matter of discretion).

The Myers Bill *directed* the Secretary of the Interior to issue leases to the permittee who complied with the terms of the bill.

2. The Ferris Bill provided that at the end of a fifty-year lease all rights should lapse unless a new lease were negotiated with the Government or unless the Government desired to take over and operate the plant itself or to hand it over to a new lessee.

The Myers Bill provided that there should be a fifty-year lease, and if at the termination of that period the Government took no steps to change the provisions of the lease or to take over the property for itself the lessee should continue in possession under the terms of the original lease.

3. The Ferris Bill prohibited the sale to any one consumer of more than fifty per cent of the total output of the plant, and also provided for regulation of interstate service by the Secretary of the Interior.

The Myers Bill provided for no limitation on output and provided for interstate regulation by the Interstate Commerce Commission.

4. The Ferris Bill provided that there should be no physical combination of plants or lines of generation, distribution, and use of power without the consent of the Secretary of the Interior.

May 24, 1916.

The Myers Bill made no provision on this point.

5. The Ferris Bill provided that in the taking over of the lessee's property at the end of fifty years, if such were done, the Government should pay the *actual* cost of lands and rights of way, and the *reasonable value* of the structures.

The Myers Bill authorized the payment of the *fair value* of the whole property.

6. The Ferris Bill excluded as elements of value, in recapture after fifty years, the value of the franchise, the good will, the profits to be earned on pending contracts, and *every other intangible element.*

The Myers Bill excluded all these except—"every other intangible element."

7. The Ferris Bill provided that in case the Government did not exercise its right to take over the properties and did not renew the lease to the original lessee, the Secretary of the Interior might give the lease to a new lessee upon payment by the latter of the value of the properties as above set forth.

The Myers Bill provided that the original lessee should have preference to renewal over and above any such new lessee upon such terms and conditions as the law and regulations then in force authorized.

8. The Ferris Bill provided that the Secretary of Interior should fix charges or rentals for the use of Government lands at such a figure as he should think best.

The Myers Bill provided specifically that the rental should be based on the value of the land to be determined by the amount of horsepower developed and should not exceed the sum of twenty-five cents per developed horsepower year.

9. The Ferris Bill provided that where the state provided no regulatory body for control of rates and services, the Secretary of the Interior should exercise that function.

The Myers Bill made no such provision.

These bills show as well as anything could the differences between the two groups in Congress and out of Congress. The most notable difference is on government control. Note the care with which Mr. Ferris provided for regulation at those points where the companies might likely slip from public control; note the absence of these provisions in the Myers Bill which seeks to give the benefit of the doubt to the power companies. A jealous care for the rights of the public is evident on the one hand, and a jealous care for the rights of the developers on the other. The anti-conservation and power groups stood firm for a minimum of government control, and with them stood all those groups who feared the evil effects upon private initiative of the heavy hand of the Government. The form of control envisaged in the Ferris Bill brought forth all those lamentations of woe which conservatives have dolefully chanted for the past hundred and fifty years.

But with the fear of government interference there came another sign for the prophets of evil to interpret. The Ferris Bill lodged in the hands of an administrative official, broad powers of discretion, and as in the earliest days of water-power controversy fear of administrative authority was unmistakable, so, too that fear here became a rallying cry for the opponents of discretionary authority on the part of executive officials. Congressmen, ever jealous for the rights of the legislature, thundered their curses on these sections of the bill. It was no difficult matter to stir up sentiment against a provision under which executive tyranny might be developed. Dislike for centralized administrative control has at times given us governmental departments with checks upon each other, checks upon themselves, and checks upon democratic efficiency.

Mr. Pinchot in testifying before the Senate Public Lands Committee on the Ferris Bill put the matter for wider discretionary powers in administrative officers in the following words:

You never can give power enough to an executive officer to be effective without at the same time giving him power enough to be unjust. My experience in the public service leads me very strongly to believe that the wise thing is to give an executive officer power enough to be effective and then watch him.[1]

Practice in other countries has sanctioned the Pinchot method. This may be illustrated by section 8 of the Province of Ontario Water-Power Act of 1898 which provides:

On compliance with the foregoing regulations and upon approval of the application by the minister in writing, he may order a lease of the water privileges to be issued by the plaintiff upon such terms and conditions, and at such rentals as may be fixed by the minister.

This is, of course, what the conservationists in this country were contending for.

The congressional point of view was expressed by Senator Jones of Washington in the Senate on February 25, 1916:

This, I may say, is really the crux of the whole controversy with reference to water-power legislation. The question of giving to some Secretary or some administrative officer the power to fix charges as he may deem proper has been, in my judgment, the real source of trouble and the real cause of the delay of legislation. . . . I further most seriously object to the plan of the Senator from Montana and those who agree with him, in that they would leave to the determination of an administrative officer the policy to be followed in levying this charge, not only to the amount but as to the manner of its levy. They would say to the Secretary, " Make a charge if you think it wise, and you fix the amount and you say how it should be deter-

[1] Hearings before the Senate Committee on Public Lands on *H. R. 16673*, 63rd Cong., 3rd Sess., p. 235.

mined." This is wrong. It is the duty of Congress to say whether or not the charge should be levied. It is our duty to determine how it should be arrived at, and it is our duty to fix the amount as nearly as possible. We are the legislative body. The policy to be followed by administrative officers should be settled by us. We know what we want to do, or we should know, and we should do it. The responsibility is ours and we should discharge it. . . . If we want these enterprises undertaken, let us not place it within the power of an administrative officer to stifle them. . . . This administrative branch of the Government has almost as much, if not more, powerful influence over legislation and policies than the legislative branch itself. We are told by officers that we can do this or we can not do that. A departmental officer said a few days ago that we could not pass a certain bill if we put a certain provision in it. They come here not to give us information but to tell us what to do and what not to do. I do not criticize them for it. They have a right to congratulate themselves for their power and influence. We ought to be ashamed of ourselves. We are to blame for this state of affairs, and the only way to correct it is for us in the laws we pass to declare our will, to fix the policies we want followed, and specify what we want done.[1]

Both the Ferris and the Myers Bills failed, and another attempt at a solution of the water-power problem had proved fruitless.

In accordance with Senate resolution 544, passed in the Sixty-third Congress, third session,[2] Secretary of Agricul-

[1] *Congressional Record*, 64th Cong., 1st Sess., pp. 3121-3124. Mr. Pinchot's terse statement on page 191 seems to be an effective answer to this.

[2] *Resolved*, that the Secretary of Agriculture be, and he is hereby, directed to furnish the Senate with all information in his possession as to the ownership and control of the water-power sites in the United States, showing what proportion of such water-power sites is in private ownershp and by what companies and corporations such sites in private ownership are owned and controlled, what horsepower has been developed, and what proportion of it is owned and controlled by such private companies and corporations, and any facts bearing upon the question as to the existence of a monopoly in the ownership and control of hydro-electric power in the United States.

ture Houston transmitted to the Senate three volumes of information on the status of the hydroelectric industry in the United States. These important reports were submitted to Congress on December 20, 1915. Prepared by Chief Engineer O. C. Merrill, these volumes constitute the most extensive report on electric-power development and monopoly that have ever been published. The reports were based on data which had accumulated for several years in the office of the chief of engineers, supplemented by investigations made in the field by district engineers of the Forest Service and by correspondence with the officials of power companies to whom were submitted for verification the greater part of the data gathered. Part I of the report contained the text; Part II contained the plates and tables concerning primary power, power generated, financial statistics, the detailed data of power development in 1915, the summary tables showing the concentration in control of this power, and maps of fourteen of the public land states showing the location of all power plants, main transmission systems, and national forest areas; Part III contained the data concerning the interrelations between public service holding companies, the relation of these companies to certain banking corporations, diagrams showing the successive steps by which certain holding companies have established their control over operating companies, and charts indicating the relation through directors or principal officers of certain public holding companies with each other.

The three principal charts in the report required the services of an officer of the Department of Agriculture and two clerks working full time for six months. The electric-power census required one officer and one clerk working ten consecutive months. A considerable outlay of money was needed for the printing of such a report; on this point the anti-conservationists raised objection. Speaking in the Senate, Senator Smoot said:

> Mr. President, I want the Senate to understand distinctly, that this $21,000 is only the beginning of the cost. There is no question but that just as soon as this report is printed as a public document there will be a request for the printing of additional copies, and they will not be for the information of the members of the Senate or the House; not at all. They will make rather an elegant set of books when printed . . . and when bound will be put into libraries throughout the country and never opened nor looked at unless the children look at the pictures contained therein.[1]

Seventeen of the Old Guard—tried and true—lined up against the printing; they were Bankhead, Brandegee, Clark (Ark.), du Pont, Harding, Jones, Lodge, Martin (Va.), Oliver, Shaproth, Smoot, Sutherland, Swanson, Thomas, Thompson, Vardaman, and Wadsworth. Among the anti-conservation group approving of the printing were Shields and Underwood. The report was printed.

The report, in digest form, received wide publicity throughout the country. To many citizens it was a revelation, to thousands of others it was confirmation of all that had been known or suspected.

The House of Representatives by this time[2] was openly committed to charges for power privileges. Its two bills—the Ferris and the amended Adamson — represented the majority opinion of the lower House of Congress. The Senate stood behind the Myers Bill on public land development and a bill introduced by Senator Shields on the navigable stream development. On the Shields Bill[3] the power interests made their last stand.

[1] *Congressional Record*, 64th Cong., 1st Sess., p. 2267.

[2] Beginning of the year 1916.

[3] Introduced as S. 3331, 64th Cong., 1st Sess.

The Shields Bill provided for the granting of power permits by the Secretary of War on a fifty-year permit basis. No compensation for the privilege was provided in the bill, the grantee being required to reimburse the Government for administrative expenses or when public lands or works were used. The recapture provisions of the bill were particularly objectionable because of their vagueness. These provisions would require the United States, if it wished to take over the property at the end of the fifty-year period, to take over and pay for all the property of the grantee dependent in whole or in part for its usefulness upon the rights granted in the act. Furthermore, the Government would have had to take over those improvements which were necessary and appurtenant or acquired and valuable or serviceable in the distribution of water. These provisions might have compelled the Government to take over everything in any way connected with a power development, no matter how remotely connected. Whole lighting systems of cities and whole manufacturing plants would have to be taken over by the government under these clauses; there was no telling where the line should be drawn. By making the recapture clause impossible, the power people were made certain of perpetual leases.

The problem of recapture caused an ever increasing amount of trouble as time passed. When should the works be taken over? Who should have preference in taking over a plant—the Government, the original grantee, or a new applicant? How much should the grantee be paid, how much of his plant should be estimated in the amount? What general procedure should be used in taking over a plant? All these questions had to be answered. The power people and their friends in Congress were all in favor of terms that would make the Government hesitate before meeting them and in this way to encourage procrastination and a perpetual grant. The conservation group was insistent that nothing should be allowed for rights granted by the Government, good will, going concern, profit in pending contracts for electrical energy, for other conditions of current or prospective business, or for any other intangible element. Besides these terms the conservationists favored allowance being made for deterioration of transmission lines and insisted that the part of the plant taken over should have to include the equipment necessary and useful for the generation of power and the transmission system from the generation plant to initial points of distribution. The power groups favored such a provision as was found in the Shields Bill which would make it compulsory for the United States to renew the lease to the original grantee, if no one else were found to take it, and to make that renewal upon the same terms and with the same restrictions as originally made; thereafter the lease would not have been subject to alteration or amendment—regardless of future legislation.

In connection with the subject of recapture it is well to note the provisions made in other countries:

France: Power plants on the national lands are developed under concession for periods not exceeding fifty years. At the expiration of this period the grantee, if the concession be not renewed, is required to restore the premises to the conditions previously existing or to deliver the plant to the nation with or without indemnity as the Government may elect. A rental is charged.

Norway: Authorizes the granting of sixty to eighty year concessions. When the concession expires the land with improvement and work reverts to the Government. Among other things various payments for the privilege are required.

Canada: Dominion laws authorize issuance of licenses for twenty-one years, renewable for three further terms of like extent, at a fixed fee, payable annually, and provide that upon the termination of a license the works may be taken over by the Government upon payment of the value of the actual and tangible works and of any lands held in fee in connection therewith.

Province of Ontario: The lease is granted for a period not exceeding twenty years, with the right of renewal of two further successive terms of ten years and with such other additional conditions as the provincial government through the appropriate minister may prescribe. On the termination of the lease, the privileges together with all dams and structures revert to and become the property of the Crown. Provision is made for the payment of compensation to the lessee of such sums as the appropriate minister may deem proper for buildings or structures of a permanent character necessary or useful for development or utilization of the water privilege.

New Brunswick: The Lieutenant Governor in Council is authorized to lease or sell rights and privileges for water-power development upon such terms and conditions as he may prescribe.

Provinces of Manitoba, Saskatchewan, Alberta, Yukon, and Northwest Territory: The Governor in council is authorized to make regulations for the diversion, taking, or use of water for power purposes, and for the construction of development works on public lands. He also may fix the fees, charges, rents, royalties, or dues to be paid and the rates to be charged.

Queensland (Australia): The law authorizes water-power development under special license for periods of ten years subject to such conditions and provisions as the Governor in council shall determine.[1]

In the above cases where recapture is not specifically

[1] Hearings House Committee on Public Lands on *H. R. 14893*, 63rd Cong., 2nd Sess., pp. 531-535.

mentioned, it is understood that provision for it is to be made by administrative regulation. Distrust of administrative control, demonstrated in another section of this work, helped to prevent the adoption of any such simple solution in the United States. Senator Norris of Nebraska endeavored to put through an amendment to the Shields Bill providing for the conservationist recapture plans, but the amendment was turned down.

The Shields Bill, first introduced in December, 1915, favorably reported on January 26, 1916, stirred up all the old discussions of former days. It was discussed for six weeks in the Senate and despite the fact that people were thinking and talking war and preparedness, the measure received a considerable amount of attention in the press. Yet the time was more propitious than any other had been for several years for putting through gift legislation. Water-power interests were not unaware of this; they strove mightily for the enactment of the Shields Bill hoping that Mr. Average Citizen as well as Mr. Average Congressman were preoccupied with the grave question of National Defense. Senator Norris sized up the situation rather gloomily as follows:

> The people of the United States are not thinking about water power now. We can take away every right possessed and they will not find it out for a long time. . . . The entire country is worked up about military preparedness and like the Senate of the United States, they are not paying much attention to water-power development because I am talking now to practically empty seats. Senators have no interest in it; the people have not any interest in it; and that is the kind of a time when the unseen Government gets in its work.[1]

Once again the subject of charges for power privileges proved an effective obstacle to progress. Senator Walsh of Montana and Senator Husting of Wisconsin championed

[1] *Congressional Record*, 64th Cong., 1st Sess., p. 3172.

the tolls amendments to the bill. In a separate chapter [1] the legal phases of this question are treated; here it is well to note the arguments of a different nature. Those opposed to tolls argued—and with good reason—that a charge by the Federal Government on power development would simply be shifted to the consumer. Many who believed in the constitutional right of the Government to make the charge and who in many ways sympathized with the conservationists opposed the imposition of the charge as practically unwise.

Those who favored charges pointed out that power companies operating on the public domain had to pay a privilege tax and that such companies would operate at a distinct disadvantage in competition with those using the navigable streams if the latter were not forced to pay. Senator Waish pointed out that a power on the Kootenai River in his State would not have to pay a cent to the Government under the Shields Bill, while a plant on the non-navigable Yaak River would pay under the public domain regulations. Yet both these plants would cover the same territory. It was further pointed out that the advantages might be equalized by a charge. To illustrate, some one may be given an opportunity to generate power by damming a navigable stream, and by so doing he may be able to produce power at thirty dollars per horsepower and sell it at a good profit at that price. If this plant can not supply all the needs of the community, some one else may build and operate a steam plant; to develop the power by steam will cost more, in this case let us say sixty dollars per horsepower. If the public service commission of the state in which these plants are situated should fix a price of fifty dollars per horsepower as the legal rate, all steam plants would go out of business; if the commission fixed the rate at sixty, sixty-five, or seventy dollars the

[1] Chapter II.

water-power plant would be making too large a profit. By a federal charge, the Government could take the excess surplus profits from the hydro plant and use it for navigation improvements either in the immediate vicinity or the surrounding regions. Illustrating what might happen from the absence of charge regulation in the competition of steam power and water power, Representative Ferris of Oklahoma described the situation as follows:

> A public utility board can not say in a given city that I shall have lights in my house at a flat rate of fifty cents a month and that my neighbor across the fence shall pay three dollars a month, merely because one is hung onto a steam power and the other to hydroelectric power.[1]

Another use for a charge may be seen in the following case. One power corporation develops and sells to another corporation that will take the power over a line of fifty miles; that corporation sells to another corporation, and that corporation to another corporation that distributes it. All of these overhead charges must be paid by the consumer. The condition could be improved if the Secretary of War could say to a corporation that one rental would be imposed upon it if it sold to an intermediate corporation, but that a lower rental would be charged if the corporation sold directly to a municipality whose citizens would reap the immediate benefit. One other case in which a charge would benefit the public can be seen from the following. Regulation, whether state or federal, touches nothing that is not in the nature of a public utility. If a grantee uses his developed power for his own manufacturing purposes, he escapes ordinary regulation. Such a person would be guided by his own ideas of justice in fixing the price of his product; he would be in an excellent position to cut under his competitors and yet enjoy large profits. A situation of this kind may very readily be reached by a government charge.

[1] *Congressional Record,* 64th Cong., 1st Sess., p. 10450.

As to the shifting of such a charge to the consumer, it should be recognized that the proponents of charges were proposing to put into the hands of the Government a means of keeping power people ever aware of their public obligations. In most cases it was expected the charge would be nominal, so small that the consumer would never feel it. Ex-Secretary of the Interior Walter Fisher, who imposed many charges for use of power on the Federal domain and who had every opportunity to watch their effect once said:

There is a difference between the principle and the practical effect of it. The difficulty is this, that because in certain aspects the exaction of compensation by the granting power theoretically may possibly have an effect upon the price paid by the consumer, that theoretical possibility is used as an objection to a very practical provision which, in my judgment, will have precisely the *opposite effect . . . those things will have no practical effect of increasing the price to the consumer.*[1]

Senator Husting of Wisconsin, speaking on this subject during the debate on the Shields Bill, said:

It is assumed . . . that . . . rates that are under the control of the Public Utility Commissions are always adjusted with such firmness that a charge of $25 or $50 a year will reflect itself in the prices that they charge. It may be a good theory, but it's a theory that rests upon the assumption that the scales of control are so finely balanced and so finely adjusted that the slightest advance in overhead expenses, no matter how slight, the rates will be immediately and promptly lowered. I can illustrate that that does not obtain in practice. I know of cities where you can buy six street-car tickets for a quarter now. You could buy them twenty-five years ago for the same price, and in the last fifteen or twenty years, although the company is getting hydro-electric power from a power dam that they own somewhere, the public continues to pay the same price, and with the cheapening

[1] Hearings Senate Committee on Public Lands on *H. R. 16673*, p. 392.

of the power, the difference between the old cost of steam power and water power goes into the company's pockets.[1]

As proposed by the conservationists the charge was to be adjusted to each particular case as the administrative official deemed for the best interest of the public. This discretion lodged in a Department Secretary caused the usual objections to "executive tyranny" and "arbitrary officials." As such it was contended that a charge would be a constant impediment to water-power development. This was not at all borne out by the development of power on the public lands under a charge provision. Despite deficiencies in the law the development of power on the public domain surpassed development on navigable streams where no charge was made. The income to the Government for development on the forest preserves may be shown by the following table:[2]

District	1915	1914	1913	1912
1	$8,772.63	$2,970.00	$2,062.74	$3,275.45
2	1,180.72	2,010.63	1,228.62	1,882.68
3	4,618.37	2,574.95	2,594.85	2,546.86
4	607.55	524.80	609.48	1,169.29
5	63,748.57	31,542.86	39,537.00	34,265.07
6	10,022.60	7,443.80	5,202.39	7,423.63
7	......	96.70	......	......
Total	$88,950.44	$47,163.74	$51,235.08	$50,562.98

The fairly desperate opposition of the anti-conservation group to charges is nowhere better illustrated than in Senator Shields' speech in the Senate on February 16, 1916.

Call it what you may please, frame it in any form, the proposition that Congress may impose conditions in such cases as this upon the owners of the beds and waters of navigable streams, is not only the commonest tyranny but blackmail in its worst form.

[1] *Congressional Record*, 64th Cong., 1st Sess., p. 3298.

[2] *Congressional Record*, 64th Cong., 1st Sess., p. 10459. See also Appendix VIII.

It is no better than the action of the grafting policeman who demands tribute of the saloon keeper over whom he has authority in enforcing police regulations, under the penalty of declaring his place disorderly and closing it up for non-payment.[1]

Three other questions that should receive notice and which were given consideration during debates on the Shields Bill were the working-out of a definition of navigability, the placing of control of water power in the hands of a commission, and the Newlands idea of a comprehensive, scientific study of all problems relating to waterways and water power with a view to a country-wide systematic development.

Senator Cummins of Iowa had spent a great deal of time in drawing up a definition of navigability to prevent the Federal Government's supervising every stream of any size in the United States. It will be remembered from the discussion of this subject in Chapter II that the control of Congress over waters is exceedingly expansive since any body of water that is navigable, or potentially navigable, or is a feeder of a stream that is navigable or potentially so, may be controlled by Congress. Even streams of relative unimportance might be regulated under such an interpretation. Senator Cummins having given up the difficult job of defining navigability, it was taken over by Senator Johnson of Maine who offered the following definition as an amendment to the Shields Bill:

The words navigable waters shall be construed to mean such streams and parts of streams which are in fact navigable and used for the transportation of merchandise in interstate and foreign commerce and also such streams as may be designated by the Secretary of War as capable of improvement for the purposes of navigation and transportation of merchandise in interstate and foreign commerce.[2]

[1] *Congressional Record,* 64th Cong., 1st Sess., p. 2642.

[2] *Congressional Record,* 64th Cong., 1st Sess., p. 3235.

The objection that one might expect was raised. Senator Thomas of Colorado believed that it gave too much power to an administrative officer—the Secretary of War. The amendment was allowed to lie over for consideration. Sometime later on during the debate on the Shields Bill, Senator Cummins introduced a compromise amendment on the subject which provided:

> The term navigable waters as used in this act and as applied to streams or parts of streams as are in their ordinary, natural condition used for the transportation of persons or property in interstate or foreign commerce, or which, through improvement heretofore or hereafter made, have been or shall become usable in such commerce.[1]

The amendment then went on to say that obstruction in other streams over which the United States might have jurisdiction would not come under the provisions of the Shields Bill but would be regulated by the Secretary of War as provided in other acts. The amendment was accepted, but as to its sufficiency as a definition there was much to be desired. It limited the application of the Shields Bill but it gave no general, adequate definition of navigability. A stream good only for the floating of logs might have come under the provisions of the amendment.

The idea of placing control of water powers in the hands of a commission was not new at the time of the consideration of the Shields Bill, but at this time it was more persistently put forward. That water power should be dealt with as a unit was the desire of many men in public life. It was also believed by some that the head of no department who was liable to be here one day and gone the next, due to the political vicissitudes which befall department chiefs, should be given charge of the administration of a great law.

[1] *Congressional Record*, 64th Cong., 1st Sess., p. 3664.

Senator Shafroth of Colorado presented the difficulties of division of authority in the matter when he said:

> We have difficulties now even in the construction of little reservoirs. For instance in the mountains of my state it seems that under the rules and regulations that are prescribed, it is necessary now not only to go to the Secretary of the Interior, but the application has to go through the Forestry Department where the land is in a forest reserve; it has to be referred to the Secretary of Agriculture . . . in streams that border upon Mexico it is necessary also to have the Secretary of State pass upon the matter; and in addition to that, the Secretary of War comes in to see whether or not a navigable stream is injured.[1]

No provision, however, was made for commission regulation although all sides were willing to admit its desirability.

On March 7, 1916, Senator Newlands of Nevada offered as an amendment to the Shields Bill his comprehensive development scheme. The amendment, in twenty sections, provided for an appropriation of sixty million dollars a year for ten years for the development of water highways in coordination with steam highways, for the storage of water for irrigation, and for the construction of huge reservoirs to stabilize the flow. The country, it was proposed, should be divided into regions corresponding to the watershed areas, and in each, after scientific investigation, a plan of development should be mapped out. The working-out of the plan would be in charge of a commission of experts and would do away with haphazard river and harbor improvements and water-power development.[2] The plan was very far-reaching. Senator Newlands deserves much credit for his broad-visioned proposal; he was looking far into the future. If a systematic disposal of water resources could have been

[1] *Congressional Record,* 64th Cong., 1st Sess., p. 2699.

[2] *Congressional Record,* 64th Cong., 1st Sess., pp. 3733-3736.

made, most of the hit-or-miss system of dredging a little here and digging a little there that has characterized our water-development system would have been eliminated. Senator Newlands spoke many times on his proposed plan but received little encouragement from his colleagues. So persistent was the Nevada Senator, that towards the close of the debate on the Shields Bill we find Senator Shields interjecting the following:

Senator Shields: I understand that Jefferson's Manual is an authority in the procedure and practice of the Senate.
President pro tempore: It has a certain degree of influence, but is not a direct authority.
Senator Shields: A point of order, Mr. President. I find in Jefferson's Manual, at page 95, this rule—"No one is to speak impertinently or beside the question, superfluously, or tediously."[1]

The Chair did not sustain the Senator's point of order. What a novel suggestion that such a rule should hold in the United States Senate! The reply of Senator Newlands was significant and by no means lacking in humor. He said that he did not mean to be tedious or long-winded but that the Senate system made for that very thing. He reminded the author of the bill that if only ten Senators were in attendance at a time and there were over ninety Senators to convince, he would have to repeat his views at least nine times!

The infrequent suggestion of government ownership as a solution of the water-power problem is not to be wondered at; its mention at all is cause for wonderment. Yet we find Senator Martine of New Jersey suggesting:

My solution of this trouble is government ownership, the government construction of all the plants to aggregate and con-

[1] *Congressional Record*, 64th Cong., 1st Sess., p. 3732.

centrate this power. I believe that not only with reference to water power, but I have believed it with reference to some other great utilities of our country. However, I realize that to urge it is almost to urge heresy.[1]

Lobbying activity was brisk on all sides during consideration of the Shields Bill. On March 9, 1916, the manufacturers of hydroelectric appliances met in New York City and formed the Water-Power Development Association. They announced that they were about to undertake a campaign of publicty for more *liberal* laws in the use of streams. Over six hundred manufacturers representing a capital of 200 million dollars were interested in the Association. Their first act was to endorse the Shields Bill, and to make public the fact that headquarters would be set up at once in the Munsey Building in Washington.[2] One of the methods adopted by this Association was to send free plate matter to country publishers to be run in the daily papers as an expression of public opinion. Subsequently this matter would be collected and sent to members of Congress conveying the impression that the articles presented the local opinion of the community in which the matter was circulated.[3] One country newspaper, *The Democrat* of Mineral Point, Wisconsin, commented rather hotly on the boiler-plate method of publicity:

If the men who are behind the scheme to pervert the minds of the people on the water-power question by sending free plate matter to country publishers had been present at the meeting of newspaper men in the senate chamber in Madison last Friday night, they would doubtless have come to the conclusion that tricks that are vain will hardly get them very far in the court of public opinion. When the matter was put up to Cortland

[1] *Congressional Record*, 64th Cong., 1st Sess., p. 3229.

[2] *New York Times*, March 10, 1916.

[3] *Congressional Record*, 64th Cong., 1st Sess., pp. 10971-10976.

Smith, president of the American Press Association, he confessed that in his opinion it was *rotten business,* and the unanimous opinion of the gathering was that the publisher who would accept the plates and publish them except as paid advertisements, plainly marked as such, would do himself and his profesison dishonor.[1]

Among those in and about the Capitol at Washington busy in behalf of the power companies were:

Josiah Newcomb, (Stone and Webster).
L. L. Nunn, (Utah Power Company).
H. J. Pierce, (promoter of Seattle, Washington).
John H. Finney, (Aluminum Company of America).
Ex-Congressman D. J. Flynn, (Electric Bonding interests).
Calvert Townly, (Westinghouse interests).
Henry L. Coafter, (du Pont interests).
Frank M. Washburn, (American Cyanamide Company).
Ex-Congressman C. B. Landis, (du Pont interests).
S. Z. Mitchell, (General Electric interests).
M. O. Leighton, (Utah Securities Company).
Frank H. Short, (Pacific Gas and Electric Company).
G. W. Worthington, (Alabama Power and Light Co.).
Ex-Congressman George W. Taylor, (Muscle Shoals Co.).

Senator Shields replying to attacks on the influence of the power lobby said:

There have been three gentlemen here, and only three so far as I know, interested in water-power development and favoring this bill. One of them is Mr. H. L. Cooper. . . . I have not seen him during this session of Congress, but the Senator from Montana (Mr. Walsh) after this bill was reported with a recommendation that it be passed, and while we were trying to get it before the Senate at the last session of Congress, carried me into the Marble Room and introduced me to him, and in a few minutes' conversation Mr. Cooper told me that he favored

[1] June 8, 1916.

the bill and that it would be a great thing for the country to have it passed, and that he hoped it would be pushed at that session. . . . . Another gentleman is Mr. H. J. Pierce of Seattle, Washington, who has been a student of water-power development for many years. . . . I have also met here Colonel George W. Worthington of Sheffield, Alabama, whom I knew before I came to the Senate. . . . These are the only gentlemen interested in this bill who have been here, so far as I know, and I venture to say that no one will charge them with any improper motives or using any improper influences.

Mr. President, I have heard no charge that this was a bill of the water-power trust, except through the communication of Mr. Gifford Pinchot, and judging by his own letters to the President and the *New York American* and others, he is the most active party now interested in this bill.[1]

Senator Shields' ignorance of the presence of many lobbyists in Washington is somewhat surprising in view of the open activities of the power groups and the faithful attendance of their representatives at hearings and legislative sessions. So far as the public knew they were not "using any improper influences." Even Senator Norris admitted their integrity when he said:

We have had men from all over this country, interested in great financial institutions, begging Congress to pass a bill similar to this one that has been introduced here. I am not finding fault with these gentlemen, but they are not here for philanthropic purposes. They are here for an honorable purpose, I concede. They are fine gentlemen, as a rule, as far as I know. I know of no exceptions.[2]

Senator Norris, although acknowledging the honesty of the power lobbyists, was quite aware of their presence.

[1] *Congressional Record,* 64th Cong., 1st Sess., pp. 3290-3291.

[2] *Congressional Record,* 64th Cong., 1st Sess., p. 3171.

Another source of outside pressure was the National Conservation Association which met in Washington in May, 1916, for the first time since the stormy session of 1913. Mr. Pinchot had little control over these meetings and the Shields and Myers Bills were endorsed by 116 to 39. The Pinchot groups charged that the convention was bound hand and foot by the power interests. In commenting on the situation, the *New Republic* of May 13, 1916, said:

> By endorsing these two water-power bills, the National Conservation Congress has clearly shown that it has become nothing but an annex to the water-power lobby, of whose activities Washington has seen so much during this past winter while the bills were pending in Congress. The Committee on Water Power, whose recommendations the National Conservation Congress endorsed, was completely controlled by representatives, among others of the Utah Power Company, the Georgia Power Company, the General Electric Company, the Alabama Power Company, and the Aluminum Company of America.

Much of the strength of the power group at this Convention was due to their clever campaign for economic preparedness. The country at large was afire with enthusiasm for military preparedness. The power people were able, under the guise of patriotism, to point out the need of the *immediate* development of water power to manufacture nitrates so essential for ammunition. So successful were they in this campaign that the press throughout the country began to call for the scalps of the Pinchot obstructionists.

The press was interested for other reasons, too. The American Newspaper Publishers' Association was anxious for prompt development of water power because of its importance in the production of print paper. The following are excerpts from papers throughout the country showing their anxiety.

The Nashville Banner [1]

It would have been well if the Shields Bill, introduced two years ago had been passed. It was opposed by some of the ultra-conservationists of the Gifford Pinchot kind and by others for reasons of a purely political nature. . . . It was claimed by the ultra-conservationists that this valuable privilege should not be let to private enterprise, to "greedy corporations" was the phrase employed, but reserved for governmental experimentation. It was a sort of Bolsheviki idea that, as usual, resulted in public injury.

The Knoxville Journal and Tribune [2]

The bill was opposed by some men who were unable to understand what it meant and by some men in Congress whose constituencies had less to derive from it than some others. It was also opposed by some wise-acres, who vainly imagine themselves to be an Atlas with the world on their shoulders.

Memphis News-Scimitar [3]

Some very ingenious gentlemen who have been subsidized by the water-power interests, have rendered very effective service in preventing legislation on that subject for several years by claiming that whatever bill is introduced is in the interest of the Power Trust. And many ignorant people have been actually persuaded to believe that this is true.

The above represents a new mode of attack—that of representing the conservation group as friends of the power trust. Whatever else the item from the *News-Scimitar* may lack, it does not lack originality. Another editorial from that same paper for December 5, 1917, is no less interesting.

It need hardly be set down here, so well is it known throughout the country, that the Pinchot interests, backed by their mil-

[1] December 1, 1917.

[2] December 17, 1917.

[3] October, 1917.

lions, have met a signal defeat by the passage of the Shields bill in the Senate. Likewise, there is no comfort for the little coterie of newspaper men in Washington, who have been paid liberally, it is said, for their distribution of scurrilous matter against Senator Shields and his bill.

The Chattanooga News [1]

The National Conservation Congress indorsed the Shields Bill by a vote of 116 to 39. The bill has been much maligned. It is by no means a "graft" measure, and the rights of the public are fully protected.

The Springfield (Ill.) State Register [2]

The great unused stands of pulpwood timber that are now controlled by the present paper makers are almost without exception in sections of the country where the available water powers lie, either in the public domain or on navigable streams. . . . The Senate of the United States can strike effectively at the heart of the Paper Trust if it passes effective water-power legislation. The people of the country should get actively behind the Shields bill and urge its passage. The paper combine that has so arrogantly defied the Government in its price manipulation naturally oppose the Shields Bill. This fact should make the people rally to its support.

The San Francisco Chronicle [3]

The crazy faction of those who call themselves conservationists insists that to enact any law which will make private development possible is to give away millions to presumably wicked and designing men. The truth is that it is merely giving them a chance to rush their money in enterprises whose entire risks they must assume, but whose charges will be fixed by public authority.

[1] May 9, 1916.

[2] August 14, 1917.

[3] August 2, 1917.

The New York Journal of Commerce [1]

The whole question of regulation of water powers on Federal-controlled lands has been the subject of much emotional, not to say hysterical, oratory. The so-called conservationists appear to feel that a water power is equivalent to a gold mine and therefore must be controlled for the benefit of the people. The fact that drouth and flood overruns in costs and disappointments in markets put hydroelectrics on the same plane as the average business enterprise is obvious. . . . Hence, to bolster up their case, the conservationists invented a fantastic myth about a menacing water-power trust, which as a matter of easily established fact does not exist.

New Bedford (Mass.) Mercury [2]

It remains to be seen how loudly Mr. Roosevelt will shriek. He has been one of the arch-conservationists. With much ado, self-righteous, indeed, he vetoed the earlier bills to permit water-power development, in particular the Snake River Dam bill, a veto for which Gifford Pinchot was credited. . . . The only water-power monopoly that has been in existence has been the group of conservationists, who have exerted a power heretofore absolutely preventing anybody from making use of a great national resource. It has been a monopoly of the worst type.

To the aid of the conservationists, came the *Outlook,* the *Nation,* the *New Republic,* the Hearst papers, and many other publications. The *Nation* of March 2, 1916, said:

The Shields Bill, now before the Senate, gives to the power interests without compensation the use of water power on navigable streams. The amount of water power these streams will supply is larger by far than all the power of every kind now in use in the United States. It pretends to, but does not, enable the people to take back their own property at the end of fifty years, for in order to do so under the bill the Government would

[1] January 2, 1918.

[2] December 27, 1917.

have to pay the unearned increment, and to take over whole lighting systems.

And in the *New Republic* of March 25, 1916, we read:

On March 7, after desultory and intermittent debate running through six weeks, the Senate passed the Shields bill. . . . The bill aims to turn over to private ownership without compensation to the public the one great natural resource that still remains in the ownership of the United States.

The Shields bill on its face purports to grant a fifty-year lease to private companies. In effect the grant is in perpetuity for terms of recapture are too onerous. . . .

That such a bill should pass the Senate is surprising but not without explanation. The western Senators, with a few notable exceptions, are opposed to federal control of property located within their states. The conservatives still hold the old fashioned view that the only thing to do with public property is to turn it over to private interests. Perhaps the chief reason why the Shields Bill received such strong support is the idea, carefully circulated by the power companies, that the public is suffering from lack of development. . . . A statement of the facts about developed and undeveloped power shows how unfounded is this claim.

In the meantime Mr. Pinchot was busy making known his views in speeches and special articles and in an open letter to President Wilson. It is important to note certain points in this letter which was dated January 29, 1916.

There is a bill on the Calendar of the Senate whose passage would be a public misfortune. It is the Shields Bill. . . . The great water-power interests are behind it, and an effort to pass it is to be made next week.

This is the second time the Shields bill has been reported in the Senate. Last year the friends of conservation were able to prevent its passage. This year, thanks to a skillful and elaborate campaign conducted by the water-power interests, there is a grave danger that it will pass.

The Shields Bill gives the use of enormously valuable public property to the water-power interests without compensation. Ostensibly it provides for a method of restoring its own property to the public at the end of 50 years. As a matter of fact it has been so drawn as to make it practically impossible for the people to take their own water powers back into their hands. This it does by opening the way for indefinite litigation, and by the use of language under which the United States might be required to take over and pay for the whole electric lighting systems of cities . . . in order to get possession again of water powers owned by the people. . . . The Shields Bill gives to the water-power interests the right to condemn or take any land they choose, public or private rights which they should never have, but which should be exercised when required for water-power development either by the states or by the National Government. . . . In not a few of its provisions the actual form of words prepared by the representatives of the water-power interests have been incorporated.[1]

President Wilson had recommended to Congress the passage of water-power legislation drawn to project the public's interest. The Senate Committee on Commerce fell heir to the task of drawing the navigable streams power bill. Owing to our system of seniority in congressional committees, Senator Shields, an opponent of what were generally supposed to be President Wilson's ideas of power development, was chairman of the committee that prepared the power bill. The President did not interfere during the debates on the Shields Bill, nor did he interpose any objections when it passed the Senate. To Representative Kent of California, a militant member of the conservation group, the President let it be known that "it would be better to let the water go on running to waste than to part with its use and control on improper terms."[2] Having been written at

[1] *Congressional Record*, 64th Cong., 1st Sess., p. 3232.

[2] The New York *Nation*, March 23, 1916.

the time of the consideration of the Shields bill, the Adamson bill, the Ferris bill, and the Myers bill the advice meant conservation or anti-conservation as you cared to interpret it.

The last act in the water-power story before the Great War was a visit by President Wilson to the Capital in January, 1917. There he conferred with Senators Shields and Bankhead and Representative Adamson. All were administration leaders in Congress, and all were of the anti-conservation group.[1] The President was anxious to get some kind of legislation through before March 4, 1917. In this he failed.

[1] *New York Times*, January 19, 1917.

CHAPTER V

Climax and Anti-Climax

1917-1920

The remaining period of the water-power fight is a bewildering legislative maze. The confusion was due in large part to the Great War; water-power legislation was subsidiary to war legislation. The water-power interests, however, never ceased to press their claims with all the vigor and strength at their command. The conservationists now had control of the House, and had the sympathy of the members of the Cabinet and the President. The weakness in the conservation support lay in the fact that so much of it was in the Government, which was at the time preoccupied with the serious problem of carrying on the most extensive war preparation ever known in American history.

Immediately following the Christmas holidays in 1917, President Wilson requested the members of the Committee on Interstate Commerce, the members of the Committee on Public Lands, the members of the Committee on Agriculture, and the members of the Committee on Rules to confer with him on the water-power problem. The chairmen of these House Committees at the time were respectively Sims, Ferris, Lever and Pou. The committees accepted the invitation; about twenty-five attended the conference. President Wilson told the Congressmen that in order to get action it would be necessary to make a composite bill of all the power bills then pending, and that in view of bringing about such a result he had asked the Secretary of War, the Secretary of the Interior, and the Secretary of Agriculture to prepare a bill providing for the construction of water powers on the forest reserves, the public lands, and on the navigable rivers. Having stated this much, the President asked if the members of the assembled committees were willing to have a special committee created composed of an equal number from each committee.[1] It was suggested that all water-power bills be handed to this committee. The President pointed out that he had invited the Committee on Rules to the conference in order to advise whether or not a rule could be secured in the House that would accomplish the purpose.[2]

Here at last we see direction given to all the efforts to secure water-power legislation. Both Houses of Congress being at odds on the water-power question, it was a foregone conclusion that nothing could be secured without authoritative pressure from outside.

In reply to the President's question of committee consolidation, Mr. Ferris, speaking for the Public Lands Committee said that his committee had no objection and would be willing to cooperate. Mr. Lever of the Agricultural Committee provoked laughter by saying that his committee had never considered any power legislation but that they were willing to assist. Mr. Sims of the Committee on Interstate and Foreign Commerce was the last to speak. His consent to the proposal was qualified. He stated that his committee had always had jurisdiction of water-power legislation dealing with navigable streams, that it was a committee of great importance; that he did not know whether his committee would agree to the proposal, but that he would submit the matter to them. This reply, however frank, was not encouraging. Mr. Sims added that he did

[1] That is, of Interstate and Foreign Commerce, Public Lands and Agriculture.

[2] *Congressional Record*, 65th Cong., 2nd Sess., pp. 9797-9799.

not see that there was any great need for water-power legislation when the cost of material and labor were such as practically to prohibit development.[1] The President admitted that he did not expect there would be any immediate development, but he added that it was very important to have legislation passed, so that as soon as the War was over and high prices were reduced development might be made.[2] There remained to be given the advice of Mr. Pou, chairman of the Rules Committee. Previous actions of the House had made Mr. Pou cautious. On the matter of forming a special, consolidated committee, he believed that such could be formed under a special rule, but he could not say whether the House would agree as it was *something new and would establish a precedent.* The President, not wishing to favor any one committee having jurisdiction over water-power, handed the bill prepared by the Secretaries to Mr. Pou of the Rules Committee.[3]

The bill provided for a license period not exceeding fifty years. Provision was made for a charge to be laid by the government for the privilege of utilizing waters on the public lands or on the navigable streams. The Government was given the option of taking over the license at the end of the lease period, of renewing the old license, or of granting a new one. On recapture by the Government, the fair value of the property taken over was to be paid; the fair value, however, was not to exceed the actual cost plus such damages as might result from severing the water-power structure proper from other property. Administration of the act was placed in the hands of the Secretaries of War, Agriculture, and Interior with an executive secretary, appointed by the President with the consent of the Senate, supervising the routine work.

[1] *Ibid.*
[2] *Ibid.*
[3] *Ibid.*

Mr. Pou had a thousand copies of the administration bill printed and distributed. It was given out broadcast throughout the country as President Wilson's approved bill. Much praise was given to it especially by Mr. Pinchot and the conservationists. The power people were not altogether happy.

As we should expect the members of the various power committees were not overwhelmingly enthusiastic about the composite committee idea. The sense of pride and importance of a congressional committee is difficult for a mere layman to fathom. But the word had come from the White House, and who was there to say nay. So the committees accepted the plan. The reception of the proposal in the House was not one of unrestricted welcome. It was indeed a petulant attitude that was shown in many quarters. The resolution offered by Mr. Pou on January 11, 1918, read as follows:

That the Speaker of the House be, and is hereby, authorized and directed to appoint a special committee of 18 members to whom all bills and resolutions hereafter introduced during the Sixty-fifth Congress pertaining to the development or utilization of water power shall be referred (notwithstanding any general rule of the House to the contrary), except, however, bills and resolutions of which the Committee on Foreign Affairs has jurisdiction under the general rules of the House.

Resolved further, That the Committee on Interstate and Foreign Commerce be, and it is hereby discharged from further consideration of H. R. 3808, H. R. 7695, H. R. 4505, H. R. 8005, S. 1419 (Shields Bill), and said bills are hereby referred to the special committee herein provided for, that the Committee on Public Lands is discharged from further consideration of H. R. 7227, and the chairman of said special committee be, and he is hereby, empowered to appoint a clerk subject to its approval.[1]

[1] *Congressional Record,* 65th Cong., 2nd Sess., p. 844.

Mr. Sanford of New York made the point of order against the resolution that the Rules Committee had no privilege to report a resolution providing for the appointment of a clerk. Mr. Pou contended there was no appropriation made.[1] The Speaker sustained the point of order. The provision for the clerk was stricken out. Sniping on the resolution continued: Mr. Johnson of Washington believed that such a committee would have itself made permanent; Mr. Stafford of Wisconsin thought it funny that the Democrats, in the light of recent history, should return to appointing committees. Mr. Johnson's speech against the resolution gives an idea of the fear that existed among certain members at this departure from precedent:

> I hope members will give attention to what is coming off in the Congress of the United States. Behind this innocent-looking resolution for a special committee is a bill without a name and without an introducer. . . . If it is necessary to pass this proposed bill which is already indexed, and reported upon by three Secretaries, if it is thought necessary by the Executive that this bill should be passed, why go through this rigmarole and red tape in the appointment of a rubber-stamp committee? . . . What does the bill propose? . . . Just one more commission! Just one more arm of Congress which will be stronger than Congress itself. The bill is bureaucratic, written by bureau chiefs, and endorsed by three Secretaries. It gives no western states any hand in the control of the water power within their confines and no share in any of the returns.[2]

Nevertheless the resolution was passed. On January 15, 1918, Mr. Raker of California introduced the administration bill in the House;[1] on January 16, 1918, the Speaker, Mr. Clark, appointed the special water-power committee

[1] *Congressional Record,* 65th Cong., 2nd Sess., p. 833.

[2] *Congressional Record,* 65th Cong., 2nd Sess., p. 846.

[3] Introduced as *H. R. 8716,* 65th Cong., 2nd Sess.

which was composed of Thetus W. Sims of Tennessee (Chairman), Scott Ferris of Oklahoma, Asbury F. Lever of South Carolina, Frank E. Doremus of Michigan, Edward T. Taylor of Colorado, Gordon Lee of Georgia, Dan V. Stephens of Nebraska, John E. Raker of California, Ezekiel S. Candler of Mississippi, Carl Hayden of Arizona, John J. Esch of Wisconsin, Irvine L. Lenroot of Wisconsin, Gilbert N. Haugen of Iowa, Edward L. Hamilton of Michigan, William L. La Follette of Washington, James C. McLaughlin of Michigan, Richard Wayne Parker of New Jersey, and Sydney Anderson of Minnesota.

One committee now sulked in its tent. Not until some months later, however, did the bitter truth come out. Note the ring of resentment in a speech by Mr. Small of that committee:

The question has been asked since this special Water-Power Committee was created as to the reason for excluding members of the Committee on Rivers and Harbors from membership on this special committee. I had never intended to refer to that question publicly in the House, although it is fair to state that a flagrant injustice was done to the Committee on Rivers and Harbors. If it was the purpose to include on the special committee members of the standing committees having jurisdiction of the authorization of government dams for navigation purposes, then necessarily the Committee on Rivers and Harbors should have been included. . . . The honorable Speaker of this House, who appointed the committee, sent for me during the consideration of the matter and informed me that he had been requested not to appoint on the special committee any members from the Committee on Rivers and Harbors because that committee had no concern or jurisdiction over dams and water-power legislation. The Speaker did not give the name of his informant, but I learned from other sources that such statement emanated from a member of this House who is a conspicuous member of the special Water-Power Committee. . . . Without intending to display the slightest personal resentment (*sic*) by any member of the Committee on Rivers and Harbors, it can be stated in all frankness that a flagrant injustice has been done to the Committee on Rivers and Harbors. I would hesitate to state that any deliberate misrepresentation in this respect was made, and, in charity, it must have been made through ignorance.[1]

Representative Sims took the blame for this deed, stating as his reason that President Wilson did not desire any committees represented other than those invited to his conference.

After the appointment of the special Water-Power Committee, Mr. O. C. Merrill, Chief Engineer of the Bureau of Forestry, went to Mr. Sims and asked that the administration bill be handed back to the Secretaries of War, Interior, and Agriculture for the purpose of making certain changes in the interest of clarity and simplicity. During the latter part of February Mr. Merrill brought to Mr. Sims a bill with changes proposed by the three Secretaries with an accompanying letter. Mr. Sims did not read the bill nor the letter, but had a thousand copies of the bill printed at once and also a thousand copies of the letter.[2]

The principal amendment in the new bill had to do with recapture. Section 14 with the old and new parts was as follows: (Parts scratched to be omitted; parts in italics are new)

Sec. 14. That upon not less than two years' notice in writing from the commission the United States shall have the right, upon or after the expiration of [any] *the original* license *or of any license subsequently issued,* to take over and thereafter to maintain and operate any project or projects, as defined in section three hereof, and covered in whole or in part by the license,

[1] *Congressional Record,* 65th Cong., 2nd Sess., p. 9898.

[2] *Congressional Record,* 65th Cong., 2nd Sess., pp. 9797-9799.

or the right to take over upon mutual agreement with the licensee all property owned and held by the licensee then valuable and serviceable in the development, transmission, or distribution of power and which is then dependent for its usefulness upon the continuance of the license, together with any lock or locks or other aids to navigation constructed at the expense of the licensee, upon the condition that before taking possession it shall pay the [fair value not to exceed actual cost of] *net investment of the licensee in* the [property] *project or projects* taken, plus such reasonable [severance] damages, if any, [as may be caused by the separation of said property from] *to* property *of the licensee* valuable, serviceable and dependent as above set forth, but not taken, *as may be caused by the severance therefrom of property taken,* and shall assume all contracts entered into by the licensee with the approval of the commission. The [value of such property] *net investment of the license in the project or projects* so taken *and the amount of such severance damages, if any,* shall be determined by agreement between the commission and the licensee, and in case they cannot agree, by proceedings in equity instituted by the United States in the district court of the United States in the district within which any of such property may be located.

[*Provided,* That such fair value shall not include or be affected by the value of any lands, rights of way, or other property of the United States licensed by the commission under this Act by the license, or by good will, going value, or prospective revenues:]

[*Provided further,* That the values allowed for water rights, rights of way, lands, or interest in lands shall not be in excess of the actual cost thereof at the time of acquisition by the lessee.] [1]

The letter which accompanied the amendments follows:

[1] *House Report 715,* 65th Cong., 2nd Sess.

WASHINGTON, FEBRUARY 27, 1918.

Hon. T. W. Sims,
House of Representatives.

Dear Mr. Sims:

It is understood your committee will take action at an early date upon various proposals which have been made concerning water-power legislation. On account of the conditions now affecting the power industry and the need of maintaining our entire industrial machinery at its highest efficiency, a satisfactory solution of the water-power problem is, in our judgment, one of the most important steps for the consideration of this Congress and one which should receive attention at the earliest possible date.

The industrial expansion which has been necessary in order to produce the materials and equipment needed in the prosecution of the war has placed unprecedented demands upon the electric power industry, to such an extent in fact that the output of commercial central stations has increased more than 60 per cent since 1914. This increase has been greatest in the manufacturing sections of the East where water-power development is comparatively limited, and has been chiefly in the form of steam-generated power, because steam power can be developed more quickly and at less capital cost than water power. This increase in power output has taken place notwithstanding advances in costs of construction and of operation.

While the form of bill which has been presented for your consideration is directly concerned with water-power development only, an adequate solution of this problem will have a favorable and stabilizing effect upon the whole power industry. Probably no considerable increase in new water-power development can be expected immediately, but legislation is urgently needed in order to put existing water-power developments, which have been made under inadequate law, into a position of security which will enable them to make extensions and to meet maturing obligations upon favorable terms.

There is also need of legislation in order that time may be given to prepare for the developments that must take place after the close of the war, if the United States is to maintain its proper place in world trade, or even to supply its domestic needs. A survey of water-power resources is needed, particularly with relation to specific districts and specific industries. The various establishments of the Federal Government which have had to do with the administration of water power should be coordinated through a single agency, and as far as practicable all agencies, federal, state, and private, should be brought into cooperation. It is urgently recommended that a federal power commission be established as provided in the proposed bill and be given ample authority to undertake this work of preliminary investigations.

Beyond the need of power development as such is the need of increasing the proportion of water power in order to reduce the drain on our coal and petroleum supplies, particularly the latter. Even if the coal supply were unlimited, the reduction in the demands upon labor and transportation equipment would be sufficient reason for substituting water power for steam power whenever possible. The petroleum supply particularly in the West where the greatest proportion is used for fuel, is being rapidly depleted, consumption has exceeded production and stocks in storage are fast disappearing. With the substitution of water power for steam power in central stations and with the electrification of railroads, a large part of the use of petroleum for fuel could be eliminated.

Water-power legislation should have in view not only the maintenance of the rights of the public in the national resources, but also the adequate protection of private capital by which such resources are developed. The bill before you aims to do both. After careful consideration, however, it is believed that certain changes in language could be made which would more clearly express the intent of the proposed legislation.

It is particularly important that the conditions which affect the disposition of the property at the termination of the license should be so definite that uncertainties will be reduced to a minimum. If the properties are not taken over, the conditions under which a new license may be secured should be entirely clear. If the properties are taken over, the price to be paid should not include alleged values not represented by investment, or, on the other hand, require needless amortization of capital during the period of the license in order to protect the investment. It is, therefore, believed advisable to define in specific language the items which should or should not enter into the price to be paid. The following definition which it is recommended should be inserted at the end of section 3 has been prepared after thorough consideration and after consultation with accounting and banking experts. It is believed to be eminently fair from the point of view of the public and of the investor. The use of this term will require certain changes in other parts of the bill, particularly section 14:

" Net investment " in a project means the actual legitimate original cost thereof as defined and interpreted in the " Classification of investment in road and equipment of steam roads, issue of 1914, Interstate Commerce Commission," plus similar costs of additions thereto and betterments thereof, minus the sum of the following items properly allocated thereto, if and to the extent that such items have been accumulated during the period of the license from earnings in excess of a fair return on such investment: (a) Unappropriated surplus, (b) aggregate credit balances of current depreciation accounts, and (c) aggregate appropriations of surplus or income held in amortization, sinking fund, or similar reserves, or expended for extensions or betterments. The term " cost " shall include, in so far as applicable, the elements thereof prescribed in said classification, but shall not include expenditures from funds obtained through donations by states, municipalities, individuals, or others.

The language of section 6 which fixes the period of the license has been changed somewhat in order to make its intent more clear and in order to make certain that there shall be no time when the holder of a license may not have the privilege of receiving a new license if the properties are not taken over either by the United States or by a new licensee.

Certain other changes, minor in character, have been made for the purpose of clarifying the language, or improving the form of the bill. All these changes are shown upon the attached copy of the confidential committee print.

Very truly yours,

NEWTON D. BAKER,
Secretary of War.
FRANKLIN K. LANE,
Secretary of the Interior.
D. F. HOUSTON,
Secretary of Agriculture.[1]

Several days after the presentation of the amendments and the letter, Representative Ferris came to Chairman Sims and asked him if he had read the suggested changes. Sims replied that he had not. It was the opinion of Mr. Ferris that some of the changes were very material. After reading them Mr. Sims agreed with him, but labored under the impression that the suggested changes had been approved not only by the three Secretaries but by the President as well. The mystery deepened when Mr. Ferris called Secretary Lane by telephone and discovered that the Secretary had not given his approval to the changes. Secretary Baker had not personally signed the letter recommending the changes, for at this time he was not in the country. Mr. Merrill, however, contended that the Secretary had authorized some one to sign for him.[2] Secretary Lane's ignorance of the changes can be seen from his testimony before the special Water-Power Committee on March 27, 1918. The following is an excerpt from the Hearings:

Mr. Ferris: Now, that brings us to a point where I feel like I ought to read to you what has been stricken out in reference to section 6 and what has been incorporated as a subsequent amendment which came along with a letter of transmittal under date of February 27, 1918. The language stricken out of section 6 page 11:

[1] *Congressional Record,* 65th Cong., 2nd Sess., p. 2942.

[2] *Congressional Record,* 65th Cong., 2nd Sess., pp. 9797-9799.

> *That unless revoked for cause, as provided in sections 13 and 26 hereof, each license under this act shall be issued for a period not exceeding 50 years.*

That is stricken out and this language is inserted instead and is printed as an amendment in italics:

> *That each license under this act shall be issued for an original period of 50 years, unless a shorter time is agreed upon between the applicant and the commission or is necessary in order that licenses for parts of the same project shall terminate on the same date. Licenses for subsequent periods of such duration and under such conditions as may be prescribed by then existing law and regulations shall be tendered as provided in section 15 hereof unless and until at the termination of the original, or of any subsequent period, the properties are taken over and compensation made as provided in sections 14 and 15 hereof.*

Now let me turn to section 14, page 20, if I may, and read what is done there. Section 14 is amended in many particulars by striking out language and inserting other language, but this language is stricken out which it seems to me is particularly pertinent, page 21, lines 17 to 24, inclusive.

> *Provided, That such fair value shall not include or be affected by the value of any lands, rights of way, or other property of the United States licensed by the commission under this act, by the license or by good will, going value or prospective revenues:*
> *Provided further, That the values allowed for water rights, rights of way, lands, or interests in lands, shall not be in excess of the actual reasonable cost thereof at the time of acquisition by the lessee.*

That language which it seems to me provided a very great safeguard for the people or whoever may want to retake the property, has in connection with these subsequent amendments been stricken out; and on yesterday I dictated a letter to you Mr. Secretary, which, of course, you have not yet seen, and likewise to Mr. Merrill, who has been actively here helping us with the bill, and to Secretary Houston and Secretary Baker, calling attention to these suggestions. Of course, if you have not seen these amendments I do not want to ask you about them in detail.

Secretary Lane: Tell me why was that last proviso stricken out?

Mr. Ferris: That is what I want to know, Mr. Secretary.

Secretary Lane: Why ask me? I would like to know about that.

Mr. Ferris: I have reason for asking that because under date of February 27, 1918, we have a joint letter of transmittal here addressed "Hon. T. W. Sims, House of Representatives, my dear Mr. Sims," which is too long to read in full, but the last paragraph of it is, I think, worthy of reading. It is as follows:

> Certain other changes, minor in character, have been made for the purpose of clarifying the language or improving the form of the bill. All these changes are shown upon the attached copy of the confidential committee print.
>
> NEWTON D. BAKER, *Secretary of War.*
> FRANKLIN K. LANE, *Secretary of the Interior.*
> D. F. HOUSTON, *Secretary of Agriculture.*

Secretary Lane: Was this proviso stricken out in that print?

Mr. Ferris: I assume so because they are the amendments that the chairman had printed along with many others, which I have not mentioned.[1]

So opposed was Mr. Ferris to this net investment provision that he filed a minority report against it when the bill was reported by the special committee to the House. On the twenty-third of August, 1918, Chairman Sims received a letter from President Wilson.

[1] *Hearings before House Committee on Water Power,* 65th Cong., 2nd Sess., pp. 455-456.

THE WHITE HOUSE,
WASHINGTON, D. C.,
AUGUST 22, 1918.

My dear Mr. Sims: I am going to venture to say to you as chairman of the special water-power committee what I hope that you will not think I am taking too great a liberty in saying, namely, that inasmuch as the House of Representatives has four times passed a water-power bill [1] as it was originally proposed by the administration and agreed upon in informal conference, I am very much in hopes that it will be the judgment of the House to respect the Committee Amendment and recur to the original bill in the form in which it was delivered to Mr. Pou of the Rules Committee for introduction and consideration by the Congress. I am very much concerned about this feature of the bill and have the privilege of being so intimately associated with those who have from time to time conferred about it that I am venturing to make this earnest suggestion.

Sincerely yours,
WOODROW WILSON.

Hon. Thetus W. Sims,
House of Representatives.

The President was evidently not in accord with the changes. On the same day on which the President wrote his letter to Mr. Sims, Mr. Sims was writing a letter to the President. The letters passed each other on the way to their separate destinations. The letter of Mr. Sims to the President follows:

[1] These four bills were as follows:
Adamson Bill (*H. R. 16053*), August 4, 1914 (Navigable streams).
Ferris Bill (*H. R. 16673*), August 24, 1914 (Public lands).
Ferris Bill (*H. R. 408*), January 8, 1916.
Adamson Bill (*S. 3331*), January 14, 1916.

House of Representatives of
the United States,
Committee on Water Power,
Washington, D. C.,
August 22, 1918.

My dear Mr. President:

General debate on the water-power bill has been closed. Further consideration has been postponed until the man-power bill passes the House, but we will probably have time to take up the water-power bill and finish its consideration before the Ways and Means Committee will have the revenue bill ready for consideration. We are, therefore, in the amendment stage of the bill, which is the all-important stage.

As the bill was finally reported by the Committee there is no matter of serious difference except the so-called net-investment amendment. As you know, Mr. Ferris is very bitterly opposed to that amendment. Mr. Doremus agrees with him, and so do I, but as chairman having charge of the bill and representing a majority of the Committee, rather than my personal views, it is rather embarrassing for me to do what I feel my duty will require me to do in the present case.

You requested the three Secretaries to prepare a bill for you. Naturally, I must suppose that they gave the preparation of that bill their most deliberate and serious consideration. You presented the bill they had prepared and given you and which met with your approval as a basis upon which you asked that a special committee be created by special rule in order that all questions of water-power legislation should be included in one bill. You stated to us at the time we met you in conference that you approved the fundamental provisions of the bill. You finally gave the bill to Mr. Pou, Chairman of the Committee on Rules, so that it might not appear that you had any feeling or preference as between the several committees that have heretofore had jurisdiction of water-power legislation.

Mr. Pou immediately had the bill printed and a thousand copies of the same distributed among the members of the House. This was all done before the Committee on Rules had brought in a rule providing for the establishment of a special committee in compliance with your request. Being satisfied with the fundamental provisions of the bill I strongly urged the Committee on Interstate and Foreign Commerce to agree to this special rule. Mr. Doremus helped me in the matter, but it was rather an uphill task to get the Committee to agree to it, but it finally did so. The fundamentals of that bill were given to the House as the deliberately considered necessary provisions of a water-power bill, carefully prepared by the three Secretaries, carefully scrutinized by yourself, and approved by all concerned. The House, feeling it to be the last word from both you and the three Secretaries, adopted the rule creating the committee. The committee was appointed, and I was honored with the chairmanship of the same. But the railroad-control bill was then up for consideration by the Committee on Interstate and Foreign Commerce. I could not call the Water-Power Committee together or take any steps whatever in the consideration of the proposed water-power bill.

Several weeks after the Committee had been created Mr. O. C. Merrill, Chief Engineer of the Bureau of Forestry in the Department of Agriculture, came to see me and stated to me that the three Secretaries requested that this bill which you had given us be referred back to the three Secretaries, that there were certain amendments which the three Secretaries wanted in the interest of clarity and simplicity. I told Mr. Merrill that the bill which you had given to us and which had been printed at the request of Mr. Pou was not a pending bill before the Committee in the sense that it could be referred by Committee action, but that if the three Secretaries desired to look over the bill with a view to changing its phraseology, thereby making it more clear and simple, they could do so and the committee would take up their suggestions and consider same when organized.

About two weeks afterwards Mr. Merrill came to my committee room late one afternoon and brought what he said was a bill with the suggested amendments. Assuming, of course, that the amendments had been submitted to you by the three Secretaries and approved by you, I never even read the bill or the letter, but went immediately to the floor of the House and had a thousand copies of the amended bill printed at once and also a thousand copies of the letter.

It was a number of days after that time when Mr. Ferris asked me if I had read these proposed amendments. I told him I had not. He suggested that I read them immediately, as he regarded the changes made in the bill fundamental. I then read the bill and found that Mr. Ferris was exactly right, that instead of changing the phraseology so that the fundamental provisions of the bill would be more easily understood that the basic provisions of the bill had been completely changed. For instance, the bill you gave us provided for a license period of not exceeding 50 years. This had been changed to a specific arbitrary 50 year period with no power to provide for a less period without the consent of the licensee. A second license period was provided for the holder of the original license, and the tender of this second was made mandatory upon the part of the commission. The recapture provisions of the bill you gave us provided for recapture upon a basis of fair value not exceeding actual cost. This provision was stricken out almost bodily and the so-called net-investment provision substituted for it.

It is evident to me that the Secretaries never considered these amendments as thoroughly as they should have been considered. I could never believe that radically fundamental changes in the bill would have been suggested and pressed by the three Secretaries without first being submitted to you and having your approval.

Now, in all fairness and justice to myself as chairman of the Water-Power Committee and to the members of the three committees and to the House of Representatives, who concurred in making a revolutionary change in the procedure of the House in order to consider a bill given to us by you, that radical and fundamental changes in that bill should not have been prepared and suggested by the Secretaries and given the stamp of administration approval, without you or any member of the committee being consulted as to the effect these proposed changes would have upon the bill.

I, of course, took it for granted that Mr. Merrill was in all good faith representing the Secretaries in doing what he did and that they were doing what you approved. I feel absolutely sure that neither the committee nor the House of Representatives would have suggested any such amendments, or consented to them on any other theory than that they had received your approval. The committee has acted on all the amendments, but the net-investment amendment is the bone of contention, and I ask you if you are willing to do so to let me know whether or not they were approved by you, especially the net investment amendment as written in the reported bill.

I would like very much to have your reply before we begin considering the bill for amendment, because I feel in all good faith I must oppose this net-investment amendment.

I must assume that the three Secretaries gave the whole matter exhaustive consideration before they handed you a bill. If they did so and then afterwards radically changed almost every fundamental provision of the bill is to me a very strange proceeding. Therefore, I can not believe that they did so with a thorough knowledge of the effect of the amendments upon the bill.

Very sincerely yours,

T. W. SIMS, *Chairman.*

The President,
The White House.

The reply of President Wilson was a denial of responsibility for the net-investment amendment and a statement of opposition to it. The letter of the President reads as follows:

THE WHITE HOUSE,
WASHINGTON, D. C.,
AUGUST 26, 1918.

My dear Mr. Sims:

Pardon me for not having replied sooner to your important letter of August 22.

[1] *Congressional Record*, 65th Cong., 2nd Sess., pp. 9657-9658.

I am free to reply to it that I did not see the draft amendments to the water-power bill which were introduced by Mr. Merrill and his associates after the bill was first put in the hands of your special committee. I do not approve of them, and it is my earnest hope that the Congress will see fit to pass the bill as it was originally drafted and provisionally agreed upon in our informal conference.

Cordially and sincerely yours,
WOODROW WILSON.[1]

Hon. Thetus W. Sims,
House of Representatives.

When the House was apprised of these letters a royal battle began on executive dictation. Representative Mondell wanted to know if this were a correspondence course in legislation. Representative Sinnott of Oregon gleefully read from Woodrow Wilson's *Congressional Government:*

No one, I take it for granted, is disposed to disallow the principle that the representatives of the people are the proper ultimate authority in all matters of government and that administration is merely the clerical part of government. Legislation is the originating force; it determines what shall be done. And the President, if he can not or will not stay legislation by the use of his extraordinary power as a branch of the legislature, is plainly bound in duty to render unquestioning obedience to Congress.[2]

Mr. Gillett of Massachusetts thought the incident illustrated the wisdom of the House rule that executive communications intended for the use of committees should be sent to the speaker of the House. This was true enough, but the question still remained—who changed the bill? It

[1] *Congressional Record,* 65th Cong., 2nd Sess., p. 9658.

[2] *Congressional Record,* 65th Cong., 2nd Sess., p. 9658. Representative Sinnott was quoting from Wilson's *Congressional Government,* Boston, 1885, p. 273.

seemed impossible to believe that a competent administrative officer such as Mr. Merrill had been guilty of misleading the Water-Power Committee. Many saw in it the influence of the Power Trust. Headlines such as the following were found in the press throughout the country:

> ONE MAN BEATS POWER COMBINE.
>
> THREE CABINET MEMBERS AND
> ALL BUT ONE COMMITTEEMAN FAVORED
> WATER-GRAB BILL.
>
> FERRIS WINS WILSON'S HELP.
>
> INSISTS ON ACTUAL COST.
>
> WINS DAVID-GOLIATH FIGHT.[1]

Here then was a situation in which an administration bill had been offered by the President, materially and mysteriously amended by three cabinet officers—none of whom knew of the changes—obediently adopted with the changes by a committee in sympathy with the administration and believing they were doing the President's bidding, and summarily disowned by the President. Debate in the House at times became quite amusing as members endeavored to fathom the mystery. Seldom were the three cabinet officers involved called by name; members simply referred to "the three Secretaries." Scores of times in the debates one reads of "the three Secretaries." So common did the phrase become that Representative Johnson of Washington called attention to the fact in the following words:

> Now, thoughtlessly we may get these distinguished gentlemen, members of the Cabinet, into the position whereby continually referring to them as the "three Secretaries," we will have them designated, as have been many others in history and literature, even as "The Three Wise Men from the East," the "Three

[1] *New York Globe*, August 17, 1918.

Black Crows," or the "Three Little Maids from School," or the "Three Musketeers," or "Three Blind Mice," or even, my friends, as "Three Men in a Boat."

Indeed the last phrase was quite appropriate.

It is not difficult to understand the reason for the amendment mystery when the facts are known.[2] No effort to deceive, no vicious pressure by lobby interests, and no desire to hold up legislation caused the amendments to be offered. There had been created in the Departments of War, Agriculture, and Interior an inter-departmental committee consisting of Mr. Merrill of the Agricultural Department, Mr. Finney and Mr. Brown of the Interior Department, and General Black, Chief Engineer of the Army, of the War Department. Before the proposition was made for a joint water-power committee these men were delegated to draft a power bill along lines suggested by the Secretaries of War, Interior, and Agriculture. They made such a draft. Just prior to the holiday recess (1917) it was submitted to the three Secretaries and by them to the President. The Secretaries and the President approved of the original draft. The difficulty seems to have arisen because the interdepartmental committee deemed it necessary to give more time and study to certain phases of the bill; they continued in session and determined upon certain perfecting amendments. Among these was the 'net-investment' amendment which if adopted required certain further changes in the bill. After a conference between the interdepartmental committee and the Secretaries, Secretary of the Interior Lane suggested that Mr. Aitchison of the Interstate Commerce Commission be consulted. The suggestion was made as Mr. Aitchison was an expert on valuation matters. Mr. Aitchison proposed

[1] *Congressional Record*, 65th Cong., 2nd Sess., p. 9803.

[2] Stated by Representative Esch, *Congressional Record*, 65th Cong., 1st Sess., p. 9956.

that for the purposes of determining *cost* in recapture, the drafters make reference to the classification for investment in road and equipment as used by the Interstate Commerce Commission in its valuation work.[1] Approval of the change by the Secretaries was not carelessly given; they could not have been ignorant of the change as Mr. Merrill conferred at length with Secretary Houston of the Department of Agriculture. Messrs. Finney and Brown discussed the proposals with Secretary Lane. The proposed changes rested for a week in the War Department. It is possible that the Secretaries may not have seen the exact wording of the final draft, but they did approve of the changes including "net investment."

The President, being a very busy man at the time, had little or no chance to study thoroughly the changes, but it is evident that he did not like the sound of the net-investment proposition and that he had been much impressed by the minority report of Mr. Ferris.

There can be no doubt of the honesty of both sides in this dispute. All were anxious to secure recapture terms fair both to the Government and to the investor. Mr. Merrill and his associates were seeking recapture terms as exact as language could express them. Representative Ferris saw in these terms a guarantee to the investor that every dollar put into a power plant would be returned; as he expressed it: "this so-called net investment amendment provides that the Government shall become an absolute insurer of all the money invested in the water-power plant."[2] Everyone interested in power development realized the importance of the recapture provisions. The power interests fully realized that their control of power sites might have

[1] The net investment plan of the Interstate Commerce Commission will be found in Appendix V.

[2] *House Report 715*, 65th Cong., 2nd Sess.

been made perpetual by difficult recapture provisions. Recapture clauses that were to apply to conditions fifty years in the future were in no sense easy to draft; and that there should have been differences of opinion on such clauses by the best friends of conservation was rather to be expected.

An interesting recapture provision submitted by Representative Sims would have provided for current compulsory amortization so that by the end of the lease period no appropriation would have to be made by Congress. Mr. Sims did not believe that Congress would ever appropriate money out of the Treasury of the United States to pay for recapture and the result would be a lease continued perhaps indefinitely. The amendment on this point offered by Mr. Sims was as follows:

That a charge of not less than 50 cents per horsepower per annum for the first 10-year period after the date of issuance of said license and $1 for the second 10-year period, and $1.50 for the third 10-year period, and $2 for the fourth 10-year period shall be levied and collected by the United States on all electric power produced by the licensee for and during said periods or for any and all further time after the expiration of said fourth 10-year period that said project property remains in the possession, use, and control of said licensee or his assignee: *Provided,* That all sums so collected from the licensee by the United States shall be considered and treated as an amortization sinking fund, upon which interest shall be credited to the licensee at the rate of 4 per cent, compounded annually on all sums so paid from date of payment, until the sums so paid in, with accumulated compound interest, shall equal the value of all the project property of the licensee except transmission lines and distribution plants. The value of said project property to be determined as provided in this act: *Provided further,* That upon the payment of said sum to the licensee or paid in discharge of any outstanding bonds or other liabilities of said licensee which at such times constitute a valid subsisting lien on said property, that all right, title, claim, and interest, which the licensee has in and to all said project property, except transmission lines and distributing plants, shall be divested out of said licensee and vested in the United States.[1]

This Amendment was rejected by the House.

The hearings on the administration power bill lasted from March 18, 1918, to May 15, 1918. The War was having its effect upon the power interests and the conservationists. A more tolerant spirit was shown by both at the House hearings. The power people had practically surrendered on the regulation by charge principle and were concentrating their efforts on the recapture clauses. Their plan was to secure as favorable conditions of recapture as possible in the face of a determined conservation House of Representatives and Administration. The power lobby at these hearings were the following who very ably presented the water-power companies' views.

Calvert Townley, Assistant to the President of the Westinghouse Electric and Manufacturing Company, New York City, formerly Vice President of the Niagara, Lockport and Ontario Power Company.

E. K. Hall, Vice President of the Electric Bond and Share Company of New York City. Mr. Hall preferred the broad general phrase "just compensation" in the place of "net investment."

John A. Britton, Vice President and General Manager of the Pacific Gas and Electric Company, San Francisco.

Harrison B. Freeman, representing the Connecticut River Company of Hartford, Connecticut.

John J. Harris, President of the Big Horn Canyon Irrigation and Power Company, Hardin, Montana.

C. F. Kelley, representing the Montana Power Company and with offices at 42 Broadway, New York City.

[1] *Congressional Record,* 65th Cong., 2nd Sess., p. 9903.

A. C. Morrison, representing the Electro-Metallurgical Company of Niagara Falls.

P. C. Krauthoff, representing Harris, Forbes, and Company of New York City, an investment bond house.

Clyde C. Dawson of Denver, Colorado, who appeared "purely as an individual and attorney." He had, however, acted in an advisory and consulting capacity for a number of water-power companies and had also represented a number of such companies in litigated cases.

M. O. Leighton, Consulting Engineer of Washington, D. C., formerly (1906-1913) Chief Hydrographer of the United States Geological Survey.

William H. Ouken, Jr., Editor of the *Electrical World,* New York City.

Henry B. Pierce of Seattle, Washington.[1]

No conservation representative appeared before the committee except in so far as that view was presented by certain public officials, such as the Secretary of the Interior, Franklin K. Lane; the Secretary of War, Newton D. Baker; the Secretary of Agriculture, David F. Houston; and Senator Thomas J. Walsh of Montana.

Various letters and resolutions from cities and civic organizations were read into the record. Sir Adam Beck, chairman of the Hydroelectric Commission of Ontario, Canada, gave an account of Ontario's experiment in public operation of hydroelectric plants. A few individuals appeared to air private views. Almost nine hundred pages of testimony were taken.

Mr. Sims, chairman of the special committee, asked (July 8, 1918) unanimous consent for the consideration of the Water-Power Bill as reported, saying that it could be disposed of in two or three days. Mr. Cooper of Wisconsin

[1] See *Hearings before the House Committee on Water-Power,* 65th Cong., 2nd Sess.

refused the unanimous consent. Later on that same day Mr. Sims again made the request; this time it was granted. Mr. Cooper was not present at the time, so there was much explaining to be done the next day. After more bickering the discussion on the bill got under way.

After argument on the bill had run on for some time, Representative Walsh of Massachusetts raised the point of order that in the bill there was an appropriation and that the Water-Power Committee had no right to appropriate money as that was the business of the Appropriations Committee. Now what was to be done? The debate that followed was an interesting discussion of House rules, but not altogether beneficial to the progress of power legislation. The ruling of the Chair on the point is, nevertheless, worth noting:

> The chair is thoroughly convinced that the Committee on Water Power which has control of this bill—Senate bill 1419—has no general power to appropriate money, and the Chair would hold so immediately if it were not for the exceptional circumstances under which this committee was created and these particular bills referred to it. Senate bill 1419, which was referred specifically to this new committee by the special resolution of the House passed on January 11 of this year, does carry appropriations. It is stated that another bill referred to specifically in the resolution and referred to this special committee on Water Power also carries appropriations.
>
> The Chair confesses that this is a rather perplexing question, but it seems to the Chair that inasmuch as a special rule was provided by the Committee on Rules, after careful consideration, which was finally adopted and known as resolution 216, in which resolution these four bills were specifically named and specifically referred to the Committee on Water Power, it does seem to the Chair that the House must be assumed to have known what it was doing, and that it knew these bills did carry some form of appropriation, and that the House thereby conferred on the committee in these particular instances, and in these

> alone, the power to make appropriations. Therefore, the Chair rules that in these specific cases the committee has jurisdiction to make Appropriations. That is as far as the Chair rules, except, as I said at the beginning, the Chair believes that this committee has no further power to make appropriations.[1]

In the original bill the secretary of the proposed Water-Power Commission was to receive a salary of $10,000 a year. When reported to the House the salary had been lowered to $5,000 a year. Representative Raker showed his contempt for the generous provision of the original bill by saying that it would "give some fellow a fat salary to run the business."[2] Not content with lowering his salary, Representative Raker proposed that the title "executive secretary" be changed to "secretary" evidently to impress upon the mind of this faithful government slave, whoever he might be, that he was a mere clerk after all. The proposal was rejected.

Following the discussion about the position of the Executive Secretary, Mr. Walsh of Massachusetts moved that the following amendment be adopted:

> The work of the commission shall, in so far as practicable, be performed by and through the Departments of War, Interior, and Agriculture, respectively.

Mr. Walsh believed that despite the commission arrangement there was a danger of each Secretary's working by himself and at cross-purposes with the other members. The comment of Representative Ferris in approving the amendment will strike a sympathetic note with any who have tried to unwind official red-tape at Washington:

[1] *Congressional Record*, 65th Cong., 2nd Sess., p. 9666.

[2] *Congressional Record*, 65th Cong., 2nd Sess., p. 9667.

[3] *Congressional Record*, 65th Cong., 2nd Sess., p. 9667.

Personally, I would like to see the action of that commission a simple action, so that when action is taken, that will be the end of it. Our departments here are scattered all over town, and I do not know how other members of the House have been impressed, but it certainly has been impressed on me when I go to transact a little business about the war or about the navy . . . that I start out in the morning and wind up at night with some additional man yet to see.

The amendment was accepted.

Representative Humphreys of Mississippi proposed that all corporations in which a majority of the stock was held by aliens should be denied a license. Representatives Sims and Esch although in sympathy with the proposition said that they feared retaliation on the part of Canada and Mexico.[2] Despite the fact that such a provision would be controlling only when the license was issued and that the very next day there might be a transfer of stock, the amendment was accepted. At any rate it satisfied the patriotism of the Representatives.

An effort on the part of Representative Harrison of Mississippi, that ever-present scourge of the Republicans, to exclude boundary streams from the jurisdiction of the Commission failed. Mr. Harrison was especially concerned about Niagara Falls and the St. Lawrence and the companies operating in that region which he desired to have treated as special cases. A similar amendment offered earlier in the discussion of the bill by Representative Humphreys of Mississippi also failed. Mr. Humphreys in defending that amendment said:

For ten years the Aluminum Company of America has been knocking at the door of Congress for the right to destroy the Long Sault Rapids in the St. Lawrence by constructing a dam

[1] *Congressional Record,* 65th Cong., 2nd Sess., p. 9668.

[2] *Congressional Record,* 65th Cong., 2nd Sess., p. 9766.

there for the purpose of developing water power. That was ten years ago, and it was estimated then that it would cost $45,-000,000. Just how many millions it will cost now, I am not prepared to say. They propose to develop at that one particular point 500,000 horsepower. . . . They have come here repeatedly and asked Congress for the privilege of developing that power, and every time Congress has refused to grant it. . . . Except for the interposition of Congress at Niagara ten years ago or more, that most wonderful of all natural spectacles of the world would have been seriously impaired. . . . There are 50,000 people . . . every year, not plutocrats, not millionaires, but clerks and people of moderate means who are able to spend a little money for a vacation, who go down the St. Lawrence River and run the rapids. This company proposes to dam the river at the foot of the Long Sault and destroy those rapids for the purpose of developing water power. They have never been able to get the consent of the Canadian Government and now by treaty under its terms this can not be done except by the two Governments acting jointly in the matter. I am not willing . . . to take from the Congress the power to act finally in that matter and delegate it to this so-called commission of Cabinet officers, which in my opinion means to delegate it to the chief of some bureau in one of the departments.[1]

The situation at Niagara had caused concern for some years. It was not alone a question of scenery; it was also a question of proper regulation of a source of great water power. The first company to develop power at the Falls received a most generous grant from the New York Legislature in the early days of power development. Some time later a second company came along and during the exigencies of the Great War merged with the first company. When the companies, at the suggestion of the War Department, merged, they made application for reorganization to the New York State Legislature. They secured from the

[1] *Congressional Record*, 65th Cong., 2nd Sess., p. 9768.

legislature a special act approving their securities, thus avoiding examination by the Public Service Commission of the state. The House Committee on Foreign Affairs refused to approve of the financial plan which had previously been approved by the state legislature. The merger went on, however.[1] There can be no doubt that these companies were in a position to make a great deal of money. They controlled one of the country's greatest power sites, where power could be developed very cheaply. The chief expense in such a development would be the power houses and extension lines. At committee hearings before Congress it was shown that power could be developed at six dollars a horsepower, and yet in some instances the companies charged one hundred dollars a horsepower. Their average charge was about twenty-nine dollars a horsepower. Across the River in the Province of Ontario the charge was about $19.40. An illustration cited by Judson King, Director of the National Popular Government League, in 1924, is interesting on this point:

Another startling illustration that I found was the cost of lighting of the international bridge over the Niagara River. This bridge is lighted on the west half by the Ontario hydro system, and it is lighted on the east half by a private company operating in the United States. The same number of lights, the same bridge, the same river, the same method of production, average monthly cost for 1921 on the Canadian side $8.43 and on the American side $43.10.[2]

Representative Dempsey of New York in the House and Senator Wadsworth of New York in the Senate opposed any interference with the Niagara companies.

[1] *Congressional Record,* 65th Cong., 2nd Sess., pp. 10043-10044.

[2] *Hearings before Senate Committee on Agriculture and Forestry on S. 139, S. 372, S. 2747, S. 3214* and *H. R. 518,* 68th Cong., 1st Sess., p. 1209.

Representatives Doremus and Humphreys were responsible for the following important amendment:

That in issuing preliminary permits or licenses hereunder the commission shall give preference to applications therefor by states and municipalities provided the plans for the same are deemed by the commission adapted to conserve and utilize in the public interest the navigation and water resources of the region.[1]

This was accepted.

Representative Ferris strove mightily to knock out the net-investment provision. About three-quarters of an hour were used in trying to agree on the amount of time to be given to debate on this amendment. The net-investment provision remained. Mr. Ferris did not, however, lose hope, for when all discussion had come to an end, and after a great deal of parliamentary maneuvering, he moved to recommit the bill. The motion was lost by a vote of 133 to 128 with 167 not voting.

The vote in the House on the final passage showed 231 for, 23 against, 2 voting present, and 174 not voting. The negative votes were cast by the following:

Ayres	Hamlin	Sears
Baer	Haugen	Sisson
Booker	Humphreys	Thomas
Cooper (Wis.)	James	Thompson
Decker	London	Webb
Doremus	McKeown	Wingo
Ferris	Nichols (Mich.)	Walsh
French	Norton	

On September 19, 1918, the Water-Power Bill reached the Senate. It was sent to the Senate as an amendment to the Shields Bill. Senator Fletcher of Florida moved to send the bill to conference at once, despite the fact that it was

[1] *Congressional Record*, 65th Cong., 2nd Sess., p. 9805.

practically an entirely new bill. Senator Cummins of Iowa believed that the changes in the bill were too vital to be settled in conference.[1] Theoretically the conferees could have adopted any matter that was contained in either bill, but could not have adopted any new matter. How much of a variation of old matter makes new matter will always remain a disputed question. Senators Cummins and Shields remained for several days irreconcilable on the question of reference to a conference committee; both opposed the charge provisions and the recapture clauses. The motion to refer to conference, however, was agreed to after Senator Walsh of Montana caused to be adopted as a substitute a proposal requiring the appointment as conferees of three members of the Committee on Public Lands and three members of the Committee on Commerce. On September 27 Senators Shields (Tennessee), Bankhead (Alabama), Nelson (Minnesota), Myers (Montana), Pittman (Nevada), and Smoot (Utah) were appointed as the Senate conferees. From the House Representatives Sims, Ferris, Lever, Esch, Sinnott, and Haugen were appointed.[2]

In the meantime a Congressional election was pending. President Wilson had issued his memorable appeal for a Democratic Congress, bringing to an end the 'adjournment of politics' which had obtained during the war period. In the November election of 1918 the Democratic majority in Congress was overturned, and the Republicans secured control of both Houses by a narrow margin. President Wilson let it be known that he would not call an extra session after March 4, 1919, as he would be in Europe and did not wish Congress in session during that time. The Re-

[1] *Congressional Record,* 65th Cong., 2nd Sess., p. 10474.

[2] In the midst of the discussion on reference Senator Borah gave his views in favor of Governmental control and ownership of water power. These will be found in Appendix VI.

publicans, on the other hand, were anxious for the calling of the new Congress in extraordinary session and were determined to hold up important business in order to bring about such a session.

On February 1, 1919, an inquiry by Senator Jones of Washington as to the reason for the delay of the conference committee report brought the following explanation from Senator Bankhead:

That substitute for the Shields bill passed the other House, came over here, and a conference was ordered.

The Senator from Tennessee (Mr. Shields) was then in the Senate and was the chairman of that conference committee. Since that time he has been unable to attend the sessions of the Senate on account of the condition of his health. The chairmanship of the conference committee by that process fell to the Senator from Alabama, and the Senator from Florida (Mr. Fletcher) was substituted on the committee of conference in the place of the Senator from Tennessee. We had two or three conferences. The House conferees came over and practically told us, "If you want any legislation on this subject, you will take the House bill." We were not quite prepared to do that without some discussion, hoping that we might get some concessions, and that matters might so shape themselves that we would have a real conference where differences could be discussed, compromises made, and each side give and take in order that we might reach a conclusion. That situation lasted to the end of the second or third conference. It appeared that the conference was in a hopeless deadlock and that it was impossible to make any progress. So the conference adjourned with the understanding that the chairman should again call it in session when he thought proper to do so.

I promptly announced that when the House conferees were willing to meet the Senate conferees in a fair spirit and were willing to discuss the differences with us without telling us practically that we would take what they offered or nothing I would call another meeting of the conference. I have been waiting, thinking perhaps that something would develop. This morning I have been advised by the chairman of the House conferees that they are willing and ready—in fact, they are getting anxious—for another conference, in order that we may take up, discuss, and agree upon the differences in the bill. So I am going to call a conference for Monday afternoon at 2 o'clock; and I do not think there is any doubt that we will be able to get an agreement within a very reasonable time. That is the way I feel about it; and I make that statement to the Senate, believing that the conferees will report an agreement after one or two further sessions of the conference.[1]

The report of the conferees was introduced in the House by Representative Sims on February 26, 1919. The bill had been sent to conference September 30, 1918.[2]

The House got the better of the bargain so far as the report was concerned. The big differences between the House and the Senate were on the recapture clauses and on charges. The charge provision came back exactly as it had passed the House, providing that the licensee shall pay the United States reasonable annual charges in an amount to be fixed by the commission. No maximum, no minimum was set up. The Senate conferees receded from their disagreement to the net-investment clause but insisted that it should be made to read in part " upon the condition that before taking possession it (the Government) shall pay the net investment of the licensee in the project or projects *not to exceed the fair value of the property taken.*" (The part in italics is new). The change was made in the interest of clarity. Other changes were made but they need not be mentioned at this point. Representatives Esch and Sims both joined in praising the measure. Many members breathed sighs of relief that now the power fight was over

[1] *Congressional Record*, 65th Cong., 3rd Sess., p. 2509.

[2] *House Report 1147*, 65th Cong., 3rd Sess.

at last.[1] Some saw in this occasion an historic moment. But all was not peace. Minority Leader Mann called attention to the fact that the Senate definition of navigable streams which was adopted read that navigable waters as used in the act

> shall be construed to include only such streams or parts of streams as are in their ordinary natural condition used for the transportation of persons or property in interstate or foreign commerce, or which through improvement heretofore or hereafter made have been or shall become usable in such commerce.[2]

He reminded the House that this took very valuable sites out of the hands of the United States, particularly falls, shallows, or rapids of a stream. Thus, such a site as Muscle Shoals would be excluded. Because of this fact many progressives joined in voting against the bill which was passed by a vote of 263 to 65. A further objection put forward by Representative Mann is worth quoting:

> here is a conference report upon an extremely important subject presented to Congress in the closing days when everybody is pressed almost beyond endurance; with an hour's discussion permitted, of which so far as I know, those opposed to it get five minutes, and the subject proposed to be disposed of in that way after a controversy lasting eight or ten years.[3]

But what more could even a Congressman say after eight or ten years of discussion? Mr. Mann omitted to say what fitting services of farewell to this veteran subject he wished. Could it have been a ceremonial that would have lasted over into the extra session of a Republican Congress? Perhaps.

[1] *Congressional Record*, 65th Cong., 3rd Sess., pp. 4630-4636.

[2] *Congressional Record*, 65th Cong., 3rd Sess., p. 4638.

[3] *Ibid.*

At any rate, the Senate dealt the mortal blow. The conservationists about Congress were worried over the navigable streams definition and its exclusion of shoals sites. Senator La Follette consulted Philip P. Wells, formerly of the Forest Service, who had been active for many years in behalf of conservation water-power legislation. Mr. Wells told Mr. La Follette of his objections to the navigable streams definition.[1] Taking advantage, therefore, of the general legislative situation Senator La Follette joined in a filibuster to prevent the power bill from being enacted. The filibuster began with Senator La Follette taking the floor at two o'clock in the morning of March 4, 1919. At five-thirty in the morning he was relieved by Senator France of Maryland; at seven-thirty Senator France was relieved by Senator Sherman of Illinois who talked until eleven-thirty, when Vice President Marshall instead of adjourning the Senate *sine die,* adjourned it *sine deo.*[2]

During the filibuster, President Wilson sat in a nearby room in the Capital surrounded by members of his cabinet and receiving Democratic leaders. He sent in word to the Senate that no matter what happened he would refuse to call an extra session. A description of this closing drama of the Sixty-fifth Congress is given in the *New York Times* of March 5, 1919.

The scene in the Senate Chamber during the closing hours of the long filibuster was one which will be remembered by all who witnessed it. Democratic Senators were sitting back in their seats smiling grimly. For one, Senator Martin of Virginia, their floor leader, made no effort to conceal his feeling of bitterness.

He is a short, stocky man, well-past middle age, with snow

[1] *Hearings before Senate Committee on Agriculture and Forestry on S. 139, S. 2372,* etc., 68th Cong., 1st Sess., p. 1265.

[2] *New York Times,* March 5, 1919.

white hair. His features are sharp cut and his face deeply lined. He was worn out and his face was almost as white as his hair as he sat immovable. His fingers played a tattoo on the desk in front of him and his face was like a graven image, picturing a mixture of anger and contempt. . . . During the closing hour of the Congress Senator Lodge several times paced the floor of the Senate Chamber, watching Senator Sherman of Illinois, who was pouring out words which it seemed would never cease. Senator Lodge spoke briefly to Senator Martin, and the report went about that he was trying to aid that adept in parliamentary law in formulating a plan which might make adoption of the bill possible.

It must not be understood that the filibuster was arranged solely against the Water-Power Bill. That was but one item. The main consideration was the forcing of an extra session. Not alone did the Water-Power Bill go down to defeat, but the very important General Deficiency Bill went the same way. The latter bill carried large appropriations for government expenses already incurred. The comment of Senator France on the situation was:

I do not believe that the American people ever condemn men who have the courage to do their duty as they see it. I believe it is apparent to the whole nation that the interests of the country demand that Congress be in session in order to deal with the pressing reconstruction problem which is upon us and which has not as yet received that careful consideration which would have resulted in constructive action.[1]

Senator Sherman who promised to defeat the General Deficiency Bill unless he dropped dead was less charitable in his remarks:

We are willing to take that responsibility. If the constitution of the League of Nations is the result of his attendance

[1] *Ibid.*

at the Paris Conference and his administration of the railroads of the United States is the result of his constant attendance upon Congress, both Paris and Washington will be better off without him. He is a superfluous luxury, anyhow.[1]

And from President Wilson came the following:

A group of men in the Senate have deliberately chosen to embarrass the Administration of the Government, to imperil the financial interests of the railway systems of the country, and to make arbitrary use of powers intended to be employed in the interest of the people.

It is plainly my present duty to attend the Peace Conference in Paris. It is also my duty to be in close contact with the public business during a session of the Congress. I must make my choice between these two duties and I confidently hope that the people of the country will think that I am making the right choice.

It is not in the interest of the right conduct of public affairs that I should call the Congress in special session while it is impossible for me to be in Washington, because of a more pressing duty elsewhere, to cooperate with the Houses.

I take it for granted that men who have obstructed and have prevented the passage of necessary legislation have taken all of this into consideration and are willing to assume the responsibility of the impaired efficiency of the Government and the embarrassed finances of the country during the time of my enforced absence.[2]

In the Sixty-sixth Congress a special Water-Power Committee was again provided in the House[3] and Representative Esch of Wisconsin was named as its chairman. Eighteen members were appointed, all but four of whom served on the first Water-Power Committee. Owing to the fact that

[1] *Ibid.*

[2] *Ibid.*

[3] May 20, 1919.

extensive hearings had been held in the preceding Congress and owing to the fact that the personnel of the new committee was almost identical with the former committee, no further hearings were held and the bill as agreed to in conference in the previous session was reported on June 24, 1919. The new members of the House made some protest against the speed with which the new legislation was being put through, yet progress continued fairly rapid despite incidental discussions of the Treaty of Versailles, prohibition, the disgraceful treatment of the bodies of dead soldiers, the St. Lawrence Ship Canal and other things. With some changes the bill passed the House without a roll call July 1, 1919. The Senate referred the bill to its Committee on Commerce of which Mr. Jones of Washington was chairman, and, on September 12, 1919, a report came forth which showed that the Senate was up to its old tricks again.

The power given the proposed commission to fix reasonable annual charges was changed in such a way that only such charges could be levied as would reimburse the United States for the cost of administering the act. On the other hand, the navigable streams definition was so changed as to give the Government charge over rapids and shoals as demanded by the conservationists in the last Congress.[1]

The legal right of the Government to make a charge was fought all over again in the Senate. Senator Lenroot led the fight in behalf of a charge, and Senator Nelson led the fight against it. After the old debate was staged once more, the Senate in Committee of the Whole divided 28 to 29 against a government charge. The vote, unusually close for a Senate vote, indicated that times were changing and that the old opposition was indeed dying out, although reluctantly yielding up the ghost.

[1] *Senate Report 180*, 66th Cong., 1st Sess.

In the course of a rather uninteresting debate Senator Williams took occasion to lecture his colleagues on their inattention to important matters before the Senate. Part of the scolding follows:

It seems to me that this is a very important point, if we are going to take care of the interests of the people at large as against the interests of the people who may fall heir to these licenses, or whatever you may choose to call them, we ought to think about it three times before we vote.

I have long since lost interest in the ordinary machinery of politics; I do not care anything about it; I contemn and despise it; but there are times when men ought to stop and think awhile before they vote.

I find at this present moment that there are five Republican Senators present and that there are six Democratic Senators present. Those eleven Senators have heard the argument; none of the others has. This is a fair sample of the utility of the United States Senate to the people of the United States. . . .

Mr. President, I withdraw my last remarks. There are two more Republicans who have come in since I have made the reference. I ask that they be recorded. That is about the way the United States Senate, the fifth wheel in the Government of this country, is carrying itself. It is not paying any attention to its public business; I am not paying any attention to mine as a member of this august body; nobody else is. Old Benjamin Franklin was about right when he said this was the fifth wheel and ought to be dispensed with. The American people are gradually rising to the height of demanding the abolition of the United States Senate simply because the United States Senate does not function; it does not operate.

Do you know, Mr. President, I feel almost tempted to demand the presence of a quorum in order to determine the pending proposition? I will not do so because that would be unclublike, and I am a member of this club.[1]

[1] *Congressional Record,* 66th Cong., 2nd Sess., p. 1496.

Senator Williams' lecture struck fire. From King of Utah there came a lengthy defense of the Senate. Senator King called attention to the fact that when Senator Williams was speaking, more than twenty committee sessions were being held and a number of hearings being conducted, that some of these committees continued in session from ten in the morning until six in the evening, that Senators work from eight to twelve hours a day and some give fourteen hours a day for weeks at a time to their duties, that it is humanly impossible for each Senator to investigate the thousands of questions presented for consideration and be present in the Senate Chamber for all sessions, and that many feel in attending certain sessions they are missing very important work. He reminded the Senator from Mississippi that some Senators had to attend as many as four committee meetings in a day.[1] These are facts worth noting, for the casual observer and visitor to the United States Senate is painfully shocked at the sparse attendance.

A letter from Gifford Pinchot, read before the final vote, declared that certain provisions of the Senate Bill were anti-public and indefensible. The first and foremost objection cited by Mr. Pinchot was the omission of a charge except for administration purposes.[2] The vote on the final passage, however, showed fifty-two in favor of the bill, eighteen against, and twenty-five not voting. The list of opponents is worth mentioning:

Borah	Kirby	Reed
Gore	Lenroot	Sheppard
Gronna	McCormick	Stanley
Harris	McKellar	Trammell
Harrison	Norris	Walsh (Mass.)
Kenyon	Nugent	Williams

[1] *Congressional Record,* 66th Cong., 2nd Sess., p. 1526.

[2] *Congressional Record,* 66th Cong., 2nd Sess., p. 1573.

On January 17, 1920, the Water-Power Bill was back in the hands of the conferees. The outlook was not bright. The whole tedious process of wrangling in conference had to be gone through once more. Not until May 4, 1920, did the House get down to debate on the report from the conference as given by Mr. Esch. The result was not as complete a victory for the House as the previous result had been.[1] The navigable streams definition inserted by the Senate was accepted. In regard to the charge, the conferees accepted neither the broad provision of the House nor the charge-for-service provision of the Senate. The conference report provided for

(a) Reimbursing the Government for the administration of the act.

(b) Rent for United States land and property used.

(c) *Expropriation to the Government of excess profits,* until the respective states should make provision for preventing excess profits—in fixing charges the commission should avoid raising the price to consumers and charges of expropriation should be adjusted from time to time by the commission as conditions required.

This provision it will be seen recognized the rights of the states to take over the charging upon which certain Senators had been for so long insistent. The adequacy of the state provisions was to be judged by the commission. The placing of a charge in the nature of an excess profits tax was much easier to accept in the post-war days than at other times. The anti-charge people could say: "This, of course, is nothing more than an excess profits tax." The conservationists could say: "Call it anything you will, it is a charge just the same." In a way it was an ideal compromise, for it is difficult to see how the proud Senate could ever

[1] *House Report 910,* 66th Cong., 2nd Sess.

have recognized the charge *per se* after years of declaiming on the utter unconstitutionality—to say nothing of the iniquity—of a charge. It was a graceful "let-down" for the vanquished, and yet not the complete victory which the conservationists had looked forward to.

The conferees also compromised on parts of the recapture clause. The Senate provision was:

That in the event the United States does not exercise the right to take over or does not issue a new license to a new licensee, or tender a new license to the original licensee, upon the terms and conditions aforesaid, which is accepted, then the commission shall issue from year to year, etc.

The House provision was:

That in the event the United States does not exercise the right to take over and does not issue a new license to the original or a new licensee, then the commission shall issue from year to year an annual license to the then licensee under the terms and conditions of the original licensee.

The conference provision read:

That in the event the United States does not exercise the right to take over or does not issue a new license to the original licensee, upon reasonable terms. . . .

In the Senate amendment the words "which is accepted" would have resulted in a perpetual license because all the original licensee would have to say to the Government when it tendered him terms would have been, "These terms are not accepted; we will not accept them," and simply stand his ground.

The bill passed the House on May 4, 1920, by a vote of 259 to 30 with 137 not voting. After some discussion in the Senate, during which Senator Lenroot opposed the adoption of any but the broadest provision for charges, the bill was passed by a vote of 45 for, and 21 against, with 30 not voting. The opponents were:

Borah	Kenyon	Norris
Capper	Keyes	Nugent
Furnald	King	Phelan
France	Lenroot	Reed
Hale	McCormick	Sheppard
Harrison	McKellar	Trammell
Henderson	Moses	Walsh (Mass.)

On May 31, 1920, the completed act was presented to the President for signature. On June 5, 1920, Congress adjourned, thus bringing about what most people thought to be a pocket veto. Dismay was apparent among government leaders; the ill-fated measure seemed to have met one more set-back. Senator Jones of Washington called the veto a great calamity to the country.

I do not know why the President did it. The excuse given, and it is nothing more than an excuse, is that it came to the President too late.

The bill was sent to the President at 1:15 o'clock P. M. on the 31st day of May. He had it throughout the week. That was ample time to study it.[1]

After almost a dozen years of wrangling, postponements and deadlocks a real water-power bill had been enacted, only to meet defeat by executive neglect—or disdain. But all was not over. On June 18, there came from the White House a statement to the effect that the President had signed the Water-Power Bill on June 11. The White House statement read:

The President having been advised by the Attorney General (Palmer) in a formal opinion that the adjournment of Congress

[1] *New York Times*, June 8, 1920.

does not deprive him of the ten days allowed by the Constitution for the consideration of a measure, but only in case of disapproval of the opportunity to return the measure with his reasons to the House in which it originated, has signed the following bills, each within the ten days period, of course.[1]

The Power Bill and others were then enumerated.[2]

President Wilson was not the first president to sign a bill after adjournment of Congress; President Lincoln signed the Abandoned and Captured Property Act of 1863 just eight days following adjournment of Congress.[3] The Committee of the Judiciary of the House of Representatives on June 11, 1864, gave it as their unanimous opinion that the act of President Lincoln was *ultra vires.* Yet on July 2, 1864, Congress amended the Captured Property Act,[4] apparently recognizing its validity. The act was not tested in the United States Supreme Court.

It has been settled that the President may sign acts within the ten-day period following a recess and many acts have been so signed.[5] It makes no difference how long this re-

[1] *New York Times,* June 19, 1920.

[2] The following were the bills signed following adjournment:

H. R. 3184, water-power bill (Public 280).

H. R. 6407, for relief of Michael MacGarvey for damage caused to set of false teeth (Private 73).

H. R. 13962, bridge, Monongahela River, Pa. (Public 283).

H. R. 13976, bridge, Alleghany River, Pittsburgh, Pa. (Public 284).

H. R. 13977, bridge, Alleghany River, Midvale, Pa. (Public 285).

H. R. 13978, bridge, Ohio River, McKee's Rocks, Pa. (Public 286).

S. 547, to authorize enlistment of non-English speaking citizens and aliens in Army (Public 281).

S. 4167, bridge, Mississippi River, St. Louis, Mo. (Public 282).

[3] For a good discussion of the power of the President to sign acts after adjournmnet of Congress, see Professor Lindsay Rogers' article in the *Yale Law Journal,* November, 1920.

[4] The original act will be found in 12 *Stat.* 820; the amendment will be found in 13 *Stat.* 375.

[5] *La Abra Silver Mining Company v. United States* (1899), 175 U. S. 423.

cess may be. As Professor Rogers points out in his article in the *Yale Law Journal* referred to above, that the difference between a recess and an adjournment is one of nomenclature only; there is no change in the status of legislative business.[1]

Since the Constitution is not clear on the question of signing bills after adjournment,[2] it would seem to be a common-sense inference that the President has ten days for deliberation—ten days which have always been greatly needed. Whether the same can be said in regard to the situation on the fourth of March every odd year, especially when a President's term comes to an end is another question. All discussion of the point is purely academic until the Supreme Court passes judgment on the question. In the meantime, however, there is much justification for the President's action in signing the Water-Power Bill. Those who are superstitious and who believe that a fatal jinx bars the progress of water-power legislation wag their heads ominously when they think of the supreme judicial test.

At any rate, the Water-Power Bill is now in force.[3]

[1] *Rules* of the House of Representatives, No. XXVI, House *Manual and Digest*, 63rd Cong., 3rd Sess.

[2] See article i, section 7.

[3] The Act will be found in full in Appendix VII.

CHAPTER VI

The Progress of the Power Act

Philip Wells, one of the foremost leaders in the fight for effective power legislation, in looking back over the struggle, wrote as follows in 1924:

The strategy of the forces fighting for it was from first to last an application of economic and political theories of the conservation movement. They fought with whatever weapons they found at hand. First and most important, the immense prestige and force of President Roosevelt, without which they would have been swept off the field at the first shock of conflict; then the Executive Power broadly conceived and boldly used; then popular agitation through press and platform; then a change of party control in the House of Representatives; then the rivalry of two House Committees; lastly the legislative filibuster in a dangerous crisis.

Litigation in which all our basic legal and constitutional contentions were upheld by the Supreme Court should not be omitted from the list. Party lines cut no figure at any time. We found strong champions in both parties and hard-hitting opponents in both. We won first the Forest Service which remained steadfast throughout; then the general public, then the Department of Interior under Garfield, losing it under Ballinger, but recapturing it under Fisher; then the War Department under Stimson, then the House Committee on Public Lands; then the House Committee on Interstate and Foreign Commerce and the House Organization; last the Senate, though we had had a steadfast, hard-fighting, bi-partisan group of allies there from the first. Conspicuous on our side in the executive departments were President Roosevelt; Gifford Pinchot and

Henry S. Graves, Foresters; Herbert Knox Smith, Commissioner of Corporations; James R. Garfield and Walter L. Fisher, Secretaries of the Interior; Henry L. Stimson and Newton D. Baker, Secretaries of War; and Oscar C. Merrill, Engineer of the U. S. Forest Service, now Executive Secretary of the Federal Power Commission. In the House we had Parsons of New York, Kent of California, Lenroot of Wisconsin (later in the Senate), Ferris of Oklahoma, Sims of Tennessee; in the Senate, LaFollette of Wisconsin, Norris of Nebraska, Dolliver and Kenyon of Iowa, Gronna of North Dakota, Husting of Wisconsin, Lane of Oregon. Of course this list is far from complete. Geographically the opposition's stronghold was in the South and far West. The Senators from these sections were the old guard and held out longest. Our stronghold was the Middle West. The electrical industry fought us fiercely and unitedly from 1906 until 1911. Then they split for a time. The Stone and Webster interests accepted our principles and agreed with the Secretary of War Stimson upon the Connecticut Dam Bill as an application of them. This bill was defeated by the combination of Southern and far Western Senators in 1913. The industry again closed ranks in opposition until 1917. By that time we had definitely captured the House Organization and the industry sent in a flag of truce. Negotiations were resumed, and a general bill, better than we could have hoped for at the outset but still defective, passed both houses and was reported from conference committee. Amendment was now impossible, but we called upon LaFollette and he stopped it by threat of filibuster in the closing hours of the Congress that expired March 4, 1919. In the next Congress, negotiations were resumed, a satisfactory bill agreed upon and passed.[1]

The fight is not yet over. The aim must now be to keep what has been fought for. In the short time of its operation vigorous attacks have been made upon the Water-Power Act by the greatest industrial wizard of our day, Henry Ford, and by the State of New York.

[1] "Our Federal Power Policy" by Philip Wells, *Survey Graphic*, March, 1924, pp. 572-573.

Muscle Shoals

One of the greatest power sites in the world today is at Muscle Shoals on the Tennessee River in northern Alabama. The Tennessee River is formed by the confluence of the French Broad and the Holston Rivers, four and one-half miles above Knoxville; it flows southwesterly through the southeastern portion of Tennessee, thence westerly across the northern part of Alabama, thence almost due north across the states of Tennessee and Kentucky, and empties into the Ohio at Paducah, about forty-seven miles above the mouth of the Ohio at Cairo, Illinois.[1] The total length of the river is 652 miles, and the total area drained is over 40,000 square miles. The Muscle Shoals[2] section extends from

[1] Table of Distances

		Miles
Junction of French and Holston		0.
Knoxville		4½
Chattanooga		188
Hales Bar (Miles below Chattanooga,	33)	221
Widow's Bar	56)	244
Belle Fonte	73)	261
Guntersville	106)	294
Decatur	160)	348
Head of Brown's Island		359
Florence (Miles below Head of Brown's Island	37)	396
Head of Colbert Shoals	58)	417
Riverton	87)	426
Paducah, Ky. (Confluence with Ohio,	226.5)	652

[2] The origin of the name *Muscle* Shoals is unknown. "According to legend, the name for the shoals comes to us from the Indians. The red man, making his way up the river, found that it took what we call muscle to put his birch canoe over the rocky shoals, and with characteristic directness called them accordingly. The early white man, being of the same opinion but finding the Indian name difficult, gave us the present translation. However the prosaic etymologists and geologists like to argue with the legend. They claim that the name was derived from an innocent little bi-valve which played a leading role in the formation of the shoals, and that the correct spelling of the name was lost in the early days, probably due to the lack of proper educational advantages in that period." C. F. Adams in the New York *Nation*, March 26, 1924.

Brown's Island, Alabama, to Florence in same state, a distance of thirty-seven miles over which the swift waters twist and swirl in a vertical fall of 134 feet. An early explorer of this region gave his first impressions of the Shoals in the following words:

> When we approached them,[1] they had a dreadful appearance. . . . The water being high, made a terrible roaring, which could be heard at some distance, among the driftwood heaped frightfully upon the points of the islands, the current running in every possible direction. . . . I know not the length of this wonderful shoal; it had been represented to me to be about 25 or 30 miles. If so, we descended very rapidly, as indeed we did, for we passed it in about three hours.[2]

As early as 1836 the state of Alabama aided by the Federal Government constructed a lock-canal, affording a depth of five feet, around the shoals. Because of obstructions above and below,[5] the canal was used but little and was soon abandoned. In 1868 the Federal Government began the construction of a canal in two divisions; one of the divisions is three and five-tenths miles long with two locks, and the other is fourteen and five-tenths miles long with nine locks. The depth afforded by these two canals, which are eight miles apart, is five feet. Only in part do they remove the barrier to navigation. In 1904 a permit was granted by Congress "to the city of Chattanooga or other private corporation" to develop power at Hales Bar.[3] From that time forward the Shoals have owed their importance to the great possibilities in the development of hydroelectricity.[4]

[1] The shoals.

[2] *Journal* (March 12, 1779), Captain John Donelson.

[3] Above at the Colbert and Bee Tree Shoals and below at Hales Bar.

[4] See Chapter II, p. 27.

[5] For an official account of the development of the Tennessee River see *House Document 1262*, 64th Cong., 1st Sess.

For a thorough understanding of the Ford proposal, it is necessary to go back to the passage of the National Defense Act of June 30, 1916.[1] Under section 124 of this act the President was authorized to:

construct, maintain, and operate, at any site or sites so designated, dams, locks, improvements to navigation, power houses and other plants and equipment . . . as in his judgment is the best and cheapest, necessary, or convenient means for the generation of electrical or other power, and for the production of nitrates or other products needed for munitions of war and useful in the manufacture of fertilizers and other useful products.

In a letter dated February 23, 1918, the President authorized the construction by the Government of a dam at Muscle Shoals to carry out the purposes of the Defense Act.[2] This dam, at first known as Dam No. 2, became known as the Wilson Dam. Situated six miles southwest of Dam No. 2, at Sheffield, Alabama, is United States nitrate plant No. 1, constructed by the United States during the War under an agreement with the General Chemical Co. at a total cost of $12,887,941.31. This plant, built under the supervision of the Ordnance Department, was expected to produce 22,000 tons of ammonium nitrate per annum. The plant, however, proved unsuccessful in a test operation and is now idle. The cost of upkeep is about $75,000 per year.[3]

Four miles northeast of nitrate plant No. 1 is plant No. 2 constructed under contract with the Air Nitrates Corporation for the production of munitions of war. The total expense of construction was over sixty-seven million dollars. The plant was built for an estimated capacity of 110,000

[1] 39 *Stat.* 166, 125.

[2] Letter of the Secretary of War, *House Document 167*, 67th Cong., 2nd Sess.

[3] *Ibid.*

tons of ammonium nitrate per year. During the short time of its operation the plant was successful. The munitions plant is now idle, but the power plant was leased, under a license revocable at any time, to the Alabama Power Company.[1] About twenty miles south of plant No. 2, and purchased in connection with it, is Waco Quarry embracing an area of 460 acres. The quarry has a crushing plant sufficient to produce 2,000 tons of crushed and sized limestone per day. The cost of the quarry including all equipment, was $1,179,076.80.[2] The quarry is not being operated.

Eighty-eight miles southeast of nitrate plant No. 2, at Gorgas, Alabama, is the Warrior steam plant. The plant was constructed under contract with the Alabama Power Company on land owned by that company. A nearby coal mine supplies fuel for operating the plant which has a capacity of 30,000 kilowatts. The power from the plant is transmitted to nitrate plant No. 2. The total cost of this plant was $4,979,782.33. The property is being operated by the Alabama Power Company on a rental basis. It brings the Government over $70,000 a year.[3]

The Wilson Dam, now completed, has a total length of 4,267 feet, of which 2,890 is a spillway, 1,221 feet is a power house section, and 156 feet are abutments and approaches. The height of the dam above low water is 95 feet. The dam will form a navigable lake eighteen miles in length. A comparison with other great dams on the basis of the number of cubic yards of masonry required is interesting.[4]

[1] *Ibid.* The lease was granted under the act of Congress of July 28, 1892 (27 *Stat.* 321).

[2] *Ibid.*

[3] *Ibid.*

[4] Figures compiled by the District Engineer, Florence, Alabama, January, 1924.

Wilson Dam	1,291,385 cu. yds.
Assuan, Egypt	1,179,000 " "
Kensico, N. Y.	942,000 " "
New Croton, N. Y.	855,000 " "
Keokuk, Iowa–Ill.	540,000 " "
Arrowrock, Idaho	530,000 " "
Olive Bridge, N. Y.	488,200 " "
Tanso, India	408,520 " "
Poona, India	360,000 " "
Roosevelt, Arizona	344,000 " "

The capacity of the Wilson Dam is estimated at 624,000 horsepower, the equivalent of about 2,500,000 tons of coal per year. The cost of the project will be about $50,000,000.

Government construction at Muscle Shoals was a war measure, and with the ending of hostilities in November, 1918, the question at once arose, "What is to be done with this vast enterprise?" The thought of the Government going into the business of manufacturing fertilizer for the farmer and thus entering into competition with private enterprise was not entertained by most officials at Washington. After the beginning of the Harding administration, Secretary of War Weeks stated that before he would recommend to the Congress the appropriation of more funds for the completion of the Wilson Dam he would first ascertain if there would be a market for the power developed from the dam.[1] Accordingly the Chief of Engineers endeavored to get offers. No one seemed to be interested. One of the companies approached—The Southern Power Company—advised against the completion of the work.[2] At this time Henry Ford and Thomas A. Edison visited the Muscle Shoals district. It is said that the comment of Mr. Ford on seeing the work was: "The destiny of the American people for centuries lies here." [3]

[1] *Congressional Record*, 67th Cong., 2nd Sess., p. 3699.

[2] *Ibid.*

[3] *The Truth About Muscle Shoals* by Richard C. Henry (Chicago), p. 27.

On July 8, 1921, came the Ford offer for developing Muscle Shoals. Congress received the proposal on February 2, 1922.[1] The Ford proposal was incorporated in a bill and introduced in the House.[2] Hearings were held before the House Committee on Military Affairs from February 8, 1922 to March 13, 1922. At these hearings appeared representatives of the power companies of the South, especially the Alabama Power Company, to oppose the Ford proposition. Mr. Ford's proposal had evidently brought visions of an aggressive and successful competitor who would place the southern power groups in an uncomfortable position. Abandoning their disinterestedness in Muscle Shoals, they now became active bidders for developing the site. Mr. Ford offered to form a corporation with a cash capital of $10,000,000. He would pay to the Government $5,000,000 for nitrate plants No. 1 and No. 2 with the Waco limestone quarry, at the same time guaranteeing to produce every year commercial fertilizer containing at least 40,000 tons of fixed nitrogen. This fertilizer he would sell to the farmer at a cost not to exceed eight per cent profit on the manufacturing cost. Nitrate plants 1 and 2, however, would be bought on condition that the Ford Corporation would have a lease of 100 years on Muscle Shoals, and that the Government would finish building the dams there. At the conclusion of the lease, Mr. Ford would have first option on the renewal of the lease. The Ford Corporation would undertake to complete the Wilson Dam (No. 2) and Dam No. 3,[3] which had never been begun. An annual rent equal to four per cent of the actual cost of construction, excluding $17,000,000 spent by the Government on the Wilson Dam

[1] *House Document No. 167*, 67th Cong., 2nd Sess.

[2] *H. R. Bill 518*, 68th Cong., 1st Sess.

[3] This dam would make the Tennessee River navigable for sixty-three additional miles. It was situated 14 miles upstream from Dam No. 2.

prior to May 31, 1922, was to be paid.[1] A sum of $55,000 would be paid yearly for the maintenance of the locks and dams. Nitrate plant No. 2 was to be maintained in a state of readiness for the manufacture of explosives in case of war. A board of nine members named by national farm organizations, the President of the United States, and the Ford corporation would judge of the fairness of prices charged.[2]

A competing offer was made by the Alabama Power Company through the Secretary of War and referred to the House Committee on Military Affairs on February 22, 1922.[3] Offers came in from other companies from time to time, and on January 8, 1924 several of these companies joined in an offer submitted in a letter to Mr. Merrill, Executive Secretary of the Federal Power Commission.[4] The companies adopted the joint name of the Associated Power Companies of the South. These companies were: The North Carolina Electrical Power Company, the Memphis Power and Light Company, the Alabama Power Company, the Central Georgia Power Company, the Yadkin River Power Company, the Tennessee Electric Company, and the Columbus Electric Power Company. The offer of the associated companies provided for a lease of Muscle Shoals under the provisions of the Federal Water-Power Act, without any option on the renewal of the lease. They agreed to manufacture 50,000 tons of nitrate a year.[5] They offered to lease one of the nitrate

[1] It is estimated that the rental would be about $2,400,000 a year.

[2] The Secretary of Agriculture or his representative was to sit as an advisory member.

[3] *House Document 192*, 67th Cong., 2nd Sess.

[4] For the letter of Mr. Merrill and the offer of the companies see *Congressional Record*, 68th Cong., 1st Sess., pp. 813-815.

[5] An excellent comparison of the two competing bills (H. R. 518—Ford and H. R. 6781—Associated Power Companies) is found in *House Report 143*, 68th Cong., 1st Sess.

plants, but made no proposition to buy the plants. The companies offered to have 90,000 tons of nitrogen available in case of war and to turn over the nitrate plant on government demand in war time. The companies agreed to devote $1,000,000 to research work on the improvement in the manufacture of fertilizers. The total rental for the fifty years offered by the companies, to be paid in annual installments, amounted to something over $150,000,000. All the provisions of the Power Act such as the right of recapture, regulation of rates and service by the state or the Government, payment for headwater improvements, and general supervision by the Federal Power Commission would apply under this offer.

Mr. Ford consistently refused to submit to the conditions of the Federal Water-Power Act. Herein his offer was open to attack from many quarters, especially from the Pinchot conservation group which in this instance found themselves allied with their old foes, the big power companies.[1] Mr. Ford also refused to give testimony in person before congressional committees. It seemed particularly unfortunate that after so many years of struggle for power legislation, efforts were being made to obtain exemption from the provisions of that legislation for one of the greatest industrial wizards the world has ever known. The provisions of the act are certainly inclusive enough, and so drawn as to relieve Congress of the troublesome task of preparing special legislation for each power project. The Act was hailed on all sides as a great step in the development of our power resources; we seemed at the time to have solved a great problem. Yet within four years Mr. Ford, with an

[1] A National Committee for the Defense of the Federal Power Act was set up with Philip A. Wells as Secretary and including practically the whole Pinchot group. Its headquarters were set up at 719 Woodward Building, Washington, D. C.

admiring and loyal host, attempted to rush the barriers set up to protect the people in the use of a great resource. Once again all the old opposition to the conservationists' plans flared up. As evidence of this, note the following:[1]

WEAKNESS OF FEDERAL POWER ACT

IS NOW EXPOSED—HOW MUCH FAT DID PINCHOT'S COMMITTEE FRY OUT OF THE POWER INTERESTS?—WILL CONGRESS ADJOURN WITHOUT DOING ANYTHING FOR THE FARMER?

FARM AND HOME'S "DIRT FARMER AT THE NATIONAL CAPITOL AT WASHINGTON" LETS MORE LIGHT IN UPON THE GOINGS ON THERE.

"Is it a blind to mislead Congress and public into believing that the Federal water-power act is all right?" This question is being raised by some of the shrewdest observers of the Muscle Shoals controversy.

"That act of June 10, 1920, regulates nothing and does not protect the people, but does aid and protect the hydroelectric interests," declares one who ought to know. Perhaps this explains why these power interests are fighting to preserve that law and the Federal Power Commission. The latter consists of the Secretaries of Treasury, Agriculture, and War, and apparently is run by the director, O. C. Merrill.

In the short time since the law was enacted—that is, up to January last—applications to the commission for permits to develop power, on navigable rivers or in rivers within public lands, reached the enormous sum of 21,500,000 horsepower, or more than twice the total water power previously developed in the United States. Licenses were granted for 7,500,000 horsepower, of which one-third is built or building.

Yet it now appears that about the only authority which the commission has in safeguarding the public is the possible right to refuse a license to an overcapitalized corporation. Director Merrill admits issuing licenses for constructing plants "the fair

[1] "Weakness of the Federal Water-Power Act," *Farm and Home*, June, 1924.

value of which will aggregate probably $100,000,000," but confesses that "because of lack of personnel we have been able to accomplish but little in the way of valuation of these projects."

How scant the commission's knowledge may be is shown by its approval of two dams across the Cumberland River from shore to shore without locks, thus completely obstructing navigation and preventing the westward movement of coal by water from the great coal fields east of Nashville. Fortunately this error was frustrated by the Chief of Army Engineers.

Fortunately, also, Congress doubtless will pass Chairman Dempsey's bill "for the preparation of a general plan for the most effective navigation improvement, in combination with the most efficient development of the potential water power on those navigable streams of the United States and their tributaries where such power development seems feasible." Until such survey, even the power grabbers will be in the dark, and may repeat the costly mistake of one corporation which by developing 25,000 horsepower spoiled what at relatively less expense would have yielded 150,000.

The Dempsey bill also would complete the survey of Tennessee River and its tributaries, where 52 dams in the upper reaches mean 3,000,000 horsepower. When a survey is completed as thorough as that of the Muscle Shoals stretch of the Tennessee, it may reveal 6,000,000 horsepower as yet undeveloped in the Tennessee, Cumberland, Warrior, Coosa, and Chatahoochee River systems. This rivals the power possibilities of the Colorado River, which latter may absorb a billion of public funds if Congress permits. The Mississippi also probably could yield as much energy.

If Muscle Shoals is not awarded to Ford it will be partly because of public protest against a perpetual franchise. Apparently the public does not know that every license issued by the Federal Power Commission is in effect a perpetual grant. Neither has a word been said against the perpetual rights on the Little Tennessee River possessed by Mellon's aluminum interests. They have 75,000 horsepower already developed, and 400,000 more in sight, dominating a vast area and a common necessity of life. Another perpetual grant to a private corporation is the dam across the Mississippi at Keokuk, Iowa. And a franchise for 99 years was granted by special act of Congress to the corporation that develops hydroelectricity at Hales Bar on the Tennessee.

If "sacrifice of the public welfare" is threatened at Muscle Shoals, some Senators are asking, "How about Keokuk, Hales Bar, Mellon's monopoly and millions that are being licensed under the Federal act?" The Senate knows, but the public may not know, that whoever operates Muscle Shoals must obey the Alabama State Public Service Commission as to rates, location of lines, distribution of current and service. Its power may be sent outside the State only when the state commission decides that it is not all needed within the state. And Director Merrill declares that, "even when the power developed enters interstate commerce, the Federal Power Commission is not expected to act unless the states directly concerned can not reach an agreement."

The latest offer for Muscle Shoals is Union Carbide Co's minimum guarantee of $120,000,000 for a 50-year lease. That company "will manage the entire properties and operate and maintain them at its own expense for the use of one-fourth of the hydroelectric energy developed there, make fertilizer, and pay a yearly rental of $175,000." This is much higher than the same company's first offer, and makes the fourth proposal in addition to the Ford offer.

How queer the true inwardness of certain propaganda down here. One Philip P. Wells, as secretary of a "national committee for the defence of the Federal power act," 719 Woodward Building, Washington, D. C., printed in the Wall Street Journal, November 13, 1922, an interview in behalf of that committee opposing the Ford offer for the reasons repeated by Governor Pinchot last month. The latter seems to have been the inspiration and leading member of the committee. At least two other gentlemen, upon learning that Secretary Wells was collecting funds from the power interests to support the committee's propaganda, resigned therefrom. It is not yet publicly known how much fat Wells fried out of the then 357 applicants for 21,000,000 horsepower. Some Senators who insist upon action before Congress adjourns point out that in 12 or 18 months there will be 360,000 horsepower ready to serve at Wilson Dam powerhouse with nothing to serve it to unless provision is made now. They protest against repeating a worse mistake than that of shutting down the Government nitrate plant since November, 1918, when farmers have most needed cheaper fertilizer.

Analysis shows that the two newest offers for Muscle Shoals merely propose cost plus for fertilizer production. It will be remembered that the Alabama Power Company's offer did not agree to operate the nitrate plants or produce any fertilizer. Even when the power group came in at last, they did not tackle nitrate plant No. 2, but offered to make their fertilizer development at No. 1 plant.

What certain Senators are trying to find out is the why of so much effort to defeat the establishment of the nitrogen industry as a key industry in the United States. It has already become a key industry in Germany. The evidence shows that Germany already has a capacity to produce 500,000 tons annually of pure nitrogen from her coke ovens and from her war-built nitrogen fixation plants. Germany thinks she possesses a monopoly of potash salts in her natural deposits.

And throughout all the international politics and readjustments from armistice down to this time the German potash syndicate seems to have skated in between all liabilities and exactions and to-day stands unfettered. All this goes to prove the truth of the latest opinion that Germany proposes to dominate the fertilizer market. Indeed, the new German process for producing urea at extraordinary low cost but very rich in nitrogen is another step in the same direction. How petty, by comparison, is the proposal to make 40,000 tons of pure nitrogen yearly at Muscle Shoals.

Further study of the Ford proposal in connection with the proposal of the Associated Power Companies reveals that Mr. Ford by having an option at release might perpetuate the control on Muscle Shoals for the Ford heirs. *Mr. Ford made no guarantee of price on fertilizers to the farmer.* He promised that his profits would not exceed eight per cent *on the cost of production.* Much, therefore, depended upon the cost of production. In debate on that subject in the House, Mr. Burton of Ohio, a vigorous opponent of the Ford offer, put these questions to Mr. McKenzie of Illinois who had charge of the Ford bill:

On what basis is this 8 per cent to be computed? Is it the value of the permanent property? Is the right of the lessee to be counted in? Is the value of the water power to be counted in? Or is this merely on the bare cost of manufacturing fertilizers?

Mr. McKenzie replied:

I will say to my distinguished friend from Ohio that I cannot answer that question categorically. I do not know.[1]

The Ford proposal required deeds from the Government for nitrate plants No. 1 and No. 2, the Waco quarry, the Gorgas-Warrior steam plant with all its appurtenances—all worth over $93,000,000—with no right to recapture. The power companies required leases only for these properties. Under the Ford proposal there would be little or no regulation of rates and service such as the Power Act requires. Mr. Ford's rental offer amounting to about $240,000,000 for one hundred years is much lower than the offer of $150,000,000 for fifty years offered by the power companies.

Mr. Ford's proposal was accepted by the House of Representatives on March 10, 1924 by a vote of 227 to 143.[2]

[1] "Mr. Ford is so Good," William Hard in the New York *Nation*, March 26, 1924.

[2] *Congressional Record*, 68th Cong., 1st Sess., p. 3927.

This success of Mr. Ford's offer may be laid to the tremendous prestige of the man who had had such phenomenal success in identifying his industrial achievements with the welfare of the people, to the current idea that the Ford offer embodied a definite promise of cheap fertilizer to the farmer, and to the activity of hordes of real estate men who had gone to Muscle Shoals, bought up large tracts of land, and hoped for great profits on their investment in the event of Ford's plan being carried out.[1] As to Mr. Ford's prestige note the comment of William Hard:

> Two reasons really are found for this extraordinarily exceptional treatment accorded to Mr. Ford.
>
> The first is that Mr. Ford is a heap big medicine man and a different man from all other men and a friend of the people and a seller of cars at a low price and a payer of high wages and a developer of the American country-side and a man who is good. He is a good man. Therefore the Water-Power Act should not apply to him. The constitution of Italy should not apply to Mussolini. The Water-Power Act of the United States should not apply to Mr. Ford. Both Mussolini and Mr. Ford are supermen. It was supposed that Italy, having had experience with Marius and Sulla and Julius Caesar, should welcome supermen beyond the law. It was not known that this republic had advanced so far toward the condition of the Roman Republic in the first century before Christ.
>
> The second reason for Mr. Ford's exemption from the common American applicants before the federal Water-Power Commission is only an intensification of the first reason. It is that Mr. Ford is so good that he has gained the respect and support of our farm organizations irrespective of the consequences to all other elements of the population.
>
> The essential combined ultimate reason is that Mr. Ford is

[1] There might also be mentioned the strength given the Ford offer by the definite approval of President Coolidge and by the opposition of the great power trust.

so good. At least he cashes in on it. He gets the largest, the most expensive, the most indefinitely and miraculously valuable public property of the United States Governement at a fraction of its value for that part of it which he buys and at 2.85 per cent interest payments on the part of it which he leases.

Naturally and with all of his native and charming and poignant and devastating wit the radical Senator from Nebraska, Mr. Norris, inquires:

" Has it come to this, that because a man is good and great, and because we have confidence in him, we should give him a special privilege and a particular inheritance that we would give to no one else? Has it come to this, that a citizen can come to Congress and, because he is honest and upright, claim that contracts made for ordinary men shall not apply to him? Should a municipality permit a Christian to charge a higher rate for lighting the homes of the city than it would permit an infidel to charge? Have we reached the point of saying that we are going to permit good men to capitalize their virtue and to be paid a premium for it out of the Treasury of the United States?"

It would be an impertinence to add anything to these remarks by Mr. Norris.[1]

As to the real estate speculators the following comment describes the situation:

Mr. Ford made that carefully hedged offer two years ago. There was no unanimity on the subject, and much agitation at the time against the acceptance of the bid; the matter was allowed to drag. Observe what happened in the meantime. Real-estate speculators descended in a body on Muscle Shoals. They plotted out the country into lots, for miles in all directions. They bought it cheap, of course, and saved most of their money for "literature." They sent this literature out in the most approved California-Florida style, by the ton load. The country surrounding Muscle Shoals was described as a second heaven. Mr. Ford was to be god, and he was only awaiting a

[1] "Mr. Ford is so Good," New York *Nation*, March 26, 1924.

mandate from Congress to come in and take his throne. The streets were shortly to be paved with gold. The response to the invitation was all that the hopeful heart of any speculator could desire. With the usual sprinkling of widows, orphans, and school-teachers came a generous arrival of farmers. All of these buyers immediately began to inform their congressmen that the country could only be saved by giving Mr. Ford Muscle Shoals. They were of course more interested in saving their investments than saving the country, but congressmen cannot be expected to know such things.

In the meantime, in addition to the ordinary selling literature, the original speculators sent out special farmer literature advertising the wholly mythical idea that Mr. Ford intended to manufacture fertilizer for the farmers at half its present cost. The farmers were charmed with the thought, and even those who had not bought land immediately began petitioning congressmen to give them cheap fertilizer by giving Mr. Ford Muscle Shoals. Farmers sent letters; their farmer-organizations sent lobbies; the sanguine speculators laid aside a fund for lobbying as well as for circulars; in the meantime Mr. Ford also began pulling his wires.

He has denied that he has ever financed any propaganda in favor of his bid. In view of Mr. Ford's action in permitting his biographer to state unblushingly that all of the Ford war-profits had been returned to the Government, Mr. Ford's asseverations or denials are perhaps not to be taken too seriously. If we accept his claim that he has never financed any direct propaganda, the evidence that he has done it by indirection seems too large to be ignored. The exact extent of this propaganda expenditure will probably never be known—just as the direct and indirect expenditure made in the attempt to put a large share of the country's oil resources in the hands of one or two men will probably never be known.[1]

By the time the bill came up for discussion in the Senate[2]

[1] "Henry Ford, Man or Superman," New York *Nation*, March 26, 1924.

[2] Actual discussion began March 21, 1924.

opposition to Mr. Ford's offer had grown considerably. Wide publicity was given to Mr. Ford's proposal and to the alternative proposals, with the result that Senatorial approval was impossible.

The Senate Committee on Agriculture and Forestry gave extensive hearings [1] on all of the Muscle Shoals bills.[2] After several weeks Senator Norris, Chairman of the committee, came forward with a report.[3] Amendments to the House bill as suggested by the report recommended that the Secretary of War should be authorized to complete the dams at Muscle Shoals; that a corporation, the Federal Power Corporation, should be created to be managed by a board of three appointed by the President with the advice and consent of the Senate; that the members of this board should hold office during good behavior, removal being secured by a concurrent resolution of the House and the Senate; that this board should have full powers of management over Muscle Shoals and over the production of fertilizers and explosives; that in case there should be surplus power above the needs of the corporation in its production of fertilizers and explosives, the board would be empowered to lease that surplus to a public or private corporation; that this corporation should turn over to the United States all earnings over $25,000,000, and should supply the Government with enough power to operate all locks built for the improvement of navigation on the Tennessee River.[4] After weeks of wrangling in the Senate Mr. Ford withdrew his offer. Mr. Underwood, with the assistance of President Coolidge endeavored to put through a special fifty-year leasing plan, but in this he failed. Mr. Norris' plan for continued government

[1] 68th Cong., 1st Sess.

[2] *S. 139, S. 2372, S. 2747, S. 3214* and *H. R. 518.*

[3] *Senate Report 678,* 68th Cong., 1st Sess.

[4] A very interesting part of this report deals with "Ford propaganda."

ownership, with the option of operation by the Government or by a private agency under strict government control, also failed. A Federal commission is now investigating the problem of the disposition of Muscle Shoals.[1] A quotation of Newton D. Baker on this subject is worth noting:

To grant Muscle Shoals to any individual or company for a hundred years, or even fifty years, grants to such company or individual industrial dominance for that period of the whole southeastern portion of our country. . . . All the figures one sees about the gifts in present values in money to Mr. Ford or other proposed lessees are trifling as compared with the growing value of the industrial power that any such lease necessarily entails. . . . I am therefore clearly of the belief that Congress should retain Muscle Shoals, provide for its operation directly by the corps of engineers of the army or by a public corporation analogous to the Panama Railroad Company, and through such operation deal with the power produced in the mass, without entering into retail operation. By so doing the public interest, which we now see to be large, will be continuously served, and as the importance of this power source grows the hand of the Government will be free to make it continuously serviceable in the highest degree as the changing public interest demands.[2]

[1] The commission has since reported. The commission is hopelessly divided over the question of government or private operation. In his message to the Sixty-ninth Congress, December 8, 1925, President Coolidge displayed some impatience over the whole matter when he said: "If anything were needed to demonstrate the almost utter incapacity of the National Government to deal directly with an industrial and commercial problem, it has been provided by our experience with this property. We have expended vast fortunes, we have taxed everybody but we are unable to secure results which benefit anybody. This property ought to be transferred to private management under conditions which will dedicate it to the public purpose for which it was conceived."

Mr. Coolidge told the Congress that he was sending on the report of the special commission "for their information." The President added, however, that it might be well for Congress to appoint a committee of its own.

[2] "Muscle Shoals—Ours," New York *Nation*, December 17, 1924.

OTHER TESTS OF THE POWER ACT

In June of 1922 the State of New York instituted a suit in the Supreme Court of the United States to test the validity of the Federal Power Act as to those portions which give the Power Commission certain rights of jurisdiction over power enterprises on navigable streams within a state. Governor Miller procured the initiation of the suit denying the authority of the Federal Government to act under the Federal Power Act in New York, especially in regard to the Niagara and St. Lawrence water powers. The Solicitor General of the United States demurred, upon which the attorneys for the State of New York got leave to amend their complaint. The new complaint was based on control of the water powers from the Barge Canal which had been built by the state. When Governor Smith came into office he sent a special message to the Legislature on the water-power question. He recommended:

That seventy-five thousand dollars ($75,000) be made immediately available to the Attorney General to enable him to defray the expenses of the action now pending and begun by the state against the federal government designed to determine the right, control and jurisdiction of the state over the navigable waters within its borders for power development.

This action should be prosecuted with the utmost care, vigor and dispatch in order that this vital question be finally determined. We have already delayed too long. While we have been debating and bickering over the enactment of laws for the progressive development of our great water power under state ownership and control the Federal Government has enacted a water-power law which challenges our right, authority, and jurisdiction over the navigable waters of our state in all matters relating to power development.

The Federal Government contends that it has the right, authority, and jurisdiction to control and dictate by license how, when, and where developments are to be made on the Niagara and St. Lawrence Rivers as well as all other navigable streams of the state. Such right and authority, if sustained, would enable the Federal Government to deprive the State of New York and its people of this priceless heritage bestowed upon us by the Creator himself. In the final analysis it would permit the Federal Government to divert the energy created by the fall of water in our streams to other states against our will. The bed of our streams over which power-creating water flows belongs to the state, or, better still, to its citizens. Our use and control of the same are threatened. I am credibly advised that a strong and determined propaganda is now being spread in support of a plan to divert the electrical energy from our border streams to territory outside the state. This we must resist with all the power that we can bring to our command.

No pending public question is of more moment to the people of this state than the development of this great resource. It has been exploited in the past in the interest of private corporations that have operated it for private gain. What remains of it must be developed in accordance with the enlightened thought of to-day, and that I take it to be by the state itself, under state ownership and state control, to the end that all of the people may be able to realize the individual benefit which should flow to them from their own resources and their own property.[1]

Not many days later Governor Pinchot of Pennsylvania wrote a letter of protest to Governor Smith:

I have read with great interest your water-power message of March 5, and I wish you every success in your effort to furnish to the people generally, at cost, electric energy from the undeveloped water-power resources within and on the borders of your State.

For your information, I enclose copy of my letter of March 5 to W. Clyde Harer, Chairman of the Committee on Appropriations of the Pennsylvania House of Representatives, recommending an appropriation of $35,000 for a survey to outline a giant power system intended finally to supply all industries

[1] *New York Evening Post,* March 6, 1923.

farms and homes in this state with cheap and dependable electric energy.

In pursuing such a plan we must make certain that the abuses and blunders which grew out of the unrestrained selfish struggle in the field of transportation are not repeated. At the same time, as one means to our end, we must insure a fair chance for reasonable profit on private investments prudently made in good faith.

After eighteen years of study and work upon this problem, I have come confidently to expect the growth of a nation-wide interlocking power system; no small part of this future power development, especially water-power development, will, I believe, be made by state municipal enterprise—some, perhaps, by national or even international undertakings. The nation is now constructing works for the installation of 480,000 water horse power at Muscle Shoals, Alabama, and vast projects are urgently pressed for development by the National Government on the Colorado, the Columbia and the St. Lawrence. You are now proposing state development for New York.

I look to see the scope of state enterprise in this field increase rather than diminish. Yet I do not expect that private enterprise, at least for many years to come, will be wholly excluded from the field, and especially not from the field of electric power generated from fuel.

Pennsylvania's power resources lie chiefly in her coal deposits. These have passed into private ownership, yet they remain, like all other private property, under the political control of the state. Having this legal status, they have always been and are now being fully shared through commerce with all sister states within practicable transportation distance.

The freedom of commerce among the several states, the unrestricted exchange across state lines of services, goods and resources guaranteed by the Federal Constitution, is the strongest man-made basis of the prosperity of each state. This consideration applies not only to energy riding in a coal car, but equally to energy floating over a wire, whether the burning of fuel or the falling of water was the source. Furthermore, really cheap power cannot be supplied to consumers unless the burning coal and the flowing water contribute their energy to a common reservoir for the common supply of industries, farms, homes and railroads.

Such a system must transcend state lines and is likely to become nation wide. The new art of electric transmission is already so developed that the giant power system with which we are immediately concerned should now include all power producers and consumers in the northern section of the United States and should perhaps draw also upon resources of water power in Canada.

If this is so, then Pennsylvania should share its fuel power with southern New York, and New York should share its water power with western Pennsylvania. Therefore, I urge you most earnestly to provide, in planning the state-owned system you have proposed, for delivering at the Pennsylvania line a due proportion of Niagara power to supply the needs of western Pennsylvania. On the other hand, by the location of giant power stations near the coal mines, by saving the valuable by-products of the fuel consumed, by the development of water power, and by the electrification of railroads, I hope and expect that power resources of Pennsylvania will be intensively developed, enormously increased, and their product greatly cheapened, not only for the people of Pennsylvania, but also for the people of New Jersey and New York.

The negotiations already informally begun by you, Governor Silzer and myself for the development, apportionment and control of the water-power resources of the Delaware River illustrate most clearly that power is an interstate problem, both as to its origin and its distribution. In that connection I desire to urge you to consider most carefully the suit begun in the Supreme Court of the United States by your predecessor in the name of the State of New York to annul the Federal Water-Power act.

That statute is the outgrowth of the conservation movement initiated by President Roosevelt and especially of measures taken by him for safeguarding public rights in water power. In the initiating and application of these measures, I had the good fortune to enjoy his confidence and support, and I was active in the fifteen years of controversy which bore fruit in the Federal Water-Power act of 1920.

This law embodies the ideal of the conservation of natural resources for the public interest to a degree greater than any other with the possible exception of the national forest laws. By it 85 per cent of the undeveloped water-power resources of the nation were saved from monopoly and dedicated to the public welfare. It is not only equitable and workable but it is accepted as such by the best opinion among water-power experts, who recognize that one of its principal purposes is to promote development.

By proceeding under the Federal Water-Power act and by accepting the preference it gives to state enterprise over private enterprise, New York can initiate the new policy under the most favorable circumstances and without the delay inseparable from litigation, and can do so without jeopardizing the interests of other states. For it is true that by this statute, and by it alone, the rights of the people of all the states in water power are now safeguarded. If the State of New York should attempt, and unhappily succeed, in overthrowing it while safeguarding the rights of her own people, she would thereby strike down the people's rights in forty-seven other states which are not ready to undertake a state ownership policy at this time. I am sure that any such result is far from your intention.

Since, therefore, the Federal Water-Power law is specifically adapted to meet the present needs of the State of New York as well as to safeguard the interests of the other states, I respectfully urge on behalf of the people of Pennsylvania and of other states as well, that you withdraw the suit begun by your predecessor and use the Federal Water-Power act as a sure and sufficient basis of the policy of state ownership which you have proposed. If you take that course, you will have the good wishes of the people throughout the nation for your success in this difficult undertaking. If not, you will put one of their most vital interests to the hazard of litigation, and actually destroy that interest in the event that your litigation should succeed.

I speak for the people of our whole Commonwealth when I say that Pennsylvania desires to live with New York, her sister state, on terms of the closest mutual helpfulness and consideration. I cannot, however, but regard with deep concern any movement which might be expected to interfere with such mutual helpfulness or lead to antagonism of any sort.[1]

In this letter is well-stated the gospel of giant power which Governor Pinchot has been so ably promoting.

It is difficult to characterize New York's action in this case as other than narrow and selfish. People of the State of New York cannot but feel a great deal of pride in the resources which the Almighty has placed within their reach; —the St. Lawrence which is capable of developing 3,000,000 horsepower and the Niagara which is capable of developing 5,400,000 horsepower.[2] Yet the development of power on a scale both great and beneficial is no respecter of state lines. Pennsylvania ships tons of coal to New York every year for power, and on that basis alone it claims a right to share the power from Niagara. New England, too, wishes to share the power from the St. Lawrence. In an editorial of March 14, 1923, the *New York Evening Post* put the case for cooperation as follows:

Putting aside mere legal aspects and looking at the question from the economic point of view, Gov. Pinchot is quite right. It is urgently desirable for all inhabitants of the great industrial section stretching from Washington to Boston to regard themselves in the same boat so far as the power problem is concerned. The superpower survey recently completed by expert engineers under Federal supervision treated this huge manufacturing district as a unit and based its plan upon the principle

[1] *New York Times*, March 10, 1923.

[2] This must of course be divided between New York and Canada.

that all power resources should be pooled. Steam-electric power can be generated in the Pennsylvania fields and supplied to southern New York and New Jersey. Hydroelectric power can be generated in northern New York and supplied in part to northern Pennsylvania and New England. For each state to set about developing power for itself alone, no matter how artificial its boundaries, would result in the waste of countless millions. New York should not try to go her own way with only that cooperation with Canada which is unescapable. She should cooperate with all her neighbors of the northeastern United States.

State development, as distinguished from private development, will be just as feasible under the Federal Water-Power act as if New York should wrest complete control of the American share of the Niagara and St. Lawrence power for itself. The act gives a preference to state or municipal applications. It is hard to think of the act, which was greeted two years ago as ending a long period of confusion and opening an era of steady development, being destroyed. It is hard to think of New York as having a right to all the power of water which rises as far west as Montana and reaches the ocean off Nova Scotia. The large view should be taken, and the large view counsels acquiescence in the law.

A conference between officials of the State of New York and the Federal Power Commission resulted in New York's withdrawing its suit. It would seem that at the conference the provisions of the Federal Power Act were clearly explained to the New York spokesmen and that no concessions were gained by the state. Indeed, the State of New York had all it agreed to before the conference was called.[1]

Another attack on the Federal Power Act was launched in the South early in 1922. The Alabama Power Company,

[1] A brief account of the conference may be found in the Hearing before the Senate Committee on Agriculture and Forestry on *H. R. 518* and other bills, 68th Cong., 1st Sess., pp. 1277-1281.

a licensee of the Federal Power Commission, proceeded to condemn lands of the Gulf Power Company and others on the Coosa River in Alabama. The Gulf Company and others began suit to test the validity of the act which gave the power of condemnation to the Alabama Power Company. The suit was instituted in the Federal District Court at Montgomery. Judge Clayton presided. It was contended by the Gulf Company that the Federal Power Act trespassed upon the power of the state to control and regulate or use its own navigable waters. It was further contended that there was by the provisions of the act a delegation of legislative functions to the Power Commission rather than the bestowal of administrative duties. The act was called an attempt on the part of Congress to invade the right of the state and to take away from the state the control and regulation of hydroelectric development. Further, it was argued that the act infringed upon the authority of the state in the matter of the transmission and distribution within the state of electric energy therein; that the effect of the legislation was to put the Government into the business of generating, transmitting, and distributing intrastate and interstate power originating at the dams constructed under Government licenses, and that this generation and transmission is aside from governmental purposes and for the benefit of private corporations.

In upholding the law Judge Clayton said:

The conclusion is that this act authorizing the constructions of dams in navigable streams to impound the water . . . for the purpose of improving navigation by the slack water method does not offend the Constitution. It was within the power of Congress to create a board called the Water-Power Commission to carry out the purpose of Congress, and to provide that such commission should select its licensees as a proper federal agency to carry out the administrative detail of this general plan, wherever applicable for the improvement of navigation. . . . It is competent for Congress to provide that the licensees who build the dams under government supervision should receive as their compensation for their outlay the surplus water at the wier, not necessary for navigation.[1]

The Power Act has not been tested in the Supreme Court. Judging from its career up to date, however, it would not seem that such a test is far off.

Conclusion

Activity under the act has been rapid. Prior to the passage of the Act of 1920, 1,430,000 horsepower had been developed on public lands and navigable streams. On June 30, 1921, there were applications under the Act for 15,000,000 horsepower pending or acted upon; on June 30, 1922, 20,000,000 horsepower; on June 30, 1923, 21,500,000 horsepower. Some of this development may not be undertaken for several years, yet increased activity is indicated by the figures.[2]

A difficulty in the operation of the Act has developed owing to the fact that the direct employment by the commission of experts is forbidden. The Act provides that the work of the Commission should be done through the personnel of the three departments of War, Interior, and Agriculture. Existing projects which come under the Act must be valued at once, as a basis for their rates, for the recapture price to be paid for them at the end of fifty years, and for the measure of their excess profits. Valuation engineers are needed but there are no valuation engineers in the War, Interior, or Agriculture Departments. Here is a serious weakness in the Act which should be remedied at once to prevent an untold number of lawsuits and controversies in

[1] 283 *Federal* 606, March 15, 1922.

[2] See the Reports of the Federal Power Commission 1921, 1922, 1923.

the future. Naturally, Mr. O. C. Merrill who was appointed Executive Secretary of the Commission has been unable to satisfy all the conservationists and, of course, not all the power people. By some conservationists it is charged that a reactionary opinion exists in the commission and even in the Secretary which discourages public ownership and operation even though the law gives preference to public corporations. It would not at all be surprising to learn that conservative ideas ruled the commission which no doubt explains the conservatism of Mr. Merrill.

In conclusion it must be emphasized that popular indifference can defeat the aims of the best legislation. The commission in Washington with its Executive Secretary—especially the latter—must meet with the representatives of great corporations whose interests are often contrary to those of the public and who are skilled in the arts of lobbying. The old interests—water-power developers and promoters, bond brokers, hydroelectric engineers who secure employment from water-power promoters, to say nothing of real estate agents—are ever on the alert to secure this concession or that favor. They have been in Washington for years and they never seem to grow tired. It is not to be assumed that these people are passing rolls of bills around among public officials; for the most part they are honest men with special interests to serve. They have the same right to be in Washington as any other citizen of the Republic. But where are the agents of the people at large? A lone and busy Executive Secretary with a borrowed office force stands between the interests and the property of the people.

APPENDIX I

Water Power in the United States

(Data gathered by the United States Geological Survey in 1924)

New York *World Almanac,* 1925, p. 288

State	*Horse Power Capacity of Existing Water Wheels*	Potential Horse Power	
		Available 90 Per Cent of the Time	*Available 50 Per Cent of the Time*
Alabama	215,863	472,000	1,050,000
Arizona	38,760	2,759,000	2,887,000
Arkansas	1,189	125,000	178,000
California	1,451,830	4,603,000	6,674,000
Colorado	87,978	765,000	1,570,000
Connecticut	136,423	65,000	110,000
Delaware	3,133	5,000	10,000
District of Columbia	666	Incl. in Md.	Incl. in Md.
Florida	7,036	10,000	18,000
Georgia	364,394	572,000	958,000
Idaho	270,918	2,122,000	4,032,000
Illinois	85,002	189,000	361,000
Indiana	29,199	40,000	110,000
Iowa	177,280	169,000	495,000
Kansas	14,504	104,000	251,000
Kentucky	1,256	77,000	184,000
Louisiana		1,000	2,000
Maine	473,188	536,000	1,074,000
Maryland	7,230	106,000	238,000
Massachusetts	343,939	106,000	235,000
Michigan	281,618	168,000	274,000
Minnesota	211,850	203,000	401,000
Mississippi		30,000	60,000
Missouri	17,970	67,000	152,000
Montana	345,040	2,550,000	3,700,000
Nebraska	19,716	183,000	342,000
Nevada	13,550	300,000	370,000
New Hampshire	235,810	186,000	350,000
New Jersey	18,902	50,000	90,000
New Mexico	1,322	116,000	186,000
New York	1,542,983	4,010,000	4,960,000
North Carolina	431,500	540,000	816,000
North Dakota	245	82,000	193,000
Ohio	29,753	55,000	166,000

APPENDIX I—*Concluded*

State	*Horse Power Capacity of Existing Water Wheels*	Potential Horse Power	
		Available 90 Per Cent of the Time	*Available 50 Per Cent of the Time*
Oklahoma	1,718	70,000	194,000
Oregon	206,865	3,665,000	6,715,000
Pennsylvania	169,996	257,000	638,000
Rhode Island	30,188	25,000	40,000
South Carolina	357,510	429,000	632,000
South Dakota	18,171	63,000	110,000
Tennessee	128,465	432,000	710,000
Texas	13,820	238,000	514,000
Utah	115,329	1,420,000	1,586,000
Vermont	167,816	80,000	169,000
Virginia	109,798	459,000	812,000
Washington	480,356	4,970,000	7,871,000
West Virginia	14,711	355,000	980,000
Wisconsin	404,282	285,000	480,000
Wyoming	7,886	704,000	1,182,000
United States	9,086,958	34,818,000	55,030,000

The data in the above table covers 3,200 water plants of 100 horse-power or more.

The increase in 1924 is about 1,160,000 horse-power, or nearly 15 per cent over 1921, when the total was 7,926,958 horse-power.

Of the 1924 horse-power, 7,348,197 horse-power is in 1,390 public utility and municipal plants, and the rest, 1,738,761 horse-power, is in 1,821 manufacturing and miscellaneous plants.

The proposed turbine capacity of projects under construction, for which licenses were issued by the Federal Power Commission in 1921, 1922 and 1923, was 2,600,000 horse-power.

The developed horse-power in Alaska is 40,000; in Hawaii, 25,000; in Porto Rico, 15,000.

The potential horse-power, available 90 per cent of the time, is 1,000,000 in Alaska, 19,000 in Porto Rico and 100,000 in Hawaii.

Assuming that all sites may eventually be developed to a point where the wheel capacity is 131 per cent of the power available 50 per cent of the time, we may say that the installed capacity will reach 72,000,000 horse-power.

The present installed capacity of plants of 100 horse-power or more is 9,087,000 horse-power, and on the above assumption of the ultimate installed capacity about 12.5 per cent of the potential water power of the country has now been developed.

APPENDIX II

Water-Power Development on National Forests under Revocable License by Companies whose First Hydroelectric Plants were Built on Public Land

(Installed capacities of development on national forest land)

Hearings Senate Committee on Public Lands, H. R. 16673, 63rd Congress, 3rd Session, p. 571

State.	*Permittee*	*Installed capacity (horsepower)*
Arizona	Arizona Power Co.	9,000
California	Mount Whitney Power and Electric	6,500
Do.	Nevada-California Power Co.	18,000
Do.	Oro. Electric Corporation	2,700
Do.	Pacific Light and Power Co.	112,000
Do.	Pacific Power Co.	4,000
Do.	San Joachin Light & Power Corporation	34,000
Do.	Sierra & San Francisco Power Co.	48,000
Do.	Tuolumne Electric Co.	800
Do.	Utica Gold Mining & Hobart Estate Companies	2,000
Do.	Western States Gas & Electric	2,000
Colorado	Central Colorado Power Co. (Shoshone plant).	18,000
Do.	Colorado Springs Light, Heat & Power Co.	3,000
Do.	Colorado Yule Marble Co.	1,750
Do.	Cuchara Lumber & Supply Co.	50
Do.	Eagle Mining & Milling Co.	130
Do.	East Lake Mining & Milling Co.	40
Do.	Glenwood Light & Power Co.	530
Do.	Green & Clear Lakes Co.	1,800
Do.	Indiana Colorado Mining & Milling Co.	250
Do.	Marion Mines & Mill Co.	100
Do.	Manhattan Milling & Power Co.	50
Do.	Ramsay, Hugh B.	20
Do.	Rico Mining Co.	300
Do.	Salida Light, Power & Utility Co.	750
Do.	Tam O'Shanter-Montezuma M. & M. Co.	140
Do.	Thistle, M. L.	125
Do.	Tin Cup Gold Dredging Co.	300
Idaho	Kitty Burton Gold Mines Co.	400
Do.	Teton Valley Power & Milling Co.	200
Montana	Anaconda Copper Mining Co.	1,470
Do.	Cooke Mining & Reduction Co.	130
Do.	Grangeville E. L. & P. Co.	420
Do.	Helena Power & Transmission Co. (Montana Power Co.)	18,760

APPENDIX II—*Concluded*

State.	*Permittee*	*Installed capacity (horsepower)*
Do.	Montana-Illinois Copper Mining Co.	150
Do.	Stover, W. H.	20
Nevada	Elko-Lamoille Power Co.	330
Oregon	City of Ashland	400
Do.	Crown-Columbia Pulp & Paper Co.	1,750
Do.	Eagle River Electric Co.	800
Do.	Eastern Oregon Light & Power Co.	2,800
Do.	Mount Hood Railway & Power Co.	11,250
Do.	West Coast Mines Co.	300
South Dakota	Dakota Power Co.	2,400
Utah	City of Manti	450
Do.	Columbus-Consolidated Mining Co.	800
Do.	Mackay Light & Power Co.	135
Do.	Michigan-Utah Mining Co.	200
Do.	Ophir Hill Consolidated Mining Co.	750
Do.	Dkougaard, C. A.	10
Do.	Skougaard, C. A.	10
Do.	Spring City Light & Milling Co.	10
Washington	Chancellor Gold Mining Co.	250
Do.	Seckman, Louis	40
Do.	Great Northern Railway	8,250
Do.	Inland Portland Cement Co	4,730
Do.	Superior Portland Cement Co.	1,500
Do.	Valley Development Co.	70
Wyoming	Babione	20
Total		325,130

APPENDIX III

CONCENTRATION OF POWER DEVELOPMENT IN THE SEVERAL STATES, SHOWING AMOUNT OF WATER POWER, STEAM AND GAS POWER, AND OF TOTAL POWER CONTROLLED BY CERTAIN CORPORATIONS AND BY MUNICIPALITIES, IN HORSEPOWER AND IN PER CENT.

Hearings House Committee on Water Power, 65th Congress, 2nd Session, pp. 125-155.

ALABAMA

Reference Nos.	Name of company	Individual totals				Cumulative totals		Individual percentages		Cumulative percentages	
		No. of stations	Water power	Steam and gas power	All power	Water power	All power	Water power	All power	Water power	All power
4	Alabama Traction, Light & Power Co.	7	72,500	18,920	91,420	72,500	91,420	87.9	57.1	87.9	57.1
39	United Gas & Electric Corporation of Connecticut	1	......	16,300	16,300	72,500	107,720	.....	10.2	87.9	67.3
36	H. M. Byllesby & Co.	1	......	9,330	9,330	72,500	117,050	......	5.8	87.9	73.1
23	Doherty Operating Co.	1	5,000	3,420	8,420	77,500	125,470	6.1	5.3	94.0	78.4
41	West Point Manufacturing Co.	2	3,950	4,200	8,150	81,450	133,620	4.8	5.1	98.8	83.5
31	Montgomery Light & Traction Co.	1	......	6,670	6,670	81,450	140,290	......	4.2	98.8	87.7
33	The Sheffield Co.	1	......	2,432	2,432	81,450	142,722	......	1.5	98.8	89.2
1	Alabama City, Gadsden & Attilla Ry. Co.	1	......	1,500	1,500	81,450	144,222	......	.9	98.8	90.1
44	Municipal stations	34	682	6,847	7,529	82,132	151,751	.8	4.7	99.6	94.8
	All other stations	32	334	8,012	8,346	82,466	160,097	.4	5.2	100.0	100.0
	Total	81	82,466	77,631	160,097	......	....	100.0	100.0	.....	.....
	Central stations and electric railways, 1912	..	9,880	73,525	83,403	......	....	.....	.....	.....	.....

APPENDIX III—*Continued*

ARIZONA

17	Ray Consolidated Copper Co.	1	......	14,700	14,700	......	14,700	.....	16.7	.....	16.7
1	Arizona Copper Co.	1	......	10,000	10,000	......	24,700	.....	11.3	.....	28.0
2	Arizona Power Co.	2	9,000	750	9,750	9,000	34,450	26.8	11.0	26.8	39.0
6	Copper Queen Consolidated Mining Co.	2	......	5,170	5,170	9,000	39,620	.....	5.9	26.8	44.9
11	Federal Light and Traction Co.	1	......	2,180	2,180	9,000	41,800	.....	2.5	26.8	47.4
21, 30	U. S. Reclamation Service and Municipal stations	6	24,250	40	24,290	33,250	66,090	72.1	27.6	98.9	75.0
	All other stations	18	380	21,685	22,065	33,630	88,155	1.1	25.0	100.0	100.0
	Total	31	36,630	54,525	88,155	......	....	100.0	100.0	.....	.....
	Central stations and elec. rys., 1912	..	817	10,198	11,015	......	....	.....	.....	.....	.....

ARKANSAS

56	United Gas & Electric Corporation of Connecticut	1	......	9,900	9,900	......	9,900	.....	18.5	.....	18.5
17	H. M. Byllesby & Co.	1	......	5,425	5,425	......	15,325	.....	10.2	.....	28.7
47	Pine Bluff Co.	1	......	5,250	5,250	......	20,575	.....	9.8	.....	38.5
1	Arkansas Light & Power Co.	7	......	3,620	3,620	......	24,195	.....	6.8	.....	45.3
53	Southwestern Gas & Electric Co.	1	......	3,350	3,350	......	27,545	.....	6.3	.....	51.6
43	Merchants Lighting Co.	1	......	3,330	3,330	......	30,875	.....	6.2	.....	57.8
28	Federal Light & Traction Co.	1	......	3,000	3,000	......	33,875	.....	5.6	.....	63.4
51	Scofield Engineering Co. of Philadelphia	1	......	1,670	1,670	......	35,545	.....	3.1	.....	66.5
41	Mammoth Springs Electric Light & Power Co.	1	1,600	......	1,600	1,600	37,145	72.7	3.0	72.7	69.5
52	Seven Cities Co	1	600	500	1,100	2,200	38,245	27.3	2.1	100.0	71.6
27	Fayetteville Gas & Electric Co.	1	......	1,020	1,020	2,200	39,265	.....	1.9	100.0	73.5
60	Municipal stations	17	......	5,262	5,262	2,200	44,527	.....	9.9	100.0	83.4
	All other stations	37	......	8,887	8,887	2,200	53,414	.....	16.6	100.0	100.0
	Total	71	2,200	51,214	53,414	......	....	100.0	100.0	.....	.....
	Central stations and elec. rys., 1912	..	3,040	39,564	42,604	......	....	.....	.....	.....	.....

APPENDIX III—*Continued*

CALIFORNIA

79	Pacific Gas & Electric Co.	13	152,080	108,540	260,620	152,080	260,620	21.1	20.5	20.1	20.5
93	Pacific Light & Power Corporation	13	117,950	79,300	197,250	270,030	457,870	16.3	15.5	37.4	36.0
128	Southern California Edison Co.	11	56,400	79,120	135,520	326,430	593,390	7.8	10.7	45.2	466.7
165	Western Power Co.	4	73,330	38,670	112,000	399,760	705,390	10.2	8.8	55.4	55.5
155	United Railway Investment Co.	5	65,600	25,330	90,930	465,360	796,320	9.1	7.2	64.5	62.7
115	San Joaquin Light & Power Co.	8	40,150	28,950	69,100	505,510	865,420	5.6	5.4	70.1	68.1
58	Nevada-California Power Co.	7	37,750	10,670	48,420	543,260	913,840	5.2	3.8	75.3	72.1
66	Northern California Power Co.	7	47,200	......	47,200	590,460	961,040	6.6	3.7	81.9	75.6
9	H. M. Byllesby & Co.	6	17,200	20,020	37,220	607,660	998,260	2.4	2.9	84.3	78.5
92	Pacific Lighting Corporation	1	......	34,202	34,202	607,660	1,032,462	.....	2.7	84.3	81.2
149	United Properties Co.	6	......	33,025	33,025	607,660	1,065,487	.....	2.6	84.3	83.8
198	Southern Pacific Co.	2	......	23,870	23,870	607,660	1,089,357	.....	1.9	84.3	85.7
58	Mount Whitney Power Co.	5	14,650	9,000	23,650	622,310	1,113,007	2.0	1.9	86.3	87.6
67	Oro Electric Corporation	3	6,000	1,300	7,300	628,310	1,120,307	.8	.6	87.1	88.2
16	California-Oregon Power Co.	2	5,300	......	5,300	633,610	1,125,607	.7	.4	87.8	88.6
173	Municipal stations	18	45,700	12,000	57,700	679,310	1,183,307	6.3	4.5	94.1	93.1
	All other stations	85	42,815	44,985	87,800	722,125	1,271,107	5.9	6.9	100.0	100.0
	Total	200	722,125	548,982	1,271,107	......	....	100.0	100.0	.....	.....
	Central stations and electric rys., 1912	....	432,327	449,232	881,559	......	....	.....	.....	.....	.....

COLORADO

14	Colorado Power Co.	7	41,750	4,870	46,620	41,750	46,620	45.2	24.0	45.2	24.0
26	Doherty Operating Co.	1	......	24,650	24,650	41,750	71,270	.....	12.7	45.2	36.7
74	Utah Securities Corporation	8	18,630	1,480	20,110	60,380	91,380	20.2	10.3	65.4	47.0
7	H. M. Byllesby & Co.	5	2,400	11,894	14,294	62,780	105,674	2.6	7.4	68.0	54.4
70	United Gas & Electric Co. of Connecticut	2	4,750	6,460	11,210	67,530	116,884	5.1	5.8	73.1	60.2
33	Federal Light & Traction Co.	3	......	10,670	10,670	67,530	127,554	.....	5.5	73.1	65.7
83	Western Light & Power Co.	1	......	10,670	10,670	67,530	138,224	.....	5.5	73.1	71.2
65	Roaring Fork Electric Light and Power Co.	1	3,600	......	3,600	71,130	141,824	3.9	1.8	77.0	73.0

APPENDIX III—*Continued*

COLORADO—*Concluded*

84	Municipal stations	10	975	2,775	3,750	72,105	145,574	1.1	1.9	78.1	74.9
	All other stations	103	20,198	28,569	48,767	92,303	194,341	21.9	25.1	100.0	100.0
	Total	141	92,303	102,038	194,341	.....	....	100.0	100.0	.....	.....
	Central stations and electric railways, 1912	....	82,205	100,331	182,536	.....	....	.....	.....	.....	.....

CONNECTICUT

12, 64	New York, New Taven & Hartford R. R. Co.	13	8,050	35,275	43,325	8,050	43,325	19.2	22.5	19.2	22.5
52	United Illuminating Co.	2	......	31,200	31,200	8,050	74,525	.....	16.2	19.2	38.7
13	The Hartford Electric Light Co.	3	3,600	20,670	24,270	11,650	98,795	8.6	12.6	27.8	51.3
42	Stone & Webster	5	16,000	6,505	22,505	27,650	121,300	38.2	11.7	66.0	63.0
37	Shore Line Electric Ry. Co.	2	......	6,780	6,780	27,650	128,080	.....	3.5	66.0	66.5
41	Stamford Gas & Electric Co.	1	......	6,080	6,080	27,650	134,160	.....	3.2	66.0	69.7
30	Ponemah Mills	1	2,500	3,304	5,804	30,150	139,964	5.9	3.0	71.9	72.7
19	Meriden Electric Light Co.	1	......	5,550	5,550	30,150	145,514	.....	2.9	71.9	75.6
9	Derby Gas Co.	1	1,000	3,567	4,567	31,150	150,081	2.4	2.4	74.3	78.0
28	Ousatonic Water Power Co.	2	3,400	......	3,400	34,550	153,481	8.1	1.8	82.4	79.8
1	Atlantic Power and Light Corporation.	2	2,300	850	3,150	36,850	156,631	5.5	1.6	87.9	81.4
10	Doherty Operating Co.	1	......	2,733	2,733	36,850	159,364	.....	1.4	87.9	82.8
71	Norwood & Westerly Traction Co.	2	......	2,470	2,470	36,850	161,834	.....	1.3	87.9	84.1
50	The Uncas Power Co.	1	2,000	......	2,000	38,850	163,834	4.8	1.0	92.7	85.1
18	Torrington Electric Co.	1	......	2,000	2,000	38,850	165,834	.....	1.0	92.7	86.1
32	Putnam Light & Power Co.	1	600	1,285	1,885	39,450	167,719	1.4	1.0	94.1	87.1
57	Municipal stations	6	......	10,890	10,890	39,450	178,609	.....	5.6	94.1	92.7
	All other stations	27	2,460	11,575	14,035	41,910	192,644	5.9	7.3	100.0	100.0
	Total	72	41,910	150,734	192,644	.....	....	100.0	100.0	.....	.....
	Central stations and electric railways, 1912	...	20,334	141,752	162,086	.....	....	.....	.....	.....	.....

DELAWARE

5	National Properties Co.	3	......	14,800	14,800	......	14,800	.....	81.8	.....	81.8
11	Municipal stations	6	......	1,535	1,535	......	16,335	.....	8.5	.....	90.3
	All other stations	7	54	1,750	1,804	54	18,139	100.0	9.7	100.0	100.0
	Total	16	54	18,085	18,139	......	....	100.0	100.0	.....	.....
	Central stations and electric railways, 1912		826	24,075	24,901	......	....	.....	.....	.....	.....

FLORIDA

29	Stone & Webster	4	1,400	8,615	10,015	1,400	10,015	19.9	21.0	19.9	21.0
11	Florida Power Co.	1	5,600	......	5,600	7,000	15,615	79.7	11.7	99.6	32.7
34	J. G. White & Co.	8	......	4,127	4,127	7,000	19,742	.....	8.7	99.6	41.4
19	Miami Electric Light & Power Co.	1	......	2,255	2,255	7,000	21,997	.....	4.7	99.6	46.1
13	General Utilities Operating Co.	1	......	2,000	2,000	7,000	23,997	.....	4.2	99.6	50.3
21	Orlando Water & Light Co.	1	......	1,350	1,350	7,000	25,347	.....	2.8	99.6	53.1
3	Bagdad Land & Lumber Co.	1	......	1,320	1,320	7,000	26,667	.....	2.8	99.6	55.9
26	St. John's Electric Co.	1	......	1,300	1,300	7,000	27,967	.....	2.7	99.6	58.6
45	Municipal stations	17	......	12,697	12,697	7,000	40,664	.....	26.6	99.6	85.2
	All other stations	27	30	7,033	7,063	7,030	47,727	.4	14.8	100.0	100.0
	Total	62	7,030	40,697	47,727	......	....	100.0	100.0	.....	.....
	Central stations and electric railways, 1912		7,100	44,604	51,704	......	....	.....	.....	.....	.....

GEORGIA

19	Georgia Railway & Power Co.	7	100,400	33,720	134,120	100,400	134,120	46.1	39.7	46.1	39.0
47	Stone & Webster	7	29,426	18,790	48,216	129,826	182,336	13.5	14.3	59.6	54.7
16	Georgia Light, Power & Railways Co.	3	33,000	4,750	37,750	162,826	220,086	15.2	11.2	74.8	65.0
60	J. G. White & Co. (Incorporated)	5	20,800	8,342	29,142	183,626	249,228	9.6	8.6	84.4	73.2
42	Savannah Lighting Co.	1	......	9,600	9,600	183,626	258,828	.....	2.8	84.4	76.8

APPENDIX III—*Continued*

GEORGIA—*Concluded*

59	West Point Manufacturing Co......	1	3,000	5,000	8,000	186,626	266,828	1.4	2.4	85.8	79.9
8	Doherty Operating Co.	4	5,800	2,000	7,800	192,426	274,628	2.7	2.3	88.5	81.0
146	Fulton Bag & Cotton Mill	1	......	6,500	6,500	192,426	281,128	.....	1.9	88.5	82.3
1	Albany Power & Manufacturing Co.	1	2,330	2,130	4,460	194,756	285,588	1.1	1.3	89.6	84.5
55	Towaliga Falls Power Co.	1	3,600	750	4,350	198,356	289,938	1.6	1.3	91.2	85.8
144	Eagle and Phoenix Mills	1	4,000	......	4,000	202,356	293,938	1.8	1.2	93.0	87.0
41	Rome Railway, Light & Power Co. .	1	1,500	2,330	3,830	203,856	297,768	.7	1.1	93.7	88.1
65	Municipal stations	75	1,500	16,127	17,627	205,356	315,395	.7	5.2	94.4	93.3
	All other stations	49	12,199	10,012	22,211	217,555	337,606	5.6	6.7	100.0	100.0
	Total *	157	217,555	120,051	337,606	......	....	100.0	100.0	.....	.....
	Central stations and electric railways, 1912		82,487	88,345	170,832	......	....	.....	.....	.....	.....

IDAHO

49	Utah Securities Corporation	10	73,507	300	73,807	73,507	73,807	48.3	45.5	48.3	45.5
25	National Securities Corporation.....	9	34,350	2,000	36,350	107,857	110,157	22.5	22.4	70.8	67.9
59	Washington Water Power Co.	1	16,300	......	16,300	124,157	126,457	10.7	10.0	81.5	77.9
46	Thousand Springs Power Co.	1	3,000	......	3,000	127,157	129,457	2.0	1.8	83.5	79.7
14	Grangeville Light & Power Co.	2	1,300	......	1,300	128,457	130,757	.8	.8	84.3	80.5
8	H. M. Byllsby & Co.	1	......	900	900	128,457	131,657	.....	.6	84.3	81.1
47, 61	United States Reclamation Service and Municipal Stations	5	14,350	......	14,350	142,807	146,007	9.4	8.8	93.7	89.9
	All other stations	43	9,553	6,800	16,353	152,360	162,360	6.3	10.1	100.0	100.0
	Total........................	72	152,360	10,000	162,360	......	....	100.0	100.0	.....	.....
	Central stations and electric railways, 1912		51,850	4,525	56,375	......	....	.....	.....	.....	.....

* Totals contain 12,649 water horse-power and 7,150 steam horse-power, total of 19,799 horse-power used in manufacture.

APPENDIX III—*Continued*

ILLINOIS

40	Commonwealth Edison Co.	4	......	511,150	511,150	......	511,150	.....	55.6	.....	55.6
191	Public Service Co. of Northern Ill.	13	5,300	55,930	61,230	5,300	572,380	9.8	6.7	9.8	62.3
231	United Light & Railways Co.	1	......	42,000	42,000	5,300	614,380	.....	4.6	9.8	66.9
64	Illinois Traction	28	4,115	35,886	40,001	9,415	654,381	7.6	4.4	17.4	71.3
105	Middle West Utilities Co.	66	4,630	29,180	33,810	14,045	688,191	8.5	3.7	25.9	75.0
33	Commonwealth Power, R. R. & Light Co.	7	......	26,480	26,480	14,045	714,671	.....	2.9	25.9	77.9
332	Chicago Surface Lines	2	......	24,000	24,000	14,045	738,671	.....	2.6	25.9	80.5
9	Aurora, Elgin & Chicago R. R. Co.	2	75	21,430	21,505	14,120	760,176	.1	2.3	26.0	82.8
3	American Gas Co.	2	1,680	16,700	18,380	15,800	778,556	3.1	2.0	29.1	84.8
27	E. W. Clark & Co. Mortgage Corp.	4	......	19,100	19,100	15,800	797,656	.....	2.1	29.1	86.9
20	H. M. Byllesby & Co.	1	......	9,600	9,660	15,800	807,316	.....	1.0	29.1	87.9
205	Rock Island Southern Ry. Co.	2	......	5,200	5,200	15,800	812,516	.....	.6	29.1	88.5
211	Southern Illinois Light & Power Co.	7	......	4,546	4,546	15,800	817,062	.....	.5	29.1	89.0
248	Municipal stations *	86	34,500	20,906	55,406	50,300	873,458	63.4	6.0	92.5	95.0
	All other stations	119	4,101	41,156	46,257	54,401	918,725	7.5	5.0	100.0	100.0
	Total	344	54,401	864,324	918,725	......	....	100.0	100.0	.....	.....
	Central stations and electric railways, 1912	...	42,562	777,849	820,411	......	....	.....	.....	.....	.....

INDIANA

65	Indianapolis Light & Heat Co.	1	......	40,900	40,900	......	40,900	.....	12.5	.....	12.5
48	Fort Wayne & Northern Indiana Tr. Co.	3	......	32,160	32,160	......	73,060	.....	9.9	.....	22.4
7	American Public Utilities Co.	2	......	24,200	24,200	......	97,260	.....	7.4	.....	29.8
92	Middle West Utilities Co.	21	4,400	19,430	23,830	4,400	121,090	54.4	7.3	54.4	37.1
139	Terre Haute, Indianapolis & Elec. Tr. Co.	8	......	22,800	22,800	4,400	143,890	.....	7.0	54.4	44.1
148	Union Traction Co. of Indiana	4	......	17,930	17,930	4,400	161,820	.....	5.5	54.4	49.6

*** Includes stations of Sanitary Drainage District of Chicago and of United States Army.**

APPENDIX III—*Continued*

INDIANA—*Concluded*

3	American Gas & Electric Co.	4	......	16,890	16,890	4,400	178,710	.....	5.2	54.4	54.8
155	The United Gas Improvement Co. ..	1	......	15,566	15,566	4,400	194,276	.....	4.8	54.5	59.6
63	Indiana & Michigan Electric Co. ...	2	1,300	13,330	14,630	5,700	208,906	16.1	4.5	70.5	64.1
32	Commonwealth Power, Railway and Light Co.	1	......	13,070	13,070	5,700	221,976	.....	4.0	70.5	68.1
28	Chicago, Lake Shore & South Bend Ry. Co.	1	......	10,000	10,000	5,700	231,970	.....	3.1	70.5	71.2
66	Indiana Railway & Light Co.	1	......	9,750	9,750	5,700	241,726	.....	3.0	70.5	74.2
245	Indianapolis & Cincinnati Traction Co.	1	......	2,670	2,670	5,700	244,396	.....	.8	70.5	75.0
169	Municipal stations	70	200	29,265	29,465	5,900	273,861	2.5	9.0	73.0	84.0
	All other stations	126	2,191	49,820	52,011	8,091	325,872	27.0	16.0	100.0	100.0
	Total	246	8,091	317,781	325,872	......	....	100.0	100.0	.....	.....
	Central stations and electric railways, 1912	...	23,915	283,508	307,423	......	....	.....	.....	.....	.....

IOWA

169	Stone and Webster	3	150,000	......	150,000	150,000	150,000	94.1	47.4	94.1	47.4
93	Iowa Railway & Light Co.	12	......	23,255	23,255	150,000	173,255	.....	7.4	94.1	54.8
77	Illinois Traction Co.	6	300	15,649	15,949	150,300	189,204	.2	5.1	94.3	59.9
27	Central Iowa Light & Power Co. ...	3	......	10,400	10,400	150,300	199,604	.....	3.3	94.3	63.2
180	Union Electric Co. of Dubuque	1	......	9,500	9,500	150,300	209,104	.....	3.0	94.3	66.2
183	United Light & Railways Co.	6	500	8,025	8,525	150,800	217,629	.3	2.7	94.6	68.9
194	Waterloo, Cedar Falls & Northern Ry. Co.	1	......	7,000	7,000	150,800	224,629	.....	2.2	94.6	71.1
3	The American Gas Co.	5	345	6,545	6,890	151,145	231,519	.2	2.2	94.8	73.3
266	Des Moines City Ry. Co.	1	......	6,750	6,750	151,145	238,269	.....	2.1	94.8	75.4
164	Sioux City Service Co.	1	......	6,400	6,400	151,145	244,669	.....	2.0	94.8	77.4
83	Interstate Power Co.	6	2,000	1,625	3,625	153,145	248,294	1.3	1.1	96.1	78.5

APPENDIX III—*Continued*

IOWA—*Concluded*

38	Continental Gas & Electric Corp. ..	7	......	3,363	3,363	153,145	251,657	.....	1.1	96.1	79.6
19	H. M. Byllesby & Co.	1	......	3,350	3,350	153,145	255,007	.....	1.1	96.1	80.7
196	Municipal stations	70	710	16,112	16,822	153,855	271,829	.4	5.3	96.5	86.0
	All other stations	145	5,576	38,821	44,397	159,431	316,226	3.5	14.0	100.0	100.0
	Total	268	159,431	156,795	316,226	......	....	100.0	100.0	.....	.....
	Central stations and electric railways, 1912		7,029	126,564	133,593	......	....	.....	.....	.....	.....

KANSAS

27	Doherty Operating Co.	4	7,000	13,570	20,570	7,000	35,430	.....	13.5	59.9	32.2
3	American Power & Light Co.	5	......	14,860	14,860	7,000	20,570	59.9	18.7	59.9	18.7
50	Illinois Traction Co.	2	......	7,491	7,491	7,000	42,921	.....	6.8	59.9	39.0
14	Bowersack Mill & Power Co.	1	1,500	1,000	2,500	8,500	45,421	12.8	2.3	72.7	41.3
67	Light and Development Co. of St. Louis	1	......	2,030	2,030	8,500	47,451	.....	1.9	72.7	43.2
103	United Gas & Electric Corporation of Connecticut	1	......	1,925	1,925	8,500	49,376	.....	1.8	72.7	45.0
65	Land & Power Co.	1	1,015	840	1,855	9,515	51,231	8.7	1.7	81.4	46.7
109	Municipal stations	90	125	26,232	26,357	9,640	77,588	1.1	24.0	82.5	70.7
	All other stations	102	2,048	30,158	32,206	11,688	109,794	17.5	29.3	100.0	100.0
	Total	207	11,688	98,106	109,794	......	....	100.0	100.0	.....	.....
	Central stations and electric railways, 1912	...	8,820	101,788	110,608	......	....	.....	.....	.....	.....

KENTUCKY

105	Louisville Traction Co.	2	......	44,130	44,130	None	44,130	None	34.5	None	34.5
6	H. M. Byllesby & Co.	1	......	33,330	33,330	"	77,460	"	26.1	"	60.6
13	Columbia Gas & Electric Co. of W. Va.	1	......	9,100	9,100	"	86,560	"	7.1	"	67.7

APPENDIX III—*Continued*

KENTUCKY—*Concluded*

42	Kentucky Securities Corporation	1	......	6,670	6,670	None	93,230	None	5.2	None	72.9
39	J. G. White & Co.	3	......	3,260	3,260	"	96,490	"	2.6	"	75.5
54	Middle West Utilities Co.	7	......	3,195	3,195	"	99,685	"	2.5	"	78.0
104	Kentucky S. W. Electric Ry., Light & Power Co.	1	......	2,500	2,500	"	102,185	"	2.0	"	80.0
78	Stone & Webster	1	......	2,350	2,350	"	104,535	"	1.8	"	81.0
16	Consolidated Coal Co.	1	......	1,500	1,500	"	106,035	"	1.2	"	83.0
52	Mayfield Water & Light Co.	1	......	1,200	1,200	"	107,235	"	.9	"	83.9
47	Light and Development Co. of St. Louis	2	......	1,055	1,055	"	108,290	"	.8	"	84.7
85	Municipal stations	18	......	7,730	7,730	"	116,020	"	6.0	"	90.7
	All other stations	68	......	11,865	11,865	"	127,885	"	9.3	"	100.0
	Total........................	107	......	127,885	127,885	......	....	.....	100.0	.....	.....
	Central stations and electric railways, 1912	...	......	108,227	108,227	......	....	.....	.....	.....	.....

LOUISIANA

26	United Gas & Elec. Corp. of Conn. .	4	......	66,665	66,665	......	66,665	.....	73.4	.....	73.4
23	Southwestern Gas & Elec. Co.	1	......	3,450	3,450	......	70,115	.....	3.8	.....	77.2
58	Shreveport Rys. Co.	1	......	2,450	2,450	......	72,565	.....	2.7	.....	79.9
12	Lake Ch..rles R. R., Light & Water Works Co.	1	......	2,370	2,370	......	74,935	.....	2.6	.....	82.5
25	Stone & Webster	1	......	1,400	1,400	......	76,335	.....	1.5	.....	84.0
1	Algiers Ry. & Lighting Co.	1	......	1,000	1,000	......	77,335	.....	1.1	.....	85.1
33	Municipal stations	25	......	8,061	8,061	......	85,396	.....	8.9	.....	94.0
	All other stations	26	160	5,284	5,444	160	90,840	100.0	6.0	100.0	100.0
	Total........................	60	160	90,680	90,840	......	....	100.0	100.0	.....	.....
	Central stations and electric railways, 1912	...	......	70,910	70,910	......	....	.....	.....	.....	.....

MAINE

25	E. W. Clark & Co. Management Cor.	16	37,330	18,390	55,720	37,330	55,720	13.4	16.4	13.4	16.4
119	International Paper Co.	7	45,750	8,095	53,845	83,080	109,565	16.5	15.9	29.9	32.3
18	Central Main Power Co.	6	20,700	6,700	27,400	103,780	136,965	7.5	8.1	37.4	40.4
132	St. Croix Paper Co.	2	25,000	......	25,000	128,780	161,965	9.0	7.4	46.4	47.8
115	Great Northern Paper Co.	1	24,500	......	24,500	153,280	186,465	8.8	7.2	55.2	55.0
134	Union Water Power Co.	1	18,400	......	18,400	171,680	204,865	6.6	5.4	61.8	60.4
130	Pepperell Mfg. Co.	1	7,000	10,800	17,800	178,680	222,665	2.5	5.2	64.3	65.6
136	S. D. Warren & Co.	6	12,200	5,000	17,200	190,880	239,865	4.4	5.1	68.7	70.7
126	Pejepscot Paper Co.	4	14,700	1,800	16,500	205,580	256,365	5.3	4.9	74.0	75.6
3	Hollingsworth & Whitney Co.	3	15,700	......	15,700	221,280	272,065	5.7	4.6	79.7	80.2
94	Rumfords Falls Power Co.	1	15,000	......	15,000	236,280	287,065	5.4	4.4	85.1	84.6
63	Main Ry. Light & Power Co.	5	2,686	2,600	5,286	238,966	292,351	1.0	1.6	86.1	86.2
110	Androscoggin Pulp Co.	2	3,522	1,100	4,622	242,488	296,973	1.3	1.4	87.4	87.6
1, 112	Atlantic Shore Ry. Co.	3	3,100	1,100	4,200	245,588	301,173	1.1	1.2	88.5	88.8
113	Edwards Mfg. Co.	1	4,000	......	4,000	249,588	305,173	1.4	1.2	89.9	90.0
13	Cabot Mfg. Co.	1	3,300	......	3,300	252,888	308,473	1.2	1.0	91.1	91.0
105	Municipal stations	5	1,996	805	2,801	254,884	311,274	.7	.8	91.8	91.8
	All other stations	77	22,705	5,036	27,741	277,589	339,015	8.2	8.2	100.0	100.0
	Total..........................	142	277,589 *	61,426 *	339,015 *	......	....	100.0	100.0	.....	.....
	Central stations and electric railways, 1912	...	95,502	34,271	129,773	......	....	.....	.....	.....	.....

* Totals include 170,272 water horsepower and 26,595 steam horsepower; total, 196,867 horsepower used in manufactures.

MARYLAND AND DISTRICT OF COLUMBIA

41	United Rys. & Elec. Co. of Baltimore	4	......	61,875	61,875	......	61,875	.....	28.0	.....	28.1
8	Consolidated Gas, Elec. Light & Power Co. of Baltimore	7	1,000	56,710	57,710	1,000	119,585	30.4	26.2	30.4	54.3
D. C. 2	Washington Ry. & Elec. Co.	1	......	53,800	53,800	1,000	173,385	.....	24.5	30.4	78.8

APPENDIX III—*Continued* MARYLAND AND DISTRICT OF COLUMBIA—*Concluded*

D. C. 1	Capital Traction Co.	1	......	16,870	16,870	1,000	190,255	.....	7.7	30.4	86.5
25	Hagerstown & Frederick Elec. Ry. Co.	2	......	5,905	5,905	1,000	196,160	.....	2.7	30.4	89.2
D. C. 4	Washington-Virginia Ry. Co.	1	......	4,170	4,170	1,000	200,330	.....	1.9	30.4	91.1
53	Baltimore & Ohio R. R. Co.	1	......	3,350	3,350	1,000	203,680	.....	1.5	30.4	92.6
20	Edison Electric Illuminating Co. of Cumberland	1	......	3,273	3,273	1,000	206,963	.....	1.5	30.4	94.1
54	Doherty Operating Co.	2	......	1,750	1,750	1,000	208,703	.....	.8	30.4	94.9
46	Municipal stations	7	......	2,533	2,533	1,000	211,236	.....	1.1	30.4	96.0
	All other stations	33	2,289	6,522	8,811	3,289	220,047	69.6	4.0	100.0	100.0
	Total	60	3,289	216,758	220,047	......	....	100.0	100.0	.....	.....
	Central stations and electric railways, 1912	.....	3,223	199,645	202,868	......	....	.....	.....	.....	.....

MASSACHUSETTS

20	Edison Elec. Illuminating Co.	3	......	140,850	140,850	......	140,850	.....	17.5	.....	17.5
170	Boston Elevated Ry. Co.	6	......	126,300	126,300	......	267,150	.....	15.7	.....	33.2
195	Massachusetts Elec. Co.	13	......	57,575	57,575	......	324,725	.....	7.2	.....	40.4
63	New England Investment Co.	7	......	53,830	53,830	......	378,555	.....	6.7	.....	47.1
70	New England Power Co. of Maine..	4	49,400	....	49,400	49,400	427,955	32.2	6.1	32.2	53.2
170	Turners Falls Power & Elec. Co....	2	36,900	....	36,900	86,300	464,855	24.0	4.6	56.2	57.8
100	C. H. Tenney & Co.	7	681	29,688	30,369	86,891	495,224	.4	3.8	56.6	61.6
115	Worcester Elec. Light Co.	2	......	21,330	21,330	86,981	516,554	.....	2.7	56.6	64.3
92	Stone & Webster	7	......	20,630	20,630	86,981	537,184	.....	2.6	56.6	66.9
110	United Elec. Light Co.	3	4,500	15,000	19,500	91,481	556,684	2.9	2.4	59.5	69.3
37	Ludlow Mfg. Association	3	9,900	8,200	18,100	101,381	574,784	6.5	2.2	66.0	71.5
23	Fall River Elec. Co.	1	......	17,330	17,330	101,381	592,114	.....	2.2	66.0	73.7
212	New York, New Haven & Hartford Ry. Co.	2	......	15,225	15,225	101,381	607,339	.....	1.9	66.0	75.6
61	New Bedford Gas & Elec. Co.	1	......	13,330	13,330	101,381	620,669	.....	1.7	66.0	77.3

MASSACHUSETTS—*Concluded*

219	Proprietors of locks and canals	1	11,262	....	11,262	112,643	631,931	7.3	1.4	73.3	78.7
167	Bliss Fabyan Co.	3	5,194	5,850	11,044	117,837	642,975	3.4	1.4	76.7	80.1
76	C. B. Parker & Co., Inc.	8	1,650	8,735	10,385	119,487	653,360	1.1	1.3	77.8	81.4
11	Cambridge Elec. Light Co.	1	......	8,670	8,670	119,487	662,030	.....	1.1	77.8	82.5
45	Mass. Lighting Co.	11	......	8,485	8,485	119,487	670,515	.....	1.0	77.8	83.5
117	Municipal stations	33	1,270	32,553	33,823	120,757	704,338	.8	4.2	78.6	87.7
	All other stations	108	32,928	65,725	98,653	153,685	802,991	21.4	12.3	100.0	100.0
	Total	226	153,685 *	649,306 *	802,991 *	......	....	100.0	100.0	.....	.....
	Central stations and elec. rys., 1912	...	26,189	597,387	623,576	......	....	.....	.....	.....	.....

* Totals include 32,348 water horsepower and 9,597 steam horsepower; total, 41,945 horsepower used in manufactures.

MICHIGAN

132	The North American Co.	12	5,133	176,572	181,705	5,133	181,705	2.4	30.2	2.4	30.2
33	Commonwealth Power Rys. & Light Co.	38	70,813	66,610	137,423	75,946	319,128	33.2	22.8	35.6	53.0
290	Detroit United Rys.	9	......	46,986	46,986	75,946	366,114	.....	7.8	35.6	60.8
174	Union Carbide Co.	1	30,800	......	30,800	106,746	396,914	14.4	5.1	50.0	65.9
103	Indiana & Michigan Elec. Co.	2	9,400	......	9,400	116,146	406,314	4.4	1.6	54.4	67.5
29	Cleveland Cliffs Iron Co.	3	8,000	......	8,000	124,146	414,314	3.8	1.3	58.2	68.8
301	Otsego Water Power Co.	1	3,000	5,000	8,000	127,146	422,314	1.4	1.3	59.6	70.1
287	Cambria Steel Co.	2	5,000	2,000	7,000	132,146	429,314	2.4	1.2	62.0	71.3
118	Menominee and Marinette Light & Traction Co.	2	5,700	1,100	6,800	137,846	436,114	2.7	1.1	64.7	72.4
120	Michigan Power Co.	2	2,000	4,670	6,670	139,846	442,784	.9	1.1	65.6	73.5
150	Peninsular Power Co.	2	5,250	833	6,083	145,096	448,867	2.5	1.0	68.1	74.5
165, 302	Stone & Webster	2	......	5,750	5,750	145,096	454,617	.....	.9	68.1	75.4
79	Escanaba Traction Co.	3	4,520	700	5,220	149,616	459,837	2.1	.9	70.2	76.3
303	Victoria Copper Mining Co.	1	4,000	......	4,000	153,616	463,837	1.9	.7	72.1	77.0
144	Oak Park Power Co.	1	......	4,000	4,000	153,616	467,837	.....	.7	72.1	77.7

APPENDIX III—*Continued*

MICHIGAN—*Concluded*

108	Ironwood & Bessemer Ry. & Light Co.	1	2,600	1,300	3,900	156,216	471,737	1.2	.6	73.3	78.3
289	Carnegie Steel Co.	1	3,850	......	3,850	160,066	475,587	1.8	.6	75.1	78.9
122	Middle West Utilities Co.	4	2,286	320	3,606	162,352	479,193	1.1	.6	76.2	79.5
183	Municipal stations	104	10,972	42,179	53,151	173,324	432,344	5.1	8.8	81.3	88.3
	All other stations	112	39,787	30,351	70,318	213,111	602,662	18.7	11.7	100.0	100.0
	Total	303	213,111 *	389,551 *	602,662 *	......	......	100.0	100.0	.....	.....
	Central stations and elec. rys., 1912	...	134,454	311,008	445,462	......	......	.....	.....	.....	.....

* Totals contains 15,850 water horsepower and 7,000 steam horsepower; total, 22,850 horsepower used in manufacture.

MINNESOTA

96	Twin City Rapid Transit Co.	3	......	66,700	66,700	......	66,700	.....	17.0	.....	17.0
68	Northwestern Power Co.	2	57,000	4,670	61,670	57,000	128,370	24.9	15.7	24.9	32.7
10	H. M. Byllesby Co.	10	43,450	18,500	61,950	100,450	190,320	18.9	15.8	43.8	48.5
81	Pillsbury-Washburn Flour Mills Co.	2	57,500	......	57,500	157,950	247,820	25.1	14.6	68.9	63.1
254	Minnesota & Ontario Power Co.	1	12,500	10,000	22,500	170,450	270,320	5.4	5.8	74.3	68.9
1	American Light & Traction Co.	1	7,800	9,000	16,800	178,250	287,120	3.5	4.3	77.8	73.2
258	Northwest Paper Co.	3	8,527	......	8,527	186,777	295,647	3.7	2.1	81.5	75.3
32	Crookston Waterworks, Power and Light Co.	1	4,000	1,600	5,600	190,777	301,247	1.7	1.5	83.2	76.8
242	Itaska Paper Co.	1	3,500	950	4,450	194,277	305,697	1.5	1.1	84.7	77.9
33	Cuyuna Range Power Co.	3	3,200	1,150	4,350	197,477	310,047	1.4	1.1	86.1	79.0
74	Otter Tail Power Co.	6	3,080	1,015	4,095	200,577	314,142	1.4	1.1	87.5	80.1
87	Public Service Co. of St. Cloud	1	3,000	1,000	4,000	203,557	318,142	1.3	1.0	88.8	81.1
105	Municipal stations	115	1,399	22,199	23,598	204,956	341,740	0.6	6.0	89.4	87.1
	All other stations	139	24,302	26,439	50,741	229,258	392,481	10.6	12.9	100.0	100.0
	Total	288	229,258 *	163,223 *	392,481 *	......	......	100.0	100.0	.....	.....
	Central stations and elec. rys., 1912	...	102,172	159,522	261,694	......	......	.....	.....	.....	.....

* These totals include 39,364 water horsepower and 14,867 steam horsepower; total, 54,231 horsepower used in manufacture.

APPENDIX III—*Continued*

MISSISSIPPI

14	Gulfport & Mississippi Coast Trac...	1	None	6,000	6,000	None	6,000	None	14.1	None	14.1
11	Doherty Operating Co.	2	"	5,295	5,295	"	11,295	"	12.5	"	26.6
2	American Public Utilities Co.	1	"	4,000	4,000	"	15,295	"	9.4	"	36.0
17	Laurel Light Railway Co.	1	"	2,120	2,120	"	17,415	"	5.0	"	41.0
10	Delta Light & Traction Co.	1	"	1,730	1,730	"	19,145	"	4.1	"	45.1
33	Vicksburg Light & Traction Co.	1	"	1,650	1,650	"	20,795	"	3.9	"	49.0
20	McComb City Electric Light & Traction Co.	1	"	1,400	1,400	"	22,195	"	3.3	"	52.3
32	United Public Utilities Co.	1	"	1,100	1,100	"	23,295	"	2.6	"	54.9
7	Columbia Railway, Light & Power Co.	1	"	1,000	1,000	"	24,295	"	2.3	"	57.2
5	Capital Light & Power Co.	1	"	800	800	"	25,095	"	1.9	"	59.1
37	Municipal stations	42	"	10,623	10,623	"	35,718	"	25.0	"	84.1
	All other stations	25	"	6,785	6,785	"	42,503	"	15.9	"	100.0
	Total........................	78	None	42,503	42,503	None	....	None	100.0	None	.....
	Central stations and elec. rys., 1912..	...	None	40,347	40,347	......	....	.....	.....	.....	.....

MISSOURI

103, 203	North American Co.	9	......	131,450	131,450	......	131,450	.....	40.2	.....	40.2
26	Doherty Operating Co.	6	20,400	49,838	70,238	20,400	201,688	98.7	21.5	98.7	61.7
54	Kansas City Ry. & Light Co.	1	......	53,300	53,300	20,400	254,988	.....	16.3	98.7	78.0
62	The Leclad Gas, Light Co.	1	......	10,000	10,000	20,400	264,988	.....	3.1	98.7	81.1
69	Light & Development Co. of St. Louis	7	......	4,810	4,810	20,400	269.798	.....	1.5	98.7	82.6
39	Federal Light & Traction Co.	1	......	4,040	4,040	20,400	273,838	.....	1.2	98.7	83.8
208	Southern Missouri Ry. Co.	1	......	3,000	3,000	20,400	276,838	.....	.9	98.7	84.7
89	Middle West Utilities Co.	7	......	2,805	2,805	20,400	279,643	.....	.8	98.7	85.5
201	Joplin & Pittsburg Ry. Co.	1	......	2,550	2,550	20,400	282,193	.....	.8	98.7	86.3
135	Municipal stations	65	......	19,501	19,501	20,400	301,694	.....	6.0	98.7	92.3
	All other stations	109	270	25,106	25,276	20,670	327,070	1.3	7.7	100.0	100.0
	Total......................	208	20,670	306,400	327,070	......	....	100.00	100.00	.....	.....
	Central stations and elec. rys., 1912.	...	1,902	306,133	308,035	......	....	.....	.....	.....	.....

APPENDIX III—*Continued*

MONTANA

23	Montana Power Co.	19	179,700	8,300	188,000	179,700	188,000	88.6	79.8	88.6	79.8
1, 57	Amalgamated Copper Co.	3	11,830	9,000	20,830	191,530	208,830	5.8	8.9	94.4	88.7
8	Clark-Missoula Power Co.	1	3,200	1,067	4,267	194,730	213,097	1.6	1.8	96.0	90.5
5	H. M. Byllesby & Co.	2	2,820	250	3,070	197,550	216,167	1.4	1.3	97.4	91.8
55	Municipal stations	2	......	1,005	1,005	197,550	217,172	.....	.4	97.4	92.2
	All other stations	38	5,345	13,071	18,416	202,895	235,588	2.6	7.8	100.0	100.0
	Total	65	202,895	32,693	235,588	......	....	100.00	100.00	.....	.....
	Central stations and electric railways, 1912	...	103,655	13,575	117,230	......	....	.....	.....	.....	.....

NEBRASKA

86	Omaha Electric Light & Power Co.	1	......	24,000	24,000	......	24,000	.....	24.3	.....	24.3
196	Omaha & Council Bluffs St. Ry. Co.	1	......	23,375	23,375	......	47,375	.....	23.7	.....	48.0
75	Lincoln Traction Co.	1	......	5,100	5,100	......	52,475	.....	5.2	.....	53.2
35	Doherty Operating Co.	2	......	2,700	2,700	......	55,175	.....	2.7	.....	55.9
70	Kearny Water & Electric Power Co.	1	1,350	1,350	2,700	1,350	57,875	12.5	2.7	12.5	58.6
21	Continental Gas & Electric Corp.	6	......	2,595	2,595	1,350	60,470	.....	2.6	12.5	61.2
111	Union Company of Omaha	1	......	1,450	1,450	1,350	61,920	.....	1.5	12.5	62.7
11	Blue River Power Co.	1	700	600	1,300	2,050	63,220	6.5	1.3	19.0	64.0
49	Grand Island Electric Co.	1	......	1,033	1,033	2,050	64,253	.....	1.1	19.0	65.1
48	Gothenburg Electric Light & Power Co.	1	500	400	900	2,550	65,153	4.6	.9	23.6	66.0
121	Municipal stations	73	5,050	14,414	19,464	7,600	84,617	46.8	19.7	70.4	85.7
	All other stations	107	3,199	10,902	14,101	10,799	98,718	29.6	14.3	100.0	100.0
	Total	196	10,799	87,919	98,718	......	....	100.00	100.00	.....	.....
	Central stations and electric railways, 1912	...	5,884	65,409	71,293	......	....	.....	.....	.....	.....

APPENDIX III—*Continued*

NEVADA

10	Stone & Webster	3	9,800	......	9,800	9,800	9,800	73.6	37.1	73.6	37.1
19	Utah Copper Co.	1	......	9,775	9,775	9,800	19,575	.....	37.0	73.6	74.1
14	United States Reclamation Service	1	2,490	......	2,490	12,290	22,065	18.7	9.4	92.3	83.5
5	Ely Light & Power Co.	2	160	1,400	1,560	12,450	23,625	1.2	5.9	93.5	89.4
4	Elko Lamoille Power Co.	2	415	300	715	12,865	24,340	3.1	2.7	96.6	92.1
17	Municipal stations	1	......	......	......	12,865	24,340	.....	.....	96.6	92.1
	All other stations	9	455	1,644	2,099	13,320	26,439	3.4	7.9	100.0	100.0
	Total	19	13,320	13,119	26,439	......	....	100.00	100.00	.....	.....
	Central stations and elec. railways, 1912	...	12,540	2,880	15,420	......	....	.....	.....	.....	.....

NEW HAMPSHIRE

70	Berlin Mills Co.	2	31,700	......	31,700	31,700	31,700	29.2	21.2	29.2	21.2
4	Amoskeag Mfg. Co.	1	22,445	......	22,445	54,145	54,145	20.7	15.0	49.9	36.2
73	International Paper Co.	2	15,300	2,350	17,650	69,445	71,795	14.1	11.8	64.0	48.0
40	Manchester Traction, Light & Power Co.	2	5,990	6,000	11,900	75,345	83,695	5.4	8.0	69.4	56.0
49	New Hampshire Electric Rys. Co.	1	......	10,670	10,670	75,345	94,365	.....	7.1	69.4	63.1
76	Pacific Mills	2	1,500	5,060	6,560	76,845	100,925	1.4	4.4	70.8	67.5
73	J. E. Henry & Sons Co.	1	1,800	2,800	4,600	78,645	105,525	1.7	3.1	72.5	70.6
75	Nashua Mfg. Co.	1	4,500	......	4,500	83,145	110,025	4.1	3.0	76.6	73.6
45	Middle West Utilities Co.	2	1,600	2,000	3,600	84,745	113,625	1.5	2.4	78.1	76.0
9	Boston & Maine R. R. Co.	3	2,190	10,050	3,240	86,935	116,865	2.0	2.2	80.1	78.2
15	Concord Electric Co.	1	2,000	1,000	3,000	88,935	119,865	1.8	2.0	81.9	80.2
72	Great Falls Mfg. Co.	1	3,000	......	3,000	91,935	122,865	2.8	2.0	84.7	82.2
78	Suncock Mills	1	3,000	......	3,000	94,935	125,865	2.8	2.0	87.5	84.2
6	W. S. Barstow & Co., Inc.	1	600	1,900	2,500	95,935	128,365	.6	1.7	88.1	85.9
68	Municipal stations	2	600	545	1,145	96,135	129,510	.6	.8	88.7	86.7
	All other stations	55	12,280	7,645	19,925	108,415	149,435	11.3	13.3	100.0	100.0
	Total	78	108,415 *	41,020 *	149,435 *	......	....	100.00	100.00	.....	.....
	Central stations and elec. railways, 1912	...	59,119	29,211	88,330	......	....	.....	.....	.....	.....

* Totals include 59,000 water horsepower and 7,410 steam horsepower; total, 66,410 horsepower used in manufacturing.

APPENDIX III—*Continued*

NEW JERSEY

47	Public Service Corporation of N. J..	16	......	232,905	232,905	......	232,905	.....	68.6	.....	68.6
1	American Gas & Electric Co.	2	......	17,675	17,675	......	250,580	.....	5.2	.....	73.8
44	Penna. R. R. Co.	1	......	10,670	10,670	......	261,250	.....	3.1	.....	76.9
38	New Jersey General Security Co. ...	3	7,200	......	7,200	7,200	268,450	72.4	2.1	72.4	79.0
30	Jersey Central Traction Co.	1	......	6,400	6,400	7,200	274,850	.....	1.9	72.4	80.9
9	W. S. Barstow & Co., Inc.	4	1,500	3,630	5,130	8,700	279,980	15.1	1.5	87.5	82.4
2	American Light & Traction Co.	1	......	3,950	3,950	8,700	283,930	.....	1.2	87.5	83.6
4	American Rys. Co.	1	......	2,725	2,725	8,700	286,655	.....	.8	87.5	84.4
20	Commonwealth Water & Light Co...	2	100	2,450	2,550	8,800	289,205	1.0	.7	88.5	85.1
66	Sayerville Electric Light & Power Co.	1	......	2,500	2,500	8,800	291,705	.....	.7	88.5	85.8
82	Municipal stations	10	112	2,885	2,997	8,912	294,702	1.1	.9	89.6	86.7
	All other stations	60	1,035	43,845	44,880	9,947	339,582	10.4	13.3	100.0	100.0
	Total........................	102	9,947	329,635	339,582	......	....	100.00	100.00	.....	.....
	Central stations and elec. rys., 1912..	...	1,569	267,043	268,612	......	....	.....	.....	.....	.....

NEW MEXICO

6	Federal Light & Traction Co.	3	......	5,158	5,158	......	5,158	.....	37.1	.....	37.1
18	Roswell Gas & Electric Co.	1	......	1,650	1,650	......	6,808	.....	11.9	.....	49.0
19	Santa Fe Water & Electric Co.	1	102	445	547	102	7,355	18.5	4.0	18.5	53.0
20	Silver City Power Co.	1	......	460	460	102	7,815	.....	3.3	18.5	56.3
17	Raton Electric Light & Power Co...	1	......	425	425	102	8,240	.....	3.1	18.5	59.4
16	Public Utilities Co.	1	350	......	350	452	8,590	63.4	2.5	81.9	61.9
14	Peoples Light & Power Co.	1	......	350	350	452	8,940	.....	2.5	81.9	64.4
25	Tucumcari Light & Power Co.	1	......	350	350	452	9,290	.....	2.5	81.9	66.9
26, 27	United States Reclamation Service and municipal stations	4	......	3,185	3,185	452	12,475	.....	22.9	81.9	89.8
	All other stations	16	100	1,322	1,422	552	13,897	18.1	10.2	100.0	100.0
	Total........................	30	552	13,345	13,897	......	....	100.00	100.00	.....	.....
	Central stations and elec. rys., 1912..	...	817	10,198	11,015	......	....	.....	.....	.....	.....

28	Consolidated Gas Co. of New York.	8	......	481,895	481,895	......	481,895	.....	21.2	.....	21.2
388	Interborough Metropolitan Co.	2	......	246,500	246,500	......	728,395	.....	10.8	.....	32.0
371	Brooklyn Rapid Transit Co.	5	......	198,025	198,025	......	926,420	.....	8.7	.....	40.7
66	Hydraulic Power Co. of Niagara Falls	3	153,000	......	153,000	153,000	1,079,420	19.1	6.7	19.1	47.4
102	The Niagara Falls Power Co.	2	115,000	......	115,000	268,000	1,194,420	14.4	5.1	33.5	52.5
97, 408	New York Central & Hudson River R. R. Co.	4	22,325	70,800	93,125	290,325	1,287,545	2.8	4.1	36.3	56.6
391	International Paper Co.	10	75,180	17,025	92,205	365,505	1,379,750	9.4	4.1	45.7	60.7
411	Pennsylvania Railroad Co.	1	......	74,700	74,700	365,505	1,454,450	.....	3.3	45.7	64.0
72	Kings County Electric Light and Power Co.	3	......	74,670	74,670	365,505	1,529,120	.....	3.3	45.7	67.3
145	Stone & Webster	4	45,800	9,000	54,800	411,305	1,583,920	5.7	2.4	51.4	69.7
5	Illuminum Company of America...	2	40,000	......	40,000	451,305	1,623,920	5.0	1.8	56.4	71.5
104	Niagara, Lockport & Ontario Power Co.	1	40,000	......	40,000	491,305	1,663,920	5.0	1.8	61.4	73.3
53	General Electric Company	3	31,000	......	31,000	522,305	1,694,920	3.9	1.4	65.3	74.7
25	Coches Company	1	30,000	......	30,000	552,305	1,724,920	3.7	1.3	69.0	76.0
387	Hudson & Manhattan R. R. Co. ...	1	......	24,000	24,000	552,305	1,748,920	.....	1.1	69.0	77.1
164	Utica Gas & Electric Co..........	5	11,800	11,000	22,800	564,105	1,771,720	1.5	1.0	70.5	78.1
418	St. Regis Paper Co.	5	19,800	2,590	22,390	583,905	1,794,110	2.5	1.0	73.0	79.1
158	United Gas & Elec. Corp. of Connecticut	2	500	18,440	18,940	584,405	1,813,050	.1	.8	73.1	79.1
432	West Virginia Pulp & Paper Co. ..	1	9,550	8,800	18,350	593,955	1,831,400	1.2	.8	74.3	80.7
160	United Gas Improvement Co.	3	350	15,720	16,070	594,305	1,847,470	.....	.7	74.3	81.4
319	Municipal stations	48	3,155	10,721	13,876	597,460	1,861,346	.4	.6	74.7	82.0
	All other stations	335	202,070	207,464	409,534	799,530	2,270,880	25.3	18.0	100.0	100.0
	Total..........	449	799,530*	1,471,350*	2,270,880*	......	....	100.00	100.00	.....	.....
	Central stations and elec. rys., 1912..	...	530,921	1,282,608	1,813,529	......	....	.....	.....	.....	.....

* Totals contain 181,238 water horsepower and 34,026 steam horsepower; total, 215,264 horsepower used in manufacturing.

APPENDIX III—*Continued*

NORTH CAROLINA

61	Southern Power Co.	4	30,000	38,010	68,010	30,000	68,010	30.3	37.6	30.3	37.6
8	Carolina Power & Light Co.	9	44,400	7,725	52,125	74,400	120,135	44.8	28.9	75.1	66.5
46	North Carolina Electrical Power Co.	3	7,530	......	7,530	81,930	127,665	7.6	4.2	82.7	70.7
66	Southern Publ. Utilities Co.	2	2,100	3,350	5,450	84,030	133,115	2.1	3.0	84.8	73.7
71	Tide Water Power Co.	1	......	5,000	5,000	84,030	138,115	.....	2.8	84.8	76.5
53	J. A. Roper Lumber Co.	3	......	4,300	4,300	84,030	142,415	.....	2.4	84.8	78.9
131	Roanoke Rapids Power Co.	1	4,100	......	4,100	88,130	146,515	4.1	2.3	88.9	81.2
127	Erwin Cotton Mills Co.	1	2,037	1,240	3,277	90,167	149,792	2.1	1.8	91.0	83.0
51	Piedmont Railway & Elec. Co.	1	......	2,500	2,500	90,167	152,292	.....	1.4	91.0	84.4
49	North Carolina Public Service Co.	2	......	2,480	2,480	90,167	154,772	.....	1.4	91.0	85.8
24	Doherty Operating Co.	1	......	2,200	2,200	90,167	156,972	.....	1.2	91.0	87.0
35	Haywood Elec. Power Co.	1	1,950	......	1,950	92,117	158,922	2.0	1.1	93.0	88.1
69	Spencer Mountain Mills	1	1,000	......	1,000	93,117	159,922	1.0	.5	94.0	88.6
28	Electric Light Co. of Elizabeth City	1	......	1,000	1,000	93,117	160,922	.....	.5	94.0	89.1
77	Municipal stations	49	1,035	8,923	9,958	94,152	170,880	1.0	5.5	95.0	94.6
	All other stations	51	4,953	4,793	9,746	99,105	180,626	5.0	5.4	100.0	100.0
	Total	131	99,105	81,521	180,626	......	....	100.00	100.00	.....	.....
	Central stations and elec. rys., 1912	131	99,105 *	81,521 *	180,626 *	......	....	.....	.....	.....	.....

NORTH DAKOTA

2	H. M. Bilesby & Co.	3	......	6,950	6,950	......	6,950	.....	36.7	.....	36.7
18	Hughes Electric Co.	1	......	1,200	1,200	......	8,150	.....	6.3	.....	43.0
32	Otter Tail Power Co.	2	......	600	600	......	8,750	.....	3.2	.....	46.2
37, 44	U. S. Reclamation Service and municipal stations	12	......	4,212	4,212	......	12,962	.....	22.3	.....	68.5
	All other stations	62	80	5,883	5,963	80	18,925	100.0	31.5	100.0	100.0
	Total	80	80	18,845	18,925	......	....	100.0	100.0	.....	.....
	Central stations and elec. rys., 1912	.....	80	16,249	16,249	......	....	.....	.....	.....	.....

* These totals contain 6,887 water horsepower and 1,365 steam horsepower; total, 8,252 horsepower used in manufacturing.

OHIO

47	Central States Elec. Corporation	1	......	135,700	135,700	......	135,700	.....	18.1	.....	18.1
387	Ohio Traction Co.	6	......	65,611	65,611	......	201,311	.....	8.7	.....	26.8
88	Doherty Operating Co.	11	1,700	63,735	65,435	1,700	266,746	8.5	8.7	8.5	35.5
62	Columbia Gas & Elec. Co.	1	......	38,930	38,930	1,700	305,676	.....	5.2	8.5	40.7
68	Columbus Railway, Power & Light Co.	6	......	34,670	34,670	1,700	340,346	.....	4.6	8.5	45.3
182	Northern Ohio Traction & Light Co.	2	2,270	31,000	33,270	3,970	373,616	11.4	4.4	19.9	49.7
184	Ohio Electric Railway Co..........	6	700	27,800	28,500	4,670	402,116	3.5	3.8	23.4	53.5
37	Cleveland Railway Co.	2	......	27,100	27,100	4,670	429,216	.....	3.6	23.4	57.1
4	American Gas & Electric Co.	11	......	25,405	25,405	4,670	454,621	.....	3.4	23.4	60.5
78	Dayton Power & Light Co.	6	100	20,120	20,220	4,770	474,841	.5	2.7	23.9	63.2
203	Republic Railway & Light Co.	2	......	16,330	16,330	4,770	491,171	.....	2.2	23.9	65.4
58	Cleveland Southwestern & Col. R. R. Co.	3	......	14,750	14,750	4,770	505,921	.....	2.0	23.9	67.4
103	East Liverpool Traction & Light Co.	3	330	14,100	14,430	5,100	520,351	1.6	1.9	25.5	69.3
238	United Service Co.	5	1,630	10,190	11,820	6,730	532,171	8.2	1.6	33.7	70.9
249	Western Ohio Railroad Co.	1	......	11,330	11,330	6,730	543,501	.....	1.5	33.7	72.4
147	Lake Shore Electric Ry. Co.	1	......	11,000	11,000	6,730	554,501	.....	1.5	33.7	73.9
64	Columbus, Delaware Marion Ry. Co.	4	......	9,660	9,660	6,730	564,161	.....	1.3	33.7	75.2
28	W. S. Barstow & Co.	3	......	6,890	6,890	6,730	571,051	.....	.9	33.7	76.1
24	Auglaize Power Co.	1	6,666	......	6,666	13,396	577,717	33.4	.9	67.1	77.0
74	Commonwealth Power, Railway and Light Co.	1	......	6,000	6,000	13,396	583,717	.....	.8	67.1	77.8
260	Municipal stations	114	175	55,795	55,934	13,571	639,651	.9	7.5	68.0	85.3
	All other stations	205	6,377	103,709	11,086	19,948	749,737	32.0	14.7	100.0	100.0
	Total.........................	395	19,948	729,789	749,737	......	....	100.0	100.0	.....	.....
	Central stations and electric railways, 1912	...	10,690	659,657	670,347	......	....	.....	.....	.....	.....

APPENDIX III—*Continued*

OKLAHOMA

9	H. M. Byllesby & Co.	5	......	17,215	17,215	......	17,215	.....	24.4	.....	24.4
48	Middle West Utilities Co.	7	1,200	9,490	10,690	1,200	27,905	68.2	15.2	68.2	39.6
138	Oklahoma Railway Co.	1	......	5,980	5,980	1,200	33,885	.....	8.5	68.2	48.1
3	American Public Service Co.	2	......	2,125	2,125	1,200	36,010	.....	3.0	68.2	51.1
18	Choctaw Railway & Lighting Co.	1	......	1,650	1,650	1,200	37,660	.....	2.3	68.2	53.4
64	Southwestern Cities Electric Co.	3	......	1,560	1,560	1,200	39,220	.....	2.2	68.2	55.6
6	Ardmore Ice, Light & Power Co.	1	......	1,525	1,525	1,200	40,745	.....	2.2	68.2	57.8
63	Shawnee Gas & Electric Co.	1	......	1,450	1,450	1,200	42,195	.....	2.1	68.2	59.9
24	Doherty Operating Co.	1	......	1,420	1,420	1,200	43,615	.....	2.0	68.2	61.9
75	Municipal stations	61	358	11,428	11,786	1,558	55,401	20.4	16.7	88.6	78.6
	All other stations	56	200	14,908	15,108	1,758	70,509	11.4	21.4	100.0	100.0
	Total	139	1,758	68,751	70,509	......	....	100.0	100.0	.....	.....
	Central stations and electric railways, 1912	...	2,135	61,462	63,597	......	....	.....	.....	.....	.....

OREGON

53	E. W. Clark & Co. Mortgage Corp.	11	80,000	35,875	115,875	80,000	115,875	51.0	52.3	51.0	52.3
94	Crown-Williamette Paper Co.	3	26,124	3,500	29,624	106,124	145,499	16.7	13.4	67.7	65.7
14	California-Oregon Power Co.	5	11,100	......	11,100	117,224	156,599	7.1	5.0	74.8	70.7
1	American Power & Light Co.	5	9,090	1,650	10,740	126,314	167,339	5.8	4.8	80.6	75.5
9	H. M. Byllesby & Co.	6	520	6,227	6,747	128,834	174,086	.3	3.0	80.9	78.5
49	National Securities Corporation	1	5,000	......	5,000	131,834	179,086	3.2	2.3	84.1	80.8
31	Eastern Oregon Light & Power Co.	5	3,700	......	3,700	135,534	182,786	2.3	1.7	86.4	82.5
81	Municipal stations	12	4,646	242	4,888	140,180	187,674	3.0	2.2	89.4	84.7
	All other stations	53	16,583	17,447	34,030	156,763	221,704	10.6	15.3	100.0	100.0
	Total	101	156,763	64,941	221,704	......	....	100.0	100.0	.....	.....
	Central stations and electric railways, 1912	...	105,302	50,163	155,465	......	....	.....	.....	.....	.....

APPENDIX III—*Continued*

PENNSYLVANIA

88	The Philadelphia Co.	10	......	161,508	161,508	......	161,508	.....	16.2	.....	16.2
85	Penn. Water & Power Co.	2	118,000	......	118,000	118,000	279,508	70.0	11.9	70.0	28.1
305	Philadelphia Rapid Transit Co.	5	......	105,730	105,730	118,000	385,238	.....	10.6	70.0	38.7
60	Lehigh Coal & Navigation Co.	4	5,367	70,500	75,867	123,367	461,105	3.2	7.6	73.2	46.3
8	American Water Works & Electric Co.	11	......	49,545	49,545	123,367	510,650	.....	5.0	74.6	51.3
19	W. S. Barstow & Co. (Inc.)	10	2,400	46,800	49,200	125,767	559,850	1.4	5.0	73.2	56.3
6	American Gas & Electric Co.	1	......	35,800	35,800	125,767	595,650	.....	3.6	73.2	59.9
116	United Gas & Electric Corp. of Conn.	3	......	22,950	22,950	125,767	618,600	.....	2.3	74.6	62.2
134	York Haven Water & Power Co.	1	20,000	......	20,000	145,767	638,600	11.9	2.0	86.5	64.2
64	Lehigh Valley Transit Co.	3	......	18,330	18,330	145,767	656,930	.....	1.8	86.5	66.0
75	Penn Central Light & Power Co.	6	2,000	16,220	16,220	147,767	675,150	1.2	1.8	87.7	67.8
126	H. D. Walbridge & Co.	2	250	14,250	14,500	148,017	689,650	.2	1.5	87.9	69.3
98	Philadelphia Electric Co.	2	......	13,920	13,920	148,017	703,570	.....	1.4	87.9	70.7
49	Erie County Electric Co.	1	......	11,770	11,770	148,017	715,340	.....	1.2	87.9	73.0
1	American Gas Co.	5	500	10,800	10,300	148,517	726,640	.3	1.1	88.2	73.0
259	Municipal stations	41	538	15,549	16,087	149,055	742,727	.3	1.6	88.5	74.6
	All other stations	243	19,478	232,856	252,334	168,533	995,061	11.5	25.4	100.0	100.0
	Total	350	168,533	826,528	995,061	......	....	100.0	100.0	.....	.....
	Central stations and elec. railways, 1912	...	133,018	775,861	908,879	......	....	.....	.....	.....	.....

RHODE ISLAND

6	New York, New Haven & Hartford R. R. Co.	1	......	46,000	46,000	......	46,000	.....	48.5	.....	48.5
3	Narragansett Electric Lighting Co.	3	......	28,260	28,260	......	74,260	.....	29.8	.....	78.3
1	Massachusetts Lighting Co.	2	......	9,800	9,800	......	84,060	.....	10.4	.....	88.7
7	Stone & Webster	3	2,485	6,650	9,135	2,485	93,195	100.0	9.6	100.0	98.3
12	Municipal stations	1	......	......	......	2,485	93,195	.....	.....	100.0	98.3
	All other stations	2	......	1,625	1,625	2,485	94,820	.....	1.7	100.0	100.0
	Total	12	2,485	93,335	94,820	......	....	100.0	100.0	.....	.....
	Central stations and elec. railways, 1912	...	2,440	92,909	29,349	......	....	.....	.....	.....	.....

APPENDIX III—*Continued*

SOUTH CAROLINA

34	Southern Power Co.	5	127,850	9,000	136,850	127,850	136,850	56.3	50.0	56.3	50.0
12	Columbia Railway, Gas & Electric Co.	2	26,000	7,330	33,330	153,850	170,180	11.5	12.2	67.8	62.2
39	Southern Public Utilities Co.	5	16,300	1,850	18,150	170,150	188,330	7.2	6.6	75.0	68.8
32	South Carolina Light, Power & Rys. Co.	2	12,000	4,000	16,000	182,150	204,330	5.3	5.9	80.3	74.7
74	Pelzer Manufacturing Co.	1	6,500	4,500	11,000	188,650	215,330	2.9	4.0	83.2	78.7
45	Union Mfg. & Power Co.	1	8,000	......	8,000	196,650	223,330	3.5	2.9	86.7	81.6
46	United Gas Improvement Co.	1	......	6,670	6,670	196,650	230,000	.....	2.4	86.7	84.0
48	Ware Shoals Manufacturing Co.	1	5,000	......	5,000	201,650	235,000	2.2	1.8	88.9	85.8
75	Tucapua Mills	1	5,000	......	5,000	206,650	240,000	2.2	1.8	91.1	97.6
1	Belton Power Co.	1	4,650	......	4,650	211,300	244,650	2.0	1.7	93.1	89.3
72	Lockhart Mills	1	2,800	......	2,800	214,100	247,450	1.2	1.0	94.3	90.3
73	Pacolet Manufacturing Co.	1	2,800	......	2,800	216,900	250,250	1.2	1.0	95.5	91.3
70	Clifton Manufacturing Co.	1	2,000	750	2,750	218,900	253,000	.9	1.0	96.4	92.3
49	Municipal stations	21	......	4,625	4,625	218,900	257,625	.....	1.7	96.4	94.0
	All other stations	22	8,112	8,300	16,412	227,012	274,037	3.6	6.0	100.0	100.0
	Total	76	227,012 *	47,025 *	274,037 *	......	....	100.0	100.0	.....	.....
	Central stations and elec. railways, 1912	...	178,555	52,051	230,606	......	....	.....	.....	.....	.....

SOUTH DAKOTA

40	Homestake Mining Co.	2	6,225	175	6,400	6,225	6,400	47.8	13.5	47.8	13.5
8	H. M. Byllesby & Co.	3	2,063	3,740	5,805	8,290	12,205	15.8	12.2	63.6	25.7
17	Consolidated Power & Light Co. of South Dakota	2	1,000	4,670	5,670	9,290	17,875	7.7	11.9	71.3	37.6
20	Dakota Power Co.	2	2,550	530	3,080	11,840	20,955	19.6	6.5	90.9	44.1
78	Municipal stations	17	......	2,356	2,356	11,840	23,311	....	5.0	90.9	49.1
	All other stations	70	1,213	22,963	24,176	13,053	47,487	9.1	50.9	100.0	100.0
	Total	96	13,053	34,434	47,487	......	....	100.0	100.0	.....	.....
	Central stations and elec. railways, 1912	...	6,913	20,835	27,748	......	....	.....	.....	.....	.....

* Totals contain 20,400 water horsepower and 5,950 steam horsepower; total, 26,350 horsepower used in manufacturing.

TENNESSEE

10	E. W. Clark & Co. Mortgage Corp...	5	45,000	30,000	75,000	45,000	75,000	46.0	40.1	46.0	40.1
9	Chattanooga & Tennessee River Power Co.	1	42,000	......	42,000	87,000	117,000	42.9	22.4	88.9	62.5
90	United Gas & Elec. Corp. of Conn...	2	......	22,970	22,970	87,000	139,970	.....	12.3	88.9	74.8
40	Memphis Consolidated Gas & Electric Co.	1	......	11,500	11,500	87,000	151,470	.....	6.1	88.9	80.9
41	Merchants Power Co.	1	......	7,330	7,330	87,000	158,800	.....	3.9	88.9	84.8
56	Tennessee Eastern Electric Co.	2	5,000	2,270	7,270	92,000	166,070	5.1	3.9	94.0	88.7
22	Doherty Operating Co.	2	3,200	800	4,000	95,200	170,070	3.3	2.1	97.3	90.8
47	Public Light & Power Co.	4	980	1,250	2,230	96,180	172,300	1.0	1.2	98.3	92.0
31	Jackson Railway & Light Co.	1	......	1,670	1,670	96,180	173,970	.....	.9	98.3	92.9
61	Municipal stations	29	300	6,646	6,946	96,480	180,916	.3	3.7	98.6	96.6
	All other stations	42	1,355	5,014	6,369	97,835	187,285	1.4	3.4	100.0	100.0
	Total..........	90	97,835	89,450	187,285	......	....	100.0	100.0	.....	.....
	Central stations and electric railways, 1912	...	27,750	94,611	122,361	......	....	.....	.....	.....	.....

TEXAS

208	Stone & Webster	11	......	71,793	71,793	......	71,793	.....	32.1	.....	32.1
5	American Power & Light Co.	19	......	46,775	46,775	......	118,568	.....	20.9	.....	53.0
232	United Gas & Electric Corporation..	1	......	15,500	15,500	......	134,068	.....	6.9	.....	59.9
4	American Light & Traction Co.	1	......	12,278	12,278	......	146,346	.....	5.5	.....	65.4
73	Doherty Operating Co.	5	......	6,290	6,290	......	152,636	.....	2.8	.....	68.2
24	American Public Service Co.	7	......	4,220	4,220	......	156,856	.....	1.9	.....	70.1
222	Texas Southern Electric Co.	5	1,800	1,552	3,352	1,800	160,208	26.6	1.5	26.6	71.6
247	Yellow Pine Paper Mills Co.	1	......	3,000	3,000	1,800	163,208	.....	1.3	26.6	72.9
70	Dallas Ice Factory, Light & Power Co.	1	......	2,350	2,350	1,800	165,558	.....	1.1	26.6	74.0
138	The Laredo Electric Ry. Co.	1	......	1,900	1,900	1,800	167,458	.....	.9	26.6	74.9
268	Austin Street Ry. Co.	1	......	1,750	1,750	1,800	169,208	.....	.8	26.6	75.7
61	Colorado River Power Co.	1	1,650	......	1,650	3,450	170,858	24.3	.7	50.9	76.4

APPENDIX III—*Continued*

TEXAS—*Concluded*

57	Citizens Electric Light & Power Co.	1	1,190	250	1,440	4,640	172,298	17.6	.6	68.5	77.0
1, 248	State and municipal stations	21	225	8,249	8,474	4,865	180,772	3.3	3.8	71.8	80.8
	All other stations	198	1,912	40,949	42,861	6,777	223,633	28.2	19.2	100.0	100.0
	Total........................	274	6,777	216,856	223,633	......	....	100.0	100.0	.....	.....
	Central stations and electric rys., 1912.	...	3,503	164,185	167,688	......	....	.....	.....	.....	.....
	UTAH										
22	Utah Securities Corporation	25	79,565	28,594	108,159	79,565	108,159	82.2	84.3	82.2	84.3
1	Beaver River Power Co.	1	2,500	......	2,500	82,065	110,659	2.6	2.0	84.8	86.3
11	L. L. Nunn	4	1,550	420	1,970	83,615	112,629	1.6	1.5	86.4	87.8
49	Municipal stations	22	7,151	650	7,801	90,766	120,430	7.4	6.0	93.8	93.8
	All other stations	24	5,968	1,950	7,918	96,734	128,348	6.2	6.2	100.0	100.0
	Total........................	76	96,734	31,614	128,348	......	....	100.0	100.0	.....	.....
	Central stations and electric rys., 1912.	...	74,688	27,186	101,874	......	....	.....	.....	.....	.....
	VERMONT										
41	New England Power Co of Maine ..	3	31,300	700	32,000	31,300	32,000	26.5	21.9	26.5	21.9
6	International Paper Co.	3	16,600	1,925	18,525	47,900	50,525	14.1	12.7	40.6	34.6
57	C. H. Tenney & Co.	7	8,964	8,370	17,334	56,864	67,859	7.6	11.9	48.2	46.5
2	American Gas Co.	2	13,000	1,330	14,330	69,864	82,189	11.0	9.8	59.2	56.3
6	W. S. Barstow & Co. (Inc.)	8	8,975	4,625	13,600	78,839	95,789	7.6	9.3	66.8	65.6
66	Vermont Marble Co.	6	8,700	1,700	10,400	87,539	106,189	7.4	7.1	74.2	72.7
99	Missisquoi Pulp Co.	1	4,400	200	4,600	91,939	110,789	3.7	3.2	77.9	75.9
37	Middle West Utilities Co.	3	1,988	2,020	4,008	93,927	114,797	1.7	2.8	79.6	78.7
93	American Woolen Co.	1	2,844	......	2,844	96,771	117,641	2.4	2.0	82.0	80.7
4	American Pipe & Construction Co...	1	2,250	530	2,780	99,021	120,421	1.9	1.9	83.9	82.6
76	Woodbury Granite Co.	3	1,250	1,330	2,580	100,271	123,001	1.1	1.8	85.0	84.4
94	Dalton Paper Mills	1	2,103	......	2,103	102,374	125,104	1.8	1.4	86.8	85.8
46	Newport Electric Co, ...	1	1,600	300	1,900	103,974	127,004	1.4	1.3	88.2	87.1

VERMONT—*Concluded*

95	Green Mountain Pulp Co.	1	1,700	......	1,700	105,674	128,704	1.4	1.2	89.6	88.3
33	Lyman Falls Power Co.	1	1,336	......	1,336	107,010	130,040	1.1	.9	90.7	89.2
80	Municipal stations	13	4,910	1,830	6,740	111,920	136,780	4.2	4.6	94.9	93.8
	All other stations	47	5,969	3,105	9,074	117,889	145,854	5.1	6.2	100.0	100.0
	Total	102	117,889 *	27,965 *	145,854 *	......	....	100.0	100.0	.....	.....
	Central stations and electric rys., 1912.	...	39,927	18,091	58,018	......	....	.....	.....	.....	.....

* Totals include 28,016 water horsepower and 2,215 steam horsepower; total, 30,141 horsepower used in manufactures.

VIRGINIA

55	Virginia Railway & Power Co.	5	19,000	46,420	65,420	19,000	65,420	20.2	31.4	20.2	31.4
7	H. M. Byllesby & Co.	3	20,900	7,500	28,400	39,900	93,820	22.1	13.6	42.3	45.0
86	Riverside & Dan River Cotton Mills.	2	13,270	11,500	24,770	53,170	118,590	14.1	11.9	56.4	56.9
2	American Railways Co.	4	7,650	9,500	17,150	60,820	135,740	8.1	8.2	64.5	65.1
35	Newport News & Hampton Railway, Gas & Electric Co.	2	......	8,280	8,280	60,820	144,020	.....	4.0	64.5	69.1
59	Virginia Western Power Co.	5	3,750	2,525	6,275	64,570	150,295	4.0	3.0	68.5	72.1
29	Municipal Service Co.	4	1,900	3,555	5,455	66,470	155,750	2.0	2.6	70.5	74.7
49	Spotsylvania Power Co.	1	4,500	......	4,500	70,970	160,250	4.8	2.2	75.3	76.9
86	The Warren-Burnham Co.	1	......	4,000	4,000	70,970	164,250	.....	1.9	75.3	78.8
83	The Bedford Pulp & Paper Co.	1	3,400	......	3,400	74,370	167,650	3.6	1.6	78.9	80.4
89	The Washington & Old Dominion R. R. Co.	1	......	3,300	3,300	74,370	170,950	.....	1.6	78.9	82.0
37	Norfolk Southern R. R. Co.	1	......	3,000	3,000	74,370	173,950	.....	1.5	78.9	83.5
10	Charlottesville & Albemarle Ry. Co.	1	......	2,300	2,300	74,370	176,250	.....	1.1	78.9	84.6
18	Emporia Hydro-Electric Power Co.	1	1,500	......	1,500	75,870	177,750	1.6	.7	80.5	85.3
68	Municipal stations	15	6,124	6,278	12,402	81,994	190,152	6.5	6.0	87.0	91.3
	All other stations	44	12,235	5,959	18,194	94,229	208,346	13.0	8.7	100.0	100.0
	Total	90	94,229 *	114,117 *	208,346 *	......	....	100.0	100.0	.....	.....
	Central stations and elec. rys., 1912.	...	66,399	94,090	160,489	......	....	.....	.....	.....	.....

* Totals include 17,830 water horsepower and 15,500 steam horsepower; totals, 33,330 horsepower used in manufactures.

APPENDIX III—*Continued*

WASHINGTON

62	Stone & Webster	11	85,300	38,160	123,460	85,300	123,460	25.8	29.1	25.8	29.1
83	Washington Water Power Co.	4	92,900	16,000	108,900	178,200	232,360	28.0	25.6	53.8	54.7
59	Spokane & Inland Emp. R. R. Co.	1	20,000	......	20,000	198,200	252,360	6.0	4.7	59.8	59.4
1	American Power & Light Co.	11	13,888	5,936	19,824	212,088	272,184	4.2	4.7	64.0	64.1
46	Northern Electric Co.	1	18,000	......	18,000	230,088	290,184	5.4	4.2	69.4	68.3
53	Olympic Power Co.	1	9,600	......	9,600	239,688	299,784	2.9	2.3	72.3	70.6
114	Great Northern Railroad Co.	1	8,500	......	8,500	248,188	308,284	2.6	2.0	74.9	72.6
38	Lewiston-Clarkson Improvement Co.	1	3,300	2,330	5,630	251,488	313,914	1.0	1.3	75.9	73.9
89	Wenatchee Valley Gas & Electric Co.	3	4,800	......	4,800	256,288	318,714	1.5	1.1	77.4	75.0
30	Inland Portland Cement Co.	1	4,000	......	4,000	260,288	322,714	1.2	1.0	78.6	76.0
25	Federal Light & Traction Co.	1	......	3,500	3,500	260,288	326,214	.0	.8	78.6	76.8
81	Washington-Oregon Corporation	2	970	2,000	2,970	261,258	329,184	.3	.7	78.9	77.5
98	Municipal stations	12	54,510	13,450	67,960	315,768	397,145	16.5	16.0	95.4	93.5
	All other stations	66	15,366	12,344	27,710	331,134	424,854	4.6	6.5	100.0	100.0
	Total	116	331,134	93,720	424,854	......	....	100.0	100.0	.....	.....
	Central stations and electric rys., 1912	...	269,641	72,060	341,701	......	....	.....	.....	.....	.....

WEST VIRGINIA

53	Virginian Power Co.	1	......	20,000	20,000	......	20,000	.....	14.4	.....	14.4
26	General Utilities Operating Co.	1	......	13,300	13,300	......	33,300	.....	9.6	.....	24.0
1	American Gas & Electric Co.	2	......	12,500	12,500	......	45,800	.....	9.0	.....	33.0
74	Union Carbide Co.	2	11,750	......	11,750	11,750	57,550	49.4	8.4	49.4	41.4
7	W. S. Barstow & Co. (Inc.)	4	......	11,000	11,000	11,750	68,550	.....	7.9	49.4	49.3
5	American Water Works & Elec. Co., Inc.	2	......	9,192	9,192	11,750	77,742	.....	6.6	49.4	55.9
46	Northern Virginia Power Co.	2	4,750	2,833	7,583	16,500	85,325	20.0	5.4	69.4	61.3
3	American Rys. Co.	1	......	6,670	6,670	16,500	91,995	.....	4.8	69.4	66.1
14	H. M. Byllesby & Co.	2	......	6,050	6,050	16,500	98,045	.....	4.3	69.4	70.4
68	Consolidated Coal Co. (Inc.)	1	......	6,000	6,000	16,500	104,045	.....	4.3	69.4	74.7
35	Martinsburg Power Co.	1	2,250	2,000	4,250	18,750	108,295	9.4	3.0	78.8	77.7

APPENDIX III—*Continued*

WEST VIRGINIA—*Concluded*

38	Monongahela Valley Traction Co.	1	......	4,000	4,000	18,750	112,295	.....	2.9	78.8	80.6
70	Harpers Ferry Paper Co.	1	2,400	......	2,400	21,150	114,695	10.1	1.7	88.9	82.3
73	Shenandoah Pulp Co.	1	2,000	......	2,000	23,150	116,695	8.4	1.4	97.3	83.7
31	Kanawha Traction & Electric Co.	1	......	2,000	2,000	23,150	118,695	.....	1.4	97.3	85.1
61	Municipal stations	6	......	1,755	1,755	23,150	120,450	.....	1.3	97.3	86.4
	All other stations	47	637	18,313	18,950	23,787	139,400	2.7	13.6	100.0	100.0
	Total	76	23,787	115,613	139,400	......	....	100.0	100.0	.....	.....
	Central stations and electric railways, 1912	...	6,036	62,889	68,925	......	....	.....	.....	.....	.....

WISCONSIN

124	North American Co.	9	450	112,355	112,805	450	112,805	0.2	25.5	0.2	25.5
35	H. M. Byllesby & Co.	2	26,800	......	26,800	27,250	139,605	11.5	6.1	11.7	31.6
197	Wisconsin River Power Co.	1	25,000	......	25,000	52,250	164,605	10.7	5.6	22.4	37.2
9	American Public Utilities Co.	6	13,350	3,695	17,045	65,600	181,650	5.7	3.8	28.1	41.0
47, 296	Consolidated Water Power & Paper Co.	2	16,500	300	16,800	82,100	198,450	7.1	3.8	35.2	44.8
300	Kimberley-Clark Co.	6	13,450	......	13,450	95,550	211,900	5.8	3.0	41.0	47.8
7	American Light & Traction Co.	2	5,600	6,356	11,956	101,150	223,856	2.4	2.7	43.4	50.5
167	Southern Wisconsin Power Co.	1	11,000	......	11,000	112,150	234,856	4.7	2.5	48.1	53.0
114	Nokoosa-Port Edwards Paper Co.	3	10,700	80	10,780	122,850	245,636	4.6	2.4	52.7	55.4
198	Wisconsin Securities Co.	2	8,000	2,470	10,470	130,850	256,106	3.4	2.4	56.1	57.8
196	Wisconsin Railway, Light & Power Co.	1	8,000	......	8,000	138,850	264,106	3.4	1.8	59.5	59.6
200	Wisconsin Traction, Light, Heat & Power Co.	1	2,550	5,330	7,880	141,400	271,986	1.1	1.8	60.6	61.4
68	Green Bay & Mississippi Canal Co.	1	6,100	900	7,000	147,500	278,986	2.6	1.6	63.2	63.0
295	Combined Locks Paper Co.	1	6,100	900	7,000	153,600	285,986	2.6	1.6	65.8	64.6
98	Menasha Woodenware Co.	2	5,600	1,400	7,000	159,200	292,986	2.4	1.6	68.2	66.2
43	Commonwealth Power Co.	1	......	6,500	6,500	159,200	299,486	.....	1.5	68.2	67.7

APPENDIX III—*Continued*

WISCONSIN—*Concluded*

321	Warsaw Paper Mills Co.	1	4,756	600	5,356	163,956	304,842	2.0	1.2	70.2	68.9
323	Wisconsin River Pulp & Paper Co.	1	5,300	......	5,300	169,256	310,142	2.3	1.2	72.5	70.0
309	Marathon Paper Mills Co.	1	5,000	......	5,000	174,256	315,142	2.1	1.1	74.6	71.2
202	Municipal stations	85	3,143	15,034	18,177	177,399	333,319	1.4	4.1	76.0	75.3
	All other stations	195	56,170	53,207	109,377	233,569	442,696	24.0	24.7	100.0	100.0
	Total	324	233,569 *	209,127 *	442,696 *	......	....	100.0	100.0	.....	.....
	Central stations and electric railways, 1912	...	94,284	177,779	272,063	......	....	.....	.....	.....	.....

WYOMING

23	Union Pacific Coal Co.	3	......	3,900	3,900	......	3,900	.....	22.3	.....	22.3
7	Federal Light & Traction Co.	2	......	3,825	3,825	......	7,725	.....	21.9	.....	44.2
27	Western Light & Power Co.	1	......	1,565	1,565	......	9,290	.....	9.0	.....	53.2
19	Penn-Wyoming Copper Co.	1	500	670	1,170	500	10,460	19.7	6.7	19.7	59.9
4	Cambria Fuel Co. of Wyoming	2	......	770	770	500	11,230	.....	4.4	19.7	64.3
15	Intermountain Railway, Light and Power Co.	1	......	700	700	500	11,930	.....	4.0	19.7	68.3
18	Natrona County Electric Co.	1	......	650	650	500	12,580	.....	3.7	19.7	72.0
14	Hot Springs Light & Power Co.	1	400	200	600	900	13,180	15.7	3.4	35.4	75.4
22	Shoshone Electric Light & Power Co.	1	400	......	400	1,300	13,580	15.7	2.3	51.1	77.7
10, 29	U. S. Army and municipal stations	5	864	371	1,235	2,164	14,815	34.0	7.1	85.1	84.8
	All other stations	16	380	2,285	2,665	2,544	17,480	14.9	15.2	100.0	100.0
	Total	34	2,544	14,936	17,480	......	....	100.0	100.0	.....	.....
	Central stations and electric railways, 1912	...	1,334	10,262	11,596	......	....	.....	.....	.....	.....

* Totals contain 74,496 water horsepower and 8,360 steam horsepower; total, 82,856 horsepower used in manufactures.

APPENDIX III—*Continued*

UNITED STATES

Name of company	No. of States	No. of Stations	Individual totals: Water power	Individual totals: Steam and gas power	Individual totals: All power	Cumulative totals: Water power	Cumulative totals: All power	Individual percentages: Water power	Individual percentages: All power	Cumulative percentages: Water power	Cumulative percentages: All power
Stone & Webster	13	62	340,211	189,643	529,854	340,211	529,854	6.39	3.57	6.39	3.57
Commonwealth Edison Co. (Ill.)	1	4	....	511,150	511,150	340,211	1,041,004	....	3.44	6.39	7.01
Consolidated Gas Co. (N. Y.)	1	8	....	481,895	481,895	340,211	1,522,899	....	3.25	6.39	10.26
North American Co.	3	30	5,583	420,377	425,960	345,794	1,948,859	.11	2.87	6.50	13.13
H. M. Byllesby & Co.	17	53	116,155	160,341	276,496	461,949	2,225,355	2.18	1.86	8.68	14.99
E. W. Clark & Co., Mortgage Corp.	4	36	162,330	103,365	265,695	624,279	2,491,050	3.05	1.79	11.73	16.78
Pacific Gas & Electric Co. (Calif.)	1	13	152,080	108,540	260,620	776,359	2,751,670	2.86	1.75	14.59	18.53
Interborough Metropolitan Co. (N. Y.)	1	2	....	246,500	246,500	776,359	2,998,170	....	1.67	14.59	20.[illegible]0
Public Service Corp. of N. J.	1	16	....	232,905	232,905	776,359	3,231,075	....	1.56	14.59	21.76
Doherty Operating Co.	14	43	43,100	180,401	223,501	819,459	3,454,576	.81	1.51	15.40	23.27
Southern Power Co. (S. Car., N. Car.)	2	9	157,850	47,010	204,860	977,309	3,659,436	2.96	1.38	18.36	24.65
Utah Securities Corporation	3	43	171,702	30,374	202,076	1,149,011	3,861,512	3.23	1.36	21.59	26.01
Brooklyn Rapid Transit Co. (N. Y.)	1	5	....	198,025	198,025	1,149,011	4,059,537	....	1.33	21.59	27.34
Pacific Light & Power Corp. (Calif.)	1	13	117,950	79,300	197,250	1,266,961	4,256,787	2.22	1.33	23.81	28.67
Montana Power Co.	1	19	179,700	8,300	188,000	1,446,661	4,444,787	3.37	1.27	27.18	29.94
International Paper Co.	5	23	156,830	29,945	186,775	1,603,491	4,631,562	2.95	1.26	30.13	31.90
United Gas & Electric Corp. of Conn.	9	17	5,250	181,110	186,360	1,608,741	4,817,922	.10	1.25	30.23	32.45
Commonwealth Power, Ry. & Light Co.	4	47	70,813	112,160	182,973	1,679,554	5,000,895	1.33	1.24	31.56	33.69
The Philadelphia Co. (Penn.)	1	10	....	161,508	161,508	1,679,554	5,162,403	....	1.08	31.56	34.77
Hydraulic Power Co. of Niagara Falls	1	3	153,000	....	153,000	1,832,554	5,315,403	2.88	1.03	34.44	35.80
Edison Electric Illuminating Co. (Mass.)	1	3	....	140,850	140,850	1,832,554	5,456,253	....	.95	34.44	36.75
Central States Electric Corp. (Ohio)	1	1	....	135,700	135,700	1,832,554	5,591,953	....	.92	34.44	37.67
Southern California Edison Co.	1	11	56,400	79,120	135,520	1,888,954	5,727,473	1.06	.91	35.50	38.58
Georgia Railway & Power Co.	1	7	100,400	33,720	134,120	1,989,354	5,861,593	1.88	.90	37.38	39.48
Boston Electric Rys. Co. (Mass.)	1	6	....	126,300	126,300	1,989,354	5,987,893	....	.85	37.38	40.33
Washington Water Power Co.	2	5	109,200	16,000	125,200	2,098,554	6,113,093	2.05	.85	39.43	41.18

APPENDIX III—*Continued*

UNITED STATES—*Continued*

Pennsylvania Water & Power Co.	1	2	118,000	....	118,000	2,216,554	6,231,093	2.22	.79	41.65	41.97
The Niagara Falls Power Co. (N. Y.)	1	2	115,000	....	115,000	2,331,554	6,346,093	2.16	.77	43.81	42.74
Western Power Co. (Calif.)	1	4	73,330	38,670	112,000	2,404,884	6,458,093	1.38	.76	45.19	43.50
American Gas & Electric Co.	5	20	....	109,970	109,970	2,404,884	6,568,063	....	.74	45.19	44.24
Philadelphia Rapid Transit Co.	1	5	....	105,730	105,730	2,404,884	6,673,793	....	.71	45.19	44.95
New York, New Haven & Hartford R. R. Co.	3	16	8,050	96,500	104,550	2,412,934	6,778,343	.15	.71	45.34	45.66
W. S. Barstow & Co. (Inc.)..........	7	32	13,475	82,545	96,020	2,426,409	6,874,363	.25	.64	45.59	46.30
New York Central & Hudson River R. R. Co.	1	4	22,325	70,800	93,125	2,448,734	6,967,488	.42	.63	46.01	46.93
American Power & Light Co.	4	40	22,978	69,221	92,199	2,471,712	7,059,687	.44	.62	46.45	47.55
Alabama Traction, Light & Power Co.	1	7	72,500	18,920	91,420	2,544,212	7,151,107	1.36	.62	47.81	48.17
United Railways Investment Co. (Cal.)	1	5	65,600	25,330	90,930	2,609,812	7,242,037	1.23	.61	49.04	48.78
Middle West Utilities Co............	9	118	16,824	69,890	86,714	2,626,636	7,328,751	.32	.58	49.36	49.36
Pennsylvania R. R. Co.	2	2	....	85,370	85,370	2,626,636	7,414,121	....	.58	49.36	49.94
New England Power Co. of Maine ...	2	7	80,700	700	81,400	2,707,336	7,495,521	1.51	.55	50.87	50.49
Lehigh Coal & Navigation Co. (Pa.) ..	1	4	5,367	70,500	75,867	2,712,703	7,571,388	.10	.51	50.97	51.00
Kings County Electric Light & Power Co. (N. Y.)	1	3	....	74,670	74,670	2,712,703	7,646,058	....	.50	50.97	51.50
San Joaquin Light & Power Corp. (Cal.)	1	8	40,150	28,950	69,100	2,752,853	7,715,158	.76	.47	51.73	51.97
Twin City Rapid Transit Co. (Minn.)	1	1	....	66,700	66,700	2,752,853	7,781,858	....	.45	51.73	52.42
Ohio Traction Co.	1	6	....	65,611	65,611	2,752,853	7,847,469	....	.44	51.73	52.86
Virginia Railway & Power Co........	1	4	19,000	46,420	65,420	2,771,853	7,912,889	.36	.44	52.09	53.30
Illinois Traction Co.	3	36	4,415	59,026	63,441	2,776,268	7,976,330	.08	.43	52.17	53.73
United Railways & Electric Co. of Baltimore	1	4	....	61,875	61,875	2,776,268	8,038,205	....	.42	52.17	54.15
Northwestern Power Co. (Minn.)	1	2	57,000	4,670	61,670	2,833,268	8,099,875	1.07	.42	53.24	54.57
C. H. Tenney & Co..................	4	18	10,730	50,728	61,458	2,843,998	8,161,333	.20	.41	53.44	54.98
Public Service Co. of No. Illinois.....	1	13	5,300	55,930	61,230	2,849,298	8,222,563	.10	.41	53.54	55.39
American Water Works & Electric Co.	3	14	....	59,097	59,097	2,849,298	8,281,660	....	.40	53.54	55.79
Consolidated Gas, Electric Light and Power Co. (Maryland)...........	1	7	1,000	56,710	57,710	2,850,298	8,339,370	.02	.39	53.56	56.18

APPENDIX III—*Continued*

UNITED STATES—*Continued*

Massachusetts Electric Cos.	1	13	....	57,575	57,575	2,850,298	8,396,945	....	.38	53.56	56.56
Pillsbury - Washburn Flour Mills Co. (Minn.)	1	2	57,500	....	57,500	2,907,798	8,454,445	1.08	.38	54.64	56.94
Washington Ry. & Electric Co. (D. C.)	1	1	....	53,800	53,800	2,907,798	8,508,245	....	.37	54.64	57.31
Kansas City Ry. & Light Co. (Mo.)	1	1	....	53,300	53,300	2,907,798	8,561,545	....	.36	54.64	57.67
Carolina Power & Light Co. (N. Car.)	1	9	44,400	7,725	52,125	2,952,198	8,613,670	.83	.35	55.47	58.02
American Gas Co.	5	17	15,525	36,350	51,875	2,967,723	8,665,545	.30	.35	55.77	58.37
United Light & Railways Co.	2	7	500	50,025	50,525	2,968,223	8,716,070	.01	.34	55.78	58.71
New England Investment Co. (Mass.)	1	4	49,400	....	49,400	3,017,623	8,765,470	.92	.33	56.70	59.04
Nevada-California Power Co. (Calif.)	1	7	37,750	10,670	48,420	3,055,373	8,813,890	.71	.33	57.41	59.37
Detroit United Railways	1	9	....	46,986	46,986	3,055,373	8,860,876	....	.32	57.41	59.69
Colorado Power Co.	1	7	41,750	4,780	46,620	3,097,123	8,907,496	.79	.31	58.20	60.00
J. G. White & Co.	4	17	20,880	25,599	46,479	3,118,003	8,953,975	.39	.31	58.59	60.31
American Public Utilities Co.	3	9	13,350	31,895	45,245	3,131,353	8,999,220	.25	.31	58.84	60.62
American Light & Traction Co.	4	5	13,400	31,584	44,984	3,144,753	9,044,204	.25	.30	59.09	60.92
Louisville Traction Co.	1	2	....	44,130	44,130	3,144,753	9,088,334	....	.30	59.09	61.22
United Gas Improvement Co.	4	9	350	43,641	43,991	3,145,103	9,132,325	.01	.29	59.10	61.51
Chattanooga & Tenn. Ry. Power. Co. (Tenn.)	1	1	42,000	....	42,000	3,187,103	9,174,325	.79	.28	59.89	61.79
National Securities Corporation	2	4	39,350	2,000	41,350	3,226,453	9,215,675	.74	.28	60.63	62.07
Indianapolis Light & Heat Co.	1	1	....	40,900	40,900	3,226,453	9,356,575	....	.28	60.63	62.35
Niagara, Lockport & Ontario Power Co. (New York)	1	1	40,000	....	40,000	3,266,453	9,296,575	.75	.27	61.38	62.62
Aluminum Co. of America (N. Y.)	1	2	40,000	....	40,000	3,306,453	9,336,575	.75	.27	62.13	62.89
Columbia Gas & Electric Co. (Ohio)	1	1	....	38,930	38,930	3,306,453	9,375,505	....	.26	62.13	63.15
Georgia Light, Power & Ry. Co.	1	3	33,000	4,750	37,750	3,339,453	9,413,255	.62	.26	62.75	63.41
Turners Falls Pow r Co. (Mass.)	1	2	36,900	....	36,900	3,376,353	9,450,155	.70	.24	63.45	63.65
Pacific Lighting Corp. (Calif.)	1	1	....	34,202	34,201	3,376,353	9,484,357	....	.23	63.45	63.88
Columbia Railway, Gas & Electric Co. (South Carolina)	1	2	26,000	7,330	33,330	3,402,353	9,517,687	.48	.23	63.93	64.11
Northern Ohio Traction & Light Co.	1	2	2,270	31,000	33,270	3,404,623	9,550,957	.05	.22	63.98	64.35
United Properties Co. (Cal.)	1	6	....	33,025	33,025	3,404,623	9,583,982	....	.22	63.98	64.55

APPENDIX III—*Concluded*

UNITED STATES—*Concluded*

Federal Light & Traction Co.	7	12	....	32,373	32,373	3,404,623	9,616,355	....	.22	63.98	64.77
Fort Wayne & Northern Indiana Traction Co.	1	3	....	32,160	32,160	3,404,623	9,648,515	.....	.22	63.98	64.99
United Illuminating Co. (Conn.)	1	2	....	31,200	31,200	3,404,623	9,679,715	.....	.21	63.98	65.20
General Electric Co. (N. Y.)	1	3	31,000	....	31,000	3,435,623	9,710,715	.58	.21	64.56	65.41
Union Carbide Co. (Mich.)	1	1	30,800	....	30,800	3,466,423	9,741,515	.58	.20	65.14	65.61
Cohoes Co. (New York)	1	1	30,000	....	30,000	3,496,423	9,771,515	.56	.19	65.70	65.80
Total for 87 corporations	48	1,040	3,496,423	6,275,092	9,771,515	3,496,423	9,771,515	65.70	65.80	65.70	65.80
Municipal stations	48	1,600	231,525	496,984	728,509	3,727,948	10,500,024	4.35	4.93	70.05	70.73
All other stations	48	4,299	1,593,751	2,752,367	4,346,118	5,321,699	14,846,142	29.95	29.27	100.0	100.0
Grand totals	..	6,939	5,321,699	9,524,443	14,846,142	....	....	.....	.....	.....	.....
Total manufacturing power included	..	....	736,197	172,210	908,407	....	....	.....	.....	.....	.....
Central stations and elec. rys., 1915	..	....	4,585,502	9,352,233	13,937,735	....	....	.....	.....	.....	.....
Central stations and elec. rys., 1912	..	....	2,942,388	8,251,311	11,193,699	....	....	.....	.....	.....	.....
Increase 1912 to 1915	..	....	1,643,114	1,100,922	2,744,036	....	....	.....	.....	.....	.....
Per cent of increase	..	....	35.8	11.8	19.7	....	....	.....	.....	.....	.....

APPENDIX IV

FROM HEARINGS BEFORE HOUSE COMMITTEE ON WATER-POWER 65TH CONGRESS, 2ND SESSION, PP. 503-507

The acts are here divided into four classes:

Class A. Those which give "perpetual" rights and contain "no restrictions."

These usually consist of acts passed previous to the general dam act of 1906 or extensions of the time limits thereof subsequent to said date.

Class B. Those based on the general dam act of 1906 or reciting the terms of that act.

Class C. Those based on the general dam act of 1910.

Class D. Acts specifically framed to meet peculiar conditions in certain cases.

CLASS A

Acts passed, 34: built, 15; horsepower, 293,530; not built, 19; percentage built, 44.

1. July 5, 1884. St. Cloud Water Power & Mill Co., Mississippi River at St. Cloud, Sauk Rapids. Perpetual; built; 2,580 horsepower.

2. April 16, 1886. Mississippi Water Power & Boom Co., Mississippi River at Brainerd, Minn. Perpetual; no restrictions; built; 800 horsepower.

3. July 3, 1886. Little Falls Water Power Co., Mississippi River at Little Falls, Minn. Perpetual; no restrictions; built; 4,300 horsepower.

4. June 6, 1892. Topeka Water & Electric Power Co., Kansas River, Shawnee County. Perpetual; no restrictions; not built.

5. January 22, 1894. The Chicago & Topeka Light, Heat & Power Co., Kansas River, Shawnee County. Perpetual; no restrictions; not built.

6. February 24, 1894. Des Moines Rapids Power Co., Mississippi River near Keokuk. Perpetual; no restrictions; not built under this act, but under act of February 8, 1901, and acts supplementary thereto.

7. June 8, 1894. Missouri River Power Co., Missouri River near Stubbs Ferry, Mont. Perpetual; no restrictions; built; Hauser Lake plant; 24,000 horsepower.

8. June 3, 1896. General authority to any person to construct, under such conditions as Secretary of War may prescribe, a dam above Stubbs Ferry, Missouri River, Mont. Perpetual; no restrictions; built; Canyon Ferry plant; 10,000 horsepower.

9. March 5, 1898. Twin City Rapid Transit Co., Mississippi River at Coon Rapids. Perpetual; no restrictions; not built under this act, but under the act of January 12, 1911.

10. May 4, 1898. Koochiching Co., Rainy Lake River, Minn. Perpetual; no restrictions. Time extended by act of May 4, 1900. Again extended by act of June 28, 1902. Rights previously granted transferred to Rainy River Improvement Co. by the act of May 25, 1905, and time extended after construction had begun by act of May 23, 1908. This last-named act placed the work under the act of 1906. Built; 12,500 horsepower.

11. February 4, 1899. Mount Carmel Development Co., Wabash River at Grand Rapids. Perpetual; no restrictions; not built; site later developed by Government with lock and dam for navigation purposes.

12. February 27, 1899. Grand Rapids Water Power & Boom Co., Mississippi River at Grand Rapids, Minn. Perpetual; no restrictions; built; 4,000 horsepower.

13. June 4, 1900. F. H. Fries and others. New River, Va., mouth of Stevens Creek. Perpetual; no restrictions; built; 2,800 horsepower.

14. February 8, 1901. Twin City Power Co., Savannah River at Dorton's Creek. Perpetual; no restrictions; not built.

15. February 8, 1901. Twin City Power Co., Savannah River, Price's Island. Perpetual; no restrictions; not built.

16. February 8, 1901. Keokuk & Hamilton Water Power Co., Mississippi River at Des Moines Rapids, near Keokuk. Time extended by acts of February 26, 1904, and February 5, 1905. Perpetual; permittee was required to replace navigation lock and dry dock which Government had previously constructed; built; 150,000 horsepower.

17. February 7, 1903. St. Croix Falls Improvement Co., St. Croix River at or near St. Croix Falls. Perpetual; no restrictions; built; 25,200 horsepower.

18. February 26, 1904. Sauk Rapids Water Power Co., Mississippi River at Sauk Rapids, Benton County, Minn. Time extended by act of March 2, 1907, and again by act of Februaryy 13, 1911, and finally extended by act of February 24, 1911. Perpetual; no restrictions; not built.

19. March 12, 1904. Minnesota Power & Trolley Co., Mississippi River, sec. 17, T. 121 N., R. 23 W. Perpetual; no restrictions; not built.

20. April 23, 1904. Watab Rapids Power Co., Mississippi River, Stearns and Benton Counties, Minn. Perpetual; no restrictions; built; 6,900 horsepower.

21. April 28, 1904. Oxbow Power Co., Missouri River, Mont., lot 3, sec. 26, T. 14 N., R. 3 W. Time extended by act of March 4, 1907. Perpetual; no restrictions; not built.

22. February 20, 1905. Sauk Rapids Manufacturing Co., Mississippi River at Sauk Rapids, near St. Cloud, Minn. Perpetual; no restrictions; not built.

23. March 3, 1905. Kirby Thomas and others. Mississippi River near Bemidji, between outlet of Lake Bemidji and Wolf Lake. Time extended by act of February 1, 1908. Perpetual; no restrictions; built; 1,000 horsepower.

24. February 16, 1906. E. A. Smith et als. Rock River at Grand Detour, Ill. Perpetual; no restrictions; not built.

25. February 23, 1906. Pea River Power Co., Pea River near Elba, Ala. Perpetual; no restrictions; not built.

26. March 16, 1906. William J. Murphy, Red Lake River near junction with Black River, Minn. Perpetual; no restrictions; built; 1,000 horsepower.

27. April 12, 1906. Capital City Improvement Co., Missouri River near Buck Rapids, Mont. Perpetual; no restrictions; built; "Holter Plant"; 53,600 horsepower.

28. June 1, 1906. Pend d'Oreille Development Co., Pend d'Oreille River at Metalline Falls. Perpetual; no restrictions; not built.

29. June 4, 1906. William R. Morrison and others, Mississippi River near Bemidji. Perpetual; no restrictions; not built.

30. June 4, 1906. Pike Rapids Power Co., Mississippi River in Morrison County, Minn. Perpetual; no restrictions; not built.

31. June 14, 1906. Mississippi River Power Co., Mississippi River above the mouth of Clearwater River, Wright County, Minn. Perpetual; no restrictions; not built.

32. June 14, 1906. Mississippi River Power Co., Mississippi River at Monticello, Minn. Perpetual; no restrictions; not built.

33. June 16, 1906. Judd Wright, Crow Wing River, near junction of Gull River. Perpetual; no restrictions; built; 400 horsepower.

34. June 28, 1906. St. Cloud Electric Power Co., dam across Mississippi River at sec. 7, T. 123, R. 27, Stearn County, Minn. Perpetual; no restrictions; not built.

CLASS B (UNDER ACT OF 1906)

(Acts passed, 21; built, 4; horsepower, 97,456; not built, 16; percentage built, 19.)

35. April 23, 1906. Northern Mississippi Traction Co., Bear River, Tishomingo County, Miss. Similar to the general dam act of 1906. Not built.

36. February 5, 1907. Albany Power & Manufacturing Co., Flint River, Ga., at Porter's Shoals. Not built.

37. February 5, 1907. Savannah River Power Co., Savannah River at Gregg Shoals. Built; 2,500 horsepower.

38. February 20, 1907. Missouri River Improvement Co., Missouri River above Fort Benton, Mo. Not built.

39. February 25, 1907. J. F. Andrews and others, Bear River, Tishomingo County, Miss. Not built.

40. February 27, 1907. Twin City Power Co., Savannah River at Dorton's Creek. Two dams; not built.

41. March 2, 1907. Hugh MacRae Co., Savannah River at Trotters Shoals. Not built.

42. March 2, 1907. Anderson Guaranty & Trust Co., Savannah River at McDaniels Shoals. Not built.

43. March 2, 1907. The Anderson Guaranty & Trust Co., Savannah River at Turner Shoals. Not built.

44. March 2, 1907. Anderson Guaranty & Trust Co., Savannah River at Middleton Shoals. Not built.

45. March 2, 1907. The Hugh MacRae Co., Savannah River at Cherokee Shoals. Not built.

46. March 2, 1907. Hugh MacRae Co., Savannah River at Calhoun Falls. Not built.

47. March 2, 1907. Hugh MacRae and others, Savannah River at Hattons Ford. Not built.

48. March 2, 1907. Herman L. Hartenstein, St. Joseph River at Mottville, Mich. Not built.

49. March 2, 1907. Pike Rapids Power Co., Mississippi River at Morrison County, Minn. Not built.

50. March 2, 1907. The J. R. Earle Development Co., Savannah River at Andersonville Shoals. Not built.

51. March 4, 1907. Alabama Power Co. at Lock 12, Coosa River, Ala. Built; 70,000 horsepower.

52. February 29, 1908. Twin City Power Co., Savannah River at Dortons Creek. Three dams. Time extended by act of June 3, 1912, and act of March 1, 1916. Not built.

53. March 6, 1908. Cahaba Power Co., Cahaba River near Centerville, Ala. Not built.

54. March 10, 1908. A. J. Smith and others, Choctawhatchee River, Newton, Dale County, Ala. Time extended by act of February 13, 1911. Not built.

55. March 16, 1908. T. H. Friel. Mulberry Fork of Black Warrior River near junction with Sipsey Fork, Walker County, Ala. Not built; site covered by Lock and Dam No. 17, Black Warrior River, built by United States.

56. August 5, 1909. J. L. Hankinson and others, Savannah River at Stevens Creek. Time extended by act of March 5, 1912. Built; 14,000 horsepower.

CLASS C (UNDER ACT OF 1910)

(Acts passed, 15; built, 2; horsepower, 34,500; not built, 13; percentage built, 13.)

57. March 3, 1905. Edward A. Smith and others, Rock River at Lyndon. Permanent grant with restrictions as to navigation. Time extended by act of February 25, 1907, and based on general dam act of 1906. New act passed February 18, 1911, in favor of same parties, based on general dam act of 1910. Not built.

58. February 25, 1907. Pend d'Oreille Development Co., Pend d'Oreille River near international boundary line. Under general dam act of 1906. Time extended by act of May 20, 1912, and based on general dam act of 1910. Not built.

59. January 12, 1911. Great Northern Development Co., Mississippi River at Coon Creek Rapids, Hennepin County. Built; 10,500 horsepower.

60. March 4, 1911. Pike Rapids Power Co., Mississippi River, Morrison County, Minn. Not built.

61. February 4, 1911. Ozark Power & Water Co., White River near Forsythe, Mo. Built; 24,000 horsepower.

62. February 15, 1911. Chucawalla Development Co., Colorado River at Pyramid Canyon. Under Secretary of the Interior. Not built.

63. February 18, 1911. Byron Water Power Co., Rock River at Byron, Ill. Not built.

64. February 18, 1911. Ivanhoe Furnace Corporation, New River, Va., at Ivanhoe. Not built.

65. February 18, 1911. Hugh MacRae Co. and others, Savannah River at Cherokee Shoals. Not built.

66. February 18, 1911. The Virginia Iron, Coal & Coke Co., New River at Foster Falls, Wythe County, Va. Not built.

67. February 24, 1911. Minnesota River Improvement & Power Co. Not built.

68. February 24, 1911. J. W. Vance and others, James River, Stone County, Mo. Not built.

69. February 24, 1911. Rainy River Improvement Co., outlet of Lake Namakan, St. Louis County, Minn. Not built.

70. March 3, 1911. Greeley-Arizona Irrigation Co., Colorado River near Parker, Ariz. Not built.

71. May 11, 1912. The Topeka Commercial Club. Two dams, Kansas River, Shawnee and Wabaunsee Counties. Not built.

72. July 5, 1912. Choctawhatchee River Light & Power Co., Choctawhatchee River at Newton, Dale County, Ala. Not built.

CLASS D

(Acts passed, 10; built, 3; horsepower, 46,000; not built, 7; percentage built, 33.)

73. April 5, 1904. Davenport Water Power Co., Mississippi River between Le Claire and Davenport. Lateral diversion subject to many stipulations as to future improvements for navigation. Time extended by act of February 5, 1907. Started but not completed.

74. April 26, 1904. Secretary of War authorized to permit the city of Chattanooga or individuals to construct dam at Hales Bar, Tennessee River. Amended as to names by act of January 7, 1905. Term, 99 years; built, 42,000 horsepower.

75. March 3, 1905. Cumberland River Improvement Co., authorized to improve Cumberland River and tributaries above Burnside, Ky., for navigation and power development. Toll

privileges to cease in 40 years; power franchise perpetual unless repealed by act of Congress. Not built.

76. May 1, 1906. Samuel S. Davis. Three dams, Rock River, Van Druffs and Carrs Islands. Built; 2,200 horsepower.

77. June 18, 1906. Charles H. Cornell, Niobrara River, sec. 22, T. 34 N., R. 27 W. Revocable by Secretary of War. Not built.

78. June 28, 1906. Batesville Power Co. to develop power at Lock and Dam No. 1, White River, Mo. Not built.

79. June 29, 1916. J. A. Omberg to construct lock and dam in White River above Lock No. 3 under direction of Secretary of War. Ninety-nine year franchise. Not built.

80. June 30, 1906. Henry T. Henderson, Little River, Ala. Grants right to divert water from public lands upon payment of price to be fixed by Secretary of the Interior. Not built.

81. February 27, 1911. Ragland Water Power Co. Complete Dam and Lock No. 4, Coosa River, Ala. Rights granted for 50 years. Not built.

82. March 2, 1907. (H. and H. Act.) The Sterling Hydraulic Co., Rock River at Sterling, Ill., in connection with Illinois and Mississippi Canal. Permanent grant in exchange for rights previously held but obliterated by United States construction. Built; 2,200 horsepower.

APPENDIX V

THE INTERSTATE COMMERCE COMMISSION DEFINITION OF NET INVESTMENT, HEARINGS HOUSE COMMITTEE ON WATER-POWER, 65TH CONGRESS, 2ND SESSION, PP. 39-44

GENERAL INSTRUCTIONS

The carrier's records shall be kept with sufficient particularity to show fully the facts pertaining to all entries made in the accounts provided herein for investment in road and equipment. Where the full information is not recorded in the general books, the entries therein shall be supported by other records in which the full details shall be shown. Such general book entries shall contain sufficient reference to the detail records to permit ready identification, and the detail records shall be filed in such manner as to be readily accessible for examination by representatives of the Interstate Commerce Commission.

1. Accounts for Investment in Road and Equipment. The accounts prescribed in this classification are designed to show the investment of the carrier in property devoted to transportation service. The carrier's investment in physical property other than transportation property is provided for in balance-sheet account No. 705, "Miscellaneous physical property." *The carrier* means the accounting carrier, except when otherwise specifically indicated. The carrier's record shall be kept in such form that expenditures for additions and betterments may be reported separately from those for original road, original equipment, and road extensions, and shall show separately the expenditures under each authorized addition and betterment project. (See balance-sheet account No. 701, "Investment in road and equipment," and No. 702, "Improvements on leased railway property.")

2. Items to be Charged. To these accounts shall be charged the cost of original road, original equipment, road extensions, additions, and betterments; also the estimated values at time of acquisition of right of way and other road and equipment property donated to the carrier, except that unless authorized by the commission no charges shall be made to these accounts after July 1, 1914, for donations received previously to that date. Applications to the commission for including such items in the road and equipment accounts shall contain full information concerning the source and character of the donations.

If the total cost of additions and betterments to any class of equipment, or any class of fixed improvements (except tracks), under a general plan, considered as a whole, is less than $200, the option may be exercised of charging the amount expended to the appropriate account in operating expenses. This rule is not to be construed as authorizing the parceling of expenditures in order to bring them within this limit.

Construction includes all processes connected with the acquisition and construction of original road and equipment, road extensions, additions and betterments.

Original road means the land and fixed improvements provided and arranged for in the original plan for the construction of a new road. When the acquisition of any such fixed improvements under the original plan is deferred, such improvements, when acquired, shall be considered as additions. Original road shall not be construed to include fixed improvements which, under the original plans for the road, it is proposed to substitute at some time subsequent to the beginning of commercial operations for the improvements originally installed and used for transportation operations, such as steel bridges substituted for trestles.

Original equipment means equipment provided and arranged for under the original plan for the construction of a new road. When the acquisition of such equipment under the original plan is deferred, such equipment, when acquired, shall be considered as additions.

Road extensions means the land and fixed improvements

provided and arranged for in the original plan for the construction of extensions of existing main lines, additional branch lines, and extensions of existing branch lines. When the acquisition of any such fixed improvements under the original plan is deferred, such improvements, when acquired, shall be treated as additions. Road extensions shall not be construed to include fixed improvements which under the original plans for the extensions it is proposed to substitute at some time subsequent to the beginning of commercial operations for the improvements originally installed and used for transportation in connection with commercial operations, such as steel bridges substituted for trestles.

Equipment means the rolling stock, boats, highway vehicles, horses, and harness devoted to transportation service, the cost of which is includible in the equipment accounts.

Fixed improvements means structures which are fixed as to location, such as tunnels, bridges, buildings, earthworks, etc.

Additions are additional facilities, such as additional equipment, tracks (including timber and mine tracks), buildings, bridges and other structures; additions to such facilities, such as extensions to tracks, buildings and other structures; additional ties laid in existing tracks; and additional devices applied to facilities, such as air brakes applied to cars not previously thus equipped. When property, such as a section of road, track, unit of equipment, shop or power-plant machine, building, or other structure, is retired from service and replaced with property of like purpose, the newly acquired property shall, for the purpose of this classification, be considered as an addition and the cost thereof accounted for accordingly. (See section 7). If, however, the property retired and replaced is of minor importance, such as a small roadway building or other structure, and is replaced in kind without betterment, the cost of the replacement shall be charged to operating expenses and no adjustment made in the road and equipment accounts.

Betterments are improvements of existing facilities through the substitution of superior parts for inferior parts retired, such as the substitution of steel-tired wheels for cast wheels under equipment, the application of heavier rail in tracks, and the strengthening of bridges by the substitution of heavier members. The cost chargeable to the accounts of this classification is the excess cost of new parts over the cost of current prices of new parts of the kind retired. (See section 12.)

Costs shall be actual money costs to the carrier. Where a portion of the funds expended by the carrier has been obtained through donations by States, municipalities, individuals, or others, no deductions on account of such donations shall be made in stating the costs. Contributions for joint expenditures should not be considered as donations. The carrier's proportion only of the cost of joint projects, such as construction of jointly owned tracks and elimination of highway crossings at joint expense, shall be included in these accounts.

3. Basis of Charges. The charges to the accounts of this classification shall be based upon the cost of the property acquired. When the consideration given for the purchase or the improvement of property the cost of which is chargeable to the accounts of this classification is other than money, the money value of the consideration at the time of the transaction shall be charged to these accounts and the actual consideration shall be described in the record in sufficient detail to identify it. The carrier shall be prepared to furnish the commission upon demand the particulars of its determination of the actual cash value of the consideration, if other than money.

4. Cost of Construction. It is intended that the accounts for fixed improvements and equipment shall include the cost of construction of such property. The cost of construction shall include the cost of labor, materials and supplies, work-train service, special machine service, transportation, contract work, protection from casualties, injuries and damages, privileges, and other analogous elements in connection with such work. The several items of cost here referred to are defined as follows:

(a) *Cost of labor* includes the amount paid for labor expended by the carrier's own employees, including the cost of labor expended for preliminary work, such as sinking test holes or making soundings for tunnels, grading, buildings, and other structures; and cost of labor expended in laying and taking up tracks for temporary use in construction, except the cost of labor expended on tracks provided for the protection of traffic during the progress of addition and betterment work. Office expenses and traveling and other personal expenses of employees, when borne by the carrier, shall be considered a part of the cost of the labor, as shall also the cost of fidelity bonds and employers' liability insurance premiums. When officers or employees are specially assigned to construction work, their pay and their traveling and incidental expenses while thus engaged shall be included in the cost of the work. No charge shall be made against road and equipment accounts for the pay of officers who merely render services incidentally in connection with extensions, additions, or betterments, although traveling and incidental expenses incurred by such officers solely on account of such work shall be included in the account to which the cost of the work is chargeable.

(b) *Cost of materials and supplies* includes the purchase price of materials and supplies, including small tools, at the point of free delivery, plus the cost of inspection and loading assumed by the carrier; also a suitable proportion of store expenses. (See special instructions for operating expense accounts, sections 16 and 17.) In calculating the cost of materials used, proper allowance shall be made for the value of unused portions and of cuttings, turnings, borings, etc.; for the value of the material recovered from temporary tracks, scaffolding, cofferdams, and other temporary structures used in construction; and for the value of small tools recovered and used for other purposes.

(c) *Cost of work-train service* includes amounts paid to others for rent and maintenance of the equipment used; cost of labor of enginemen, trainmen, and engine-house men, including the wages of engine crews and train crews held in readiness for such service; and the cost of fuel and other supplies consumed in connection with the operation of work trains. It shall also include the cost of maintaining the carrier's own equipment while used in construction service and a fair rent for such equipment while so used. Amounts charged for rent of such equipment used in construction shall concurrently be credited to the appropriate income account for hire or equipment. No "rent" or return upon the investment in such equipment shall be charged for the use of equipment acquired with the proceeds of securities sold, when the interest upon such securities is charged to the accounts of this classification.

(d) *Cost of special machine service* includes the cost of labor expended and of materials and supplies consumed in maintaining and operating steam shovels, scrapers, rail unloaders, ballast unloaders, pile drivers, dredges, ditchers, weed burners, and other labor-saving machines; also rents paid for use of such machines. (See Note A under account No. 37, "Roadway machines," and text of general account 11, Equipment, seventh paragraph.)

(e) *Cost of transportation* includes the amounts paid to other companies or individuals for the transportation of men, materials and supplies, special machine outfits, appliances, and tools in connection with construction. Freight charges paid foreign lines for the transportation of construction material to the carrier's line shall be included, so far as practicable, as a part of the cost of the material, when such charges are borne by the carrier. A fair allowance representing the expense to the carrier of such transportation in transportation service trains over the carrier's own line also shall be included. When the cost of such transportation is not assignable to specific work, it shall be included in account No. 43, "Other expenditures—Road." Amounts thus charged for transportation in transportation service trains over the carrier's line shall be credited to operating expense general account VIII, Transportation for Investment—Cr.

(f) *Cost of contract work* includes amounts paid for work performed under contract by other companies, firms, or individuals, and costs incident to the award of contract.

(g) *Cost of protection from casualties* includes expenditures for protection against fire, such as payments for discovery or extinguishment of fires, cost of detecting and prosecuting incendiaries, witness fees in relation thereto, amounts paid to municipal corporations and others for fire protection, and other analogous items of expenditure in connection with construction work.

(h) *Cost of injuries and damages* includes expenditures on account of injuries to persons or damage to property when incident to constructive projects, and shall be included in the cost of the work in connection with which the injury or damage occurs. It also includes that portion of premiums paid for insuring property applicable to the period prior to the completion or coming into service of the property insured. Insurance recovered on account of compensation paid for injuries to persons incident to construction shall be credited to the accounts to which such compensation is charged, and insurance recovered on account of damages to property incident to construction shall be credited to the accounts chargeable with the expenditures necessary for restoring the damaged property. The cost of injuries and damages incident to the removal of old structures, or parts thereof, shall be charged to Operating Expenses or Profit and Loss, as may be appropriate, except that such costs in connection with the removal of old structures which are incumbrances on newly acquired lands shall be included in account No. 2, "Land for transportation purposes," or No. 3 "Grading," as may be appropriate. (See sections 7 and 8.)

(i) *Cost of privileges* includes compensation for temporary privileges, such as the use of public property or streets, in connection with the construction of the property of the carrier.

5. Excavated Material. The cost of disposing of material excavated in connection with construction shall be considered as a part of the cost of the work, except when such material is used for filling, the cost of removal and dumping shall be equitably apportioned between the work in connection with which the removal occurs and the work in connection with which the material is used.

6. Items to be Credited. To these accounts shall be credited the ledger value of property retired.

Ledger value of property is the value at which the property is carried in the property investment account in the general ledger of the carrier. In case the value of any item of property is not shown separately in the ledger the ledger value of that item shall be its proportionate share of the value of the entire group in which the particular property is included.

Property retired means property which is sold, abandoned, demolished, or otherwise withdrawn from transportation service.

Salvage from retired property is the value of material recovered from property retired. When such material is retained and again used by the carrier, the value shall be computed upon the basis of fair prices for the material in its condition as recovered. When such material is sold, the net proceeds of the sale shall be considered as the value of the material.

7. Property Retired and Replaced. When a unit of property other than land or equipment—such as a section of road, side, or yard track, shop or power plant machine, building, or other structure—is retired from service and replaced with property of like purpose, the ledger value of the retired property shall be credited to the appropriate accounts of this classification at the time that the property is retired from service. The amount of this credit shall be charged concurrently as follows:

An amount equal to the credit balance in the accrued depreciation balance-sheet account with respect to the property retired shall be charged to that account and the remainder (less salvage and insurance recovered, if any), together with the cost of demolishing the property, if demolished by or for the carrier, shall be charged to the accounts in operating expenses appropriate for the cost of repairs of the property before retirement. The accounting for the salvage shall be in accordance with the disposition made of the material recovered.

If, however, the property retired and replaced with property of like purpose is of minor importance, such as a small roadway building or other small structure, and is replaced in kind without betterment, the cost of the replacement shall be charged to operating-expense accounts and no adjustment made in the road and equipment accounts.

If so authorized by the Interstate Commerce Commission,

the carrier may charge to profit and loss any extraordinarily large item representing the cost of property retired and replaced, instead of charging such item to operating expenses. The carrier shall file with the commission a statement of the cost and a description of the property retired and the reasons which, in its judgment, indicate the propriety of charging the cost of such property to profit and loss.

The provisions of this section are applicable in accounting (at the time of retirement) for the cost of property abandoned, even though the new property has been actually installed previously to the date of the demolishment of the abandoned property.

When the renewals to be made to an important building or other structure will constitute the major portion of its value when renewed, the property, when taken out of service, shall be considered as retired and accounted for as provided above, and for the purposes of this classification the renewed property shall be considered as an addition, and the appraised cost thereof shall be included in the accounts of this classification, consideration being given to the secondhand portions remaining therein. In no case shall the charge for the renewed property exceed the cost (at current market prices of labor and material) of new property of equal capacity and equal expectation of life in service, less a suitable allowance on account of the secondhand parts remaining therein.

8. Property Retired and Not Replaced. When a unit of property other than land or equipment—such as a section of road, side or yard track, shop or power plant machine, building, or other structure—is retired from service and not replaced, the ledger value shall be credited to the appropriate property accounts at the time that the property is retired from service. The amount of this credit shall be concurrently charged as follows:

An amount equal to the credit balance in the accrued depreciation balance-sheet account with respect to the property thus retired shall be charged to that account, and the remainder (less salvage and insurance recovered, if any), together with the cost of demolishing the property if demolished by or for the account of the carrier, shall be charged to the appropriate profit and loss account. The accounting for the salvage shall be in accordance with the disposition made of the material recovered.

9. Equipment Retired. The instructions for accounting for equipment retired are contained in the text of the general account II, Equipment.

10. Land Retired. When any land, the cost of which is included in the accounts of this classification, is retired, the ledger value shall be credited to account No. 2, "Land for transportation purposes." If the land is retained by the carrier, its estimated value shall be charged to balance-sheet account No. 705, "Miscellaneous physical property," the necessary adjustment of the difference between the ledger value and the estimated value on account of the loss in the property due to its retirement from transportation service shall be made through profit and loss. If sold, the difference between the ledger value credited to account No. 2 and the amount received for the land shall be adjusted in profit and loss.

11. Adjustment for Converted Property. When property, such as a unit of equipment, a building, or other facility of one class, is converted into property of another class, so that the amount of investment in such property must be transferred from one account of this classification to another, the ledger value shall be credited to the appropriate road-and-equipment account. Proper account shall be taken of any salvage recovered in the process of conversion. The amount of the balance in the accrued depreciation balance-sheet account, with respect to the property thus converted shall be charged to that account. The appraised cost of the property converted (consideration being given to the secondhand portions remaining therein) shall be included in the appropriate account of this classification. The charge for the converted property in no case shall exceed the cost (at current market prices of labor and material) of new property of equal capacity and equal expectation of life in service, less a suitable allowance on account of the secondhand portions remaining therein. The ledger value of the

property before conversion, plus the cost of conversion, less the sum of the estimated value of the property as converted, the amounts charged to accrued depreciation accounts, and the salvage recovered, shall be charged to the operating-expense accounts, appropriate for the costs of repairs of the fixed improvements or for the retirement of equipment before conversion.

12. Expenses in Connection with Additions and Betterments. The cost of removing old material from equipment and from buildings, bridges, wharves, tracks, and other fixed improvements, shall be charged to the appropriate operating-expense accounts. Such charges shall include the cost of removing old foundations and filling old excavations, and restoring condition of grounds after addition and betterment work; rearranging or relocating existing tracks; relocating telegraph and telephone poles of lines, fences, track and other signals, buildings, bridges, trestles, culverts and other structures, and farm and highway crossings, including crossing gates and alarms, when the provisions of section 8 of these instructions are not applicable; and maintaining or protecting traffic during the progress of addition and betterment work, including the cost of constructing, maintaining, and removing temporary tracks required for maintaining traffic during the progress of the work.

13. Interpretation of Item Lists. Lists of "items," "details," etc., have been given as a part of this classification for the purpose of clearly indicating the application of the accounting rules in specific cases. The lists in every case are to be considered as merely representative, and not as excluding from any account analogous items which happen to be omitted from the list appended. On the other hand, the appearance of an item in a list warrants the inclusion of the item in the account concerned only when the text of the account also indicates inclusion, inasmuch as the same items frequently appear in more than one list. The item of boilers, for example, will be found under accounts Nos. 18, 27, 37, 44, and 45, and the proper charge in any one instance must be determined by the text of the account.

14. Submission of Questions. To the end that uniformity of accounting may be maintained from year to year, carriers shall submit all questions of doubtful interpretation of the accounting rules to the commission for consideration and decision.

APPENDIX VI

Address of Senator Borah on Government Ownership, United States Senate, September 19, 1918

Congressional Record, 65th Cong., 2nd Sess., pp. 10477-10478

Water power is monopolistic in its nature, and, therefore lends itself to artificial monopoly. In determining upon a system or a policy of development this fact should not be forgotten. Even if there were no water-power monopoly at the present time there would inevitably come to be one from the very nature of the subject matter with which we deal. It is not necessary, therefore, for us to be diverted or unduly affected by the presence or absence of a power trust or a power monopoly at this time. It is sufficient that we know that in the very nature of things we are to have either a monopoly owned and controlled by the Government or public authority or owned and controlled by private interests tempered by supposed regulation. Some effective and drastic policy of either public ownership or public control is undoubtedly elemental in the framing of any plans or scheme to deal with this subject matter. I am for public ownership and control. I have come to this conclusion after years of study rather slowly. But to my mind there is no alternative if we are going to dedicate this great natural beneficence to the people as a whole . . . . .

In 1913 I ventured to say on this floor, speaking without reference to our natural resources. . . . "I am in favor of absolute public ownership. The leasing system is a delusion, so far as our natural resources are concerned." The more I have studied the question and the further I have carried the investigation the more firmly I am convinced that the leasing system will bring no proper service to these utilities, and that we should adopt, without further experimenting, public ownership, development, and control of our water power. . . . I believe the Government should retain its present water power, and through municipalities, and the states, and the political divisions of the states, and the Government, develop and control them.

It would seem, as a matter of theory at least . . . that that which is peculiarly and fundamentally for the common use, which not only by nature itself but by the laws of use seems singularly dedicated to the common service, ought to be discharged so far as possible, of the burden of private gain. That which seems set apart for the common use and to which every member of the community is to be admitted in the way of enjoyment ought not to be so operated as to be of special benefit to anyone. The water power is interwoven with and inseparably a part of the common service and welfare of the community. . . . Whatever profits there are should go to the people in better and cheaper service. The leasing system in no sense relieves the business of private gain. . . . Theoretically public ownership will give lower rates, better service, a greater diffusion of wealth, and more prosperous communities.

(He then goes on to show where public ownership and operation of water power has operated successfully in Europe, and in certain American cities and in the province of Ontario, Canada) . . . .

. . . Under the leasing system the people who now own the developed power of the country will secure the leases. There will be no independent operators who come into the field against five groups which now practically control the water power of the United States. It does not make any difference to me, whether there is a discrimination or not; that discrimination already exists in the economic and financial position which will surround the development of power. Will any independent go into the field to compete under a lease with the tremendous organizations which already have the basis of their financial and economic strength in their present ownership?

APPENDIX VII

The Federal Water-power Act

(Approved, June 10, 1920; Vol. 41, *Statutes at Large*, p. 1063)

(Public—No. 280—66th Cong. H. R. 3184)

An Act To create a Federal Power Commission; to provide for the improvement of navigation; the development of water-power; the use of the public lands in relation thereto, and to repeal section 18 of the River and Harbor Appropriation Act, approved August 8, 1917, and for other purposes.

Be it enacted by the Senate and House of Representatives of the United States of America in Congress assembled. That a commission is hereby created and established, to be known as the Federal Power Commission (hereinafter referred to as the commission), which shall be composed of the Secretary of War, the Secretary of the Interior, and the Secretary of Agriculture. Two members of the commission shall constitute a quorum for the transaction of business, and the commission shall have an official seal, which shall be judicially noticed. The President shall designate the chairman of the commission.

Sec. 2. That the commission shall appoint an executive secretary, who shall receive a salary of $5,000 a year, and prescribe his duties, and the commission may request the President of the United States to detail an officer from the United States Engineer Corps to serve the commission as engineer officer, his duties to be prescribed by the commission.

The work of the commission shall be performed by and through the Departments of War, Interior, and Agriculture and their engineering, technical, clerical, and other personnel except as may be otherwise provided by law.

All the expenses of the commission, including rent in the District of Columbia, all necessary expenses for transportation and subsistence, including, in the discretion of the commission, a per diem of not exceeding $4 in lieu of subsistence incurred by its employees under its orders in making any investigation, or conducting field work, or upon official business outside of the District of Columbia and away from their designated points of duty, shall be allowed and paid on the presentation of itemized vouchers therefor approved by a member or officer of the commission duly authorized for that purpose; and in order to defray the expenses made necessary by the provisions of this Act there is hereby authorized to be appropriated such sums as Congress may hereafter determine, and the sum of $100,000 is hereby appropriated, out of any moneys in the Treasury not otherwise appropriated, available until expended, to be paid out upon warrants drawn on the Secretary of the Treasury upon order of the commission.

Sec. 3. That the words defined in this section shall have the following meanings for the purposes of this Act, to wit:

" Public lands " means such lands and interest in lands owned by the United States as are subject to private appropriation and disposal under public-land laws. It shall not include " reservations," as hereinafter defined.

" Reservations " means national monuments, national parks, national forests, tribal lands embraced within Indian reservations, military reservations, and other lands and interests in lands owned by the United States, and withdrawn, reserved, or withheld from private appropriation and disposal under the public-land laws; also lands and interests in lands acquired and held for any public purpose.

" Corporation " means a corporation organized under the laws of any State or of the United States empowered to develop, transmit, distribute, sell, lease, or utilize power in addition to such other powers as it may possess, and authorized to transact in the State or States in which its project is located all business necessary to effect the purposes of a license under this Act. It shall not include " municipalities " as hereinafter defined.

" State " means a State admitted to the Union, the District

of Columbia, and any organized Territory of the United States.

" Municipality " means a city, county, irrigation district, drainage district, or other political subdivision or agency of a State competent under the laws thereof to carry on the business of developing, transmitting, utilizing, or distributing power.

" Navigable waters " means those parts of streams or other bodies of water over which Congress has jurisdiction under its authority to regulate commerce with foreign nations and among the several States, and which either in their natural or improved condition, notwithstanding interruptions between the navigable parts of such streams or waters by falls, shallows, or rapids compelling land carriage, are used or suitable for the use for the transportation of persons or property in interstate or foreign commerce, including therein all such interrupting falls, shallows, or rapids; together with such other parts of streams as shall have been authorized by Congress for improvement by the United States or shall have been recommended to Congress for such improvement after investigation under its authority.

" Municipal purposes " means and includes all purposes within municipal powers as defined by the constitution or laws of the State or by the charter of the municipality.

" Government dam " means a dam or other work, constructed or owned by the United States for Government purposes, with or without contribution from others.

" Project " means complete unit of improvement or development, consisting of a power house, all water conduits, all dams and appurtenant works and structures (including navigation structures) which are a part of said unit, and all storage, diverting, or forebay reservoirs directly connected therewith, the primary line or lines transmitting power therefrom to the point of junction with the distribution system or with the interconnected primary transmission system, all miscellaneous structures used and useful in connection with said unit or any part thereof, and all water rights, rights of way, ditches, dams, reservoirs, lands, or interest in lands, the use and occupancy of which are necessary or appropriate in the maintenance and operation of such unit.

"Project works" means the physical structures of a project.

"Net investment" in a project means the actual legitimate original cost thereof as defined and interpreted in the "classification of investment in road and equipment of steam roads, issue of 1914, Interstate Commerce Commission," plus similar costs of additions thereto and betterments thereof, minus the sum of the following items properly allocated thereto, if and to the extent that such items have been accumulated during the period of the license from earnings in excess to a fair return on such investment: (a) Unappropriated surplus, (b) aggregate credit balances of current depreciation accounts, and (c) aggregate appropriations of surplus or income held in amortization, sinking fund, or similar reserves, or expended for additions or betterments or used for the purposes for which such reserves were created. The term "cost" shall include, in so far as applicable, the elements thereof prescribed in said classification, but shall not include expenditures from funds obtained through donations by States, municipalities, individuals, or others, and said classification of investment of the Interstate Commerce Commission shall in so far as applicable be published and promulgated as a part of the rules and regulations of the commission.

Sec. 4. That the commission is hereby authorized and empowered—

(a) To make investigations and to collect and record data concerning the utilization of the water resources of any region to be developed, the water-power industry and its relation to other industries and to interstate or foreign commerce, and concerning the location, capacity, development costs, and relation to markets of power sites, and whether the power from Government dams can be advantageously used by the United States for its public purposes, and what is a fair value of such power, to the extent the commission may deem necessary or useful for the purposes of this Act.

In order to aid the commission in determining the net investment of a licensee in any project, the licensee shall, upon oath, within a reasonable period of time, to be fixed by the commission, after the construction of the original project or any addition thereto or betterment thereof, file with the commission, in such detail as the commission may require, a statement in duplicate showing the actual legitimate cost of construction of such project, addition, or betterment, and the price paid for water rights, rights of way, lands, or interest in lands. The commission shall deposit one of said statements with the Secretary of the Treasury. The licensee shall grant to the commission or to its duly authorized agent or agents, at all reasonable times, free access to such project, addition, or betterment, and to all maps, profiles, contracts, reports of engineers, accounts, books, records, and all other papers and documents relating thereto.

(b) To cooperate with the executive departments and other agencies of State or National Governments in such investigations; and for such purpose the several departments and agencies of the National Government are authorized and directed upon the request of the commission to furnish such records, papers, and information in their possession as may be requested by the commission, and temporarily to detail to the commission such officers or experts as may be necessary in such investigations.

(c) To make public from time to time the information secured hereunder, and to provide for the publication of its reports and investigations in such form and manner as may be best adapted for public information and use. The commission, on or before the first Monday in December of each year, shall submit to Congress for the fiscal year preceding a classified report showing the permits and licenses issued under this Act, and in each case the parties thereto, the terms prescribed, and the moneys received, if any, on account thereof.

(d) To issue licenses to citizens of the United States, or to any association of such citizens, or to any corporation organized under the laws of the United States or any State thereof, or to any State or municipality for the purpose of constructing, operating, and maintaining dams, water conduits, reservoirs, power houses, transmission lines, or other project works necessary or convenient for the development and improvement of navigation, and for the development, transmission, and utilization of power across, along, from or in any of the navigable waters of the United States, or upon any part of the public lands and reservations of the United States (including the Territories), or for the purpose of utilizing the surplus water or water power from any Government dam, except as herein provided: *Provided*, That licenses shall be issued within any reservation only after a finding by the commission that the license will not interfere or be inconsistent with the purpose for which such reservation was created or acquired, and shall be subject to and contain such conditions as the Secretary of the department under whose supervision such reservation falls shall deem necessary for the adequate protection and utilization of such reservation: *Provided further*, That no license affecting the navigable capacity of any navigable waters of the United States shall be issued until the plans of the dam or other structures affecting navigation have been approved by the Chief of Engineers and the Secretary of War. Whenever the contemplated improvement is, in the judgment of the commission, desirable and justified in the public interest for the purpose of improving or developing a waterway or waterways for the use or benefit of interstate or foreign commerce, a finding to that effect shall be made by the commission and shall become a part of the records of the commission: *Provided further*, That in case the commission shall find that any Government dam may be advantageously used by the United States for public purposes in addition to navigation, no license therefor shall be issued until two years after it shall have reported to Congress the facts and conditions relating thereto, except that this provision shall not apply to any Government dam constructed prior to the passage of this Act: *And provided further*, That upon the filing of any application for a license which has not been preceded by a preliminary permit under subsection (e) of this section, notice shall be given and published as required by the proviso of said subsection.

(e) To issue preliminary permits for the purpose of enabling applicants for a license hereunder to secure the data and to perform the acts required by section 9 hereof: *Provided, however,* That upon the filling of any application for a preliminary permit by any person, association, or corporation the commission, before granting such application, shall at once give notice of such application in writing to any State or municipality likely to be interested in or affected by such application; and shall also publish notice of such application for eight weeks in a daily or weekly newspaper published in the county or counties in which the project or any part thereof or the lands affected thereby are situated.

(f) To prescribe rules and regulations for the establishment of a system of accounts and for the maintenance thereof by licensees hereunder; to examine all books and accounts of such licensees at any time; to require them to submit at such time or times as the commission may require statements and reports, including full information as to assets and liabilities, capitalization, net investment and reduction thereof, gross receipts, interest due and paid, depreciation and other reserves, cost of project, cost of maintenance and operation of the project, cost of renewals and replacements of the project works, and as to depreciation of the project works and as to production, transmission, use and sale of power; also to require any licensee to make adequate provision for currently determining said costs and other facts. All such statements and reports shall be made upon oath, unless otherwise specified, and in such form and on such blanks as the commission may require. Any person who, for the purpose of deceiving, makes or causes to be made any false entry in the books or the accounts of such licensee, and any person who, for the purpose of deceiving, makes or causes to be made any false statement or report in response to a request or order or direction from the commission for the statements and report herein referred to shall, upon conviction, be fined not more than $2,000 or imprisoned not more than five years, or both.

(g) To hold hearings and to order testimony to be taken by deposition at any designated place in connection with the application for any permit or license, or the regulation of rates, service, or securities, or the making of any investigation, as provided in this Act; and to require by subpoena, signed by any member of the commission, the attendance and testimony of witnesses and the production of documentary evidence from any place in the United States, and in case of disobedience to a subpoena the commission may invoke the aid of any court of the United States in requiring the attendance and testimony of witnesses and the production of documentary evidence. Any member, expert or examiner of the commission may, when duly designated by the commission for such purposes, administer oaths and affirmations, examine witnesses and receive evidence. Depositions may be taken before any person designated by the commission or by its executive secretary and empowered to administer oaths, shall be reduced to writing by such person or under his direction, and subscribed by the deponent. Witnesses summoned before the commission shall be paid the same fees and mileage that are paid witnesses in the courts of the United States, and witnesses whose depositions are taken and persons taking the same shall severally be entitled to the same fees as are paid for like services in the courts of the United States.

(h) To perform any and all acts, to make such rules and regulations, and to issue such orders not inconsistent with this Act as may be necessary and proper for the purpose of carrying out the provisions of this Act.

Sec. 5. That each preliminary permit issued under this Act shall be for the sole purpose of maintaining priority of application for a license under the terms of this Act for such period or periods, not exceeding a total of three years, as in the discretion of the commission may be necessary for making examinations and surveys, for preparing maps, plans, specifications, and estimates, and for making financial arrangements. Each such permit shall set forth the conditions under which priority shall be maintained and a license issued. Such permits shall not be transferable, and may be canceled by order of the commission upon failure of permittees to comply with the conditions thereof.

Sec. 6. That licenses under this Act shall be issued for a period not exceeding fifty years. Each such license shall be conditioned upon acceptance by the licensee of all the terms and conditions of this Act and such further conditions, if any, as the commission shall prescribe in conformity with this Act, which said terms and conditions and the acceptance thereof shall be expressed in said license. Licenses may be revoked only for the reasons and in the manner prescribed under the provisions of this Act, and may be altered or surrendered only upon mutual agreement between the licensee and the commission after ninety days' public notice.

Sec. 7. That in issuing preliminary permits hereunder or licenses where no preliminary permit has been issued and in issuing licenses to new licensees under section 15 hereof the commission shall give preference to applications therefor by States and municipalities, provided the plans for the same are deemed by the commission equally well adapted, or shall within a reasonable time to be fixed by the commission be made equally well adapted, to conserve and utilize in the public interest the navigation and water resources of the region; and as between other applicants, the commission may give preference to the applicant the plans of which it finds and determines are best adapted to develop, conserve, and utilize in the public interest the navigation and water resources of the region, if it be satisfied as to the ability of the applicant to carry out such plans.

That whenever, in the judgment of the commission, the development of any project should be undertaken by the United States itself, the commission shall not approve any application for such project by any citizen, association, corporation, State, or municipality, but shall cause to be made such examinations, surveys, reports, plans, and estimates of the cost of the project as it may deem necessary, and shall submit its findings to Congress with such recommendations as it may deem appropriate concerning the construction of such project or completion of any project upon any Government dam by the United States.

The commission is hereby authorized and directed to investigate and, on or before the 1st day of January, 1921, report to

Congress the cost and, in detail, the economic value of the power plant outlined in project numbered 3, House Document numbered 1400, Sixty-second Congress, third session, in view of existing conditions, utilizing such study as may heretofore have been made by any department of the Government; also in connection with such project to submit plans and estimates of cost necessary to secure an increased and adequate water supply for the District of Columbia. For this purpose the sum of $25,000, or so much thereof as may be necessary, is hereby appropriated.[1]

Sec. 8. That no voluntary transfer of any license, or of the rights thereunder granted, shall be made without the written approval of the commission; and any successor or assign of the rights of such licensee, whether by voluntary transfer, judicial sale, foreclosure sale, or otherwise, shall be subject to all the conditions of the license under which such rights are held by such licensee and also subject to all the provisions and conditions of this Act to the same extent as though such successor or assign were the original licensee hereunder: *Provided,* That a mortgage or trust deed or judicial sales made thereunder or under tax sales shall not be deemed voluntary transfers within the meaning of this section.

Sec. 9. That each applicant for a license hereunder shall submit to the commission—

(a) Such maps, plans, specifications, and estimates of cost as may be required for a full understanding of the proposed project. Such maps, plans, and specifications when approved by the commission shall be made a part of the license; and thereafter no change shall be made in said maps, plans, or specifications until such changes shall have been approved and made a part of such license by the commission.

(b) Satisfactory evidence that the applicant has complied with the requirements of the laws of the State or States within which the proposed project is to be located with respect to bed and banks and to the appropriation, diversion, and use of water

[1] This section refers particularly to the Great Falls of the Potomac River.

for power purposes and with respect to the right to engage in the business of developing, transmitting, and distributing power, and in any other business necessary to effect the purposes of a license under this Act.

(c) Such additional information as the commission may require.

Sec. 10. That all licenses issued under this Act shall be on the following conditions:

(a) That the project adopted, including the maps, plans, and specifications, shall be such as in the judgment of the commission will be best adapted to a comprehensive scheme of improvement and utilization for the purposes of navigation, of water-power development, and of other beneficial public uses; and if necessary in order to secure such scheme the commission shall have authority to require the modification of any project and of the plans and specifications of the project works before approval.

(b) That except when emergency shall require for the protection of navigation, life, health, or property, no substantial alteration or addition not in conformity with the approved plans shall be made to any dam or other project works constructed hereunder of a capacity in excess of one hundred horsepower without the prior approval of the commission; and any emergency alteration or addition so made shall thereafter be subject to such modification and change as the commission may direct.

(c) That the licensee shall maintain the project work in a condition of repair adequate for the purposes of navigation and for the efficient operation of said works in the development and transmission of power, shall make all necessary renewals and replacements, shall establish and maintain adequate depreciation reserves for such purposes, shall so maintain and operate said works as not to impair navigation, and shall conform to such rules and regulations as the commission may from time to time prescribe for the protection of life, health, and property. Each licensee hereunder shall be liable for all damages occasioned to the property of others by the construction, maintenance, or operation of the project works or of the works appurtenant or accessory thereto, constructed under the license, and in no event shall the United States be liable therefor.

(d) That after the first twenty years of operation out of surplus earned thereafter, if any, accumulated in excess of a specified reasonable rate of return upon the actual, legitimate investment of a licensee in any project or projects under license the licensee shall establish and maintain amortization reserves, which reserves shall, in the discretion of the commission, be held until the termination of the license or be applied from time to time in reduction of the net investment. Such specified rate of return and the proportion of such surplus earnings to be paid into and held in such reserves shall be set forth in the license.

(e) That the licensee shall pay to the United States reasonable annual charges in an amount to be fixed by the commission for the purpose of reimbursing the United States for the costs of the administration of this Act; for recompensing it for the use, occupancy and enjoyment of its lands or other property; and for the expropriation to the Government of excessive profits until the respective States shall make provision for preventing excessive profits or for the expropriation thereof to themselves, or until the period of amortization as herein provided is reached, and in fixing such charges the commission shall seek to avoid increasing the price to the consumers of power by such charges, and charges for the expropriation of excessive profits may be adjusted from time to time by the commission as conditions may require: *Provided*, That when licenses are issued involving the use of Government dams or other structures owned by the United States or tribal lands embraced within Indian reservations the commission shall fix a reasonable annual charge for the use thereof, and such charges may be readjusted at the end of twenty years after the beginning of operations and at periods of not less than ten years thereafter in a manner to be described in each license: *Provided*, That licenses for the development, transmission, or distribution of power by States or municipalities shall be issued and enjoyed without charge to the extent such power is sold to the public without profit or is used by such State or municipality for State or municipal purposes, except that as to projects constructed or to be constructed by States or municipalities primarily designed to provide or improve navigation licenses therefor shall be issued without charge; and that licenses for the development, transmission, or distribution of power for domestic, mining, or other beneficial use in projects of not more than one hundred horsepower capacity may be issued without charge, except on tribal lands within Indian reservations; but in no case shall a license be issued free of charge for the development and utilization of power created by any Government dam and that the amount charged therefor in any license shall be such as determined by the commission.

(f) That whenever any licensee hereunder is directly benefited by the construction work of another licensee, a permittee, or of the United States of a storage reservoir or other headwater improvement, the commission shall require as a condition of the license that the licensee so benefited shall reimburse the owner of such reservoir or other improvements for such part of the annual charges for interest, maintenance, and depreciation thereon as the commission may deem equitable. The proportion of such charges to be paid by any licensee shall be determined by the commission.

Whenever such reservoir or other improvement is constructed by the United States the commission shall assess similar charges against any licensee directly benefited thereby, and any amount so assessed shall be paid into the Treasury of the United States, to be reserved and appropriated as a part of the special fund for headwater improvements as provided in section 17 hereof.

(g) Such further conditions not inconsistent with the provisions of this Act as the commission may require.

(h) That combinations, agreements, arrangements, or understandings, express or implied, to limit the output of electrical energy, to restrain trade, or to fix, maintain, or increase prices for electrical energy or service are hereby prohibited.

(i) In issuing licenses for a minor part only of a complete project, or for a complete project of not more than one hundred horsepower capacity, the commission may in its discretion waive such conditions, provisions, and requirements of this Act, except the license period of fifty years, as it may deem to be to the public interest to waive under the circumstances; *Provided,* That the provisions hereof shall not apply to lands within Indian reservations.

Sec. 11. That if the dam or other project works are to be constructed across, along, or in any of the navigable waters of the United States, the commission may, in so far as it deems the same reasonably necessary to promote the present and future needs of navigation and consistent with a reasonable investment cost to the licensee, include in the license any one or more of the following provisions or requirements:

(a) That such licensee shall, to the extent necessary to preserve and improve navigation facilities, construct, in whole or in part, without expense to the United States, in connection with such dam, a lock or locks, booms, sluices, or other structures for navigation purposes, in accordance with plans and specifications approved by the Chief of Engineers and the Secretary of War and made part of such license.

(b) That in case such structures for navigation purposes are not made a part of the original construction at the expense of the licensee, then whenever the United States shall desire to complete such navigation facilities the licensee shall convey to the United States, free of cost, such of its land and its rights of way and such right of passage through its dams or other structures, and permit such control of pools as may be required to complete such navigation facilities.

(c) That such licensee shall furnish free of cost to the United States power for the operation of such navigation facilities, whether constructed by the licensee or by the United States.

Sec. 12. That whenever application is filed for a project hereunder involving navigable waters of the United States, and the commission shall find upon investigation that the needs of navigation require the construction of a lock or locks or other navigation structures, and that such structures can not, consistent with a reasonable investment cost to the applicant, be provided in the manner specified in section 11, subsection (a) hereof, the commission may grant the application with the provision to be expressed in the license that the licensee will install the necessary navigation structures if the Government fails to make provision therefor within a time to be fixed in the license and cause a report upon such project to be prepared, with estimates of cost of the power development and of the navigation structures, and shall submit such report to Congress with such recommendations as it deems appropriate concerning the participation of the United States in the cost of construction of such navigation structures.

Sec. 13. That the licensee shall commence the construction of the project works within the time fixed in the license, which shall not be more than two years from the date thereof, shall thereafter in good faith and with due diligence prosecute such construction, and shall within the time fixed in the license complete and put into operation such part of the ultimate development as the commission shall deem necessary to supply the reasonable needs of the then available market, and shall from time to time thereafter construct such portion of the balance of such development as the commission may direct, so as to supply adequately the reasonable market demands until such development shall have been completed. The periods for the commencement of construction may be extended once but not longer than two additional years and the period for the completion of construction carried on in good faith and with reasonable diligence may be extended by the commission when not incompatible with the public interests. In case the licensee shall not commence actual construction of the project works, or of any specified part thereof, within the time prescribed in the license or as extended by the commission, then, after due notice given, the license shall, as to such project works or part thereof, be terminated upon written order of the commission. In case the construction of the project works, or of any specified part thereof, have been begun but not completed within the time prescribed in the license, or as extended by the commission, then the Attorney General, upon the request of the commission, shall institute proceedings in equity in the district court of the United States for the district in which any part of the project is situated for the revocation of said license, the sale of the works constructed, and such other equitable relief as the case may demand, as provided for in section 26 hereof.

Sec. 14. That upon not less than two years' notice in writing from the commission the United States shall have the right upon or after the expiration of any license to take over and thereafter to maintain and operate any project or projects as defined in section 3 hereof, and covered in whole or in part by the license, or the right to take over upon mutual agreement with the licensee all property owned and held by the licensee then valuable and serviceable in the development, transmission, or distribution of power and which is then dependent for its usefulness upon the continuance of the license, together with any lock or locks or other aids to navigation constructed at the expense of the licensee, upon the condition that before taking possession it shall pay the net investment of the licensee in the project or projects taken, not to exceed the fair value of the property taken, plus such reasonable damages, if any, to property of the licensee valuable, serviceable, and dependent as above set forth but not taken, as may be caused by the severance therefrom of the property taken, and shall assume all contracts entered into by the licensee with the approval of the commission. The net investment of the licensee in the project or projects so taken and the amount of such severance damages, if any, shall be determined by agreement between the commission and the licensee, and in case they can not agree, by proceedings in equity instituted by the United States in the district court of the United States in the district within which any such property may be located: *Provided*, That such net investment shall not include or be affected by the value of any lands, rights of way, or other property of the United States licensed by the commission under this Act, by the license, or by good will, going value, or prospective revenues: *Provided further*, That the values allowed for water rights, rights of way, lands, or interest in lands shall not be in excess of the actual reasonable cost thereof at the time of acquisition by the licensee: *Provided,* That the right of the United States or any State or municipality to take over, maintain, and operate any project licensed under this Act at any time by condemnation proceedings upon payment of just compensation is hereby expressly reserved.

Sec. 15. That if the United States does not, at the expiration of the original license, exercise its right to take over, maintain, and operate any project or projects of the licensee, as provided in section 14 hereof, the commission is authorized to issue a new license to the original licensee upon such terms and conditions as may be authorized or required under the then existing laws and regulations, or to issue a new license under said terms and conditions to a new licensee, which license may cover any project or projects covered by the original license, and shall be issued on the condition that the new licensee shall, before taking possession of such project or projects, pay such amount, and assume such contracts, as the United States is required to do, in the manner specified in section 14 hereof: *Provided,* That in the event the United States does not exercise the right to take over or does not issue a license to a new licensee, or issue a new license to the original licensee, upon reasonable terms, then the commission shall issue from year to year an annual license to the then licensee under the terms and conditions of the original license until the property is taken over or a new license is issued as aforesaid.

Sec. 16. That when in the opinion of the President of the United States, evidenced by a written order addressed to the holder of any license hereunder, the safety of the United States demands it, the United States shall have the right to enter upon and take possession of any project, or part thereof, constructed, maintained, or operated under said license, for the purpose of manufacturing nitrates, explosives, or munitions of war, or for any other purpose involving the safety of the United States, to retain possession, management, and control thereof for such length of time as may appear to the President to be necessary to accomplish said purposes, and then to restore possession and control to the party or parties entitled thereto; and in the event that the United States shall exercise such right it shall pay to the party or parties entitled thereto just and fair compensation for the use of said property as may be fixed by the commission upon the basis of a reasonable profit in time of peace, and the cost of restoring said property to as good condition as existed at the time of the taking over thereof, less the reasonable value of any improvements that may be made thereto by the United States and which are valuable and serviceable to the licensee.

Sec. 17. That all proceeds from any Indian reservation shall be placed to the credit of the Indians of such reservation. All other charges arising from licenses hereunder shall be paid into the Treasury of the United States, subject to the following distribution: Twelve and one-half percentum thereof is hereby appropriated to be paid into the Treasury of the United States and credited to "Miscellaneous receipts"; 50 per centum of the charges arising from licenses hereunder for the occupancy and use of public lands, national monuments, national forests, and national parks shall be paid into, reserved, and appropriated as a part of the reclamation fund created by the Act of Congress known as the Reclamation Act, approved June 17, 1902; and 37½ per centum of the charges arising from licenses hereunder for the occupancy and use of national forests, national parks, public lands, and national monuments, from the development within the boundaries of any State shall be paid by the Secretary of the Treasury to such State; and 50 per centum of the charges arising from all other licenses hereunder is hereby reserved and appropriated as a special fund in the Treasury to be expended under the direction of the Secretary of War in the maintenance and operation of dams and other navigation structures owned by the United States or in the construction, maintenance, or operation of headwater or other improvements of navigable waters of the United States.

Sec. 18. That the operation of any navigation facilities which may be constructed as a part of or in connection with any dam or diversion structure built under the provisions of this Act, whether at the expense of a licensee hereunder or of the United States, shall at all times be controlled by such reasonable rules and regulations in the interest of navigation, including the control of the level of the pool caused by such dam or diversion structure as may be made from time to time by the Secretary of War. Such rules and regulations may include the maintenance and operation by such licensee at its own expense of such lights and signals as may be directed by the Secretary of War, and such fishways as may be prescribed by the Secretary of Commerce; and for willful failure to comply with any such rule or regulation such licensee shall be deemed guilty of a misdemeanor, and upon conviction thereof shall be punished as provided in section 25 hereof.

Sec. 19. That as a condition of the license, every licensee hereunder which is a public-service corporation, or a person, association, or corporation owning or operating any project and developing, transmitting, or distributing power for sale or use in public service, shall abide by such reasonable regulation of the services to be rendered to customers or consumers of power, and of rates and charges of payment therefor, as may from time to time be prescribed by any duly constituted agency of the State in which the service is rendered or the rate charged. That in case of the development, transmission, or distribution, or use in public service of power by any licensee hereunder or by its customer engaged in public service within a State which has not authorized and empowered a commission or other agency or agencies within said State to regulate and control the services to be rendered by such licensee or by its customer engaged in public service, or the rates and charges of payment therefor, or the amount or character of securities to be issued by any of said parties, it is agreed as a condition of such license that jurisdiction is hereby conferred upon the commission, upon complaint of any person aggrieved or upon its own initiative, to exercise such regulation and control until such time as the State shall have provided a commission or other authority for such regulation and control: *Provided,* That the jurisdiction of the commission shall cease to determine as to each specific matter of regulation and control prescribed in this section as soon as the State shall have provided a commission or other authority for the regulation and control of that specific matter.

Sec. 20. That when said power or any part thereof shall enter into interstate or foreign commerce the rates charged and the service rendered by any such licensee, or by any subsidiary corporation, the stock of which is owned or controlled directly or indirectly by such licensee, or by any person, corporation, or association purchasing power from such licensee for sale and distribution or use in public service, shall be reasonable, nondiscriminatory, and just to the customer, and all unreasonable discriminatory and unjust rates or services are hereby prohibited and declared to be unlawful; and whenever any of the States directly concerned has not provided a commission or other authority to enforce the requirements of this section within such State or to regulate and control the amount and character of securities to be issued by any of such parties or such States are unable to agree through their properly constituted authorities on the services to be rendered or on the rates or charges of payment therefor, or on the amount or character of securities to be issued by any of said parties, jurisdiction is hereby conferred upon the commission, upon complaint of any person aggrieved, upon the request of any State concerned, or upon its own initiative, to enforce the provisions of this section, to regulate and control so much of the services rendered, and of the rates and charges of payment therefor as constitute interstate or foreign commerce, and to regulate the issuance of securities by the parties included within this section, and securities issued by the licensee subject to such regulations shall be allowed only for the bona fide purpose of financing and conducting the business of such licensee.

The administration of the provisions of this section, so far as applicable, shall be according to the procedure and practice in fixing and regulating the rates, charges, and practices of railroad companies as provided in the Act to regulate commerce, approved February 4, 1887, as amended, and that the parties subject to such regulation shall have the same rights of hearing, defense, and review as said companies in such cases.

In any valuation of the property of any licensee hereunder for purposes of rate making, no value shall be claimed by the licensee or allowed by the commission for any project or projects under license in excess of the value or values prescribed in section 14 hereof for the purposes of purchase by the United States, but there shall be included the cost to such licensee of the construction of the lock or locks or other aids of navigation and all other capital expenditures required by the United States, and no value shall be claimed or allowed for the rights granted by the commission or by this Act.

Sec. 21. That when any licensee can not acquire by contract or pledges an unimproved dam site or the right to use or damage the lands or property of others necessary to the construction, maintenance, or operation of any dam, reservoir, diversion structure, or the works appurtenant or accessory thereto, in conjunction with an improvement which in the judgment of the commission is desirable and justified in the public interest for the purpose of improving or developing a waterway or waterways for the use or benefit of interstate or foreign commerce, it may acquire the same by the exercise of the right of eminent domain in the district court of the United States for the district in which such land or other property may be located, or in the State courts. The practice and procedure in any action or proceeding for that purpose in the district court of the United States shall conform as nearly as may be with the practice and procedure in similar action or proceeding in the courts of the State where the property is situated: *Provided,* That United States district courts shall only have jurisdiction of cases when the amount claimed by the owner of the property to be condemned exceeds $3,000.

Sec. 22. That whenever the public interest requires or justifies the execution by the licensee of contracts for the sale and delivery of power for periods extending beyond the date of termination of the license, such contracts may be entered into upon the joint approval of the commission and of the public-service commission or other similar authority in the State in which the sale or delivery of power is made, or if sold or delivered in a State which has no such public-service commission, then upon the approval of the commission, and thereafter, in the event of failure to issue a new license to the original licensee at the termination of the license, the United States or the new licensee, as the case may be, shall assume and fulfill all such contracts.

Sec. 23. That the provisions of this Act shall not be construed as affecting any permit or valid existing right of way heretofore granted or as confirming or otherwise affecting any claim, or as affecting any authority heretofore given pursuant to law, but any person, association, corporation, State, or municipality, holding or possessing such permit, right of way, or authority may apply for a license hereunder, and upon such application the commission may issue to any such applicant a license in accordance with the provisions of this Act, and in such case the provisions of this Act shall apply to such applicant as a licensee hereunder: *Provided*, That when application is made for a license under this section for a project or projects already constructed, the fair value of said project or projects, determined as provided in this section, shall for the purposes of this Act and of said license be deemed to be the amount to be allowed as the net investment of the applicant in such project or projects as of the date of such license, or as of the date of such determination, if license has not been issued. Such fair value may, in the discretion of the commission, be determined by mutual agreement between the commission and the applicant or, in case they can not agree, jurisdiction is hereby conferred upon the district court of the United States in the district within which such project or projects may be located, upon the application of either party, to hear and determine the amount of such fair value.

That any person, association, corporation, State, or municipality intending to construct a dam or other project works across, along, over, or in any stream or part thereof, other than those defined herein as navigable waters, and over which Congress has jurisdiction under its authority to regulate commerce between foreign nations and among the several States, may in their discretion file declaration of such intention with the commission, whereupon the commission shall cause immediate investigation of such proposed construction to be made, and if upon investigation it shall find that the interests of interstate or foreign commerce would be affected by such proposed construction, such person, association, corporation, State, or municipality shall not proceed with such construction until it shall have applied for and shall have received a license under the provisions of this Act. If the commission shall not so find, and if no public lands or reservations are affected, permission is hereby granted to construct such dam or other project works in such stream upon compliance with State laws.

Sec. 24. That any lands of the United States included in any proposed project under the provisions of this Act shall from the date of filing of application therefor be reserved from entry, location, or other disposal under the laws of the United States until otherwise directed by the commission or by Congress. Notice that such application has been made, together with the data of filing thereof and a description of the lands of the United States affected thereby, shall be filed in the local land office for the district in which such lands are located. Whenever the commission shall determine that the value of any lands of the United Sttates so applied for, or heretofore or hereafter reserved or classified as power sites, will not be injured or destroyed for the purposes of power development by location, entry, or selection under the public-land laws, the Secretary of the Interior, upon notice of such determination, shall declare such lands open to location, entry, or selection, subject to and with a reservation of the right of the United States or its permittees or licensees to enter upon, occupy, and use any part or all of said lands necessary, in the judgment of the commission, for the purposes of this Act, which right shall be expressly reserved in every patent issued for such lands; and no claim or right to compensation shall accrue from the occupation or use of any of said lands for said purposes. The United States or any licensee for any such lands hereunder may enter thereupon for the purposes of this Act, upon payment of any damages to crops, buildings, or other improvements caused thereby to the owner thereof, or upon giving a good and sufficient bond to the United States for the use and benefit of the owner to secure the payment of such damages as may be determined and fixed in an action brought upon the bond in a court of competent jurisdiction, said bond to be in the form prescribed by the commission: *Provided,* That locations, entries, selections, or filings heretofore made for lands reserved as water-power sites or in connection with water-power development or electrical transmission may proceed to approval or patent under and subject to the limitations and conditions in this section contained.

Sec. 25. That any licensee, or any person, who shall willfully fail or who shall refuse to comply with any of the provisions of this Act, or with any of the conditions made a part of any license issued hereunder, or with any subpoena of the commission, or with any regulation or lawful order of the commission, or of the Secretary of War, or of the Secretary of Commerce as to fishways, issued or made in accordance with the provisions of this Act, shall be deemed guilty of a misdemeanor, and on conviction thereof shall, in the discretion of the court, be punished by a fine of not exceeding $1,000, in addition to other penalties herein prescribed or provided by law; and every month any such licensee or any such person shall remain in default after written notice from the commission, or from the Secretary of War, or from the Secretary of Commerce, shall be deemed a new and separate offense punishable as aforesaid.

Sec. 26. That the Attorney General may, on request of the commission or of the Secretary of War, institute proceedings in equity in the district court of the United States in the district in which any project or part thereof is situated for the purpose of revoking for violation of its terms any permit or license issued hereunder, or for the purpose of remedying or correcting by injunction, mandamus, or other process any act of commission or omission in violation of the provisions of this Act or of any lawful regulation or order promulgated hereunder. The district courts shall have jurisdiction over all of the above-mentioned proceedings and shall have power to issue and execute all necessary process and to make and enforce all writs, orders and decrees to compel compliance with the lawful orders and regulations of the commission and of the Secretary of War, and to compel the performance of any condition imposed under the provisions of this Act. In the event a decree revoking a license is entered, the court is empowered to sell the whole or any part of the project or projects under license, to wind up the business of such licensee conducted in connection with such project or projects, to distribute the proceeds to the parties entitled to the same, and to make and enforce such further orders and decrees as equity and justice may require. At such sale or sales the vendee shall take the rights and privileges belonging to the licensee and shall perform the duties of such licensee and assume all outstanding obligations and liabilities of the licensee which the court may deem equitable in the premises; and at such sale or sales the United States may become a purchaser, but it shall not be required to pay a greater amount than it would be required to pay under the provisions of section 14 hereof at the termination of the license.

Sec. 27. That nothing herein contained shall be construed as affecting or intending to affect or in any way to interfere with the laws of the respective States relating to the control, appropriation, use, or distribution of water used in irrigation or for municipal or other uses, or any vested right acquired therein.

Sec. 28. That the right to alter, amend, or repeal this Act is hereby expressly reserved; but no such alteration, amendment, or repeal shall affect any license theretofore issued under the provisions of this Act, or the rights of any licensee thereunder.

Sec. 29. That all Acts or parts of Acts inconsistent with this Act are hereby repealed: *Provided*, That nothing herein contained shall be held or construed to modify or repeal any of the provisions of the Act of Congress approved December 19, 1913, granting certain rights of way to the city and county of

San Francisco, in the State of California: *Provided, further,* That section 18 of an Act making appropriations for the construction, repair ,and preservation of certain public works on rivers and harbors, and for other purposes, approved August 8, 1917, is hereby repealed.

Sec. 30. That the short title of this Act shall be "The Federal Water Power Act."

Approved, June 10, 1920.

Amendment to the Federal Water Power Act

(41 Stat., 1353)

An Act to amend an Act entitled "An Act to create a Federal Power Commission; to provide for the improvement of navigation; the development of water power; the use of the public lands in relation thereto; and to repeal section 18 of the River and Harbor Appropriation Act, approved August 8, 1917, and for other purposes," approved June 10, 1920.

Be it enacted by the Senate and House of Representatives of the United States of America in Congress assembled, That hereafter no permit, license, lease, or authorization for dams, conduits, reservoirs, power houses, transmission lines, or other works for storage or carriage of water, or for the development, transmission, or utilization of power, within the limits as now constituted of any national park or national monument shall be granted or made without specific authority of Congress, and so much of the Act of Congress approved June 10, 1920, entitled "An Act to create a Federal Power Commission; to provide for the improvement of navigation; the development of water power; the use of the public lands in relation thereto; and to repeal section 18 of the River and Harbor Appropriation Act, approved August 8, 1917, and for other purposes," approved June 10, 1920, as authorizes licensing such uses of existing national parks and national monuments by the Federal Power Commission is hereby repealed.

Approved, March 3, 1921.

APPENDIX VIII

FEDERAL POWER COMMISSION,
WASHINGTON, SEPT. 2, 1925.

Dear Prof. Kerwin:

I have your inquiry of August 27, and in reply am enclosing for your information tabulations giving the amounts collected by the Commission as fees under section 17 of the Federal water power act, and final distribution and credit of these amounts on the books of the Treasury as required by that section under the interpretations given by the Comptroller of the Treasury.

Figures recently compiled indicate that $242,291.75 will be collected as fees from licensees during the present fiscal year, and that in the succeeding fiscal year these collections will total about $290,000.

Very truly yours,

O. C. MERRILL,
Executive Secretary.

Prof. Jerome G. Kerwin,
425 So. Manning Blvd.,
Albany, N. Y.

Enc. 3189.

1922

To the general fund of the Treasury		$4,397.96	
To the indefinite appropriation (under administration of the War Department). Maintenance and operation of dams and other improvements of navigable waters		4,370.83	
To the reclamation fund, special fund		108.55	
To payments to States under the Federal Water Power Act, special funds		81.40	
To Alabama	$0.48		
To California	39.82		
To Colorado	1.43		
To Idaho	8.30		
To Montana	23.08		
To Nevada	6.72		
To South Dakota	1.57		
To Indian fund: Proceeds of labor, Fort Hall Indians		4.83	
			$8,963.57

1923

To the general fund of the Treasury		$12,825.21
To the indefinite appropriation (under administration of the War Department): Maintenance and operation of dams and other improvements of navigable waters		12,386.41
To the reclamation fund		1,755.20
To payments to States under Federal water power act, special funds		1,316.41
To Alabama	$0.94	
To Arizona	58.14	
To California	1,126.56	
To Colorado	5.24	
To Idaho	33.26	
To Montana	55.74	
To North Carolina	.60	
To Oregon	34.05	
To South Dakota	1.88	
To Indian funds		1,236.00
To proceeds of labor, Fort Hall Indians	$1,236.00	
Total		$29,519.23

1924

To the general fund of the Treasury		$24,109.42
To the indefinite appropriation (under administration of the War Department): Maintenance and operation of dams and other improvements of navigable waters		23,421.72
To the reclamation fund		2,750.77
To payments to States under Federal water power act, special funds		2,063.07
To Alabama	$0.93	
To Arizona	86.62	
To California	1,832.97	
To Colorado	30.94	
To Idaho	53.44	
To Minnesota	1.81	
To Montana	12.79	
To North Carolina	1.16	
To Nevada	.82	
To New Mexico	1.71	
To Oregon	35.48	
To South Dakota	1.88	
To Washington	.67	
To Wyoming	1.85	
To Indian funds		1,368.44
To proceeds of labor—		
Fort Hall Indians	$36.00	
Lac Court Oreilles Indians	1,200.00	
Agua Caliente or Palm Springs Indians	19.55	
Shoshone and Arapahoe Indians	112.32	
Paiute Indians	.57	
Total		$53,713.42

1925

To the general fund of the Treasury		$59,645.52
To the indefinite appropriation (under administration of the War Department): Maintenance and operation of dams and other improvements of navigable waters		58,185.14
To the reclamation fund		5,841.53
To payments to States under Federal water power act, special funds		4,381.14
To Alabama	$39.37	
To Alaska	34.02	
To Arizona	97.30	
To California	3,973.15	
To Colorado	45.18	
To Idaho	91.07	
To Minnesota	9.90	
To Montana	24.24	
To Nevada	.98	
To New Mexico	3.94	
To North Carolina	1.16	
To Oregon	35.74	
To South Dakota	1.87	
To Washington	1.00	
To Wisconsin	1.82	
To Wyoming	20.40	
To Indian funds		1,422.19
To proceeds of labor—		
Agua Caliente or Palm Springs Indians	$25.00	
Fort Hall Indians	36.00	
Klamath Indians	27.04	
Lac Court Oreilles Indians	1,200.00	
Morongo Indians	2.00	
Rincon Indians	4.15	
Shoshone and Arapahoe Indians	125.50	
Total		$129,475.52

UNITED STATES DEPARTMENT OF AGRICULTURE
FOREST SERVICE

WASHINGTON, SEPTEMBER 8, 1925.

Professor J. G. Kerwin,
425 South Manning Boulevard,
Albany, New York.

Dear Sir:

A copy of your letter of August 27 to Mr. O. C. Merrill, Federal Power Commission, relative to receipts on account of water power has been referred to this office for information as

to such receipts prior to the passage of the Water Power Act of 1920.

Receipts from this source for the Fiscal Years 1912 to 1920, were as follows:

1912	$50,562.98
1913	51,235.08
1914	47,163.74
1915	88,950.44
1916	101,096.32
1917	106,389.48
1918	93,976.35
1919	72,322.06
1920	89,837.65
Total	$701,534.10

It is understood Mr. Merrill has furnished figures representing receipts subsequent to 1920.

Very truly yours,

Chief, Finance and Accounts.

INDEX